Haven and Home

Haven and Home

A History of the Jews in America

Abraham J. Karp

SCHOCKEN BOOKS · NEW YORK

All rights reserved under International and Pan-American
Copyright Conventions. Published in the United States by
Schocken Books Inc. New York. Distributed by
Pantheon Books, a division of Random House, Inc., New York.

Library of Congress Cataloging in Publication Data
Karp, Abraham J.
  Haven and Home
  Bibliography: p.
  Includes index.
  1. Jews—United States—History.   2. United
States—Ethnic relations.   I. Title.
El84.J5Kl68   1984   973'.04924   84–5530

ISBN 0–8052–0817–8 (paperback)

ACKNOWLEDGMENTS

''The Nineteen Eighties,'' condensed from *Judaism*, Spring, 1981. Copyright
1981 by *Judaism*. Reprinted by permission.

''The American Jew Today,'' condensed from *Newsweek*, March 1, 1971.
Copyright 1971 by Newsweek, Inc. All rights reserved. Reprinted by permission.

''What It Means to Be Jewish,'' condensed from *Time*, April 10, 1972. Copyright 1972 by Time, Inc. Reprinted by permission.

Designed by Dan Zedek

Manufactured in the United States of America
9 8 7 6 5 4

For my grandchildren
Sarah Terez Karp
Joshua Yale Karp
Aaron Isaac Karp
Beth Ariel Karp
with gratitude and hope

Contents

Preface

JEWS ARRIVED IN AMERICA, ANCIENTS IN THE NEW WORLD. TWO THOUSAND years of planting communities in lands of the Diaspora had prepared them for entry into this newest of societies.

Nowhere more fully than in America have the Jews experienced Emancipation and Enlightenment, which they have come to accept both as a right and as a mandate. In America, the Jews have undergone the fullest testing of their will and ability to retain a group identity in a free, open society. The Jews alone in America are members of a group which is simultaneously religious, cultural and ethnic. In their historic experience, the American Jews viewed themselves as communicants of a religious group, as participants in a cultural community, and as members of an ethnic fellowship. In response to their personal and communal needs, in accommodation to the social and political climate of the time, one or another aspect was emphasized.

In the context of Jewish history, the Jews' experience in America shows them entering the most "modern" of societies, a free nation continually freeing itself of imported and inherited prejudices. As the Jews migrated from Europe to America, they moved from membership in a legally defined community, which one entered by birth and could leave only by a willed act of dissociation, to membership in a voluntary community. Culturally, they moved from a self-contained civilization to full participation in the life of the larger community. Economically, they found opportunities in an expanding economy unmatched in the Old World.

The Jews could not help but notice that religious pluralism and cultural diversity were deeply rooted in the promise and practice of America, and they felt it their American duty to strengthen and broaden those traits. Democratic government in America was based on the notions of partners in covenant between the government and the governed, each covenanting party with rights and responsibilities, power and duties. The idea of covenant relationship is as old as the Jewish people; through the Jews, its content and rhetoric entered the life of Western man. It is not surprising that Jews would feel at home in a nation in which people and rulers relate to one another in covenantal forms. Because the rights extended to Jews had been denied their brethren in other countries, they would view them as a gift even when the nation proclaimed them to be their natural and inherent right. The gratitude they felt inspired them to use those rights in the service of the nation which had granted them, and therefore, Jews felt a special need to be visibly useful and productive members of the society which had opened the doors of such opportunity for them.

Three eras overlap in the historic experience of the Jew in America. Until the end of the nineteenth century, America was a haven to be sought, and being accepted by the host community was the dominant theme in the personal and communal life of American Jews. America extended freedom and offered equality which permitted Jews to establish their communal identity and the institutions that sustained it. They perceived that America accepted religious diversity and encouraged voluntary religious communities. During the latter part of the nineteenth century, American Jews established their tripartite religious communal identity—Orthodox, Conservative and Reform; at the same time, they adopted the assimilatory life-style that American egalitarianism encouraged.

In the first decades of the twentieth century, the challenge for Jews was to turn the American haven into a home. A network of organizations and institutions labored at integrating immigrant Jews into the economic, social and cultural fabric of the larger community. The organized community thus established and "at home" in America was able to test the limits and possibilities of the American experience.

Since World War II, Jews have felt at home in America, able to enter segments of the economy formerly closed to them. They have taken a central role in American cultural life, and they have been in the forefront of the postwar thrust to extend equality and opportunity to those to whom these had been denied. The Jews' sense of security in America has enabled them to make the plight of their brethren abroad their chief concern, and to make philanthropy and political activism their dominant domestic priority.

In its youthful idealism, America had accepted a vision of high purpose. Herman Melville, who understood what obsesses nations as he knew what possesses men, joined America and Israel in his description of a society propelled by purpose: "And we Americans are peculiar, chosen people, the Israel of our times; we bear the ark of the liberties of the world." Jefferson was certain that this nation would "grow to multiply and prosper until we exhibit an association powerful, wise and happy, beyond what has yet been seen by men." Walt Whitman hailed America as the "custodian of the future of humanity."

The experience of the Jew in America can provide some indication of what manner of "custodian" America has been. It also serves to instruct how one group has striven to fulfill its dual and complementary commitment to the political society and to its own religio-cultural-ethnic group, with "both grace and integrity."

In this history which concerns itself most particularly with the social, religious and cultural aspects of the American Jewish historical experience, I have followed the sage observation of Justice Oliver Wendell Holmes that "Life is painting a picture, not doing a sum." As the narrative moves from the volatile immigrant experience, the presentation becomes more episodic, retrospective and interpretive—more like a slide show than a motion picture. Sharply etched incidents that suggest and encompass the larger meaning of an experience are given special attention throughout the narrative in sections entitled "Source" and "Focus."

The author is indebted to colleagues Eugene D. Genovese, William B. Hauser and Christopher Lasch at the University of Rochester for incisive comments and helpful suggestions. Milton R. Konvitz of Cornell and author-scholar Abraham Rothberg have helped me see more clearly and express myself better. For their encouragement and guidance, and for their friendship, I am greatly beholden. The editorial assistance of Priscilla Fishman of Jerusalem, and Schocken editor Bonny Fetterman, went beyond the demands of duty. I am pleased also to acknowledge the help of Howard M. Sachar of George Washington University and Charles E. Silberman.

My wife and co-worker Deborah has seen the manuscript through all its stages with the constant, patient and demanding ministrations of a gifted writer and scholar.

To all, my deep gratitude and abiding affection.

Part One
Seeking a Haven

The great advantage of the Americans is, that they arrived at a state of democracy without having to endure a democratic revolution; and that they are born equal, instead of becoming so.

—Alexis de Tocqueville

1.

In Colonial
America

IT WAS CHRISTOPHER COLUMBUS, THE DISCOVERER HIMSELF, WHO FIRST
linked the Jew and the New World. In a letter to the king and queen
of Spain which opens his *Journal of the First Voyage*, he writes: ". . . having expelled the Jews from your dominions, Your Highnesses, in the
same month of January, ordered me to proceed with a sufficient ar-
mament to the said region of India. . . ."[1]

The linking of the historical events of expulsion and discovery
points up one of the ironies of history: The expulsion brought to an
end the greatest Jewish community of the medieval world, Spanish
Jewry. Part of the newly discovered world, the United States, is today
home for the largest community in the history of the Jewish people.

The first to be notified of the discovery of the New World was
not Ferdinand or Isabella, but Luis de Santangel, the grandson of a Jew
converted to Catholicism, who had himself done public penance as a
Marrano. As comptroller general of Aragon, he had persuaded the
queen to permit Columbus to undertake his journey, and through personal investment he had guaranteed the expenses of the first journey.
A letter written by Columbus on February 15, 1493, to Santangel quickly
appeared in print in both Spanish and Latin. One month later, a letter
almost identical in content and style was sent to Gabriel Sanchez, the
royal treasurer. Like de Santangel, Sanchez was a New Christian. His
brothers and sisters had died at the stake as Marranos or crypto-Jews—
officially Catholic, yet loyal to the faith of their fathers unto death.

During the previous century, from 1391 to 1492, riots, massacres
and forced conversions had reduced the Jews of Spain in numbers, status

and security. The converts, known as New Christians, were suspect as
to their loyalty to the new faith. In the late fifteenth century, King
Ferdinand and Queen Isabella instituted the Inquisition in Spain, giving
the Church the power to stamp out "heresy." In 1492, the last act of
the drama was staged: expulsion of the Jews from Spain.

Faced with the choice of conversion or exile, some Jews em-
braced the Cross, but about 150,000 remained loyal to the Jewish faith
and accepted exile. Most of the exiles made their way across the border
to Portugal, which first permitted them to enter but later subjected
them to forced baptism, in the process creating its own Marranos.

Portugal had been most successful in its journeys of discovery,
and a lucrative trade route to India had been opened. What it lacked,
however, was a class of entrepreneurs skillful and daring enough to
turn trade opportunities into profits. The Crown, seeing its New Christians as a group which could provide the solution to this problem, gave
them the opportunity to enrich the state and themselves. A royal decree
in 1507 permitted them to travel and settle abroad, to trade on land and
sea, and to export merchandise and money.

Envy, however, added to religious prejudice, motivated the introduction of the Inquisition to Portugal. For the next two centuries,
Jewish communities in Western Europe and the Americas would be
enriched by Marranos fleeing the Iberian Peninsula.

COLONIZING THE NEW WORLD

The southern continent of the New World was the first to be
exploited and colonized by Europe. Spain and Portugal plundered its
gold, exported its dyewoods and established vast sugar plantations.
Between 1580 and 1640, the two nations jointly controlled a colonial
empire unprecedented in size. That empire offered challenge and opportunity to the mercantile talents of the New Christians of the Iberian
Peninsula. In sizable numbers they came to settle, among them some
who still cherished memories of the ancestral Jewish faith and way of
life. The Church, ever concerned for the true piety of its adherents,
sent the Holy Office to the New World to discourage lapses into heresy.
The literature of inquisitorial activity in the New World provides evidence of the zealousness of the Church, as well as of the tenacity of
Judaism.

Professing Jews could not legally reside in Spanish or Portuguese
lands, yet some Jews did live in the Americas in the sixteenth century.
They came, traded and left. Among them was Antonio de Montezinos,
who on August 18, 1644, arrived in Amsterdam via South America.
To the Jewish community there, by whom he was called Aaron Levi,
he brought a fanciful account of a discovered Lost Tribe of Jews in the

New World, namely, the Indians. This was the first of many such tales identifying the Indians with the Lost Tribes of Israel.

In 1621 the Dutch West India Company was chartered as a mercantile-military enterprise to establish the Dutch presence in the New World. The Dutch believed that the most promising land to subdue was Brazil, which had itself been taken by the Portuguese from the Spanish king. The first Dutch military adventure, the capture of the port of Bahia, indeed proved to be an easy success. Portuguese sources record that New Christians in Bahia welcomed the invading fleet, which carried several dozen Jews. Together in 1624, the two groups established the first Jewish community in the New World. It disappeared almost as soon as it came into being, for within a year, a joint Spanish-Portuguese fleet retook Bahia.

Holland, then the world's leading mercantile power, prepared for another attempt at conquest. Five years later, in 1630, the northern Brazilian province of Pernambuco was successfully invaded, and its leading city, Recife, became a flourishing outpost of the Dutch West India Company. This time, too, Jews partook in the enterprise as soldiers and traders. Many more followed from Holland and were joined by resident New Christians returning to their ancestral faith. To encourage settlement and economic development, the company adopted a liberal policy of religious toleration, promising that "the liberty of Spaniards, Portuguese and natives, whether they be Roman Catholics or Jews, will be respected."

By 1645 the Jewish population of Dutch Brazil numbered roughly a thousand, a figure not attained in North America until more than a century later. Congregation Zur Israel maintained a synagogue, two schools, a cemetery and religious functionaries. The first rabbi to serve in the Western Hemisphere, Isaac Aboab da Fonseca, had come to Recife from Amsterdam in 1642, accompanied by a large number of immigrants.

Although the Jews were legally tolerated and protected by the company, they suffered discrimination at the hands of both their Calvinist and Catholic neighbors. The Jewish community soon began to dwindle, with many leaving for Amsterdam and some emigrating to the West Indies. The situation of the community became precarious during the period of the Reconquest, in which the Portuguese tried to recapture their lost territories. With the rising power of England challenging the Netherlands, the Dutch were faced with war in both the Old World and the New, and the New was neglected. Recife fell to Portugal in 1654, and the Jewish community, now shrunken to six hundred, had no choice but to disperse. Of the fleeing refugees, twenty-three eventually made their way to North America, to the Dutch settlement of New Amsterdam.

THE FIRST ARRIVALS

In early September 1654, the French frigate *Sainte Catherine* lowered its sails in the harbor of New Amsterdam, where the Hudson River meets the Atlantic Ocean. On board were the twenty-three Jewish refugees. These four men, six women and thirteen young people were to found the first Jewish community in what is now the United States.

New Amsterdam had been established by the Dutch West India Company. The company was promoting immigration to New Netherlands, and the Jews of Holland were among those who had responded to the invitation to make their home in the New World. Thus, the refugees were preceded by at least two coreligionists, Jacob Barsimson and Solomon Pietersen.

Pietersen was evidently a merchant who came to trade, for, within a year, he was no longer in New Amsterdam. Barsimson, the first Jewish settler in New Amsterdam, had a longer and more eventful career in the colony.

Some two weeks after the arrival of the twenty-three from Recife, Governor Peter Stuyvesant wrote to his employers, the Dutch West India Company in Amsterdam, that "The Jews who arrived would nearly all like to remain here . . ." but he "deemed it useful to require them in a friendly way to depart." He gives as reasons for his decision the fact that because of "their customary usury and deceitful trading with Christians, [they] were repugnant to the inferior magistrates, as also to the people having the most affection for you" and "the Deaconry also fearing that owing to their present indigence they might become a charge in the coming winter."[2]

The merchants of the city asked for the departure of the Jews because they wanted to prevent competition in trade. While the Jews were currently without resources, Stuyvesant and the burghers of New Amsterdam believed that this was only a temporary condition. Stuyvesant's negative view of Jews was based on his experience as governor of Curaçao, where he had witnessed their commercial success; he felt that they had deceived him there, ostensibly coming to farm, but quickly turning to trade.

On March 18, 1655, Domine Johannes Megapolensis, a predikant of the Dutch Reformed Church in New Amsterdam, wrote a letter to his superiors, the Classis of Amsterdam, concerning the arrival of the Jews.

Last summer some Jews came here from Holland in order to trade. Afterwards some Jews, poor and healthy, also came here on the same ship with Domine Polhemius . . . we have had to spend several hundred guilders for their support. They came several times to my house, weeping and bewailing their misery, and when I directed them to the Jewish merchant, they said he would not lend them a single stiver. Now again in the Spring, some have come from Holland, and report that a great many of that lot would yet follow and then build here their synagogue.[3]

He asks his superiors to intervene with the Dutch West India Company, sponsors of the settlement, to have these newcomers "sent away from here."

The Reverend Mr. Megapolensis was particularly disturbed by the possibility that the Jews would "build here their synagogue." A year earlier he had been successful in preventing the establishment of a Lutheran congregation. In company eyes, economic policy dictated that New Netherlands be hospitable to all who would come and freedom of religious worship would certainly be an inducement for colonization. Nevertheless, the Dutch Reformed establishment had to be maintained. Upon the urging of the New Amsterdam predikanters and the Classis, the company instructed Stuyvesant "not to receive any similar petitions." Megapolensis feared that this time the company might give in to economic pressure and permit a synagogue, and thereby extend freedom of public religious worship to all. To forestall such a possibility, he would see to it that Jews were not permitted to settle in the colony.

The Jews threatened with expulsion had a powerful ally in the Amsterdam Jewish community. It was in the latter's interest that Jews be permitted to live and trade in all parts of the Dutch empire. It would enable the Jewish merchants of Amsterdam to establish loyal and reliable business relationships in the New World with family members and coreligionists.

When Stuyvesant's recommendation arrived, the Jews of Amsterdam presented an opposing petition, arguing that preventing Jews from residing in New Netherlands would be regarded as an unfriendly act which would be "of no advantage to the general Company but rather damaging."[4] They further suggested to the Dutch that they faced a common enemy in Spain and Portugal. The Jews of Brazil had been loyal and economically useful to the Dutch in their struggles against the Iberian powers. Furthermore, French and English, competitors in the New World, permitted Jews to live and trade in their territories. Finally, they urged the directors to consider that "many of the Jewish nation are principal shareholders of the Company."[5]

This proved to be an irresistible argument to a company trying to recoup the loss of its Brazilian enterprise by developing New Amsterdam. On April 26, 1655, the company instructed Stuyvesant: "these people may travel and trade to and in New Netherlands and live and remain there, provided the poor among them shall not become a burden to the Company or to the community, but be supported by their own nation. You will now govern yourself accordingly."[6]

While the rights of Jews to live and trade were still being debated, the subjects of the controversy in the Dutch settlement went about demanding and establishing these rights. Abraham de Lucena was arrested for selling on Sunday, a deed forbidden to Jews even in the mother city. A heavy fine was imposed, but there is no record that it was ever paid. There is ample evidence that by 1656 Jews were engaged in commerce. A year later they were given burgher rights, permitting them to sell at retail and engage in crafts. The rights to engage in the lucrative fur trade and to own a house, denied by local authorities in New Amsterdam, were granted by the company directors in Holland.

Nor were the Jews in New Amsterdam hesitant to assert their right to practice their religion. Jacob Barsimson refused to honor a summons issued on Saturday, for in doing so he would be dishonoring the Sabbath. His religious scruples were respected, and no default was entered against him "as he was summoned on his Sabbath." After a contest with Stuyvesant and with the help of the Jews of Amsterdam, the right "to exercise in all quietness their religion within their houses" was granted by the company in June 1656.[7] Thus, Congregation Shearith Israel of New York can justly claim a life coextensive in time with the Jewish community in that city, but public worship was officially denied the Jews as it was to all groups other than the established Dutch Reformed Church.

More Jews came from the mother country, but finding the atmosphere of New Amsterdam economically and politically oppressive, most returned to Holland. It is estimated that in the decade 1654–64 the Jewish community in New Amsterdam never numbered more than fifty individuals. New Amsterdam was primarily a trading center; merchants came, conducted their business and left.

In 1663, the Torah scroll borrowed from the Amsterdam community, the symbol of Jewish life and vehicle for its religious expression, was returned to the mother country, acknowledging that Jewish communal life had come to an end in the Dutch colony. The company was losing interest in what was obviously a bad investment. A Dutch trading post could not survive, squeezed by British New England in the north and the tobacco colonies in the south. In 1664, Dutch New Amsterdam became British New York. The only Jew on the list of those taking the oath of allegiance to Britain was Asser Levy.

From Levy's arrival on the *Sainte Catherine* in 1654 to his death in 1682, he had had a multifaceted career. He is described by Jacob R. Marcus, historian of colonial Jewry, as a "merchant, furtrader, owner of real estate, executor of estates, factor for Dutch merchants, attorney and arbitrator, butcher and slaughterhouse owner, liquor merchant, exporter to Barbados, and money lender" in New Amsterdam, Albany and New York. Of greater interest is his career as activist for Jewish rights. Only a year after his arrival, he sought but was denied the right to serve in the volunteer militia fighting the Swedes. In the same year, he and Jacob Barsimson demanded the right to stand guard rather than pay a tax of exemption. The request was denied, and they were informed that "consent is hereby given them to depart whenever and whither it pleases them." Both chose to remain. Two years later, in 1657, Asser Levy petitioned for burgher rights, which were granted when he proved that he had had such rights in Amsterdam. When, in 1660, he was licensed to serve as a butcher, he was excused from slaughtering hogs. In the year 1671, he served on a jury, a rare privilege for a Jew in colonial times; he lent money to the Lutherans to build their church; and he helped a poor Jewish peddler in New England to have a fine abated, the court doing so "as a token of their respect to . . . Mr. Assur Levy."[8]

In the inventory of his estate we find listed: two brass candlesticks, one Sabbath lamb [sic], three silver goblets, one ditto cup with two ears, one ditto spice box, a parcel of old books, nine pictures. The candlesticks and goblets were evidently for Sabbath and holiday rituals, the spice box was for *havdalah* (ceremony for conclusion of the Sabbath) and the cup with two ears may have been used for the ritual washing of the hands of the Priests by the Levites (of whom Asser Levy was one) in the synagogue.

IN THE COLONIES

Arguing against extending rights to Jews, Governor Stuyvesant claimed, "Giving them liberty, we cannot refuse the Lutherans and Papists." What was true of New Amsterdam was true in the other colonies as well. Most of the colonies were organized by particular groups or sects for themselves to the exclusion of all others. Strong anti-Jewish feelings existed in seventeenth- and eighteenth-century Europe, as the economic and social pressures of urbanization and the growth of the national states added fuel to long-standing, religiously inspired hatreds. Some of these prejudices also crossed the sea. There were, however, factors unique to the New World which operated to mitigate anti-Jewish sentiments and to lay the foundation first for toleration and later for legal equality. In colonial America land was plentiful, people were not. Individuals with skills were a precious commodity. America was the frontier of Europe, and the Jews, no less than other segments of the population, became the beneficiaries of the opportunities which a frontier society provided. Because the Jews in colonial

America worked largely in mercantile enterprises, they were in an advantageous position to benefit from a country whose frontiers and economy were expanding. Such a frontier community also presents spiritual hazards. In an established community, successive generations enjoy the spiritual and institutional legacy of preceding generations. In new communities, everything must be created: schools had to be founded, churches built, scholars and clergy imported. This was a problem for the general community, but experienced most acutely by Jews, who were few in number and scattered throughout the colonies.

As we have seen, the Jews of New Amsterdam, while still petitioning for rights of domicile and trade, established a congregation, Shearith Israel. The congregation's initial holding was a cemetery, its request to "purchase a burying place" having been granted in February 1656. Near the end of the century it seems that the congregation had rented a house to serve as a synagogue: a document of 1700 refers to "the Jews' synagogue" on Mill Street. The year 1728 saw the erection or expansion of churches in New York City by the Dutch, Lutheran and Baptist congregations. In December of that year, for £700, a loaf of sugar and a pound of Bohea tea, the Jews purchased a lot adjoining the house they used as a synagogue to build a permanent house of worship. On Passover, 1730, the Mill Street Synagogue was dedicated. The congregation had received contributions from coreligionists in Boston, Barbados, Jamaica, Dutch Guiana, Curaçao and London for the building of the first synagogue in North America.

Three decades later, in 1758, the flourishing Jewish community of Newport, Rhode Island, built their beautiful synagogue, today a national shrine. In 1773, eight leading Jews of Philadelphia

> resolved unanimously that in order to Support our Holy Worship and Establishing it on a more solid Foundation than it is at present
>
> We the underwritten do mutually agree and promise to pay annually to the Parnas or Gabai for the time being the several sums annexed to our names . . . which money is to be appropriated for the use of the Synagogue (and Charitable uses) now Established in the City of Philadelphia.[9]

Barnard and Michael Gratz and Levy Marks pledged the sum of £10 each.

In colonial America, congregation and community were synonymous, and the congregation served all communal needs. Six synagogues served colonial Jewry. All used the Sephardic (Spanish and Portuguese) ritual, though the majority of congregants were Ashkenazi (descendants of Jews of Central and Eastern Europe). Thus a draft of a constitution for Philadelphia's Mikveh Israel Congregation was written in Yiddish because the congregants were German immigrants, but the synagogue ritual was Sephardic. By 1716, Ashkenazim outnumbered Sephardim in New York's Shearith Israel, but its rite has remained Sephardic to the present day. This anomaly may reflect the immigrants' perception of the rite as not so much Sephardic as "American."

By the end of the colonial period, congregations had been established in New York and Newport; Philadelphia and Lancaster, Pennsylvania; Richmond, Virginia; Charleston, South Carolina; and Savannah, Georgia. Religious functionaries were imported or trained. Kosher meat was obtained, marriages were solemnized, boys were circumcised and burial grounds were consecrated.

Colonial Jewry probably numbered no more than 1000, at most 1500 members, while the Jewish community of England was tenfold in size; yet it was in colonial New York, rather than metropolitan London, that the first English translation of the prayer book was published in 1761—a fifty-two-page booklet of the evening services of the New Year and the Day of Atonement. Five years later, Isaac Pinto published his translation of the liturgy for the Sabbath and the High Holy Days "*According to the Order of the Spanish and Portuguese Jews*" (i.e., Sephardic rite). The introduction to the volume explains that Hebrew "being imperfectly understood by many, by some not at all, it has been necessary to translate our Prayers in the Language of the Country wherein it hath pleased the divine Providence to appoint our Lot." Because of the small size of the Jewish community in the New World, linguistic acculturation proceeded at a far more rapid pace than in England. There was a need for English translations of the prayer book both in the colonies and in the British West Indies. In the last decades of the eighteenth century, multivolume editions of both the Sephardic and Ashkenazic prayer books, with Hebrew text and English translations, were published in London and imported by Jewish communities in America.

The distinction between Ashkenazic and Sephardic Jews in Europe continued in the New World. A Church of England minister in Savannah, Georgia, the Reverend S. Quincy, reported in 1735, "We have here two sorts of Jews, Portuguese and German. The former are more lax in their religious observance, having professed Christianity in Portugal or the Brazils."[10] Three years later the Reverend Mr. Bolzius reports:

> Some Jews in Savannah complained to me the other day that the Spanish and Portuguese Jews persecute the German Jews in a way no Christian would persecute another Christian. . . . They want to build a synagogue, but the Spanish and German Jews cannot come to terms. . . . The Spanish and Portuguese Jews are not so strict insofar as eating is concerned. . . . They eat, for instance,

beef that comes from the warehouse. . . . The German Jews, on the other hand, would rather starve than eat meat they do not slaughter themselves.[11]

Formal adherence to a congregation was the public posture of the colonial Jew, but personal religious observance often fell victim to the free atmosphere of the frontier. The small size of the Jewish community and its dispersion throughout the colonies made intermarriage an accepted reality in the frontier society, where often the choice was between religious loyalty *cum* bachelorhood and marriage out of the faith.

The majority of colonial Jews retained their Jewish identity, going to considerable lengths to establish the institutions and support the functionaries which Jewish living requires. Malcolm Stern writes of "Two Jewish Functionaries in Colonial Pennsylvania," the *mohalim* (ritual circumcisers) Barnard Jacobs and Mordecai Moses Mordecai. Jacobs, a resident of Heidelberg, Pennsylvania, performed thirty-three circumcisions between 1757 and 1790. Mordecai, we learn in a letter from the Mikveh Israel Congregation of Philadelphia to Rabbi Saul Lowenstamm of Amsterdam, "secretly performed a Jewish marriage rite between the girl (the daughter of Myer Hart of Easton) and her Gentile and this is why her father was appeased. That same night there was a banquet at the father's house for all the family."[12]

Intermarriage on the Pennsylvania frontier, the desire of the father for a Jewish wedding ceremony, the readiness of a Jewish lay functionary to aid the father in his attempt to keep his descendants within the faith, the disapproval of the organized religious community for the apparent disregard of Jewish law is a drama reenacted in America again and again. The letter cited above concludes: "the matter touches the very roots of our faith, particularly in this country where each acts according to his own desire; unfortunately, many marry Gentile women. . . . The congregation has no power to discipline or punish anyone."[13]

COLONIAL MERCHANTS

The migration of Jews to America in the seventeenth and eighteenth centuries was part of the general shift of the center of the Western world from the Mediterranean to the Atlantic. The European Jew, engaged in trade and finance, turned to the Americas, which the mercantile nations were opening up for exploitation. Jews of both West and East European origin made their away across the Atlantic to settle in the port cities of New York, Philadelphia, Newport, Charleston and Savannah, where they could engage in trade with the West Indies and Europe.

Members of the Sephardic Gomez family of New York were prominent in commercial and communal affairs throughout most of the eighteenth century. Leon Huhner, chronicler of early American Jewry, writes:

> The first of the name to come to New York . . . was Lewis Moses Gomez, whose father had fled from Spain and lived in France for a number of years before going to England, where he obtained "Letters of Denization" permitting him to reside in America "with all the privileges of one of the most favored subjects." He settled in New York in 1703. . . . He engaged in various large enterprises, particularly in the exportation of wheat on an enormous scale. . . . Daniel Gomez [his] son engaged in the West Indian trade at an early age, along with father and brothers. . . . In the *New York Gazette* on June 24, 1751, he announces a new importation from Liverpool, comprising "earthenware in casks and crates, Cheshire cheese, loaf sugar, cutlery ware, pewter, grindstones, coals, and sundry other goods too tedious to mention." But far more interesting than the commercial activities . . . were several real estate operations by Gomez, and his enterprise in the Indian trade . . . [which] became perhaps the most important source of their wealth.[14]

Two other important Jewish figures in colonial America were Barnard and Michael Gratz, who began their careers on the docks of Philadelphia in the 1750s. These merchant brothers, natives of Langendorf, Silesia, traveled extensively throughout the colonies, organizing a variety of business ventures. "It was the special ambition of the Gratz brothers as young merchants to be ship owners, trading around the world in every port open to American and British ships," writes William Vincent Byars. "They never gave up the attempt and they met all the success on the ocean that could be expected under the system of Imperial control of colonial trade."[15]

Perhaps the most enterprising and successful of the Jewish colonial merchants was Aaron Lopez of Newport who owned a fleet of whalers and engaged in shipping and trade. In his diary the Reverend Dr. Ezra Stiles, later president of Yale, wrote of him:

> He was a merchant of the first eminence; for honor and extent of commerce probably surpassed by no merch[an]t in America. He did business with the greatest ease and clearness—always carried about with him a sweetness of behav[ior], a calm urbanity [and] an agreeable and unaffected politeness of manners.
>
> Without a single enemy and the most universally beloved by an extensive acquaintance of any man I ever knew. His benef-

icence to his fam[il]y and connexions, to his nation [the Jews], and to all the world is almost without a parallel.[16]

This paragon of business acumen and personal virtue was a former Marrano who, at age twenty-one, escaped with his wife and family from Portugal to Newport. Upon their arrival in 1752, he and his wife remarried in accordance with Jewish law; he changed his name from Duarte to Aaron, and his wife's name from Anna to Abigail. Within a decade he was a leading member of his community.

America was also a haven for the impoverished. The plight of the poor of London in the 1720s moved James Edward Oglethorpe, member of Parliament, and some of his friends to establish a philanthropic colony for the resettlement of British paupers in the territory south of the Savannah River, between the Carolinas and Florida. Of the six thousand Jews residing in London in 1730, many were poor and supported by the Jewish community. The board of the Bevis Marks Synagogue (Sephardic) appointed three of its leading members to "interest themselves with those who have permission to arrange settlement in the English colony," with the aim of removing some of these poor Jews from the relief rolls of London Jewry. Their petition to the Georgia trustees to permit Jewish settlers in the new colony was hotly debated. While the discussion continued, the Jewish commissioners seized the initiative, chartered a ship and sent forty-two Jews to the New World. Chosen from both the Sephardic and Ashkenazic communities, they were a varied group. A few were people of some substance, but most had received free passage.

JEWS AND THE REVOLUTION

The War of Independence held out the promise of greater freedom, and most Jews joined the revolutionary cause. The Continental Army had its share of Jewish soldiers and officers. One of the first to fall in the cause of liberty was Francis Salvador of South Carolina. Among those who distinguished themselves on the field of battle were Solomon Bush, David S. Franks, Isaac Franks and Major Benjamin Nones. Another David Franks remained loyal to the Crown, as did Isaac Hart, who lost his life because of his Tory sympathies.

The papers of the Continental Congress contain a memorial from Haym Salomon, Philadelphia, August 25, 1778:

That your memorialist was some time before the Entry of British Troops at the said City of New York and soon after taken up as a Spy. . . . That being at New York he has been of great Service to the French and American prisoners and has assisted them with Money and helped them off to make their Escape—That this and his close connexions with such of the Hessian officers as were inclined to resign has rendered him at last so obnoxious to the British Head Quarters that he was already pursued by the Guards and on Tuesday the 11th inst, he made his happy Escape from thence. . . .

Your Memorialist has upon this Event most irrecoverably lost all his Effects and Credits to the amount of Five or Six thousand Pounds Sterling and left his distressed Wife and Child of a Month old at New York waiting that they soon have an opportunity to come out from thence with empty hands.

In these circumstances he most humbly prayeth to grant him any Employ in the way of his Business whereby he be enabled to support himself and his family—[17]

In Philadelphia, Haym Salomon aided the revolutionary cause, serving as "Broker to the Office of Finance." James Madison wrote in 1782: "I have for sometime past been a pensioner on the favor of Haym Salomon, a Jew broker." He confesses, "The kindness of our little friend in Front Street . . . will preserve me from extremities . . . he obstinately rejects all recompense."[18] Salomon, the American patriot, was also a loyal Jew. His standing in the Philadelphia Jewish community was such that he, a Polish Jew, was elected one of the four members of the *mahamad* (trustees) of the Sephardic congregation Mikveh Israel.

The *hazzan* (cantor-minister) of the Philadelphia congregation was another patriot, the Reverend Gershom Mendes Seixas, who had served as spiritual head of New York's Congregation Shearith Israel, but who, with others of his congregation, had fled that city when it was captured by the British. Carrying with him the ceremonial objects of the synagogue, he declared that he would live and serve only with men loyal to the revolutionary cause. Seixas was the first Jewish clergyman born in America, the son of a Sephardic father and an Ashkenazic mother. He personified the amalgam of national backgrounds which was to typify the American Jew, and the American legend of the "self-made man." Educated in the school maintained by Congregation Shearith Israel, he was sent as a young man to learn a trade, but instead, fashioned a career as a clergyman.

After the revolution, Seixas returned to his New York congregation, which he served until his death in 1816. A respected public figure, he was present in an official capacity at the inauguration of President George Washington, and served as a trustee of Columbia College for more than thirty years. To honor him, the college struck a medal with his likeness, bearing the legend "Gershom M. Seixas, Congregationis Hebraeae Sacerdos Novi Eboraci" (Priest of the Hebrew Congregation of New York).

Since the days of Asser Levy in New Amsterdam, the Jews of America had been zealous in pursuit of equal rights. The assertion of liberty and equality that the revolution engendered emboldened them to petition for the removal of laws and ordinances that discriminated against them. In December 1783, Haym Salomon and Gershom Mendes Seixas joined other members of the Mikveh Israel *mahamad* in a memorial to the Pennsylvania Council of Censors. The Commonwealth of Pennsylvania ordered that every member of the General Assembly had to take an oath that contained the phrase: "I do acknowledge the Scriptures of the Old and New Testament. . . ." The petitioners pointed out that "this religious test deprives the Jews of the most eminent rights of freemen."

The commonwealth might lose valued immigrants, they argued, if it persisted in its discriminatory laws. Moreover, the Jews of the United States had earned equality of rights by their participation in the revolutionary cause:

> The Jews of Charlestown, New York, New-Port, and other posts occupied by the British troops, have distinguishedly suffered for their attachment to the Revolution principles. . . .
>
> The Jews of Pennsylvania . . . have served some of them in the Continental army; some went out in the militia to fight the common enemy; all of them have cheerfully contributed to the support of the militia and of the government of this state.[19]

FOCUS
An Emissary from the Holy Land

The Reverend Ezra Stiles, minister of the Second Congregational Church at Newport, Rhode Island, attended Purim services in the local synagogue on March 8, 1773. He reported:

> There [in the synagogue] I saw Rabbi Carigal I judge aet. 45. lately from the city of Hebron, the Cave of Macpelah in the Holy Land. He was one of the two persons that stood by the Chusan at the Taubah or reading Desk while the Book of Esther was read. He was dressed in a red garment with the usual Phylacteries and habiliments, the white silk Surplice; he wore a high brown furr Cap, had a long Beard. He has the appearance of an ingenious & sensible Man.[20]

The rabbi was a son of the Hebron community, who had traveled widely in the Near East and Europe and twice to the Americas, acting on occasion as itinerant rabbinic functionary. In the summer of 1772 he came to Philadelphia. After a month there, and five and a half months in New York, he arrived in Newport March 3, 1773.

The Reverend Mr. Stiles had a vast curiosity about Jews and Judaism. He recorded his observations in voluminous diaries. We learn from him that no less than six rabbis visited Newport between 1759 and 1775. Stiles sought them out, conversed with them and described them and their conversations. Moses Malki was a native of Safed, while Moses Bar David was "born at Apta, Poland." Rabbi Carigal impressed him most. They spent much time together and Stiles kept notes on topics they discussed:

> March 30:
> the Gemara, the 2 Talmuds (of which he preferred the Babylonish), the Changes of the Hebrew Language in different Ages . . . showed me a passage in the *Zohar* which he said that the *Russians should conquer the Turks.* . . .
> June 14:
> on ventriloquism & the Witch of Endor . . . showed me a passage of St. *Augustin* de Civitate Dei in a Hebrew Book of *David Nieto* . . .
> July 15:
> whether the Rabbins of this Age thought themselves to have any particular Reasons for expecting the Messiah immediately.

Carigal supplied information about the Jews in other lands, and particularly the Holy Land, noting that there were about one thousand families of Jews and twelve synagogues "in all Judea or Holy Land A.D. 1773." Stiles also learned that there were three rabbis "settled in America, one in Jamaica, one in Surinam and one in Curaçao," but "none on the Continent of North America." Carigal himself planned to settle in Antigua.

The Congregationalist minister was a frequent visitor and guest at the synagogue. On May 28, Shavuot, Stiles reports that he heard a sermon in the synagogue in Spanish (Ladino?) by Carigal which lasted for forty-seven minutes. Among those in attendance were Governor Wantan, Judge Oliver and Judge Auchmuty. Though there were few listeners who understood any part of the lengthy sermon, the occasion was auspicious for the congregation. Dignitaries of Church and State were present; and the preacher in exotic dress, speaking a strange tongue, must have lifted a small group of immigrant Newport merchants to the status of sons of Patriarchs and Prophets. To preserve the memory of this occasion, Abraham Lopez, a native of Portugal and ex-Marrano, was entrusted with the task of translating it into English. Printed after Carigal left Newport, it was the first Jewish sermon to be published in America:

> *A Sermon Preached at the Synagogue, in Newport, Rhode Island, Called "The Salvation of Israel", on the Day of Pentecost, or Feast of Weeks, the 6th Day of the Month of Sivan, the year of Creation 5533,*

*or, May 28, 1773. Being the Anniversary of giving the Law at Mount
Sinai: By the Venerable Hocham, the Learned Rabbi, Haijim Isaac
Karigal, of the City of Hebron, near Jerusalem in the Holy Land.*[21]

Four years later Carigal died in Barbados. The affection which
Stiles bore for him survived parting and death. When the Newport
clergyman was called to become the fifth president of Yale, he suggested
to Aaron Lopez, the leader of the Newport Jewish community, that a
picture of Carigal be "deposited in the Library of this college." Lopez
was pleased that the likeness of the rabbi would be preserved "in so
distinguished a seminary," and in due time, a portrait done by Samuel
King was deposited in the Yale Library.

In an analysis of the First Federal Census in 1790, Ira Rosenswaike
notes that one-third to one-half of the adult male Jews were foreign-
born, that few of the immigrants had come in family groups and that
a substantial number of the immigrant single men married women born
in the New World. He estimates the Jewish population as from 1300
to 1500: residing in New England, 150; New York, 350; Pennsylvania,
250; Virginia, 200; Maryland, 50; South Carolina, 300; Georgia, 100;
New Jersey, Delaware, North Carolina, 100.[22] Jews were about one-
thirtieth of 1 percent of the total population. Yet, small as it was in
number, the Jewish community was perceived as an important and
integral part of the new nation. The Western world, raised on the Bible,
was acquainted with the ancient as well as modern Hebrews, and in
colonial America the works of Josephus were second in popularity only
to the Bible itself. The Jewish heritage served as one of the primary
components of American cultural life and its democratic tradition.

The Jews of colonial America participated eagerly in the building
of the nation and in the founding of the republic. For a people long an
object of scorn and persecution in the many lands of their dispersion,
this new government, professing equality for all its inhabitants, had
special significance and promise. The Jewish communities showed their
desire to share in the birth of the nation formally by addressing letters
of congratulations to George Washington, "The First President of the
United States." "The Hebrew Congregations in the Cities of Philadelphia, New York, Richmond and Charlestown" joined "in affection"
to express their homage. Individual letters were framed by "The Hebrew Congregation of the City of Savannah, Georgia" and "The Hebrew Congregation in Newport, Rhode Island."[23] Washington's warm
reply quoted the Prophets of Israel, joining them in the hope that the
"children of the stock of Abraham . . . shall sit in safety under . . . vine
and figtree." In his mind, as in the minds of most of his countrymen,
the Jews of the early republic were associated with their Biblical fore-
bears.

SOURCE
Four Letters at the Birth of the Nation

How did European Jews conceive of America?

An article published in the June 1783 issue of the *Deutches Museum* of Leipzig reflects the perception of America as a vast land needing settlers and cultivation, and as a society tolerant to Jews. The author suggests that America ought welcome the sore-beset, hardworking German Jew, who in appreciation would make a most loyal citizen and "would gladly contribute twofold taxes."

A Memorial Sent by German Jews to the President of the Continental Congress

Many of us . . . have learned with much satisfaction, from the peace made by the mighty American States with England, that wide tracts of land had been ceded to them which are as yet almost uninhabited. More than a century may elapse before the inhabitants of the thirteen united provinces will so increase as to populate and cultivate even the land which is already possessed by these provinces in such a degree as a duchy in our country is populated and cultivated. Your religion cannot prohibit you from leaving these deserts to us for cultivation; besides, you have been for a long time tolerating Jews near you. Whether policy might forbid you that, I do not know. At all events you have the legislative power in your hands, and we ask no more than to be permitted to become subjects of these thirteen provinces, and would gladly contribute twofold taxes for their benefit if we can only obtain permission to establish colonies at our own cost and to engage in agriculture, commerce, arts and sciences. Do we not believe in the same God as the Quakers do? Can our admission become more dangerous and precarious than that of the Quakers? Supposing that two thousand families of us would settle in a desert of America and convert it into a fertile land, will the old inhabitants of the provinces suffer by it? Let the conditions be stated to us, gracious President, under which you will admit us; we will then consider whether we can accept and keep them.

You would be astonished, most mighty President, . . . at the perseverance of a German Jew, if you could witness it. The great, nay, perhaps the greatest part of them, spend almost their whole life on the highway in the pursuit of retail business, and the trader consumes for his own person nothing but a herring and a penny loaf; the nearest brook or well has to supply his drink. All that he earns besides he conscientiously lays aside in order to bring it home on Friday to supply food and clothing for wife and chil-

dren. . . . During these one and a half days when he enjoys some-
what better food and rests in the bosom of his family he forgets
the wretched life which he is compelled to take up again on the
next Sunday. Granted that a Jew has at last become possessor of
a capital that would suffice to support a family, still he will not be
able to marry the woman he loves. Most of the time and in most
of the German provinces he is obliged to acquire protection money
for a sum which reduces his property to a half or one-third. But
love overcomes this difficulty too. He strains his energies anew,
again completes his capital and then seeks for permission to marry.
If he obtains it, the experience just described is repeated, for he
has to pay dearly for this permission and the expenses of a wedding
are not less among Jews than among Christians.

Here and there something has been done for us, but this
may be likened to the taking off of two pounds from one who
carries a burden of two tons.[24]

The American Jew looked beyond toleration. Over thirty years
of residence in America emboldened Jonas Phillips, merchant patriot
of New York and Philadelphia, to demand that rights promised by the
Declaration be guaranteed by the Constitution, "for myself, my children [of whom he had twenty-one] and posterity . . . and all the Israelites through the 13 united states of America."

Jonas Phillips to the Federal Convention
To His Excellency the president and the Honorable Members of
the Convention assembled

I the subscriber being one of the people called Jews of the
City of Philadelphia, a people scattered & dispersed among all
nations do behold with Concern that among the laws in the Constitution of Pennsylvania, there is a Clause Sect 10 to viz—I do
believe in one God the Creatur and governor of the universe the
Rewarder of the good & the punisher of the wicked—and I do
acknowledge the Scriptures of the old & New testament to be given
by divine inspiration—to swear & believe that the new testament
was given by divine inspiration is absolutely against the Religious
principle of a Jew, and is against his Conscience to take any such
oath—By the above law a Jew is deprived of holding any publick
office or place of Government which is Contradictory to the bill
of Right Sect 2 viz

That all men have a natural & unalienable Right to worship
almighty God according to the dictates of their own Conscience
and understanding & that no man ought or of Right can be Compelled to attend any Religious Worship or Creed or support any

place of worship or Maintain any minister contrary to or against his own free will and Consent, nor can any man who acknowledges the being of a God be Justly deprived or abridged of any Civil Right as a Citizen on account of his Religious sentiments or peculiar mode of Religious Worship . . . and that no authority can or ought to be vested in or assumed by any power whatever that shall in any case interfere or in any manner Controul the Right of Conscience in the free Exercise of Religious Worship.—

It is well known among all the Citizens of the 13 united states that the Jews have been true and faithfull whigs, & during the late Contest with England they have been foremost in aiding and assisting the states with their lifes & fortunes, they have supported the cause, have bravely fought and bled for liberty which they can not Enjoy.—

Therefore if the honourable Convention shall in their Wisdom think fit and alter the said oath & leave out the words to viz— and I do acknowledge the scripture of the new testament to be given by divine inspiration, then the Israelites will think themself happy to live under a government where all Religious societys are on an Equal footing—I solicit this favour for myself and my children & posterity, & for the benefit of all the Israelites through the 13 united states of America.

Your Most devoted obed. Servant

JONAS PHILLIPS

PHILADELPHIA 24th *Ellul* 5547 or *Sepr* 7th 1787.[25]

On August 17, 1790, the newly elected president, George Washington, honored Newport, Rhode Island, with a visit. The following morning, prior to his departure, deputations called upon the president to present to him expressions of affection and devotion. Moses Seixas, warden of Kahal Kadosh Yeshuat Israel, the Hebrew congregation of Newport, presented to him a letter which begins: "Permit the children of the stock of Abraham to approach you with the most cordial affection and esteem for your person and merits, and to join with our fellow citizens in welcoming you to Newport."

The letter contains an invocation to the God of Israel "beseeching Him that the Angel who conducted our forefathers through the wilderness into the promised land, may graciously conduct you through all the difficulties and dangers of this mortal life . . ." Seixas seized the opportunity to remind the president of the American Jews' association with the Biblical drama of liberation from foreign bondage and new nationhood. He suggests that no people have greater cause for loyalty to the new nation than the Jews, "Deprived as we heretofore have been of the invaluable rights of free citizens . . . we now behold a Government erected by the majesty of the people . . . a Federal Union whose basis is philanthropy, mutual confidence and public virtue." And Seixas adds his perception of what made this government unique and distinguished: "a Government which gives to bigotry no sanction, to persecution no assistance . . ."[26]

Here is a perception of America by a leader of American Jewry at the birth of the nation. In the context of the event and the way it is phrased, it is an expression of expectation as well. The heirs of a people who have suffered persecution in the Old World now look to the New World, the new nation and its newly elected president to afford this new community of Jews the freedom and equality so long denied them, and he places this eloquently worded expectation on public record.

In his reply "To the Hebrew Congregation in Newport, Rhode Island," George Washington borrowed the felicitous phrase of Seixas, as his own characterization of the new nation. The phrase became a formal and often quoted pronouncement by one of the Founding Fathers of America's purpose.

> George Washington's Letter to the New Port, R.I.
> Congregation, 1790

Gentlemen:

While I receive with much satisfaction your address replete with expressions of affection and esteem; I rejoice in the opportunity of assuring you that I shall always retain a grateful remembrance of the cordial welcome I experienced in my visit to New Port from all classes of Citizens.

The reflection on the days of difficulty and danger which are past is rendered the more sweet from a consciousness that they are succeeded by days of uncommon prosperity and security. If we have wisdom to make the best use of the advantages with which we are now favored, we cannot fail, under the just administration of a good government, to become a great and a happy people.

The Citizens of the United States of America have a right to applaud themselves for having given to mankind examples of an enlarged and liberal policy, a policy worthy of imitation.

All possess alike liberty of conscience and immunities of citizenship. It is now no more that toleration is spoken of, as if it was by the indulgence of one class of people, that another enjoyed the exercise of their inherent natural rights. For happily the government of the United States, which gives to bigotry no sanction, to persecution no assistance, requires only that they who live under its protection should demean themselves as good citizens, in giving it on all occasions their effectual support.

It would be inconsistent with the frankness of my character not to avow that I am pleased with your favorable opinion of my administration, and fervent wishes for my felicity.

May the children of the Stock of Abraham, who dwell in this land, continue to merit and enjoy the good will of the other inhabitants, while every one shall sit in safety under his own vine and fig-tree, and there shall be none to make him afraid.

May the Father of all mercies scatter light and not darkness in our paths, and make us all in our several vocations useful here, and in his own due time and way everlastingly happy.

G. Washington[27]

Rebecca Samuel, a young Jewish woman of Petersburg, Virginia, wrote a letter in Yiddish to her parents in Hamburg, Germany. Her perception of America in the 1790s is of a land of economic opportunity but spiritual peril for Jews.

Dear Parents:

I hope my letter will ease your mind. You can now be reassured and send me one of the family to Charleston, South Carolina. This is the place to which, with God's help, we will go after Passover. The whole reason why we are leaving this place is because of [lack of] *Yehudishkeit* [Jewishness].

Dear parents, . . . Jewishness is pushed aside here. There are here [in Petersburg] ten or twelve Jews, and they are not worthy of being called Jews. We have a *shohet* here who goes to market and buys *terefah* [nonkosher] meat and then brings it home. On Rosh Ha-Shanah [New Year] and on Yom Kippur [the Day of Atonement] the people worshipped here without one *sefer torah* [Scroll of the Law], and not one of them wore the *tallit* [a large prayer shawl worn in the synagogue] or the *arba kanfot* [the small set of fringes worn on the body], except Hyman and my Sammy's godfather. The latter is an old man of sixty, a man from Holland. He has been in America for thirty years already; for twenty years he was in Charleston, and he has been living here for four years. He does not want to remain here any longer and will go with us to Charleston. In that place there is a blessed community of three hundred Jews.

You can believe me that I crave to see a synagogue to which I can go. The way we live now is no life at all. We do not know what the Sabbath and the holidays are. On the Sabbath all the Jewish shops are open; and they do business on that day as they do throughout the whole week. But ours we do not allow to open.

With us there is still some Sabbath. You must believe me that in our house we all live as Jews as much as we can.

As for the Gentiles, we have nothing to complain about. For the sake of a livelihood we do not have to leave here. Nor do we have to leave because of debts. I believe ever since Hyman has grown up that he has not had it so good. You cannot know what a wonderful country this is for the common man. One can live here peacefully. Hyman made a clock that goes very accurately, just like the one in Buchenstrasse in Hamburg. Now you can imagine what honors Hyman has been getting here. In all Virginia there is no clock [like this one], and Virginia is the greatest province in the whole of America, and America is the largest section of the world. Now you know what sort of a country this is. It is not too long since Virginia was discovered. It is a young country. And it is amazing to see the business they do in this little Petersburg. . . .

When Judah comes here, he can become a watchmaker and a goldsmith, if he so desires. Here it is not like Germany where a watchmaker is not permitted to sell silverware. . . . Hyman has more to do in making silverware than with watchmaking. He has a journeyman, a silversmith, a very good artisan, and he, Hyman, takes care of the watches. This work is well paid here, but in Charleston, it pays even better.

All the people who hear that we are leaving give us their blessings. They say that it is sinful that such blessed children should be brought up here in Petersburg. My children cannot learn anything here, nothing Jewish, nothing of general culture. My Schoene [her daughter], God bless her, is already three years old. I think it is time that she should learn something, and she has a good head to learn. I have taught her the bedtime prayers and grace after meals in just two lessons. I believe that no one among the Jews here can do as well as she. And my Sammy [born in 1790], God bless him, is already beginning to talk.

Your devoted daughter and servant, Rebecca, the wife of Hayyim,
the son of Samuel the Levite.[28]

2.

The Early
Republic

THE WAR ENDED, INDEPENDENCE WON, THE ELECTED LEADERS OF THE RE-
public looked to England for friendship, and turned against their former
ally, France, which had mounted its own revolution. As the century
drew to an end, the country was divided between Federalists and Republicans, between those who favored the traditional stability represented by England, and those who hailed the revolutionary ideals of
France. The publication of the correspondence of the XYZ Affair,
which disclosed a demand by French political leaders for a bribe, brought
anti-French sentiment to a head and laid the groundwork for the Alien
and Sedition Acts. Suspicion, suppression, bitterness and recrimination
poisoned the atmosphere of the republic.

On March 23, 1798, President John Adams designated May 9
as a day for fasting, prayer and national humiliation. The citizens were
enjoined to repair to their houses of worship. The Jews of New York
met in their synagogue, recited appropriate psalms and heard a sermon
delivered by the Reverend Gershom Mendes Seixas.

Unlike the great majority of his colleagues in the pulpit, Seixas
did not attack the French, the first nation in Europe to grant Jews
citizenship. He stated "We are threatened with all the horrors of war
by a great, a conquering nation," yet he reminded his congregation
that "but a few years past" the same nation, "was looked upon to have
been highly instrumental in procuring liberty and independence to the
United States of America, when we were oppressed by the ravages and
devastations of an enraged enemy, who sought to deprive us of our
invaluable rights and privileges." He mentions neither France nor Eng-

land by name, but the reference was clear to all his listeners. Nor does he consider foreign threats to be the sole problem facing the infant republic. Equally dangerous, and more distressing, are internal divisiveness and enmity. Citing precedent and verse, he pleads for "friendly disposition toward each other." He recognizes the diversity of the nation "collected from different countries, each bringing with him the prejudices of the government he was brought up in." Such a heterogeneous society must, more than others, adhere to "the grand principles of benevolence towards all our fellow creatures."

Seixas is not unmindful of the special situation of the Jew in this new nation: "It hath pleased God to establish us in this country where we possess every advantage that other citizens of these states enjoy."[1]

Seixas perceives in the wars which plague nations, and the depravity which corrupts individuals, the "pangs of the Messiah," and he argues that "we must necessarily be led to believe that the glorious period of redemption is near at hand, and that our God will make manifest His intentions of again collecting the scattered remnants of Israel, and establishing them according to His divine promise." A pious Jew, he places God's promise of ingathering and redemption above a welcome, but perhaps temporary, haven. Still the haven that America offered in the here and now was not spurned because of the belief in divine redemption. In the first two decades of the republic, the Jewish population increased from less than two thousand to just under three thousand. In the next three decades, 1820–50, when the general population multiplied two and one-half fold, the Jewish population soared to some 50,000—a seventeenfold increase.

This phenomenal growth took place despite the fact that the American Jewish community was adversely affected by intermarriage and assimilation. As in most immigrant societies, men outnumbered women. A Jew wishing to marry within his faith often had either to return to his native country to seek a mate or import a bride. For many of the younger generation, the more ready reaction was to marry a Gentile. In the free and open society of America, the children of such marriages generally entered the majority Protestant community, and therefore the rate of attrition among the native-born generation of Jews was high. The spurt in the community's growth was due to one major factor—immigration.

Immigration demands three conditions: an intolerable situation in the country of origin, the promise of a better or more hopeful situation in a new place and the freedom to leave and settle in a new land.

America was open to immigration, and the conditions of the Jew in Europe were such as to make the enterprise most attractive. Initially, however, there were two factors which militated against it.

In the first decade of the nineteenth century the French Revolution's promise of "Liberty, Equality, Fraternity" was spread by the Napoleonic armies throughout Europe, bringing with it political emancipation for Jews in Western Europe. It gave new freedom to the Jew, and his future in Europe seemed destined to become more secure. Why brave an unknown continent when in the new Europe the Jew would enjoy equality of status and opportunity? The dangers of travel in Europe during the Napoleonic wars also contributed to slowing Jewish emigration to the merest trickle.

Convened in 1815 to restore Europe to its pre-Napoleonic terms, the Congress of Vienna set off a wave of reaction. Newly granted rights including political emancipation for Jews were revoked, and new oppressive measures enacted and enforced. Within the revised continental situation, the Jews suffered greatly. Their distress was particularly acute in the south German states. The social upheaval which followed the Napoleonic wars caused a population flow from German rural areas to urban centers with negative consequences, political and economic, for the Jewish townsmen. The unsuccessful revolutions of 1830 and 1848, and the reaction which set in afterward gave further cause for uneasiness within the Jewish community. The hopes raised by the French Revolution were shattered. After the false dawn of Napoleonic freedoms faded, the option of America looked brighter.

The American Jewish poet Penina Moise penned a welcome to the immigrants:

> If thou art one of that oppressed race,
> Whose pilgrimage from Palestine we trace,
> Brave the Atlantic—Hope's broad anchor weigh,
> A Western Sun will gild your future days.

From *Fancy's Sketch Book*, Charleston, 1833

In the 1830s and particularly in the forties, Jews arrived in America in significant numbers, mainly from Bavaria. They founded congregations in the existing communities and established new congregations in Boston, Hartford, New Haven, Albany, Syracuse, Rochester and Buffalo in the Northeast; Baltimore, Columbia, Augusta, Columbus, Mobile, New Orleans and Galveston in the South; and Cincinnati, Cleveland, Chicago, Louisville, Milwaukee, Pittsburgh, Columbus and Indianapolis in the Midwest. The De Sola-Lyons Calendar of 1854[2] listed ten congregations in the new state of California.

In 1820, the American Jewish community was largely native-born, English-speaking, small in number and rapidly assimilating. Only thirty years later it was largely a German-speaking, immigrant community beginning to establish the institutional framework that would answer its needs and lay the foundation for the community of the future.

ECONOMIC LIFE

Jews of the early Republic remained largely merchants, as they had been in colonial America. As they became integrated in American society, they entered an ever-widening area of economic pursuits. We find Jewish mechanics—carpenters, tailors, watchmakers. There were continual attempts to settle Jews on the land. In 1838 a group of Jews from New York City established an agricultural settlement in Ulster County, New York, which they named "Scholem." Apparently it did not last long, but it has the distinction of being the first of a large number of similar enterprises in nineteenth-century America.

The German Jewish immigration introduced the peddler in large numbers. In *Memoirs of American Jews*, Jacob R. Marcus writes:

> They were city peddlers and country peddlers. The former sold notions, cigars, stationery and jewelry; the packs of the latter, as a rule, contained clothing and dry goods. At best, the foot peddler was a beast of burden. He staggered under a heavy load that was never less than forty pounds. . . . At times he walked as much as twenty-five miles a day. . . . He could speak little English: he was homesick and footsore. . . .[3]

Peddling was a transitional occupation. Each peddler looked for a suitable place to establish a business and settle down. "From pack-on-back, to store, to department store" describes the economic career of a number of Jewish merchants. Some former peddlers and shop-keepers rose to great wealth, like the Seligman, Lehman and Straus families, but the great majority of Jews remained small merchants. Typical of mid-nineteenth-century Jewish economic life was the town of Bangor, Maine. Of its six heads of Jewish families, two were in the dry-goods business, one was a clothing merchant and three were peddlers.

The American generation of the 1820s through the 1840s grew up in freedom and some entered the arts, the professions and public service, a few with modest success. Daniel L. M. Peixotto became president of the Medical Society of the City and County of New York, and Dr. Jacob De La Motta served as secretary of the Medical Society of South Carolina. Samuel B. H. Judah and Jonas B. Phillips were playwrights and literary figures of some distinction. Isaac Harby was a newspaper writer and editor in Charleston, South Carolina. Naphtali Phillips published the semi-weekly newspaper *The National Advocate*, which Mordecai Manuel Noah edited.

FOR POLITICAL EQUALITY

In a report sent to Hannah Adams for inclusion in her *History of the Jews* (Boston, 1812),[4] the Reverend Gershom Mendes Seixas writes: "The United States is, perhaps, the only place where the Jews have not suffered persecution, but have, on the contrary, been encouraged and indulged in every right of citizens."

This theme was repeated by Jew and non-Jew alike, but the reality of everyday political and social life was often different from the boast. In America, however, bigotry could be countered vigorously and without fear.

In 1813, Mordecai Manuel Noah was appointed consul at Tunis. Two years later he received a letter from James Monroe, then secretary of state, reading:

> At the time of your appointment, Consul at Tunis, it was not known that the religion which you profess would form any obstacle to the exercise of your Consular functions. Recent information, however . . . proves that it would produce a very unfavourable effect. In consequence of which the President has deemed it expedient to revoke your commission.[5]

Noah was quick to protest this discrimination, first in a pamphlet published in Washington in 1816, and again and at length in his *Travels*. . . . He was joined in his protest by a number of prominent American Jews, among them Isaac Harby, then editor of *The Southern Patriot*. When was it "discovered that *religion* disqualifies a man from the exercise of his political functions?" Harby inquires in a letter to Monroe. "Or has this doctrine *ever* been known, since the first hour of the establishment of our invaluable Constitution. . . . An objection, on the score of religion, would sound to them [the framers of the Constitution] 'most monstrous and unnatural.' They know no religious distinctions. One great character of *citizenship* alone prevails."[6]

SOURCE
A Defense of the Jews

French-born Benjamin Nones arrived from Bordeaux in 1777. Two years later, serving the revolutionary cause in General Casimir Pulaski's Legion, he was cited for bravery. "His behaviour . . . has been marked by a bravery and courage which a military man is expected to show for the liberties of his country."[7]

After the war, he became a leader of the Philadelphia Jewish community and of the Democrat-Republicans. His "bravery and courage" were again called upon when he, his people and his cause were scurrilously attacked in an anonymous letter in the Federalist journal, the *Gazette of the United States*, on August 5, 1800. Nones framed a reply and counterattack which was printed as a broadside and distributed in Philadelphia. It was promptly republished as a feature in the Republican newspaper, the *Aurora*, on August 13, 1800.

> *To the printer of the* Gazette of the United States
> Sir,

I am accused of being a *Jew*, of being a *Republican*, and of being *Poor.*

I *am* a Jew. I glory in belonging to that persuasion, which even its opponents, whether Christian, or Mohamedan, allow to be of divine origin—of that persuasion on which Christianity itself was originally founded and must ultimately rest—which has preserved its faith secure and undefiled, for near three thousand years, whose votaries have never murdered each other in religious wars, or cherished the theological hatred so general, so unextinguishable among those who revile them. A persuasion, whose patient followers have endured for ages the pious cruelties of Pagans, and of Christians, and persevered in the unoffending practice of their rites and ceremonies, amidst poverties and privations; amidst pains, penalties, confiscations, banishments, tortures and deaths, beyond the example of any other sect, which the page of history has hitherto recorded. . . .

But I am a Jew. I am so: and so were Abraham, and Isaac, and Moses and the prophets, and so too were Christ and his apostles; and I feel no disgrace in ranking with such society, however it may be subject to the illiberal buffoonery of such men as your correspondents.

I am a *Republican!* Thank God I have not been so heedless and so ignorant of what has passed, and is now passing in the political world. I have not been so proud or so prejudiced as to renounce the cause for which I have *fought* as an American, throughout the whole of the revolutionary war, in the militia of Charleston, and in Polaskey's legion, I fought in almost every action which took place in Carolina, and in the disastrous affair of Savannah, shared the hardships of that sanguinary day, and for three and twenty years, I felt no disposition to change my political any more than my religious principles. . . .

I am a Jew, and if for no other reason, for that reason am I a republican. In the *monarchies* of Europe we are hunted from society, stigmatized as unworthy of common civility, thrust out as it were from the converse of men; objects of mockery and insult. . . . Among the nations of Europe we are inhabitants every where: but citizens no where *unless in republics.* Here, in France, and in the Batavian republic alone, we are treated as men and as brethren. In republics we have *rights,* in monarchies we live but to experience *wrongs.* . . .

How then can a Jew but be a Republican? in America particularly. Unfeeling and ungrateful would he be if he were callous to the glorious and benevolent cause of the difference between his situation in this land of freedom and among the proud and privileged law-givers of Europe.

But I am *poor*; I am so, my family also is large, but soberly and decently brought up. . . . I know that to purse-proud aristocracy poverty is a crime, but it may sometimes be accompanied with honesty even in a Jew: I was bankrupt some years ago; I obtained my certificate and was discharged from my debts. Having been more successful afterwards, I called my creditors together, and eight years afterwards, unsolicited, I discharged all my old debts. I offered interest which was refused by my creditors, and they gave me under their hands without any solicitations of mine, as a testimonial of the fact, (to use their own language) "as a tribute due to my honor and honesty. . . ."

Your humble servant,
Benjamin Nones.[8]

PHILADELPHIA, August 11, 1800.

FOCUS
A Plea for the Maryland Jew Bill, 1824

In 1776, the year the Declaration of Independence proclaimed that "all men are created equal," Maryland adopted a constitution. Its preamble, known as the Declaration of Rights, states: "It is the duty of every man to worship God in such manner as he thinks most acceptable to Him: all persons professing the Christian religion are equally entitled to protection in their religious liberty."

Religious liberty is declared—for Christians. And to give practical application to the declaration, Article 35 provides: "No other test or qualification ought to be required on admission to any office of trust or profit than such oath of support and fidelity to the State . . . and a declaration of belief in the Christian religion."

The new nation established, the Constitution adopted and the Bill of Rights enacted, "Solomon Etting and others" petitioned the Maryland Assembly in 1797: "a sect of people called Jews . . . are deprived of invaluable rights of citizenship and praying to be placed on the same footing as other good citizens."[9]

The petition was termed "reasonable," but was not acted upon, a fate which befell subsequent ones. In 1804 the struggle ceased, not to be pressed again for fourteen years. In 1818, a champion arose in the person of Thomas Kennedy. He asked the legislature of which he was a member to appoint a committee "to consider the justice and expediency of placing the Jewish inhabitants on equal footing with the Christians." An eight-year struggle ensued in the legislature, in the press and in the ballot. Kennedy was joined by Ebenezer S. Thomas, Judge Henry Brackenridge and Colonel William G. D. Worthington. The Jewish community of Baltimore, now grown to some 150, was led in the endeavor by Solomon Etting and Jacob Cohen, leading members of the leading families.

A vote in 1819 defeated what was now called "The Jew Bill," 50–24, the Republicans voting in favor, the Federalists against. Four years later a broader bill was again defeated, and Kennedy lost at the polls in 1823. Elected a year later, he continued his struggle for justice and full equality. The promise of America was not to be denied, and in 1825 an enfranchising bill was passed and confirmed a year later. It provided:

> that every citizen of this state professing the Jewish Religion . . . appointed to any office of public trust . . . shall . . . make and subscribe a declaration of his belief in a future state of rewards and punishments, in the stead of the declaration now required . . .[10]

The spoken and printed word played their part in the struggle and victory. None was more informative or effective than the Speech of Colonel W. G. D. Worthington delivered on Thursday, January 29, 1824, in the Maryland legislature and published in Baltimore in 1824.[11] Mr. Worthington held a variety of positions in government service and was named "colonel" by the city of Baltimore. He was obviously acquainted with many Jews, and it seems most likely that Solomon Etting provided him not only with information but with motivation as well.

The pleas of Kennedy for justice, and the skillful legal argument of Brackenridge were lofty and idealistic, but Worthington's practical emphasis was more telling and persuasive.

Speech of Colonel Worthington,

Delivered on Thursday, 29th of January, 1824, in the Maryland Legislature on abolishing the Religious Test.

Mr. Speaker: On a subject of this high importance, I feel a deep solicitude. . . .

I shall divide my subject into two parts: . . .

1st.—This disqualification is against the spirit of our constitution, and the letter of that of the United States, and against the genius and character of the governments of our State and Union, and the age in which we live.

2d.—It is against the policy of our country.

Sir:— . . . The whole scope of the Declaration of Rights, and the constitution of Maryland go to promulgate and establish our unrestrained and liberal form of government. It exists only in this character, and breathes only this spirit—so that this religious restriction, seems to be an alien and disjointed member of that compact—an intruder, an interpolator. . . . It must be recollected too, that this basis of our state rights was framed at so early a period as August, '76, when something of a monarchical and colonial prejudice, and narrow-mindedness, still hung about us—passing upwards, from dependence to freedom!

Not so with the Constitution of the Union—that was framed many years after, when we had passed from colonial misgovernment. . . . There, we have a right to look for, and there we see, this *wily enemy to equal rights*, could find no habitation nor resting place; . . . *No Religious Test* stands in high relief over the very portals of the temple and Intolerance falls broken and prostrate at the sight! This was no hasty principle engrafted in the Constitution—it grew out of the *plighted faith* of the patriots and heroes of the revolution, and the wishes of the states after the dissolution of the confederacy. . . .

Thus, Sir, we see, that Toleration—that *No Religious Test*, was the very corner stone laid by our illustrious progenitors. . . . We have now twenty-four states, eleven of which have been added since the Revolution; in every one of which, a *Religious Test* has been expressly excluded—what can be a stronger proof of the genius and spirit of the age in which we live? Even in the old states, but two or three retain a test—in the others, it is expressly excluded. A person was, some year or so past, elected in the North Carolina legislature; she has a *strict test*—his seat was attempted to be vacated; it was determined that the State Test was repugnant to the constitution of the United States, *and he retained his seat!*—he was a Jew! What does this shew, but that an isolated and odious disability like this, is swept away before the age.

It is certainly not only the policy of the union, but of each particular strata, to encourage the emigration of moral, enterprising, and affluent citizens to their shores. This assertion is now received as a political axiom.—The state, which creates or retains disqualifications, on any description of persons, will throw them into other states which have not such disqualifications, and thereby injure herself. Should this honourable House negative this bill, who could blame those gentlemen of the Hebrew Church, who have signed the memorial before you, from quitting your state with their families, their connexions, and wealth, and choosing some other state, where they enjoy equal rights and favour, with all its citizens. Some persons may think that we should lose but little, either in character, wealth, or numbers; but I assure you, I have a document here, which confutes such a conclusion. Before I left Baltimore, I wrote on a small scrip of paper some half dozen queries, and requested Solomon Etting, Esq. to have them faithfully and truly answered, and transmit them to me. . . . This is Mr. Etting's original statement, which I will read through as it is written.

Solomon Etting's Answers to Col. Worthington's Queries

Question 1st.—The number of Jews in the State of Maryland?

Answer—Supposed, at least, *one hundred and fifty*.

Ques. 2d.—The wealth of the Jews in the State of Maryland?

Ans.—General wealth difficult to ascertain; among a few heads of families, we may estimate *half a million of dollars*.

Ques. 3d.—The number of Jews in the U. States?

Ans.—At least estimate, six thousand.

Ques. 4th.—The wealth of the Jews in the U. States?

Ans.—This is equally difficult to ascertain with question 2d. Among the *heads of families*, in the principal cities, we may fairly estimate the wealth at *ten millions of dollars*.

Ques. 5th.—What offices have been held, or are now held by members of the profession?

Ans.—To enumerate these, in detail, would be extremely tedious and difficult; we will mention a few within immediate recollection.

Sol. Bush—Colonel in the American Revolution, a distinguished officer, and who died after the revolution of the wounds received, or effects arising out of them.

There were many valuable members, *officers, principally*, in the revolution, from the South chiefly, who were nearly all cut off and destroyed early in the war; they were ever at their posts, and always foremost in hazardous enterprizes.

Reuben Etting—Marshal of Maryland, appointed by Mr. Jefferson, and who continued in office until his removal from the state.

Ditto—Captain of a volunteer corps, raised very early in Baltimore, long under his command, and grew so numerous as to require being divided into companies and thrown into the 5th regiment of Maryland militia.

Solomon Etting—Captain 5th regiment Maryland militia, appointed by Governor Paca.

B. I. Cohen—Lieutenant in Columbian Volunteers, attached to the 5th regiment Maryland militia, appointed by Charles Ridgely, of Hampton, Esq.

M. M. Noah—Major in Pennsylvania, Counsul to *Tunis* for the *American government*, and on his return to the country, appointed by the legislature of New York to the important station of SHERIFF of their metropolis.

A. A. Massias—Major in the U.S. army during the late war, and retained in the service at the reduction of the army; he is now pay-master for the southern department.

U. P. Levy—Lieutenant in the Navy of the United States; has repeatedly distinguished himself in the service—last commander of the U. S. schooner Revenge, and lately sailed for London and Paris, as bearer of despatches to the ministers of the government at those places.

. . . This test is a restriction on the people—it says, they shall not elect a man for a particular service, unless he declare, *after* his election, that he possesses a particular superadded qualification which the people, who may have elected him, think has nothing to do with that service. The people have cause to complain, and a large majority of them do—it is vulgarly called a Jew Bill; it might as well be called a Mahomedan, or Persian Bill. . . .

It is against the spirit of the age—it is against the spirit of your Declaration of Rights: and on that rock, the Constitution of the Union, I build my argument. . . .

The "person . . . elected in the North Carolina legislature" referred to in Worthington's speech was Jacob Henry. He was elected in 1809. A challenge was raised. He defended his rights in a speech which has become a classic. "Conduct alone is the subject of human laws," he argued. "A man ought to suffer civil disqualifications for what he does and not for what he thinks." He was allowed to take his seat, by exempting legislative office from state constitutional restrictions which were not removed till 1868.

Solomon Etting (1764–1847) was born in York, Pennsylvania, and has the distinction of being the first native-born Jew in America to become a *shohet* (ritual slaughterer). He moved to Baltimore, organized the Baltimore East India Company and served as a director of the first American railroad company, the Baltimore and Ohio. He was equally active in the civic life of the city, and led the struggle for the "Jew Bill."

Solomon Bush, born in Philadelphia in 1753, was appointed deputy adjutant general for the state militia of Pennsylvania in 1777. He fought in the Revolution and, when wounded, was retired with the rank of lieutenant colonel. A fervent patriot and abolitionist, he was unsuccessful in his quest for public office.

Reuben Etting (1762–1848), elder brother of Solomon, in 1801 was appointed by President Jefferson as federal marshal for Maryland. As a Jew, he could not have held any office in that state.

Abraham A. Massias (1772–1848) of Charleston, South Carolina, from 1802 to 1809 served in the New York militia. Following his service in the War of 1812, he remained in the army, retiring in 1820 with the rank of major.

Uriah P. Levy (1792–1862) of Philadelphia and New York served in the navy as a high-ranking officer. His six courts-martial and two dismissals he attributed to anti-Semitism and jealousy. Reinstated, he led the battle for the abolition of flogging in the navy.

Worthington continues his argument:

Suppose Rothschild, with his immense wealth . . . be driven to seek asylum in this western hemisphere . . . the moment he re-collected this test . . . he would turn in loathing from you to live in some *Free State*. No more than a month or two ago, a Protestant church involved in debt, in N. Orleans . . . set up at public sale . . . was bought by Mr. Judah Touro, a Jew. . . . Did he convert it into a warehouse or . . . make money on it? No: he gave it back, at a moderate rent to the pastor and congregation.

Judah Touro was a New Orleans merchant and philanthropist, who bequeathed $205,000 to Jewish institutions and $148,000 to Christian and non-sectarian purposes. His last will and testament reads like a directory of Jewish institutions in America in 1855. His beneficence enabled Sir Moses Montefiore to build the first Jewish neighborhood in Jerusalem outside the walls of the Old City.

He concludes:

Israel prays to you in her oppression and tribulation! Hear her— you have no excuse. . . . It rests with you, who have the power to restore health to the daughter of her people!

INSTITUTIONS OF RELIGION

The early nineteenth century was marked by a great religious revival throughout America. De Tocqueville was struck by the power religion had over the lives of the American people. Churches were built and filled. Religious concerns such as salvation, the state of man's soul, the power of grace, the need of baptism were topics of conversation and controversy. The clergy was esteemed, and newspapers, magazines and countless books and pamphlets recorded their words and views. Laws were enacted to preserve the sanctity of the Sabbath.

The Jews could not help but be influenced by this atmosphere. Pious Jews founded congregations and erected synagogues for their own spiritual needs; Jewish nonbelievers helped maintain them because it was the American thing to do. In city after city, a small group of Jews would establish the Jewish community by organizing a congregation.

The *Savannah Republican* of April 21, 1820, reports:

> On Wednesday the Grand Lodge of Georgia, and the subordinate Lodges of this city, assembled in Solomon's Lodge room, for the purpose of making the necessary arrangements for the laying of the cornerstone of a Hebrew Synagogue, about to be erected in this city.

The assemblage then proceeded to consecrate the ground and lay the stone. After an "anthem from a band of music," Thomas U.P. Charlton, Masonic Grand Master of Georgia and mayor of Savannah, spoke:

> This ceremony is a beautiful illustration of our happy, tolerant and free government. Everyone here is permitted to adore the Eternal after the dictates of his conscience. . . .

The erection of a synagogue was an event of public celebration; the institution endowed the Jewish community with a place in the general community. The establishment of congregations and construction of synagogues led to the publication of prayer books. In 1826, when the Jewish community throughout America numbered no more than some six thousand, Solomon Henry Jackson, the first Jewish printer in New York, published *The Form of Daily Prayers According to the Custom of the Spanish and Portuguese Jews*. It contained the traditional prayers in Hebrew, "carefully Revised and Corrected by E.S. Lazarus" (the grandfather of the poet Emma Lazarus), and an English translation by the publisher-printer himself.

Solomon Henry Jackson had left his native England for America in the late 1780s. He married the daughter of a Presbyterian minister who bore him five children. But when his wife died after twenty years of marriage, he left his rural home, took his children with him to New York, raised them as Jews and devoted the rest of his life in defense of Judaism and in the service of the Jewish community.

The Jackson prayer book sought to adapt the traditional liturgy to the requirements of the New World. The translator-publisher notes in "To the Public" that "it was thought best to adapt the prayer [He

Who Brings Salvation to Kings] to our republican institutions. . . .
Martyrdom having ceased, and the liberality of mankind assuring us it
will no more be revived, it was thought best to omit the [martyrology]
prayer *Those Who Were Burned at the Stake for the Sanctification of God's
Name. . . .*"

The prayer book met with only limited subscription, for its
republican stance made it unfit for use in the West Indies or England
itself. Moreover, it followed the Sephardic liturgy, while the new congregations being established by the fast-growing number of immigrants
were all Ashkenazi.

A decade later, the Reverend Isaac Leeser, German-born *hazzan*
of the Sephardic Mikveh Israel Synagogue, produced a six-volume
prayer book, *Siftei Zadikim,* a truly distinguished work of translation,
typography and bookmaking. This prayer book also followed the liturgy of the Spanish and Portuguese Jews, but was specifically devised
not only for the Jews of the United States, but for those of the West
Indies and England as well. It therefore included both "A Prayer for a
Royal Government" and "A Prayer for a Republican Government."
Nor was the growing Ashkenazic community forgotten by Leeser who,
in 1848, published *Sidur Divrei Zadikim, The Book of Daily Prayers for
Every Day of the Year According to the Custom of the German and Polish
Jews.* Meant for the United States alone, the book omitted the "Prayer
for a Royal Government."

The nascent awareness of the singular needs of a native-born
generation of American Jews became apparent as early as 1824. In that
year, forty-seven members of Beth Elohim Congregation in Charleston, South Carolina, presented a "Memorial" to the community leadership asking that the service be abridged, that portions be repeated in
English and that a sermon in English become part of the service. The
petition was rejected, and on November 21, the dissenters founded a
new congregation, The Reformed Society of Israelites. Isaac Harby,
the moving spirit of the society, describes the goals in *The North American Review* as the establishment of

> order and decency in worship, harmony and beauty in chanting,
> the inculcation of morality and charitable sentiments upon indi-
> viduals, and the promotion of piety toward the Deity. In these
> things, the Society believes, consist religion, virtue and happiness;
> in these, the salvation of every rational and immortal being.[12]

The Society issued its own prayerbook, reflecting its own philosophy:

> In the total absence of any well digested form of service for the
> Sabbath, as well as other occasions, adapted to the feelings, opin-
> ions and dispositions of many, who differ from their brethren of

the ancient Synagogue, it is hoped, and believed that this collection [a prayer book] will in great measure supply the deficiency.[13]

The prayer book begins with the enumeration of Articles of Faith, ten in number. It contains prayers for public worship, as well as newly composed prayers for the rite of circumcision, the naming of a daughter, the marriage ceremony, etc.—all with accompanying instructions for the conduct of the ritual.

The preface also expresses the hope that at a future period the society will "present to the Israelites of the United States, a new and enlarged edition of the whole form of prayer. . . ."

The society went out of existence three years later, so that the hopes were never realized. The anticipated "enlarged edition" would appear only a quarter of a century later. So ended the initial American attempt to establish Reform Judaism. A later, viable venture into Reform Judaism was an importation from Germany which found a hospitable environment in America and flourished on its adopted soil as nowhere else in the world.

IN DEFENSE OF JUDAISM

America welcomed the Jews and zealous American Christians attempted to welcome them into the Christian faith. The Reverend Dr. Ezra Stiles said of Aaron Lopez, "He was my intimate Friend and Acquaintance!" then ruefully added: "Oh, how often have I wished that sincere pious and candid mind could have perceived the Evidence of Christianity, perceived the Truth as it is in Jesus Christ."

In the early nineteenth century, missionary activity was pressed with vigor. There was no quorum of Jews in Boston in 1822, when the pious ladies of the Hub of the Universe felt called to organize The Baptist Female Society of Boston and Vicinity for Promoting Conversion of the Jews. Six years earlier a national society, The American Society for Evangelizing the Jews, had been formed, and when refused a charter under that name it changed the word Evangelizing to Meliorating the Condition of. Under its new name it began widespread activity which lasted some forty years.

Much of the early activity of the society revolved about the person of the Reverend Joseph Samuel Christian Frey. Born Joseph Levi, in Germany, he served as a minor Jewish religious functionary. After his conversion he turned to professional missionary activity in England and the United States. A prolific writer, he published books, tracts and journals. The first of the latter was a monthly *Israel's Advocate, or the Restoration of the Jews Contemplated and Urged,* which started publication in 1823. Within a year, Solomon Henry Jackson began the publication of *The Jew, Being A Defence of Judaism Against All Adversaries and Particularly Against the Insidious Attacks of Israel's Advocate.* In the preface he writes:

> We have enlargement; we have assurance of life. . . . There is no further occasion for the trembling heart, since, like other men, we are secured in life, and property; in short in equal rights, among which are conceded the right of conscience;—and, as other men, when our peculiar religious tenets, and our character, as a people, are attacked, we have the right of defence . . .

For two years, this first Jewish periodical in America was published monthly, engaging in vigorous polemic and argument.

The missionaries carried their activities to the very door of the synagogue. In a letter published in *The United States Gazette*, in 1836, Isaac Leeser states that an agent of the American Tract Society, "visited our place of worship on last Sabbath . . . after the conclusion of the service, he posted himself at the entrance, and as the congregation was leaving the synagogue, he handed copies of a tract . . . contravening the tenets which we profess, to ladies, gentlemen and even children. . . ." He writes the letter in warning, that should this recur, "much as we deprecate any violence or disturbance, we cannot answer for the forbearance of the zealous ones among us, who might perhaps be induced in their honest indignation, to eject an impertinent intermeddler, mildly if they can, forcibly if they must."

TO AID BRETHREN ABROAD

The spiritual energy of American Jews was not expended merely within the framework of the local community. It spilled over into a concern for broader Jewish problems, and its spokesman in such matters was Mordecai Manuel Noah, the most fascinating American Jew of the first half of the nineteenth century. He was one of the first American dramatists whose plays were well received by contemporary audiences. He edited a number of newspapers and attained considerable political influence. He was a man of pronounced opinion and forceful character who apparently delighted in controversy. His opponents were as many and varied as his friends. His public service included the offices of surveyor of the port of New York, high sheriff, and, as mentioned earlier, consul to Tunis.

Noah's active and creative imagination expressed itself most fully in his activities on behalf of Jews and Judaism. He was the first to advocate the establishment of a Jewish agricultural settlement and a Jewish college in America. The newspapers and journals of the day recorded his views on Judaism. In the *Odd Fellows Offering for 1851,* we find an article on Simhat Torah; to *The Occident,* he submitted a chemist's report on imported olive oil which had been adulterated with lard; to a contemporary volume of recipes, he sent his own method for making kosher wine.

Of greatest interest, in historical perspective, is Noah, the proto-Zionist. In 1818 he looked forward to the day when the Jewish people would establish a just and honorable government in the Holy Land: "Never were prospects for the restoration of the Jewish nation to their ancient rights and dominion more brilliant than they are at present."[14]

In the meanwhile, he attempted, in 1825, to establish a home and refuge for Jews in America on Grand Island in the Niagara River— as a "night's lodging" till their eventual restoration of Palestine. As a Jew he looked to the reestablishment in Palestine of a Jewish state. As an American, he was convinced that America could serve as a haven and refuge for his scattered, sorely beset brethren.

But long before the Jews would once again "possess themselves . . . of Syria," an event took place in its capital city, which had signal influence on the course of Jewish history. In February 1840, the head of a Franciscan monastery in Damascus disappeared. Thirteen Jews, including three rabbis, were accused of murdering the monk to use his blood for ritual purposes. They were arrested and tortured. Some "confessed" under torture, but later repudiated their confessions. The Damascus Affair became an issue of international interest. Anti-Jewish riots broke out in the Middle East, and anti-Jewish defamation was propagated by the clerical press of France, Belgium and Italy. The British government intervened in behalf of the accused. Eventually, through the exertions of British and French Jewry, led by Adolphe Crémieux and Sir Moses Montefiore, the accused were acquitted and released.

American Jewry did not remain indifferent during this period. Since colonial days American Jews had been concerned with the plight of fellow Jews. Traveling collectors for Palestinian charities were welcomed and generously supported. Now was a time for united Jewish action. Mass meetings held in New York, Philadelphia, Richmond and other sizable Jewish communities petitioned the American government to use its good offices to help the accused.

Clearly, areas of common interest united all American Jewish communities. Should not American Jewry then form a union where mutual concerns could be discussed and joint action planned? Isaac Leeser seized the opportunity and attempted to form a Union of American Israelites. A circular signed by representatives of "the Sephardim . . . the Ashkenazim and of the Polish synagogues . . ." of Philadelphia was circulated. It contained plans for a national religious authority, a system of elementary and higher Jewish education and a union of congregations, and urged the convening of a conference to consider them. But as Leeser wrote retrospectively, "the conference did not meet; no rabbinical authority was instituted, no school was erected, no union was established, and the incipient division and party strife were permitted to take what shape they pleased." Leeser blamed the lack of success on the opposition of the leaders of Shearith Israel of New York, who feared that the union would be dominated by the numerically superior German Jews.[15]

As we shall see, it was two decades later, in 1859, that American Jewry united and the Board of Delegates of American Israelites was established. But the idea of a union and the conviction that American Jewry was *community* were already present as the Jews of America entered the second half of the nineteenth century.

FOCUS
American Jewry Responds to the Damascus Affair

The event was deemed so newsworthy that the *Pennsylvania Inquirer and Daily Courier* devoted two-thirds of its news page to it. Its August 31, 1840, issue contains six columns of an article headlined PERSECUTION OF THE JEWS/THE MEETING IN PHILADELPHIA, as well as an editorial apology and explanation:

> We have been compelled to crowd out several articles intended for this morning's paper, in order to make room for the official account of the recent meeting in this city, in relation to the persecuted Jews of Damascus. It possesses the deepest interest. We have printed a few extra copies of the *Inquirer*, for the accommodation of such of our citizens as desire to forward copies to friends at a distance.

The editors of the *Inquirer* were correct in assuming that the Philadelphia meeting would be of interest to "friends at a distance." Similar meetings were held in New York, Charleston, Richmond, Cincinnati and Savannah. Every American Jewish community of size met to protest the Damascus Affair and to petition and urge the government of the United States to use its good offices to effect the release of the Jews undergoing torture in the prison at Damascus.

News of the outrage was apparently slow in reaching the Jews in America. The meeting of New York Jews was held almost two months after that of the Board of Deputies in London. But, once aroused, American Jewry moved with dispatch and boldness. Meeting followed meeting, and strong representations were made to the State Department and the president. The Jews of New York informed President Martin Van Buren "we are persuaded [of what] is the unanimous opinion of the Israelites throughout the Union, that you will cheerfully use every possible effort to induce the Pasha of Egypt to manifest more liberal treatment towards his Jewish subjects."

"The Israelites of Charleston" drafted a set of Resolutions which they sent to President Van Buren with a covering letter expressing the hope "that the efforts of civilized Europe, in the protection of a suffering, inoffensive and calumniated Race, will find a ready effective and moral support from our country."

The last resolution was of parochial Jewish interest and was not sent to the president. It read: "*Resolved,* That a Committee of five be appointed to confer with the Richmond Committee, and others, in relation to the objects of the meeting." Richmond Jewry sent a letter to the president "that in common with their brethren" they express thanks to him for "the voluntary act of the Chief Magistrate of this Great Republic, in behalf of the persecuted Jews of the East." The leaders of the individual communities of American Jews perceived in themselves a sense of national community. Expressing what they termed "The unanimous opinion of the Israelites throughout the Union," they felt it their right and duty to demand that their government act in their interest as they conceived this interest to be, couching it always, of course, in language of broad humanitarian principles.

A pamphlet entitled *Proceedings of A Meeting Held at the Synagogue Mikveh Israel Philadelphia . . . the 27th of August, 1840,* on the theme "Persecution of the Jews in the East"[16] provides information about the events in Damascus and the protest meeting. The leaders and officers were:

Hyman Gratz, born in the City of Brotherly Love in the year of the Declaration of Independence, made his fortune in the insurance industry and gave liberally to civic and Jewish institutions. His attachment to the Mikveh Israel Congregation was particularly strong and his legacy provided the foundation for the Gratz College. Abraham Hart was only thirty years old in 1840, but was already a prominent publisher and leader of the Jewish community. Philadelphia-born, of German-Dutch parentage, he assumed the presidency of Mikveh Israel a year later. The president of the meeting, John Moss, a native of England, was a respected elder of the community who could look back at a distinguished career in business, civic, political and religious activities.

The main speaker was the Reverend Isaac Leeser. The purpose of his address was to repudiate the blood-libel accusation: "We ask, where is the historical evidence that such a thing ever took place?" He argues that American Jews living in freedom and security should not look down upon Jews whose spirit has been deadened by "ages of suffering" and, therefore, are unable to "rise up against their oppressors." On the contrary, he pleads, "let us admire their patient endurances, for having remained true to our faith under every trial." Leeser is eloquent in his exposition of the traditional Jewish stance of assuming mutual responsibility:

> As citizens, we belong to the country we live in; but as believers in one God . . . as the inheritors of the Law, the Jews of England, and Russia, and Sweden, are no aliens among us, and we hail the Israelite as a brother, no matter if his home be the torrid zone, or where the poles encircle the earth . . . oceans may intervene between our dispersed remnants . . . mountains may divide us, but . . . the Israelite is ever alive to the welfare of his distant brother, and sorrows with his sorrows, and rejoices in his joy.

Abraham Hart offered a resolution to give practical expression to Leeser's eloquence: "*Resolved,* That we invite our brethren of Damascus to leave the land of persecution and torture and to seek asylum in this free and happy land. . . ."

The three Christian ministers present expressed humanitarian support and stood ready to offer help.

A Committee of Correspondence, appointed "to correspond with other Committees in this country and Europe," undertook the drafting of a letter to the president of the United States. It speaks in the name of the "Jewish inhabitants of Philadelphia . . . in conjunction with our brethren of other cities."

On August 17, 1840, the American secretary of state wrote to David Porter, American minister to Turkey:

> the President has directed me to instruct you to do everything in your power with . . . the Sultan . . . to prevent and mitigate these horrors . . . the "persecution and spoilation" of Jews in "Mahomedan dominions."

The secretary of state adds:

> The President is of the opinion that from no one can such generous endeavors proceed with so much propriety and effect, as from the Representative of a friendly power, whose institutions, political and civil, place on the same footing, the worshippers of God, of every faith and form, acknowledging no distinction between the Mahomedan, the Jew, and the Christian.[17]

The involvement of the United States State Department in the Damascus Affair may have brought about a new perception of America's role in world affairs. America was like other nations, but also different, in being a power that places "on the same footing . . . the Mahomedan, the Jew, and the Christian," and that difference allowed it to play a unique role in international relations.

FOCUS
Mordecai M. Noah: From Ararat to Zion

In his address at the consecration of the synagogue of Congregation Shearith Israel in 1818, Mordecai Manuel Noah touched on a wide variety of Jewish experiences, interests and prospects. The most interesting of all is his assertion that the time was propitious for a return of the Jews to their homeland.

> . . . they will march in triumphant numbers, and possess themselves once more of Syria, and take their rank among the governments of the earth. This is not fancy. I have been too much among them in Europe and Africa—I am too well acquainted with their views and sentiments in Asia, to doubt their intentions. . . .
> Let us then hope that the day is not far distant when . . . we may look forward toward that country where our people have established a mild, just and honourable government, accredited by the world, and admired by all good men.[18]

Noah soon realized that his vision bore no resemblance to contemporary reality. A Jewish nation resident in the ancient homeland was a far-off dream, but why not a Jewish commonwealth, an "asylum," "a city of refuge" in America? Two years later, in 1820, he petitioned the State of New York to sell him Grand Island, near Buffalo, for such a settlement. A committee of the State Legislature reported favorably on his request, but no bill was passed. Five years later Noah persuaded a friend to purchase a section of Grand Island. He immediately set about dedicating it in a manner worthy of a two-millennial dream fulfilled. Booming cannon announced the day of dedication, September 15, 1825. Military and Masonic formations, government officials and the gathered representatives of organizations and institutions joined in a grand march to a local church, where the dedication was to take place. (There were not enough boats to convey the assembled multitude to Grand Island.)

Noah, as self-designated "Governor and Judge of Israel," presided at the solemn occasion, garbed in a red judicial robe trimmed with ermine, a medal dangling on his breast. The band blared out the Grand March from *Judas Maccabeus*, the Biblical lesson was read by the minister, psalms were recited, and the new "Judge of Israel" issued his *Proclamation to the Jews*.[19] It urged the immigration of the Jewish youth of the world to the new commonwealth, delcared that polygamy was abolished, and that prayer "shall forever be said in the Hebrew language"; and levied a poll tax of three shekels or one Spanish dollar "upon each Jew throughout the world, for the purpose of defraying the various expenses of re-organizing the government, of aiding emigrants in the purchase of agricultural implements, providing for their immediate wants and comforts, and assisting their families in making their first settlements . . . in the furtherance of the laudable objects connected with the restoration of the people and the glory of the Jewish nation."

But even as Noah's practical sense directed him to place the venue of the new Jewish commonwealth in the United States, he viewed it only as a temporary haven. Beyond it was the promised restoration to the ancient homeland, which would establish a permanent state for God's chosen nation. Ararat was a "city of refuge" "where our people may so familiarize themselves with the science of government . . . as may qualify them for their great and final restoration to their ancient heritage."

Ararat did not progress beyond proclamation and dedication, and in 1837, in his *Discourse on the Evidences of the American Indians Being the Descendants of the Lost Tribes of Israel,* Noah returned to the dream of the restoration:

> The Jewish people must now do something for themselves; they must move onward to the accomplishment of that great event, long promised, long expected. . . . Syria will revert to the Jewish nation by *purchase.* . . . Under the co-operation and protection of England and France, this re-occupation of Syria . . . is at once reasonable and practicable. . . . a just, a tolerant and liberal government . . . [will] be a bulwark to the interests of England and France. . . .[20]

Seven years later, the return to Zion became the subject of a "Discourse on the Restoration of the Jews," delivered at the Tabernacle in New York on October 28 and December 2, 1844.[21] It was not a "scientific" address, but a Zionist polemic.

> I confidently believe in the restoration of the Jews . . . and believing that political events are daily assuming a shape which may finally lead to that great advent, I considered it a duty to call upon the free people of this country to aid us in any efforts which, in our present position, it may be deemed prudent to adopt. . . .[22]

The discourse appeals to American Christians to aid in restoring a Jewish state in Zion, and seeks to convince them why it is in their interests as Christians and as Americans to do so.

In the 1837 *Discourse,* Noah argued that a Jewish state in Palestine would serve the interest of England and France, and directed his "appeal" to them. In 1844, America is asked to assume a leadership role in the return of the Jews to their homeland.

In those few years, America had successfully weathered a financial crisis and was entering a period of national expansion. The young nation, suddenly aware of its own power and potential, sought adventure abroad which would permit the expression and display of that power. It was also the time of great millennial urgings in America. Noah sensed that the time was ripe to harness these religio-national sentiments in service of his dream for his people—national restoration to the ancient homeland. In his *Discourse on the Restoration of the Jews* he suggests that if the missionary societies are truly solicitous of the "temporal and eternal welfare of Israel," as they claim, they should cooperate with the temporal by aiding in the restoration and leave the eternal to the Eternal God. Making judicious use of Biblical quotations, he argues that true Christians should aid in the return of the Jews to their Homeland.

The argument he makes and the proposals he puts forth are forerunners of the classic Zionist assertions of later generations:

Jewish ability is adequate to the task: "The Jews are in a most favorable position to repossess themselves of the promised land, and organize a free and liberal government."

It can only be Palestine: "Every attempt to colonize Jews in other countries has failed."

Noah proposes a practical step-by-step program: "The first step is to solicit from the Sultan of Turkey permission for the Jews to purchase and hold land."

Special aid should be provided: "Those who desire to reside in the Holy Land and have not the means, may be aided by . . . societies to reach their desired home of repose."

Noah, the practical visionary, sees "ports of the Mediterranean occupied by enterprising Jews. The valley of the Jordan will be filled by agriculturists from . . . Germany, Poland and Russia."

He pleads that "Restoration is not for us alone, but for millions unborn. . . . Let my people go . . . and they will go, not all, but sufficient to constitute the elements of a powerful government."

He argues that America, the land of liberty, must take leadership, so that "The liberty and independence of the Jewish nation may grow out of a single effort which this country may make in their behalf. . . . They want only PROTECTION, and the work is accomplished."[23]

In *The Occident*, Leeser notes that "the address of Judge Noah has excited a good deal of attention among our Christian fellow citizens, more so at least than among ourselves. . . ." As a matter of fact, the attention it excited among Jews was almost wholly critical. Noah was taken to task for turning to the Christian world and for courting the aid of "conversion-societies." Leeser argued that the plan was not only impractical but dangerous. He had little faith in the goodwill of the European nations, but rather feared "the grasping policy of modern Christian nations."

> An independence so feeble as to be prey to the designing powers of modern Europe . . . we do not desire nor wish our people to establish; they had better remain as they are now, scattered over all the earth, rather than expose themselves to an extermination by some modern Haman.[24]

In a long letter to the editor of *The Occident*, Noah addressed himself to Leeser's criticisms and argued that if there was danger, it was "not from Christians, but from ourselves. Danger from apathy, from indifference—danger from a want of nationality."[25] He persisted in his argument that the aid and cooperation of the Christian world was to be solicited; the return to Zion could not succeed without "their good feelings—their powerful protection." But the work of restoration must be begun by the Jews themselves, and begun at once.

"We in this generation may be impelled to commence the good work, which succeeding generations will accomplish,"[26] said Mordecai Manuel Noah, half a century before Theodor Herzl wrote *Der Judenstaat*, over a century before the proclamation of Israel's statehood.

FOCUS
The Beginning of American Jewish Journalism

The appearance of the first issue of *The Occident and American Jewish Advocate* in April 1843 marked the beginning of American Jewish journalism. Almost two decades earlier Solomon Henry Jackson had begun publication in New York of *The Jew*, but that monthly was devoted exclusively to antimissionary polemics. In the first issue of *The Occident* the introductory remarks of its editor, Isaac Leeser, indicated that the second part of its title described its purpose, "the spread of whatever can advance the cause of our religion, and of promoting the true interest of that people . . . descended from the stock of Abraham."[27] For more than a quarter of a century, *The Occident* reflected the totality of Jewish interests. Its pages were open to "controversial articles," and the philosophy, passions and prejudices of Leeser gave its particular point of view a sense of mission.

The Occident remained a monthly from 1843 to 1869 (with the exception of the two years, March 1859–March 1861 when it appeared as an eight-page weekly). Each issue contained a sermon or editorial article, excerpts from Jewish literature, literary notices or criticism, domestic and foreign news items, articles on Jewish life in America, both historical and contemporary, and correspondence and comment dealing with issues in Jewish life.

In the first issue Julius Stern, a Philadelphia Jew, interested in synagogal reform, and publisher of the short-lived pioneer German journal, *Israelit*, proposes the establishment of "a colony in some of the western territories" for immigrant "Israelites of Germany." He is hopeful that the colony might grow to become a state, where the citizens would be able to enact their own legislation.

A report on the fifth anniversary examination of the Sunday School of Religious Instruction of Israelites of Philadelphia contains the information that "the whole population of Jews in Philadelphia is scarcely more than fifteen hundred" and that "among the scholars are several German children who have acquired nearly all their English in this school."

The American Society for Meliorating the Condition of the Jews, the same missionary group that *The Jew* was created to answer, is the object of a brief article. The editor promises that this subject will be referred to in the future as well.

The spirit of righteous zeal in the pages of *The Occident* is evident in the pain with which Leeser discloses the shortcomings of American Israel, and in the indignation with which he attacks those he believes to be the enemies of Jews and Judaism—bigots and missionaries from without, reformers and isolationists within the Jewish ranks. With fervor he pleads for a united Jewish community, unified in its promotion of education, culture and religious observance, and he offers plans for institutions and organizations which would serve, teach and inspire a growing Jewish community.

Born in Germany in 1806, Isaac Leeser (d. 1868) was brought to America in 1824 by an uncle living in Richmond. While a clerk in his uncle's store he helped the Reverend Isaac B. Seixas in his religious school. He came to the attention of Jews beyond his community through a masterful defense of Jews and Judaism in a Richmond newspaper. This led to his appointment in 1829 as *hazzan* of Philadelphia's Mikveh Israel Synagogue. A year later, he began his literary career with publication of *Instruction in Mosaic Religion* (1830), *The Jews and the Mosaic Law* (1833), a translation of the Sephardic prayer book in six volumes (1836–37) followed by a translation of the Pentateuch (1845) and the first translation of the entire Bible into English by a Jew (1854). He wrote textbooks, catechisms, and ten volumes of sermons, addresses and translations.

Equally important were Leeser's pioneering efforts in the organization of the Jewish community and its institutions. As early as 1841, he began to make public pleas for a united American Jewish community. His persistent advocacy prepared the ground for the formation, in 1859, of the Board of Delegates of American Israelites, the first organization representative of American Jewry. He was the first to propose a Sunday school, and to suggest that "it would be best to establish elementary schools in every district." He helped to establish the Hebrew Education Society, and to found Maimonides College, the first—though short-lived—Jewish theological seminary in America. As early as 1836, he urged the need for widows' and orphans' homes, an idea which he continued to nurture until the Jewish Foster Home was established in Philadelphia in 1855.

Editorial articles in volume I of *The Occident* contain proposals which are repeated and elaborated in subsequent volumes. Included are a plea for the retention of Hebrew as the language of worship, a proposal for a network of Jewish day schools and an appeal for Jewish unity in action and opinion. He calls for communal unity to replace congregational divisiveness, "a union of the disjointed members which now constitute our American congregations . . . a FEDERATIVE union, which leaves every Synagogue or every city perfectly at liberty to manage its own internal affairs."

The Occident also printed appeals to American Jewry from communities outside America. A letter from Adolphe Crémieux to Mordecai Manuel Noah pleads for "assistance, in carrying out a great and pious work, from our brethren in the United States." Four schools, two for boys and two for girls, had been established in Alexandria and Cairo, Egypt, "in behalf of the western Jews, and in their name. . . ." Crémieux now turns to the Jews of America to join the "western Jews." Noah introduces the letter with the observation, "Although the application comes at a time when constant assistance is required for poor emigrants who are flocking to this free country, nevertheless, it may be in the power of those who have been favoured by fortune, to transmit something in aid." He concludes with a suggestion repeated in many subsequent appeals: "It is advisable, therefore, for our friends to form committees in any part of the Union, where this letter reaches, and raise subscriptions."

The first subscription list in 1843 lists readers not only in New York, Philadelphia, Baltimore, Charleston, Richmond, Cincinnati, St. Louis and New Orleans, but also in small towns in the East such as Franklin, Huntingdon, Mercersburg and Mauch Chunk, Pennsylvania; Bull's Ferry and Bridgeton, New Jersey; and Southern hamlets such as Beaufort, Cheraw, Columbia, Georgetown, Sumterville and Camden, South Carolina; Danville, Cynthiana, Elkton, Hopkinsville and Madisonville, Kentucky; Holly Spring, Oxford, Pontotoc and Hernando, Mississippi; in Canada, the West Indies and England.

3.

The Emerging Community

IN CINCINNATI'S *DIE DEBORAH* (1855), A GERMAN-LANGUAGE WEEKLY, DR. W. Rottenheim, a Reform rabbi of that city and himself an immigrant, encouraged his fellow German Jews to follow him to the "great country,"

> . . . Far, far from where the sun sets
> A glorious blessed land
> Across the trackless ocean
> Extends a brother's hand.
> There, there shall be our haven,
> To which our course we'll bend
> There will the dire oppression
> At last forever end.[1]

A half decade earlier, Viennese writer Leopold Kompert, deeply distressed by anti-Jewish disturbances in Prague and Bohemia, concluded that the appropriate and prudent Jewish response would be mass migration to America. A supporter of the Revolution of 1848, he had little faith that it would alleviate the plight of the Jew.

> No help has come to us! The sun of freedom has risen for the Fatherland; for us it is merely a bloody northern light . . . Because slavish hordes . . . do not understand the spirit of freedom, *we* must pay for it . . . We hold our head ready for every blow of the club . . . To the oppressed and downtrodden, the expelled and impoverished and plundered . . . to all of whom "liberty" has brought calamity . . . to all these we say: "For us no help has come. Seek it out in far-off America!"[2]

Viennese editor and publisher Isidor Busch echoed the cry, "Yes, on to America! Become human beings, become free." He heeded his own advice and departed for America where he became a respected citizen of Missouri, and an active abolitionist.

As early as 1837, the German *Allgemeine Zeitung des Judentums* began to report emigration from Germany to America.

> They are emigrating indeed. We have young men who have completed their apprenticeship . . . who meet all the requirements . . . yet cannot obtain letters of protection and domicile . . . . What else should they do but seek a new fatherland . . .?[3]

Two reports in 1839 declare:

> From certain places, in which there are 30-40 Jewish families, 15-20 persons or more are leaving . . . mostly young and hard-working people. A. Riedenburg . . . an old man of eighty-five has decided to migrate to America.
>
> Not only artisans and merchants are emigrating but also men of the learned class, since the prospects for rabbinical or medical positions are not particularly bright owing to the vast number of candidates.[4]

In the years 1840–50, the Jewish population of the United States increased from 15,000 to 50,000. In the next decade, it tripled. This tenfold increase in twenty years was due both to worsening economic and political conditions in post-Napoleonic Europe and a rapidly expanding America which opened doors to needed population. The Jews, mainly from southern Germany, were part of a German wave of immigration which settled the Midwest.

From time to time, the German Jews read of anti-Semitic excesses in America. A report from New York, September 20, 1850, in the *Allgemeine Zeitung* told of a blood-libel accusation and riot.

> Who would believe that the wild appetite for Jew-baiting crosses over even to North America? . . . A shocking event occurred last Sunday. It was the eve of the Day of Atonement for the Jews and they were all in the synagogue. . . . A rumor spread that the Jews had murdered a Gentile girl for their holiday. About 10:30 a crowd of some 500 men burst into the house, broke down the doors and literally pulled from their beds the sleeping women. . . . A most shocking riot was perpetrated. Everyone who resisted was knocked down. . . . The remarkable thing about the affair is that three Irish policemen were the leaders of this raging mob.[5]

But they also read in the *Wiener Jahrbuch for Israeliten* for 1846 that in America,

Prosperity is growing day by day; those who had immigrated as beggars are rich after 6-10 years; and the name German Jew has become here a name of honor and of guarantee of integrity and honesty.[6]

The Occident described the variety of Jewish economic pursuits in 1857.

The clothing, shoe, dry goods and liquor, together with jewelry and rarely the grocery trade are nearly everywhere their sole pursuit. . . .
We do not mean, however, to assert that the above-enumerated are the only means of support of the Jews in America; for we know well enough that we have lawyers, medical doctors, bankers, some politicians, a few teachers, authors and ministers, some shipping merchants and auctioneers, and a very few farmers, and here and there a butcher, a baker, a distiller, a brewer, a tavern-keeper, a manufacturer, a miner, a billiard-table maker, an apothecary, a smith, a produce and cattle-dealer, a painter and glazier. . . .

Peddling, though widespread, was looked down upon by some:

Many . . . try their luck at peddling among the farmers, and in the small towns . . . of these . . . many have done well and become at length merchants of higher pretensions. Nevertheless this system must come to an end; it is nearly overdone now; besides which it is illegal in several states; for even could a license for peddling be secured, it will be at such a high rate, and clogged with so many restrictions, as to be unattainable by the poor. . . . The very nature, moreover, of seeking a livelihood by means of small trading of this sort, has a debasing influence on the mind.[7]

The plight of the peddler in mid-nineteenth-century America is movingly described in the journal kept by Abraham Kohn in 1842.

This week I went, together with my brother Juda, from Boston to Worcester . . . I regret that the people here are so cold to immigrants and that their watchword seems to be, "Help yourself, that's the best help . . ." Thursday was a day of rest owing to twelve inches of snow. On Friday and Saturday business was very poor, and we did not take in $2 during the two days. . . . Both of us were in a bitter mood, for during the whole week of driving about in bitter cold we had earned no money. I long for the beautiful days in my beloved homeland. Will they ever return? . . .
On Monday the 12th to Lyndenborough; Tuesday to Wil-

ton; Wednesday to Mason Village; Thursday, New Ipswich; Friday, Ashburnham; on Saturday we came to Westminster. . . . It was extremely cold this week . . . At some places the snow was three to four feet deep, and we could hardly get through with the sleigh. How often we thanked God that we did not have to carry our wares on our backs in this cold! To tramp with a heavy pack from house to house in this weather would be terrible. . . .

Dear good mother, how often I recall your letters, your advice against going to America, "Stay home you can win success as well in Germany." But I wouldn't listen; I had to come to America . . . living a life that is wandering. . . . It is hard, very hard indeed to make a living this way. Each day I must importune some farmer's wife to buy my wares, a few pennies worth. No, I must stop this business, the sooner the better.[8]

As many peddlers did, Kohn did stop "this business"; he settled in Chicago, entered the clothing business and became a leader in the Jewish and general community, an organizer and president of the city's first congregation, Kehilath Anshe Mayriv, and a prominent political figure who in 1860 was appointed city clerk. In that year, he presented newly elected President Abraham Lincoln with an American flag, on which he inscribed in Hebrew the passage from the Book of Joshua "be strong and of good courage."

A report in *Die Deborah* in 1860 speaks of the great progress made by the immigrants.

How wonderfully, how very beneficially conditions have changed since 1837! In those days, when a Europe-weary Jewish journeyman used to tie up his valise and say "I am emigrating to America," it meant that he was a black sheep who was good for nothing . . . If stout-hearted youth . . . came to his parents and said, "Let me go across the sea," the parents wept and resisted, as if their son were going to the other world. . . . If an educated Jew . . . expressed determination to go to live in the land of freedom . . . [no one] could understand how an educated man could so lower himself as to prefer distant America, the land of the uneducated, the land of the blacks and Indians to Europe. How conditions have changed! These humble artisans, these youthful adventurers have since then become the supporters of their kinfolk in the old fatherland. . . .

Many, very many of these beggarly-poor emigrants are nowadays at the head of business concerns that own enormous property . . . To be sure, not all of them have reached such heights. . . . Yet we can count hundreds. . . . The signs of their enterprises blaze in all the big commercial cities of the Union, such as New York, Philadelphia, Cincinnati, St. Louis, New Orleans. . . .[9]

ACROSS THE CONTINENT

By the middle of the century the American Jewish community stretched from New York to San Francisco; more than one hundred congregations and an even larger number of charitable, social and cultural organizations served its needs. The "List of Jewish Institutions, Religious, Charitable, etc." in *A Jewish Calendar for Fifty Years,* published in Montreal in 1854, presents a picture of organized Jewish life in cities large and small.

Twenty congregations served New York City. Among them: Shearith Israel, Portuguese Minhag; B'nai Jeshurun, Polish Minhag; Anshe Chesed, German Minhag; Benai Israel, Netherland Congregation; Ahabat Chesed, Bohemian Minhag; Imanuel, the first Reform Jewish congregation in New York.

Among New York's forty-four charitable and educational societies, we find: The North American Relief Society for the Indigent Jews in Palestine; The Jewish Orphan and Indigent Asylum; The Jews' Hospital; The Jewish Dispensary; Hebrew Benevolent Society; Society for the Education of Poor Children and Relief of Indigent Persons; The Montefiore Mutual Benefit Society; Bachelors' Hebrew Benevolent Loan Association; Young Men's Hebrew Benevolent Association for the distribution of fuel during the winter; Society of Brother Love; Widow and Orphan Society; Hebrew Young Men's Literary Association; The Constitutional Grand Lodge . . . of the Order of B'nai Brith; The Jewish Theological Seminary and Scientific Institute; Hebrew National School; Polonies Talmud Torah.

Philadelphia listed five congregations. First among them was Mikveh Israel, established in 1782 with a synagogue on Cherry Street: "They have been worshipping on this site for 72 years." Rodeph Sholom, organized in 1802, was the first Ashkenazic congregation in America. "The Mikvah [ritual bath] is on the southwest part of the synagogue building, and the School for Hebrew, English and German instruction is in the basement." Among the seventeen societies were: United Hebrew Beneficent Society (1822); United Hebrew Beneficent Fuel and Saving Society (1842); Ladies Hebrew Benevolent Society (1819); The Widow and Orphan Society (1844); Hebrah Hesed Veemet for attendance on the sick and the dead (1844); Hebrew Ladies Sewing Society (1838); American Jewish Publication Society (1846); Hebrew Sunday School (1838); Hebrah Bikur Holim Ugmilut Hasadim (1814); The Independent Order of B'nai Berith "consisting of three lodges and nearly three hundred members" (1850).

Cincinnati, the "Queen City," was served by four congregations, two German and two Polish, and eleven societies. Among the latter were:

The Hebrew Beneficent Society, "extending aid to the needy and the sick, and for mutual benefit in sickness and during the seven days of mourning."

The English Ladies' Benevolent Society "for assistance of Jewish females and orphans."

Hebrah Tipheret Israel, "to defray expenses of the Mikvah and for other good purposes."

Relief Fund Society for the Poor Jews in Palestine, "to remit money direct to Jerusalem, and to obviate the necessity of sending messengers to collect money."

The Jews Hospital Society, "Physician, M. Bettman, M.D."

Hebrah Kadishah, "To attend to the sick, the dying and the dead."

The German Ladies' Relief Society "to relieve deserving persons in distress," and

The Old German Ladies' Benefit Society, "for the mutual benefit and for the assistance of Jewish females and orphans."

Congregations were listed in the venerable communities of Newport (1658), Savannah (1733), Charleston (inc. 1791) and Richmond (1791). Charleston could also boast of the oldest American Jewish charitable organizations: Hevrah Gemilut Hasadim (1750); Hebrew Benevolent Institution (1791) and Society for the Relief of Orphans and Indigent Children (1801). In Baltimore there were four congregations, including the Reform, Har Sinai.

One could travel across the continent along either the northern or southern routes and worship in synagogues in Boston, Massachusetts: Ohabay Shalome (1842) and Beth Israel (1849); Hartford, Connecticut: Beth Israel (1847); New Haven, Connecticut: Mishkan Israel (1852); Albany, New York: Beth El (1838), Beth Jacob (1847), Anshe Emet (1850); Utica, New York; Syracuse, New York: Keneset Shalome (1846); Rochester, New York: Berith Kodesh (1847); Buffalo, New York: Beth El (1847), Beth Zion (1850); Cleveland, Ohio: Anshe Hased (1841), Tipheret Israel (1850); Detroit, Michigan: Beth El (1850); Chicago, Illinois: Anshay Mangarib [sic] (1847); and St. Louis, Missouri: Polish Congregation (1842). A southern route would offer synagogue worship in Washington, D.C.; Wheeling, Virginia; Wilmington, North Carolina; Richmond, Virginia; Charleston, South Carolina; Columbia, South Carolina; Savannah, Georgia; Mobile, Alabama; New Orleans, Louisiana; Galveston, Texas; and organized communal life in Talbotton and Augusta, Georgia; Bolivar, Nashville and Memphis, Tennessee;

Claiborne, Alabama; Clinton, Vicksburg and Natchez, Mississippi; and in communities of similar size in the Midwest.

On arriving in California, travelers would have a choice of three congregations in San Francisco: Immanuel, Shearith Israel and Shaar Ashamaim [sic]. If in need, they could turn to the Hebrew Benevolent Society or the Eureka Society "consisting of German Jews." If they fell ill in Stockton, the Society of Lovely Nation would care for them; and if they didn't recover, it would accord them proper Jewish burial. In the 1850s, Jews had organized institutions for worship and mutual aid in Los Angeles, Sacramento, San Diego, Nevada City, Maryville, Sonora and Colluma on the Yuba River.

Los Angeles was typical of the new frontier communities. In 1850 it boasted eight Jews described as ". . . all under thirty years of age, single, and classified as merchants. . . . Six had arrived from Germany, the other two from Poland." A decade later, the professional Jewish traveler, I. J. Benjamin II, records:

> About one hundred Jews are living in Los Angeles, most of whom are young people. . . . They form an enterprising and intelligent part of the population and have come from all parts of the world. They live in peace with their neighbors and engage in trade or are professionals. Some own a number of vineyards.[10]

Dr. Gustav Gottheil, rabbi of America's most prestigious congregation, Temple Emanu-El of New York, attempted to explain the Jewish immigrant experience to his fellow Americans in an article in *The North American Review* in 1878, "Position of the Jew in America." Writing at a time which saw the waning of immigration from Western Europe and the beginnings of migration from Eastern Europe, his words describe both.

> When, thirty or forty years ago, the current of Hebrew immigration set in strongly, what encouragement did it find? Beyond freedom to use his brains and his arms (and we have no desire to underrate these primary conditions of success), very little indeed. Only in some of the larger cities of the Union had Hebrew families resided long enough to secure for themselves a recognized position, both social and commercial. . . . It was different with the later settlers, who were unused to their surroundings, and too scantily provided with the means that command respect in mercantile circles. They encountered distrust, and not seldom humiliating treatment. They soon quitted the centres of trade, and were scattered over the inhabited parts of the union. . . .
> Suspicion and contempt met him [the Jew] at every step,

and forced him not seldom, to hide his origin and to bury his faith
in his bosom. Unless he did that, he could not ply his trade, nay,
would be refused shelter and food. On this free soil he was often
obliged to perform the rites of his religion and offer his prayers
behind locked doors. It was not until personal contact had proved
him to be a man, that he could safely avow himself a Jew. Nor
had he, in his wide wanderings, the support which his competitors
found everywhere in their organized churches; as yet no such existed for him. He was thrown upon his own resources in every
respect, and in sickness and death, which he faced often enough
in traveling over the prairies, or camping in the swamps, or ven-
turing into the neighborhood of pioneer settlers. . . .

He had, however, been nerved and equipped for the battle
by the severe school through which his fathers and himself had
passed. He had not been spoiled by the world, expected no favors,
and was, therefore, not liable to be much disappointed when he
found the old prejudice still confronting him. Hard work and self-
denial were his wont. Besides, his family affections, deep, holy,
permanent, were his guardian angels, to save his feet from falling.
The father, who sought here relief from the vexations of oppressive
rule, kept the remembrance of wife and children constantly in
mind, and deep down in his bosom. The prospect of being reunited
with them was the vision of his hope, which nerved his arm and
sustained his courage; the young man who came here in search of
a better future than his home offered him, knew of no higher
ambition than to become the benefactor of his kindred. The more
he learned to love his new home, the more intense grew his yearning for his dear ones to share his happiness.[11]

JUDAISM IN THE AMERICAN SETTING

Isaac Leeser visited Baltimore in February 1851, and reported:

It is now about seventeen years ago that the first serious
organization was attempted to unite the scattered few into a regular
religious community, and now there are two orthodox congregations, each with its regular hazzan and preacher and a properly
organized school, in addition to which there is a Reform Society,
worshipping after the form of the Hamburg Temple. . . . We could
only find time to visit the oldest synagogue, though it is not yet
four years old, in Lloyd Street, both to look at the school (which
is kept in the basement) on Thursday, and to attend worship on
the Sabbath, and though we did not find all as we could have
wished it, we saw enough to please any friend of Israel. There

were assembled about two hundred children of both sexes in four classrooms, under as many teachers, two of whom are for Hebrew, and the others for English.

On the Sabbath, the [Lloyd Street] synagogue was filled almost to its full capacity, and we should judge that the space was not large enough for all those who belong to the congregation; hence we should not be surprised that before many years a new synagogue will have to be erected to accommodate the constantly increasing number of Israelites in the flourishing city of Baltimore.[12]

Leeser's report reflects the *two* unique and distinctive features of American Judaism: the synagogue as the central institution of Jewish life and the pluralistic character of the religious community.

Soon a threefold religious division obtained in the Baltimore Jewish community, which set the pattern for American Jewry.

The first ordained rabbi to serve in the United States, Rabbi Abraham Rice, became the Rabbi of the Stadt Schul, Nidchei Yisrael in 1840. He was recognized as *the* rabbinic authority in America by traditional Jews, and became a champion of Orthodoxy through the spoken and written word.

The first congregation in America to be established as a *Reform* congregation was Baltimore's Har Sinai Verein in 1842. Thirteen years later Har Sinai bought to America and to its pulpit one of the intellectual giants of Reform, David Einhorn. His prayer book *Olat Tamid* served as the model for the official Reform *Union Prayerbook*.

The third tendency in Judaism, the middle ground between Orthodoxy and Reform, "positive historical Judaism," was also given institutional expression in mid-nineteenth-century Baltimore. Oheb Shalom, organized in 1853, may very well have been the first congregation organized as a Conservative (although this term came to be used only later) congregation. It brought to its pulpit the scholarly Benjamin Szold. He, too, composed a prayer book, *Abodath Israel,* which in English translation came to be known as the "Jastrow prayer book" and which was used by many moderate Reform and Conservative congregations.

Baltimore had its three rabbis, each with a different prayer book in hand, each foreshadowing a path which a whole movement would follow.

Three factors unique to America affected the shaping of the Jewish community: *freedom, frontier* and *immigration*.

Alexis de Tocqueville observed:

In France I had almost always seen the spirit of religion and the spirit of freedom pursuing courses diametrically opposed to each other; but in America I found that they were intimately united, and that they reigned in common over the same country . . . Nothing struck me more forcibly than the general equality . . .[13]

The Jews in America early felt that freedom and equality were theirs in full measure. They expressed it and acted upon it, nowhere more boldly than in the field of religion.

Separation of church and state was the legal expression of freedom and equality in the religious sphere. No religion was favored by the government above another. In lieu of an established church, each individual house of worship was deemed a valued addition to the spiritual life of the community—synagogue as well as church.

The lay ministers in the American churches had their counterparts in the Jewish community, as I. J. Benjamin describes in his *Three Years in America*:

A shoemaker, tailor, furrier, harness-maker, village schoolmaster, butcher or anybody of almost any occupation or handicraft has on occasion been transformed into a shepherd of souls . . . [they] conduct services . . . [and] supervise the observance of the laws concerning food; some of them also preach, write and become men of importance without the least knowledge of Judaism and its sacred writings.[14]

The Methodist circuit rider might meet in his rounds the itinerant *maggid* (preacher) or *shohet* or *meshulah* (emissary for religious charities) who represented the Jewish religion in the frontier communities. Most men who called themselves rabbis were teachers who also preached, brothers in spirit to the Presbyterian minister-schoolmaster and the Baptist farmer-preacher.

America was the frontier of world Jewry. It attracted the maverick, the adventurous, as well as those who left home for prudent reasons. Some learned and dedicated rabbis came to America, but there were those like the penitent apostate Henry Gersoni. A rabbinical student converted to Greek Orthodoxy, he spent ten months among the missionaries in London, recanted publicly in Paris, came to America and led congregations in Atlanta and Chicago.

The people who organized congregations and built synagogues were growing lax in religious observance. Reform Judaism, which was sweeping community after community, was characterized by loyalty to the synagogue as an institution, but a radical break with the traditional practices and observances of Judaism.

The Jewish experience in America can only be understood against the background of immigration, the community continually changing as new immigrants were arriving. Isaac Mayer Wise was one of the first rabbis to see the synagogue as an Americanizing agency, with the task of turning the benighted European into a free American. In 1858 he stated: "We need English preachers and we must become American Jews as speedily as possible." The reforms he effected in his synagogue and recommended for others were in good measure because of his desire to make the synagogue such an institution, and his zeal for establishing a rabbinical seminary in the United States was due to his conviction that a rabbi in America must Americanize as well as Judaize.

Freedom, Frontier and Immigration exerted their influence in strengthening the synagogue as an institution and in furthering the denominational division that took place within the religious community.

In the middle of the nineteenth century, Judaism found expression within two frameworks—Traditionalist and Reform—whose chief spokesmen were, respectively, Isaac Leeser and Isaac M. Wise.

Leeser had faith that America would be hospitable to a traditionally religious and highly cultured Jewish community, if only the Jews willed it and matched will with enterprise. As we have seen, he set out to establish the institutions which would fashion such a community.

Wise, an enormously energetic religious teacher from Bohemia who was to become the architect of the Reform movement in America, believed that Judaism would in time become the religion of all enlightened modern men. First, however, it had to be modernized, democratized and Americanized. He entered a rabbinic career and became the exponent of a moderate, pragmatic Reform Judaism, responsive to the pressures and exigencies of contemporary American life. The prayer book that he prepared and vigorously promoted presented a modified traditional worship service with Hebrew text and facing German or English translations. Modernity called for the elimination of prayers for the restoration of sacrifices, while references to a Messiah and return to a homeland were omitted because in his view America was Zion, and "Washington our Jerusalem." Wise entitled this prayer book *Minhag America* (The American Rite).

Overriding disputes over ritual differences and liturgical preferences was the generally shared conviction that American Jewry needed unity, American Judaism some kind of central authority. Reform and Traditionalist elements joined together in a conference in Cleveland in 1855. The rabbis recognized that unity demanded compromise. Leeser's compromise consisted in attending a conference planned and dominated by Reform Jews, Wise's in accepting the Talmud as the authoritative interpretation of the Bible.

But the conference did not lead to unity; instead, it strengthened division and led to further subdivision. Leeser and Wise dissolved their "partnership" with recriminations which grew progressively harsher. A group of Reform rabbis from the East, led by Rabbi David Einhorn of Baltimore, attacked the Cleveland Conference, declaring that its platform would "condemn Judaism to a perpetual stagnation," and rejected the Reform group led by Wise as retrogressive and opportunistic. The rift between the moderate, practical Reform of the West and the radical, ideological Reform of the East was to divide the movement for three decades. On the Traditionalist side, whatever chance Leeser had of exerting influence on the East European Orthodox immigrants who were beginning to reach America he dissipated by having consorted with the Reformers.

In Philadelphia in the late 1860s, Reform and Traditionalist groups undertook enterprises which would foster their respective interests. Supported by the Board of Delegates of American Israelites and the Hebrew Education Society of Philadelphia, Leeser organized and served as provost of Maimonides College, which opened its doors to four students in 1867 and closed six years later.

In an attempt to heal the rift in Reform Jewry, a rabbinic conference was convened in Philadelphia in 1869. The leading spirit of the conference was the radical Reformer David Einhorn. The resolutions adopted reflected his ideology, repudiating the concepts of Jewish nationality and separateness, and declaring the Jewish Diaspora, traditionally perceived as "Exile," as a divinely ordained opportunity for the Jews to fulfill "their high priestly task to lead the nations in the true knowledge and worship of God." The one "practical" resolution declared that because Hebrew has become "incomprehensible for the overwhelming majority of our present-day coreligionists . . . in the act of prayer Hebrew must take second place behind a language which the worshippers can understand."[15]

Isaac M. Wise was not prepared to follow Einhorn's extreme ideology; he viewed radical Reform as a divisive force. Wise's essential commitment was not to Reform, but to a united American Judaism. Gifted organizer that he was, he understood that congregations could be united through participation in a project rather than through agreement on resolutions. A "Jewish Theological Institute" was the vehicle he chose as a rallying center for a Union of American Hebrew Congregations which would find room for Jewish groups of all religious viewpoints.

A theological institution, the Hebrew Union College, was launched in 1875, and Wise was able to attract to his enterprise Traditionalists like Sabato Morais, the *hazzan*-minister of the Mikveh Israel Congregation in Philadelphia. But by the first ordination celebration, the college had become Reform, and the Traditionalists became convinced of the need to found a seminary of their own.

SYNAGOGUES

In America, religious practice and ideology were not fashioned in conferences or seminaries, but in individual congregations. The congregations of colonial America had all been Sephardic, and they continued their distinctive ritual even after a majority of their membership were Ashkenazic. New immigrants from Western and Eastern Europe were pleased and proud to be associated with the existing Spanish-Portuguese synagogues which, in their eyes, had the twin virtues of being "native American" and aristocratic. Not till the beginning of the nineteenth century was the first Ashkenazic synagogue founded, Rodeph Shalom of Philadelphia; and it was only in 1825 that a group of English Jews left the Sephardic Shearith Israel to organize the Ashkenazic B'nai Jeshurun in New York.

Congregations proliferated as the Jewish community in America grew. A contemporary account reports:

Last week [September 1841] a new synagogue was consecrated in Attorney Street [New York City] making, I believe, five Jewish synagogues in this city, comprising in all about ten thousand of this ancient people. The congregation of the new synagogue are German emigrants, driven from Bavaria, the Duchy of Baden, etc. by oppressive laws. One of these laws forbade Jews to marry; and among the emigrants were many betrothed couples, who married as soon as they landed on our shores. . . . If not as "rich as Jews," they are now most of them doing well in the world, and one of the first proofs they gave of prosperity, was the erection of a place of worship.[16]

In the decade from 1850 to 1860, as we have noted, the Jewish population of the United States increased from some 50,000 to approximately 150,000. The immigrants came mainly from Central European countries, but among them were a growing number of Jews from Eastern Europe. The Russian suppression of the Polish uprising of 1860–63, in which Jews had taken part, gave the Jews new cause to leave the Polish provinces. Many of the "German" Jewish immigrants came from the areas along the border between Eastern and Western Europe—Posen, Silesia, Bohemia and Slovakia.

By 1860 there were perhaps two hundred congregations, permanent and temporary (meeting for the High Holy Days only), in more than one hundred cities and towns. In addition to the old Sephardic synagogues, the traditional synagogues of West European ritual, and the Reform congregations, the first East European synagogue, the Beth Hamidrash Hagadol, was founded in New York in 1852. A contemporary report in *The Occident* states:

> Its founders were few, and they established it in poverty. . . . in affliction, deprivation and straightness they watched over its early rise. . . . Now [1857] it is supported by about eighty men in Israel.

As a typical East European synagogue,

> It is open all the day. . . . There is daily a portion of the law expounded publicly . . . every evening, when the people rest from their daily task . . . there are persons who study the law for themselves, either in pairs or singly . . . it is filled with all sorts of holy books . . . on Sabbaths and festivals, in the evening and morning . . . the house is full to overflowing.[17]

Across the continent, the synagogue experience might be quite different, as we shall now see.

SOURCE
Religion and Rights in the Far West

Lewis A. Franklin, a pioneer California Jew, bristles with righteous indignation. He seeks redress for an "untoward outrage," and asks that it be publicized so that the "perpetrators be marked with the rebuke of scorn. . . ."

The story he tells is of an incident which took place one Yom Kippur day (1859) on the farthest frontier. It tells much about life on the frontier and the Jews who settled there. They were cut off from the main centers of Jewish residence, but they wished to retain association with their faith. Scattered as they were, they came together to join in worship.

This letter appeared first in Dr. Julius Eckman's San Francisco Jewish journal, *The Gleaner*. It was reprinted on the front page of the December 22, 1859, issue of *The Occident*.

The San Diego Contempt Case

> Editor Gleaner: . . . The occurrences which have disgraced civilization in this, our remote little town of San Diego . . . know no parallel in the annals of the civilized world. An offence has been committed against all decency, and I, in common with all my coreligionists, call upon you to give publicity to the matter. . . .
>
> Know, then, that in this town and county of San Diego, there number some twelve or fourteen Israelites. These scattered

few of God's chosen people, agreed to unite in the observance of the sacred festival of the New Year, as well as in the solemnities of the Day of Atonement. . . . On the eve of that memorable day, a worthy citizen named M. Manasse journeyed fifty miles to be with us, *and complete the number designated and requisite to form a Congregation.*

Between the hours of twelve and one o'clock, P.M., the deputy sheriff presented himself at the door of the room set apart by us as a temporary Synagogue, and calling Mr. M., requested him, in the name of the Grand Jury, then in session, to appear and testify in matters and things then under their investigation. This Mr. M. declined to do, pleading as an excuse that he was engaged in his devotions. Ere a quarter of an hour had elapsed, this same minion of the law reappeared, opened the door of our temporary temple, and straightway walked up to Mr. M., with a paper in hand, and said, "Mr. M., I have a subpoena for you." At this juncture I and every other member present protested against the service of any process in a place of worship, resolutely telling the sheriff that Mr. M. neither would nor should attend unless forced, as we were then engaged in divine service—that Mr. M. was indispensable to the requisite number to form our congregation, and that that apartment was for the time being, a Synagogue. Before this official again retired, he stated that he [the undersheriff] was of the opinion that the proceedings he was taking were improper, and that he told the District Attorney that he would prefer losing fifty dollars to making the service, but that he had no alternative. He further stated that many honorable citizens cried shame at the authorities for this outrage. His last remark, however, was—"he guessed he could get a writ of attachment and *make* him go." Upon this threat Mr. M. suggested the propriety of our locking the door, so as to prevent further intrusion.

In less than half an hour that same deputy sheriff was heard at the door, demanding entrance, which, not being granted, he burst open the door, walked in, laid hands on Mr. M., and spite of all remonstrance, insisted on executing his functions. With one voice the whole assembly told this intruder that force alone could convey Mr. M. from our midst. He again left, but speedily returned with a posse, who unceremoniously rushed in. With this body all remonstrance or protest was futile, so Mr. M. consented to accompany them. He was immediately ushered into the presence of that august body of inquisitors, miscalled Grand Jurors; but lo! he refused to be sworn on that day! In their indignation they remanded Mr. M. to the court room of the Court of Sessions, where he was subjected to a severe cross-examination on the scruples he enter-

tained, and, persisting in his refusal to be sworn, the *learned* judge
ordered him into the custody of the sheriff until he should relent
and testify. The sheriff had no sooner crossed the threshold of the
court house door, than he told Mr. M. that he might proceed
whither he pleased, he, the sheriff, being answerable for his appearance at sundown. At nightfall sure enough, Mr. M. appeared
before the Grand Jury, and after answering such questions as were
then propounded to him, he was set at liberty. . . .

Although we are but few in number here, we are yet resolved to seek redress for this untoward outrage, and with this
object, a full statement of the facts is being forwarded to one of
the most able counsel in the State, for him to represent us in any
action which he, in his wisdom, thinks he can sustain in the Supreme Court of this State.

Very truly yours,
Lewis A. Franklin

FOCUS
The Rabbi in America

The periodical literature of the 1850s, 1860s and 1870s reflects
the vigor and volatility of Jewish life at that time. Community after
community experienced communal tensions brought on by religious
disputations on law and ritual, conflicts in which the rabbis—sometimes
victors, often defeated—were key figures.

America was a frontier society where religious experimentation
could be bold, deviation from tradition radical. Many of the rabbis who
came to America were caught up in the enthusiasm for the new and
uncharted, and carved out careers of imaginative leadership. Some found
that boldness and innovation were not always appreciated, particularly
when the spirit of adventure which had caused the young Jew to emigrate was replaced in middle age by the settled newcomer's desire for
respectable conformity. The synagogue often became the arena of conflict between the immigrant's need for security, provided by adherence
to tradition, and his desire for social acceptance in the host society,
which seemed to demand change in life-style and religious forms. Most
rabbis recognized the legitimacy of both tradition and change in personal
and synagogal life, becoming virtuosos of accommodation.

The earliest document touching upon the rabbinic office in America
is a petition sent "to his Excellency, Robert Hunter, Esq. Captain
General and Governor in Chief of the Provinces of New York" on
September 13, 1710, by Abraham Haim de Lucena "Minister of the
Jewish Nation":

> That your Petitioner's Predecessors, ministers of the Jewish Nation, residing at the city of New York by reason of their ministerial function, have from time to time been Exempted by the Government, not only from bearing any office Civil or Military within the City, but likewise been excused from Several Duties and Service Incumbent upon the Inhabitants of this city.[18]

The American rabbinate is thus coextensive in time with the American Jewish community; in 1710 de Lucena already speaks of "predecessors." The rabbi considered himself and was considered by the general community not only as a Jewish functionary but also as an American clergyman. America recognized the worth of the clergy to the well-being of the general community, and the rabbi as a member of the American clergy benefited from such status.

The earliest rabbinic functionary was the Sephardic *hazzan*-minister, the most noted of whom was Gershom Mendes Seixas, whose ministry spanned the Revolution. He expanded the *hazzan*'s function beyond the role of precentor of the liturgy, adding occasional preaching and civic leadership closer to the role of the American Protestant clergy and the West European *rabbiner*.

In the middle of the nineteenth century the Sephardic *hazzan* began to be joined by an ever-growing number of rabbis arriving from Western Europe. Not all had rabbinic ordination, but they entered upon the rabbinic office with energy and many with considerable ability. The most noted *hazzan* of the midcentury, Isaac Leeser, who began life in America as a clerk, had the grace never to call himself rabbi; Reverend or Minister he felt to be descriptive of his office. He readily admitted his lack of formal training and was always apologetic for the meagerness of his rabbinic learning. But in this he was an exception. Others readily conferred ordination and doctorates upon themselves.

Isaac Mayer Wise (1819–1900) was twenty-six years old, a teacher and religious functionary in Radnitz, a small town in Bohemia, when he decided to emigrate to America. Here he declared himself a rabbi, and added Dr. to the rabbinic designation.

His co-worker, Max Lilienthal (1815–1882), a German-ordained rabbi engaged by the Russian government to modernize Jewish education, fled to America when he realized that he was serving the czar against the best interest of his fellow Jews and Judaism.

Bernhard Felsenthal (1822–1908) came to carve out a career in finance, but was drawn to the pulpit and arranged for a private rabbinic ordination in America.

Benjamin Szold (1829–1902) lacked a seminary ordination necessary for major rabbinic positions in Europe. America offered better prospects, and Baltimore was the beneficiary.

David Einhorn (1809–1879) came with a solid reputation as religious thinker and ideologist of Reform. His radical position limited opportunities in Europe and he accepted a call to Baltimore's Har Sinai Verein Congregation.

Moshe Aaronson (1805–1875) was the first East European ordained rabbinic scholar to come to America. His *Pardes Habinah* and *Pardes Hachochmah* gave him some reputation in Russia, but his contentious nature, he concluded, was more suitable for "wild" America.

Hardly a promising group to assume the religious fashioning of the emerging American Jewish community! But history records that each one went on to carve out for himself a distinguished career and to make a signal contribution to the establishment of Jewish religious life in America. It may well be that the very inadequacies in training, the failings of fortune, drove them all the harder to succeed in their chosen vocations. Suffice it to say that America provided a fruitful arena for the flourishing of their talents.

We have already noted Leeser's career as editor, author, translator and organizer.

Wise edited the weekly *The American Israelite* (first called *The Israelite*), wrote learned and popular books and gave institutional organization to Reform Judaism, founding the Union of American Hebrew Congregations, the Hebrew Union College and the Central Conference of American Rabbis.

Lilienthal wrote prose and poetry, pioneered in education in New York and partook of civic leadership in Cincinnati.

Felsenthal left a rich bibliography of monographs and articles which anticipated the ideological emphases of Conservative Judaism and Reconstructionism. He was also a participant in early American Hebraic and Zionistic activities.

Szold composed prayer books, textbooks and the first important work of Hebraic scholarship in America, a commentary on the Book of Job in Hebrew. He founded the first "modern" congregational schools.

Einhorn continued his ideological formulations of Radical Reform, and, as noted earlier, wrote the prayer book *Olat Tamid* which became the model for the *Union Prayerbook*, founded and edited the German monthly *Sinai* for its seven years of publication, inspired the Philadelphia Conference and influenced the next generation of Reform leadership.

Moshe Aaronson established respect for rabbinic scholarship in America, engaged in legal correspondence with the European rabbinate and was the first American religious leader to plan *aliyah* ("going-up"— immigration to the land) to Palestine. He died on the way, but his posthumous *Mattaei Moshe* was published in Jerusalem in 1878.

These rabbis and their colleagues were men of many parts. Since they were the sole professional functionaries in the community they launched a multiplicity of enterprises and undertook a variety of tasks— preachers, teachers, organizers, writers, translators, liturgists, editors, communal architects and administrators. Their careers trained American Jewry to expect the rabbi to be a "master of all trades."

The calling was fraught with the hazards of low income, job insecurity and confrontations with congregational leadership. One incident in the career of one rabbi illustrates the tension and trauma in the lives of many.

The story of a rabbi and his congregation, the Rev. Dr. Maurice Mayer, is told in the Minute Books of Beth Elohim, Charleston, S.C.:[19]

Jan. 3, 1858. A resolution of the board of trustees:
. . . we most earnestly request the Rev. Dr. Mayer will scrupulously avoid all remarks or allusions impugning the conduct of members— . . . the expressed opinions of the Rev. Dr. in *doctrinal* points have been in conflict with the cherished principles of some members, which caused the withdrawal of their presence from divine worship, . . . the Board feels it incumbent upon them respectfully to require that the Rev. Dr. should hereafter *write out* his sermons . . . subjects could be judiciously selected and matter materially condensed. . . .
Jan. 5, 1858. Reply of Dr. Mayer:
. . . due regard for the dignity of the ministerial station, forbids my acquiescing . . . I, therefore, feel myself compelled . . . to resign my office as Minister of your Congregation. . . .
Jan. 6, 1858. Board to Dr. Mayer:
. . . there was no intention of insult . . . their sole desire . . . a course which would add to the harmony and keep together the small number we now have.

Dr. Mayer thereupon withdrew his resignation.

This took place when Judaism was heralded as a prophetic faith. The rabbi was a prophet in the pulpit, thundering forth timeless prophetic pronouncements. All was harmony so long as the prophetic wrath smote the sinners of Jerusalem. When the conduct of members in Charleston was impugned, prophecy gave way to prudence. The rabbi then could no longer escape confronting that which he knew and they knew, that if a prophet he was, he was a "court prophet," prophesying to "eat bread."

June 6, 1858. The board of trustees "protest against their Rev'd Minister's continuing to appear before the public as a student of law."
June 7, 1858. In his reply, Dr. Mayer states that he must study law for "the duty of self preservation."

Dr. Mayer gave up the study of the law, but on August 20, 1858, Dr. Mayer left for the North according to advice of his physician, for his health had been "greatly impaired. . . . It would be hazarding my life were I to dally any longer."

Many rabbis found their rewards questionable at best: fleeting gratitude of those pleased by accommodation; lasting enmity and contempt of those who pronounced them destroyers of the faith. In moments of self-searching, many must have concluded that to serve both the desires of the congregants and the demands of the faith was a futile enterprise. Moments of introspection over, they set about to accomplish as best they could their multifaceted task: teachers of the young, preachers to the elders, organizers of institutions, editors of periodicals, translators, authors of books, ambassadors to the Gentiles. The multiplicity of functions demanded of the rabbi, as his role evolved in America, ability and interests far broader than those traditionally associated with the rabbinic role. Isaac M. Wise, writing to a young American studying for the rabbinate in Europe in 1859, advised: ". . . you know that a Rabbi here must have more universal knowledge than one in Europe, he being closer connected with the world at large and being placed in a juxtaposition with the whole community."[20] The young rabbinical student was Simon Tuska.

FOCUS
From an American University into the American Rabbinate[21]

Simon Tuska decided early in his student years at the University of Rochester that he would devote his life to "the Jewish ministry. . . . I will devote myself to the sacred cause of my religion, of humanity, of my country." He was the son of the Reverend Mordecai Tuska, "Rabbi, Reader . . . *Shohet* . . . *Mohel*" of the Rochester Jewish community who was called there in 1849, shortly after his arrival from Hungary. In 1852, the young Tuska was awarded one of the first scholarships to the recently founded University of Rochester.

At the university, Tuska specialized in Greek and Latin, but his chief interest was Judaism, so he supplemented his university training with the study of rabbinical literature under his father's guidance. When Isaac Mayer Wise visited Rochester in 1854, he was delighted with the young man's deep interest in Jewish studies and encouraged him to prepare for the rabbinate.

While still a student, Tuska wrote a fifty-two-page book called *The Stranger in the Synagogue; Or the Rites and Ceremonies of the Jewish Worship, Described and Detailed,* which found a local publisher,[22] and in it presented a concise description of the Jewish holidays and how they are observed in the synagogue, noting that

> In many synagogues some unsocial customs ordered by the Rabbis are reformed, and the vain traditions of the Talmud rejected . . . most of the ceremonies prescribed in the Talmud are more interesting to Christians than they are approved of by the majority of the Jews. . . .

Both *The Occident* and *The Israelite* published Tuska's essays and translations. Isaac Mayer Wise, editor of *The Israelite*, became his guide and mentor and encouraged him to prepare for the rabbinate.

Upon his graduation from the university, Tuska enrolled as a special student in the Rochester Theological Seminary. Lest Wise be disturbed about a prospective rabbi studying theology at a Christian seminary, Tuska reassured him, "I have become so fully convinced of the fundamental principles of our faith, that I do not fear to confront in personal debate, the arguments of the most learned of Christian divines." He added that, while attending lectures in systematic theology, he planned to "take out the cream, leaving the whey for others."[23]

Tuska's chief reservation about entering the rabbinate was a language barrier. Most congregations at the time conducted their services in Hebrew, with German as the language for congregational readings, preaching and instruction.

> If I am ever to accomplish some good by sermons, they must be delivered by me in English; and there are few congregations in this land, who can fully appreciate an *English* discourse. This will not cease to be the case until the rising American-born generation will have come to manhood. Then, no doubt, a fair field of labor will be spread before the *English* preacher.[24]

Late in 1857, Tuska decided to go abroad to prepare for the rabbinate, which Wise announced in the January 8, 1858, issue of his *Israelite*:

> Our young friend Tuska of Rochester, has now decided definitely to go to Breslau, in Prussia, and study Hebrew theology. He is the first American Israelite who goes to Germany for the purpose of studying Hebrew theology; and we wish not only that he may succeed well, but also that other young men may soon follow his example. It is a sad truth, that we suffer a perceptible want of thorough theologians, and, therefore, any body who has brass enough in his face, styles himself a reverend or a rabbi. . . .
>
> Also, this is a sad fact, that many of our learned men are not sufficiently acquainted with the vernacular of the country, the

field in which they are expected to toil, the religious wants of the community, and position of Israel in this country and its relations to other religious sects. . . .[25]

The Jewish Theological Seminary in Breslau was the leading institution of its kind in the world. Founded and headed by Dr. Zacharias Frankel, a noted scholar and expounder of the positive-historical school of Judaism, its faculty consisted of some of the world's leading authorities in Jewish theology, literature, law and history. Tuska was deeply impressed with and very fond of his professors, particularly Frankel and Heinrich Graetz, the great Jewish historian.

Tuska reported a conversation with Dr. Frankel:

I, of course, told him of the lack of English preachers among us— which most persuaded me to prepare for the Ministry, in which I might make myself more useful to my American brethren than in anything else. Dr. F[rankel] congratulated me on being the first American youth who crossed the ocean for so holy a purpose.[26]

While at Breslau, Tuska became friendly with Benjamin Szold, whom Tuska described as a young rabbi who

preferred to decline the honorable post [Stockholm] he might otherwise have so easily obtained because the congregation had made it a condition, that he should introduce the prayer book in the Swedish language. . . . But as the service would in this way have utterly lost its Jewish type and color, Mr. S[zold] could not conscientiously submit to that condition.[27]

In Prague, he visited the celebrated Rabbi Solomon Judah Rapoport. Tuska's coming to Europe to study was a revelation to Rapoport. "Why, I am most agreeably surprised that there is still a sense for Jewish learning among your practical countrymen. I always thought that Judaism was on the decline in America."[28]

During his stay in Breslau, Tuska remained in communication with Wise and Wise continued to guide him. "Louisville is waiting for you," he informed Tuska, "and I can manage it that they wait till you return."[29].

Louisville was not sufficient a lure for Tuska but Temple Emanu-El in New York was. The rabbi of the congregation, Dr. Samuel Adler, was a respected scholar and spiritual leader, whose native language was German. The congregation needed a rabbi who could preach in English, for, to the sons and daughters of the German-speaking immigrants who founded Temple Emanu-El, English was the native tongue. In 1860 Tuska returned to New York City to preach a probationary sermon, which failed to win him the position. The Berith Kodesh congregation of Rochester, which his father had served, refused to consider him, for his religious views were deemed too radical.

Memphis, Tennessee, however, was more receptive. After preaching both an English and a German sermon, Tuska was unanimously elected in 1860 for three years as regular preacher in the synagogue and instructor in its religious school. He was destined to spend the remainder of his all-too-brief life in Memphis. He led his congregation through the very difficult Civil War years and through the Reconstruction. In the latter sixties, the congregation flourished so, that Isaac M. Wise called it "one of the best organized and most peaceful Reform Congregations in our country."

It was the sad duty of Rabbi Wise, Tuska's friend and mentor, to report Tuska's death in 1871. He was mourned by the whole Memphis community: clergymen, lawyers, judges of courts, county and city officials, journalists and leading merchants attended the funeral service. Tuska was only thirty-six when he died. One of America's pioneer rabbis, he set the pattern for American rabbinic training, university degree plus theological seminary studies. He recognized the need for English-speaking, American-trained rabbis for the rapidly growing American Jewish community. Among the manuscripts he left were guidelines for a seminary for Reformed Judaism in America.

The need for American-born and American-trained rabbis was felt by concerned leaders of the community. Following Simon Tuska's example, Temple Emanu-El sent young men to Germany for rabbinic training. Of these Bernard Drachman returned to serve as an Orthodox rabbi, and Felix Adler to found the Ethical Culture movement. As we have noted, the tradition-oriented Maimonides College did not last. The first viable seminary to train American rabbis, the Hebrew Union College, was established by that master builder of the Reform movement, Isaac Mayer Wise, on October 3, 1875, in Cincinnati. The first class consisted of seventeen students, one a college freshman, thirteen high-school students, three yet to enter high school. Twelve of the students were American-born, five, European.

As vital as the training of rabbis was, both Traditionalist and Reform groups recognized the need to provide basic Jewish education for the communities in which the future rabbis would labor. The Jewish community copied educational techniques from its Protestant neighbors. Thus in Philadelphia, the Hebrew Sunday School was organized in 1837.

In the forties and fifties many congregations or individuals opened schools for Jewish children which provided a full curriculum of general and Jewish subjects. A typical school would include in its Hebrew curriculum, Hebrew reading, translation of the prayers and the Pentateuch, some Hebrew grammar, Jewish religion taught through a catechism and Biblical history. Secular studies included reading, writing, arithmetic, grammar, geography, spelling, composition, rhetoric, music and language instruction in German or French. The outstanding private schools (which boarded students as well, at a fee of about $200 for board and tuition) were the Misses Palache's school for girls and Dr. Max Lilienthal's school for boys. Hyman B. Grinstein, in *The Rise of the Jewish Community in New York,* reports: "Lilienthal's students wore a special uniform; they used German and French in everyday conversations. . . . It became the outstanding Jewish school in New York City."[30] There was a sharp division in the Jewish community on the question of Jewish all-day schools. Some maintained that only such schools could provide an adequate education for the Jewish child. Others opposed them as being separatist and divisive.

In the late 1850s, the American free public-school system was secularized, and specifically Christian readings and practices were moderated in many schools. Immediately, enrollment in Jewish all-day schools began to decline. Within the decade, economic factors and a desire for full integration into the American society had their effect; the Jewish child was being educated in the public schools. Attempts at forming congregational afternoon and evening schools were, with some notable exceptions, sporadic and haphazard. Jewish education was to remain at a low level until decades later when communal institutions and agencies took over the responsibility.

SOURCE
The First Jewish Sunday School

The Hebrew Sunday school illustrates the influence of the American environment on Jewish religious life in America. The content of instruction was drawn from the Jewish religious tradition; the institution providing instruction was cast in an American mold, the Sunday school.

The first Jewish Sunday school was opened in Philadelphia in 1837. At the suggestion and urging of the Reverend Isaac Leeser, Miss Rebecca Gratz, leader in culture and philanthropy, organized the school, became its superintendent and "its moving spirit," as Rosa Mordecai reports in her "Recollections of the First Hebrew Sunday School":[31]

> The room in which we assembled was a large one. . . . On the table was a much worn Bible containing both the Old and the New Testaments, a hand-bell, Watts' Hymns, and a penny contribution box "for the poor in Jerusalem."
>
> Here Miss Gratz presided. A stately commanding figure, always neatly dressed in plain black, with thin white collar and

cuffs, close-fitting bonnet over her curled front, which time never touched with grey; giving her, even in her advanced years, a youthful appearance. Her eyes would pierce every part of the hall and often detect mischief which escaped the notice of the teachers. . . .

Miss Gratz always began school with the prayer, opening with "Come ye children, hearken unto me, and I will teach you the fear of the Lord." This was followed by a prayer of her own composition, which she read verse by verse, and the whole school repeated after her. Then she read a chapter of the Bible, in a clear and distinct voice, without any elocution, and this could be heard and understood all over the room. The closing exercises were equally simple; a Hebrew hymn sung by the children, then one of Watts' simple verses, whose rhythm the smallest child could easily catch as all repeated "Send me the voice that Samuel heard," etc.

Many old scholars can still recall the question: "Who formed you child and made you live?" and the answer: "God did my life and spirit give"—the first lines of that admirable "Pyke's Catechism," which long held its place in the Sunday school, and was, I believe, the first book printed for it. The "Scripture Lessons" were taught from a little illustrated work published by the Christian Sunday School Union. Many a long summer's day have I spent, pasting pieces of paper over answers unsuitable for Jewish children, and many were the fruitless efforts of those children to read through, over, or under the hidden lines. . . .

Both Rev. Isaac Leeser and the Rev. Dr. Morais were constant visitors. The former with his strongly marked face, gold spectacles, and inexhaustible fund of ever-ready information was a most welcome sight to the young teachers, puzzled by the questions of their big, clever scholars. He knew every child and teacher, called each by name, and nothing was too trivial or too intricate to claim his clear explanation.

Mr. Morais was then young, active, and full of enthusiasm, always ready to lead the Hebrew hymns or take the class of an absent teacher. . . .

The annual examination was held about Purim time. . . . The classes . . . were called up to "stand and recite," by Mr. Abraham Hart. . . . Every child was really examined, and each book recited in whole or in part. . . . The first prize was always a Bible, or, rather, a Bible and two books were given to each class. These books were most carefully selected by Miss Gratz herself, and handed by her to each child with a kind, encouraging word, often with a written line on the fly-leaf. As the happy children went out orderly by class, through the back door, each was given an orange and a pretzel.

LITERARY ACTIVITY

The creation and promotion of Jewish literature in midcentury and in the decades which followed was largely the enterprise of Isaac Leeser and Isaac Mayer Wise. Besides editing and publishing the first Jewish periodical in America, *The Occident,* for twenty-five years, Leeser, as we have noted, also prepared and published children's textbooks, translated the Bible into English, organized the first Jewish Publication Society (1845), which published fourteen small volumes of popular literature known as The Jewish Miscellany series, and produced volumes of his own sermons and addresses. In 1854 Wise founded the weekly, *The Israelite,* and for many years wrote most of its articles. A year later he began publication of *Die Deborah* in German. He also wrote historical and polemical works and popular novels, helped to establish Bloch and Company, the first publishing house devoted to Jewish literature, and initiated publication of the *Annual Proceedings of the Union of American Hebrew Congregations.*

In addition to *The Occident* and *The Israelite,* other Jewish periodicals, like the *Asmonean* and *The Jewish Messenger* in New York, *Sinai* in Baltimore and *The Gleaner* in San Francisco, boasted readers and influence.

This period also marked the appearance of the Yiddish and Hebrew press in America; the *Yiddische Zeitung* appeared in 1870, *Ha-Zofeh ba-Arez ha-Hadasha* a year later, edited for its five years by Zvi Hirsch Bernstein. They served the new immigrants as a tie to the Old World and an introduction to the New. In their pages Jews could become acquainted with American authors and poets in translation. Longfellow's "Excelsior" appeared in *Ha-Zofeh* in a Hebrew translation by Henry Gersoni. In addition, contributions by American Jews began to appear in European Hebrew periodicals. In 1864, for example, *Ha-Magid* (published in Lyck, Prussia) contained reports and articles from San Francisco, St. Louis, Detroit, Chicago and New York.

The first Hebrew book written and printed in America, Joshua Falk's *Avney Yehoshua,* a homiletical commentary on the *Ethics of the Fathers,* was published in 1860. The second, M. E. Holzman's *Emek Refaim* (1865), is of greater interest, for, as a spirited attack on Reform Judaism and its leaders, it reflects the American scene.

To be sure, books in Hebrew had appeared in America since 1735 when Judah Monis, an apostate Jew who taught Hebrew at Harvard, published *A Grammar of the Hebrew Tongue* "for the Use of the Students of Harvard-College at Cambridge, in New England." Other Hebrew grammars, lexicons, prayer books and editions of classic texts followed, but these were books *about* rather than *in* Hebrew and were generally directed toward Christian ministers and their more scholarly congregants. The first Hebrew Bible in America was published in Philadelphia in 1814. With a Latin introduction and notes, its Hebrew unpointed, it was intended for the Christian Bible student and scholar. A subsequent edition in 1848 took the Jewish reader into account, for it had the editorial supervision of Isaac Leeser. Leeser's Pentateuch with Hebrew text and his own English translation, published three years earlier, was meant for Jewish congregational use.

Hebrew prayer books had been printed in America since Eliezer S. Lazarus's edition of 1826. Isaac Leeser had done yeoman service in translating both the Sephardic and Ashkenazic prayer book, and other editions of the traditional *Siddur* and the holiday *Mahzorim* were prepared by W. L. Frank, publisher and printer of New York.

A prayer book prepared specifically for women, *Roochamah: Devotional Exercises for the Use of the Daughters of Israel, Intended for Public and Private Worship On the Various Occasions of Woman's Life*, appeared in 1852. The editor, the Reverend Morris J. Raphall of New York, argues the need of such a work, especially in America "where Hebrew educational institutions for both sexes are in their infancy . . . girls' schools can scarcely be said to exist."

The first prayer book for children, *Order of Prayers for Hefzi-Bah Hebrew School, Temporarily compiled for the Devotion of the Solemn Holidays of the Year 5621*, was published anonymously in San Francisco in 1860. It is a miniature pamphlet of 114 pages of English text interspersed with brief Hebrew sections. A handwritten inscription on the flyleaf of one copy indicates the editor to be the Reverend Julius Eckman, rabbi, educator and editor in San Francisco, and states that it was "compiled by the editor of the 'Gleaner,' and published at his responsibility and expense without any aid from the Synagogue or its offices, which he hitherto sought in vain."

Three Reform prayer books appeared in the 1850s, each more radical than its predecessor. The first, *The Order of Prayer for Divine Service*, prepared by L. Merzbacher, rabbi of Temple Emanu-El in New York, was a revised form of the traditional prayer book. It contained the Hebrew text with English translation, and its main concession to Reform was its abridgement. It was an unsuccessful undertaking, for, since the prayer book departed from tradition, it could not be used in Traditional congregations, while its revisions were so slight as to make it unacceptable to Reform congregations.

Isaac M. Wise's *Minhag America* was a more successful attempt at adapting the prayer book for American congregations. He visualized it as a force for "Americanization" through the modernization of thought and ritual in conformity to the "refinements" of the age, as well as a factor in the unification of American Jews who had brought from their home communities a variety of liturgical forms. *Minhag America* retained the form of the traditional prayer book, but omitted passages which did not conform to "the wants and demands of the time." Thus, for example, where the Merzbacher prayer book reads, "send a redeemer to their children's children," Wise writes ". . . bringest redemption to their descendants."

Radical Reform ideologist David Einhorn was critical of Wise's prayer book, and a year after it appeared he published his own contribution to synagogue liturgy, *Olat Tamid, Gebetbuch für Israelitische Reform Gemeinde*. As its title indicates, it was a German-language prayer book which incorporated Hebrew prayers. These were emended to conform with the theology of the author-editor, which he presented as the authentic Judaism of the age. For example, both Wise's and Einhorn's prayer books contain special services for Tisha B'Av, the fast day marking the destruction of Jerusalem. Wise terms the day "one of national mourning," and its liturgy is chosen from traditional sources. Einhorn's volume has a morning service "for the Anniversary of the Destruction of Jerusalem" which includes a long prayer by the reader. It reads in part:

> . . . Not as a disowned son Thy first born went out into strange lands, but as Thy emissary to all the families of man. The one temple in Jerusalem sank into the dust, in order that countless temples might arise to Thy honor and glory all over the wide surface of the globe . . . Grant, O God, that Israel may recognize the aim of his meanderings and tend toward it with undivided strength and cheerful courage. . . .

The "mission" idea, central to the mid-nineteenth-century Reform ideology, finds expression and emphasis in Einhorn's prayer book: The purpose of Jewish existence is to be a prophet-people to the nations. Dispersion is not punishment but opportunity; exile is not banishment but a divine gift of exalted destiny. The day of mourning for Jerusalem becomes a day of celebratory consecration.

The spirit which animated the editors and translators of these varied prayer books, from Lazarus to Einhorn, was one and the same, a deep concern for the spiritual welfare of an ancient people settled in a new world. The editors differed in their understanding of that welfare out of the conviction that American Jewry is a pluralistic community joined by common concerns but diverse in spiritual attitudes and needs. It would seem that the true *Minhag America* is the variety of liturgies it has produced and the recognition of the place and worth of all.[32]

INSTITUTIONS AND ORGANIZATIONS

Fully two-thirds of the American Jewish community were immigrants in 1860, mainly pack peddlers, storekeepers, small merchants and artisans. Shared hazards brought the immigrant Jew closer to comrades, and loneliness made him seek out those who, like himself, longed for home and yearned for companionship. Early in their American experience, Jewish immigrants established institutions which cared for human needs in exemplary fashion. Away from home, they established social clubs, literary societies and congregations which provided them with a homelike atmosphere. Away from family, they joined fraternal orders whose secret ritual shared with "brothers" substituted for the intimacy of family life and traditional communal concourse. The fraternal orders cared for sick members and provided death benefits for bereaved families. The last rites and final honors, which in a normal situation family would provide, now became the duty of one's fraternal brothers. Most congregations of the time provided similar benefits, including visits to the sick, attendance at funerals, payment of funeral expenses and often some financial settlement for widow and orphans.

The first of the Jewish fraternal orders, the Independent Order B'nai B'rith, was organized in New York in 1843. Soon lodges spread throughout the country and eventually throughout the world. The orders Kesher Shel Barzel, Free Sons of Israel, B'nai Abraham, and B'nai Moshe soon followed. These not only served the needs of the member brothers, but often spearheaded social welfare endeavors in the community and, through correspondence, conventions and joint enterprises, helped unite scattered Jewish communities.

The report of the First Anniversary Meeting of the Jewish Foster Home Society of Philadelphia, held on February 12, 1856, reads:

> With much satisfaction were presented the members of this youthful household, twelve in number, to their friends and patrons; their beaming faces radiant with health and happiness. . . . much improvement can be observed in their deportment and the development of their mental capacities, several of the children being now able to read both English and Hebrew, with tolerable accuracy and fluency. . . . [33]

Several years later, the Jews of Philadelphia met to dedicate a Jewish hospital. The B'nai B'rith fraternal order had initiated the project, and seven hundred persons pledged five dollars a year. In 1866 it opened its doors to patients "of ages ranging from six to eighty. . . ." Jewish foster homes and Jewish hospitals were also established in New Orleans, New York and Cincinnati.

JEWS AND THE CIVIL WAR

On the great issue of the day, slavery, American Jewry was as divided as the rest of the nation. In the South there were Jewish slave owners and Jewish slave merchants. "No Jewish political figure of the Old South ever expressed any reservations about the justice of slavery or the rightness of the Southern position" states historian Bertram W. Korn.[34] Judah P. Benjamin, senator from Louisiana, upheld the morality and legality of the institution of slavery in the halls of Congress. Literary figures like Isaac Harby, Edwin DeLeon and Jacob N. Cardozo placed their pens in its service. The Jews of the North (by now the great majority of the Jewish community) were generally opposed to slavery and contributed workers to the abolitionist cause. Political figures like Isidor Busch of St. Louis and Philip J. Joachimsen of New York were leaders in the antislavery ranks. The scholarly writer, Michael Heilprin, was an active abolitionist.

The same division of opinion obtained among the rabbis of the time. Rabbi George Jacobs of Richmond rented slaves for household work. His townsman, the Reverend J. M. Michelbacher, believed slavery to have been ordained by God, pronouncing in prayer: ". . . the man servants and maid servants Thou hast given unto us, that we may . . . bear over them." These sentiments were shared by their colleagues Simon Tuska of Memphis and James K. Gutheim of New Orleans. The rabbinic "hero" of the proslavery forces, however, was Morris J. Raphall of New York. His sermon, "The Bible View of Slavery," was published and republished, hailed and widely quoted. Stating that he himself was not in favor of slavery, and that a distinction was to be made between the slavery of the Bible and Southern slavery, he nevertheless made the case that the Bible does not prohibit slavery; indeed, Biblical law guaranteed the right to own slaves. He was particularly strong in his attack on abolitionists who "denounce slaveholding a sin," and addressed "the reverend gentleman from Brooklyn" (Henry Ward Beecher) accusingly: "When you remember that Abraham, Isaac, Jacob and Job—the men with whom the Almighty conversed . . . were slaveholders, does it not strike you that you are guilty of something very little short of blasphemy?"[35]

The sermon elicited many rabbinic rejoinders. In Manchester, England, Rabbi Gustav Gottheil (later rabbi of Temple Emanu-El, New York) preached and published two sermons in opposition to Raphall's views.[36] The chief attack came from Rabbi David Einhorn of Baltimore, who devoted four articles in his monthly, *Sinai*, to it.

> Is it anything else but a deed of Amalek, rebellion against God, to enslave human beings created in His image? . . . Can *that* Book mean to raise the whip and forge chains, which proclaims, with

flaming words, in the name of God: "Break the bonds of oppression, let the oppressed go free and tear every yoke!"[37]

In a sermon preached at the end of the war, the Reverend Bernhard Felsenthal of Chicago, an outspoken abolitionist, said:

Four millions of men, children of the same heavenly Father . . . were held in slavery! And now they were freed. . . . And should not the nation rejoice? . . . The white people have become emancipated just as well as the black people. . . .[38]

Before peace came, Jews in gray fought against Jews in blue. The Civil War was, after all, not a Jewish but a national issue and conflict. Jews responded to and engaged in the conflict as Americans, Northerners or Southerners, in general espousing the views and joining the ranks of the community and state in which they lived. Both Leeser and Wise remained silent on the issue, neutral in the conflict. They were, they felt, religious leaders who should stand aside from and above partisan political conflict.

During the war, they and other Jewish leaders became involved in two issues which were of particular Jewish interest. One was the right of Jews to serve as chaplains in the armed forces which was not resolved; the second was the notorious Order #11 issued by Major General U. S. Grant on December 17, 1862: "The Jews, as a class, violating every regulation of trade established by the Treasury Department and also department orders, are hereby expelled from the department within twenty-four hours. . . ."[39] Jewish reaction was instant and vigorous. Resolutions were adopted and transmitted to Washington. Delegations of Jews descended on the capital. Concerted Jewish activity brought its results. As soon as President Lincoln was apprised of the matter, he ordered cancellation of the decree.

DEFENDING JEWISH RIGHTS

The man who had informed the Jewish community of General Grant's order and appealed to the president was Cesar J. Kaskel of Paducah, Kentucky. When he arrived in Washington, he consulted with Adolphus S. Solomons, a member of the Executive Committee of the Board of Delegates of American Israelites. This first union of American Jews had emerged from Jewish activity relating to two international issues. The first was opposition to a Swiss-American treaty signed in 1850, in which the United States tacitly acquiesced to disabilities of Jews in Swiss cantons. The second was a protest of the Mortara Affair. The spiriting away of six-year-old Edgar Mortara from his parents in 1858 by the papal authorities in Bologna, Italy, and his conversion to

Catholicism evoked indignation in all Protestant countries. Protest
meetings were held in many American cities.

Since Isaac Leeser's abortive attempt to form a Union of American Israelites, two decades had elapsed in which the Jewish community
had tripled in size and had established public institutions, fraternal orders
of national scope and a significant, spirited press. This time the Reverend
Samuel M. Isaacs' proposal for a meeting of Jewish congregations to
launch a unifying organization met with a positive response, and the
Board of Delegates came into being in 1859. The Board of Delegates
made important contributions to overseas Jewish communities oppressed by disabilities or suffering persecution, and also served to tie
American Jewry in a formal, organized manner to the Jewish communities of other countries. In itself, however, it suffered a double
disability. It never attracted the Reform elements of the Jewish community, and it limited itself to "foreign relations." A growing, self-
conscious Jewish community needed a body that would address itself
to Jewish life in America.

The Union of American Hebrew Congregations, formed in 1873,
seemed to promise such a concern and program, and the Board of
Delegates was later integrated into the Union. Initially the UAHC had
limited itself in purpose, calling upon "all the congregations of the West
and South to form a union" to establish a "Jewish Theological Institute." In time, it became clearly denominational, and by the late eighties,
as the national federation of Reform congregations it bade fair to become
the organization of American Jewry.

In its concern for the rights of Jews abroad, the American Jewish
community displayed a high degree of seriousness and enterprise as the
case of Peixotto's mission to Romania discloses. The plight of the Jews
in Romania moved the leaders of American Jewry to urge upon the
government of the United States an unprecedented diplomatic enterprise. Benjamin F. Peixotto, a leader of B'nai B'rith, was appointed
United States consul to Bucharest. The letter he carried from President
U. S. Grant describes the purpose of the appointment:

> Executive Mansion
> December 8, 1870
>
> The bearer of this letter, Mr. Benjamin Peixotto . . . has
> accepted the important, though unremunerative position of U.S.
> Consul to Roumania . . .
> Mr. Peixotto has undertaken the duties of his present of-
> fice . . . as a missionary work for the benefit of the people he
> represents—a work in which all citizens will wish him the greatest
> success.
>
> U. S. Grant [40]

American Jewry and the American government were joined in a humanitarian enterprise, the former supplying the finance, the latter its diplomatic favor.

By 1880 the Jewish community had a network of institutions and organizations across the continent, a trilingual press, a corps of able, scholarly rabbis and a rabbinic seminary. The first attempt at a Jewish population survey, undertaken by the Board of Delegates of American Israelites in 1877, placed the number of Jews in the United States at 230,257. In the post–Civil War economic and industrial expansion, some significant fortunes had been made. The community enjoyed affluence and influence. But there were problems as well. It was a community divided between Reform and Traditional groups, and within these groups between moderate and radical elements. The affluence which came to some few also divided the community economically, and the beginning of a labor movement in America accentuated that division. The rift between Western and Eastern European communities was already pronounced. Spiritual values and cultural concerns were outdistanced by the desire to "move up" and "get ahead."

4.

American Judaism

SYNAGOGUES: REFORM AND ORTHODOX

REFORM CAME TO CHICAGO IN 1858. ITS LEADING SPIRIT WAS BERNHARD Felsenthal who arrived in America in 1854 from Bavaria, and continued his profession of teacher of Jewish children in Lawrenceburg and Madison, Indiana. He began to publish his Reform sentiments in *The American Israelite, Die Deborah* and *Sinai*. When he settled in Chicago in 1858, he became the leader of a "few young men" in founding the Juedische Reformverein which evolved into the city's first Reform congregation, Sinai.

Felsenthal's account of the beginnings of the congregation discloses an emphasis on the formulation of an ideological base for a ritual and liturgy, and on an insistence on the free congregational nature of the synagogue and the religious independence of its individual members.

A dozen years later an East European congregation was established in Rochester, New York. Soon there was a second. In 1874 the two joined to form Beth Israel. The Traditional ritual it followed had long since been set down in codes and further defined in usage; its liturgy was that of the Traditional prayer book.

SOURCE
The Beginnings of the Chicago Sinai Congregation
By Bernhard Felsenthal

In 1858, in Chicago, there were two Jewish congregations, *Kehillath Anshe Ma'arabh,* a congregation whose founders had been, and the majority of whose members then still were, emigrants who had come over from southern Germany; and *K. Bene Shalom,* a congregation whose members hailed from the Prussian province of Posen and adjacent parts of Germany. In the synagogue of the first named congregation the *Minhag Ashkenaz* had been adopted; the synagogue of the other congregation was conducted in accordance with *Minhag Poland.* Officially, both congregations stood upon solid orthodox grounds.

But there were then already a few younger men in Chicago who were not satisfied with existing affairs in Judaism. They were strongly inclined towards "Reform."

The present writer and his friends agreed to come together and to found, if possible, a society for the purpose of fostering Jewish reform.

On Sunday, June 20, 1858, at 3 P.M., in the office of Greenebaum Brothers . . . the *"Juedische Reformverein"* was instituted. . . . Almost three years thereafter the association changed its name to *Sinai Congregation.* . . .

The secretary [B. Felsenthal] submitted a paper containing 27 theses. [The preamble read:]

We are deeply convinced that Israel has been called by God to be the Messiah of the nations and to spread truth and virtue on earth. In order to fulfill this high mission, Israel has to undergo a process of purification in its own midst. This object will be best accomplished in free and blessed America where no material forces check spiritual progress. The special mission of American Israel, therefore, is to place Judaism before the world, purified in doctrine and conduct, and so to become a shining example for Israelites the world over. In order to do our share in this work, we organize to-day a Jewish Reform Society.

The Religious Basis of a Reform Congregation

1. As sacred days we consider the weekly Sabbath, which shall be celebrated according to tradition on Saturdays, and the seven Biblical holy days, to wit: First and Seventh days of Passover, one day of Pentecost, one New Year's Day, one day of Atonement, one day of Tabernacles and one day of Atzereth.

2. Besides, there shall be distinguished in public worship the days of Chanukkah and Purim, New Moon and Chol-Hammoed and the ninth day of Abh. . . .

4, 5. The Torah shall be read in a cycle of three years . . . in the original Hebrew. The Prophetic portions, however, shall be read either in the mother tongue intelligible to the congregation or in the language of the country.

6. Of the traditional prayer-book, there shall be retained some portions which scientific investigation has recognized as most ancient and which on that account already possess a high degree of religious power. We reserve the right to make such changes as are necessary to bring these prayers in harmony with our convictions. . . . Prayers and hymns in the vernacular shall have a prominent place.

7. From the liturgy everything that is contrary to the convictions of the congregation, shall be eliminated. . . .

8. Services shall be held with the greatest possible solemnity, and, if feasible, shall be made more impressive by solemn choral song and organ music.

9. In the public worship of the congregation, there shall be no discrimination made in favor of the male against female worshippers. . . .

From public worship there shall be removed wailing over oppression and persecution, also the prayers for the restoration of the sacrificial cult, for Israel's return to Palestine, the expression of the hope for a personal Messiah and of a resurrection of the body.

Bombastic words, exaggerations and bad taste shall have no place in public worship. Therefore, all unnecessary repetition shall be done away with.

. . . The exalting and inspiring thought shall be strongly and emphatically accentuated, that Israel is a priestly nation among the nations on earth, the people chosen by God to bring about the Messianic kingdom, i.e., the kingdom of truth, of virtue and of peace. [1]

FOCUS
An East European Congregation on American Soil [2]

In the decades after the Civil War, while the great majority of American synagogues were turning to Reform, a new kind of congregation was being introduced to the American scene, the East European Orthodox synagogue.

Typical was Beth Israel of Rochester, New York. Its history

discloses a determined effort to insulate itself against the deleterious influences of the American environment. The synagogue had to be kept as a refuge from the spiritually corroding forces which assailed the immigrant community. For the East European immigrants, their synagogue was more than a house of worship. It offered fellowship in planning and enterprise, in celebration and in contention; and it afforded them the variety of interpersonal relationships and confrontation which a true community provides.

On Sunday, June 28, 1874, seven representatives each of two small East European congregations met as a joint committee for the purpose of consolidation. Officers, trustees and a *gabbai* (lay official) for the cemetery were elected. Both groups met on the following Wednesday to bring the Scroll of the Torah and the other ritual objects into the Sheves Ahim synagogue, which would house the new, united congregation. An expenditure of up to five dollars was authorized for the move. Thus was the Beth Israel Congregation of Rochester, New York, born, for forty years the leading Orthodox synagogue of that city.

The first Jewish settlers had arrived in Rochester from Germany before 1840. A congregation, Berith Kodesh, was formed in 1848 and in the course of time came to serve both West and East European Jews. A news item in *The Occident* (December 1855) reports: "The congregation consists of Germans, Englishmen and Poles, who all are acting in harmony. Some, indeed, would have liked to have a mode of worship similar to the Emanuel Temple at New York; but they will not desire to introduce any reform which might lead to disunion."[3] In the 1860s, Berith Kodesh began veering toward Reform, just as a small but steady influx of Jews from Eastern Europe began to arrive in Rochester. Small congregations, or *hevras,* were formed to purchase burial grounds, and it was these groups that merged to form Beth Israel congregation.

The early years of Beth Israel were marked by congregational growth, the acquisition of expanded synagogue facilities and the professionalization of its religious functionaries. The beginning of differences between "traditionalists" and "progressives" can be found in the vote on where the hazzan should stand, at the center *bimah* (synagogue platform) or at the pulpit. The cantor moved to the pulpit, and a curtain was hung between the synagogue proper and the women's section.

Twice in less than a decade the men of Beth Israel made plans for a synagogue building of their own. In 1878, the congregation bought a house and renovated it. Each member contributed five dollars, and committees of three were formed to solicit contributions from the "German Jews" and the "Polish Jews." The dedication of the new synagogue was a joyous celebration for the East European Jewish community in Rochester. Three years earlier their wealthy German brethren had built a temple; now, after years in a rented hall, they were to have their own synagogue. The entire Jewish community was invited to the celebration. Dr. Max Landsberg, the radical Reform rabbi of Berith Kodesh, now a congregation of wealth and prestige, gave the dedicatory address in English. A band played. Leaders of the congregation marched in the Torah procession (for which honor they had bid from eighty-seven cents to two dollars). The immigrants from White Russia and Lithuania were now beginning to feel at home in the New World.

With an eye to the future, the congregation decided to undertake an educational program. Moshe White was elected *hazzan*-reader-teacher. Tuition was set at three dollars per year, and a board of education was appointed. Two years after its inauguration the school was closed.

An issue that split the congregation was the building of a fence for the congregrational cemetery. Mr. Nusbaum, the president, was determined to build the fence to protect the consecrated ground. To his opponents, a new synagogue building was top priority. When the president arranged to have the fence built, the vice-president convened a special meeting, which voted *not* to begin building the fence.

One result of the acrimony was the formation of a breakaway congregation, called "the Nusbaum Minyan." It constituted a threat to the parent congregation, which adopted a constitutional amendment: "It is forbidden for a member to attend the Nusbaum Minyan. If a member attends either weekdays or Sabbaths, he is to be fined 50 cents for the first violation and one dollar for the second. A third offense brings expulsion."[4]

It may very well be that this controversy was an aspect of the basic difference between "traditionalists" and "progressives." Traditionalist concerns led to emphasis on the cemetery; commitment to progress led to labors for a school and a new synagogue building.

An aspect of this division was expressed in the controversy over the language in which the constitution and bylaws be printed. After considerable debate an agreement was reached to print in both English and Yiddish, but when it was found that it would be too costly to do so in both languages, the trustees voted not to print them at all.

Rochester did not have an Orthodox rabbi until 1883. In the West European congregation in America, the rabbi was central; in the East European *hevra,* he was at best peripheral. The immigrant from Western Europe knew a congregation where preaching was central and a rabbi-preacher a necessity. For the East European, the synagogue was a place for prayer which could be led by a layman, and if by a professional, a cantor. The *rov* (rabbi) of Eastern Europe was a communal rather than congregational functionary.

In June 1883 Rabbi Abba Hayim ben Yitzhak Isaac Levinson petitioned Beth Israel to serve as its rabbi. A month later he was elected for a year at a salary of $150. The duties of the rabbi were not spelled out, but we may assume that they were nominal. The great majority of the membership apparently viewed him as a communal functionary, to be supported by the Beth Israel Congregation among others. The part-time *shamash* (sexton) and funds collector received a salary equal to that of the rabbi; the cantor's salary that year was almost three times greater! The congregation's view of the status and functions of a rabbi was later stated in the public press by the president:

> A rabbi is not a minister. He does not belong to one congregation, but to the city. His duties, only to a very small extent, resemble the duties of a Christian minister. He is an interpreter of the divine law, not a spiritual adviser. His duty is chiefly to interpret the law as it is written and apply it to particular cases as they are brought to him for decision. Moreover the feeling which animates all Orthodox Jews, of obligation to preserve the knowledge of the law and to support students of the law simply as students, is their principal motive in keeping a rabbi.[5]

Supervision of *kashrut* (dietary laws) in the community was among the primary duties of the rabbi. However, when Rabbi Levinson sought to examine the *shohatim* (ritual slaughterers) of the community, one of them ignored his authority. At a special meeting, the congregation voted to stand behind the rabbi. But controversy must have arisen in the city, for action had to be taken at the trustees' meeting a week later to protect the rabbi. It was voted that any nonmember who abused the rabbi not be permitted into the synagogue, and no outside preachers be permitted to speak. Both of the above motions were passed only by the president's tie-breaking vote. The rabbi remained vulnerable to criticism, and the congregation's Minute Books for the following two years were filled with accounts of slanderous remarks against him, and punishments meted out to congregational offenders, including proclamation of a *herem,* a ban, by the Beth Din.

In a description of Jewish religious life, Moshe Weinberger wrote in *Jews and Judaism in New York* (1887):

> The purpose of most of the Orthodox congregations is to assemble twice daily, or on Sabbaths, for worship, to visit the sick and help them, to bury the dead and pay them last respects, and to help a fellow member in time of need. But the highest purpose is to build a synagogue—grand and beautiful.[6]

In this matter, Beth Israel was not to be outdone. The congregation began to talk of building a synagogue only three years after moving into its renovated house. Impetus was given to the project when a sister congregation, B'nai Israel, requested an amalgamation with the Beth Israel Congregation. The rolls of Beth Israel were now swollen by nineteen new members. The aim was to have a new synagogue for the Holy Days of 1886. On August 29 of that year, the building completed, a committee was appointed to make arrangements "to move with a parade" and the event was duly reported in the local press.

Congregation Beth Israel was not just a body of like-minded believers joined for public worship, but primarily a group of Jews, recent immigrants all, who came together to fashion a fellowship-community. As a community, the *hevra* extended care and a helping hand to it members. Visitation in sickness, proper burial and assistance to the bereaved family were guaranteed by the laws of the *hevra,* but help went beyond that to those in need. Free cemetery land for the indigent, postponement of monetary obligations where indicated and direct aid when requested were common.

Beth Israel gave its members the sense of security and status that a community provides. America made hardly an impress upon it. It may very well have sought to remain insulated against American influences so that it would remain the unchanged *hevra* the immigrant knew in his European hometown. The *hevra*-congregation was the safe harbor to which one could return for services or meetings with cronies, after being tossed about the uncharted waters of peddling in the countryside or laboring in a not-too-friendly city. In a real sense, Beth Israel was the most comfortable and secure haven which the immigrant Jew in Rochester had in the first decades of mass immigration.

RELIGIOUS IDEOLOGIES

"Perhaps one third of the Jews in the United States are still orthodox, another third neglect religion except on the greatest days of the religious year . . . another third are in various stages of Reform . . . ," James Parton wrote in 1870. [7] The East European immigration of the following decades added to the first two groups, and introduced a new phenomenon in Jewish religious life in America—the active antireligionists. The latter, comprised of Socialists, Anarchists and a variety of Freethinkers, launched all manner of antireligious projects. Periodicals in Yiddish and Hebrew, books and pamphlets were published to argue the falsity of religious doctine, to portray organized religion as a regressive, reactionary force. Perhaps the most dramatic antireligious projects were the Yom Kippur "balls," held on Kol Nidre night, "to eat, drink and make merry," while most Jews were in prayer and fasting, observing the holiest day of the Jewish calendar.

Within organized religious life, there was heightened contention which eventually led to the divisions into Orthodox, Conservative and

Reform movements. To be sure, there were those who pleaded for one uniform American Judaism. In his *The Voice of Truth* (1870), Jacob Goldman, who had traveled widely in the United States, argues:

> The Jehudim of the different parts of Europe etc. have brought into this country their different "minhagim" [rites]. . . . Our Rabbis, D.D.'s, Reverends, Preachers . . . are holding on to their various minhagim . . . in the name of God, in the name of all Israelites whose hearts are still accessible . . . in the name of all Jewish American citizens, prepare . . . a code of minhagim common to all, and to be adopted by all of us survivors of the year 1870! Look upon our posterity! They are no longer Polander, German, Russian, English, Portuguese; they are Americans, and will and can have nothing more useful than "a Minhag of America."[8]

The Union of American Hebrew Congregations, established in 1873, and its Hebrew Union College, founded two years later, were intended to serve all American Jewry, but the issues which divided American Jewry were stronger than the wish to establish an "American Judaism." Which prayer book was to be accepted for "American Judaism"—the traditional, the moderate Reform *Minhag America* of Isaac Mayer Wise, or the radical *Olat Tamid* of David Einhorn? An increasing number of leading congregations were holding their main religious service of the week on Sunday morning. Others denounced this as rank apostasy. There were those who were meticulous in their observance of *kashrut*; others termed *kashrut* a remnant of an ancient barbaric cult and poked fun at "kitchen Judaism."

The conflict came to a dramatic head in 1883 at the banquet celebrating the first commencement of the Hebrew Union College. The first course was shellfish, causing observant Jews to leave the dinner and the movement. Visible insult had been added to the long-standing verbal attack on Jewish traditional practice. Such disparity of views on religion, law and custom could not help but lead to a split within American Jewry.

The break was, of course, long in the making. For three decades, Reformers and Traditionalists had been engaged in battle, attack and counterattack filling the pages of the contemporary Jewish press, *The Occident, The Israelite, Sinai* and *The Asmonean*. After the death of Isaac Leeser in 1868, when Traditionalist forces were left without an effective leader or spokesman, the field was open for Reform, and spread it did. Virtually all leading congregations and rabbinical personalities were to be found in its camp.

Ironically, the increasing immigration of East European Jews, a community far removed in ideology and practices, had some effect on structuring the Reform movement. The radical and moderate elements of that group found a reason for rapprochement in their desire to remain separate from the new immigrants. It has been suggested that radical Reform gained the victory over moderate Reform, because "native" Jews became convinced that its more extreme form of religious life and worship would keep the new immigrants out of their temple.

AN AMERICAN REFORM JUDAISM

For a generation, the moderate, practical Reform of Wise and the radical, ideological Reform of Einhorn were in contention, but the logic of consolidation eventually defeated the dynamics of confrontation. The contending groups met in two conferences, in Philadelphia in 1869 and in Pittsburgh in 1885, and their consolidation into a unified movement was confirmed by the platforms adopted. At the conference held in Philadelphia, fifteen rabbis adopted a platform of seven resolutions which clearly follow the ideology of Einhorn.

> It proclaimed that "The Messianic goal of Israel is not the restoration of the old Jewish state . . . but the union of all men as children of God. . . . " and emphasized "The selection of Israel as a people of faith . . . [with a] universal mission. . . ."[9]

In 1869, Reform was at the threshold of making its triumphant sweep through organized Jewish religious life in America. The resolutions adopted in Philadelphia were in a sense a battle cry. It was a declaration drawn from the European experience, an ideological declaration of the "Jewish mission" idea which served the German Jews well as they stood in confrontation with a world which bade them enter. Einhorn remained rooted in German ideology even when serving as rabbi in Baltimore, Philadelphia and New York. The seven resolutions could just as well have been adopted at a conference in Berlin as in Philadelphia. Einhorn's contribution was the *Reform* component of *American Reform Judaism*.

Sixteen years later, the disciple and son-in-law of David Einhorn, Dr. Kaufmann Kohler, convened a conference in Pittsburgh, "in view of the wide divergence of opinion and of the conflicting views prevailing in Judaism today . . . in continuation of the work done in Philadelphia in 1869."

The Platform reiterated the mission idea, but placed its central emphasis on other pronouncements.

> First— . . . We hold that Judaism presents the highest conception of the God-idea . . . We maintain that Judaism preserved and defended . . . this God-idea as the central truth for the human race. Second— . . . We hold that modern discoveries of scientific re-

searchers in the domain of nature and history are not antagonistic to the doctrines of Judaism . . .

Third— . . . Today we accept as binding only the moral laws.

Fourth— . . . We hold that all such Mosaic and Rabbinical laws as regulate diet, priestly purity and dress . . . [are] altogether foreign to our present mental and spiritual state . . . Their observance in our days is apt . . . to obstruct . . . modern spiritual elevation.

Fifth— . . . We consider ourselves no longer a nation but a religious community, and therefore expect neither a return to Palestine . . . nor the restoration of the laws concerning the Jewish state.

Sixth— . . . We recognize in Judaism a progressive religion, ever striving to be in accord with the postulates of reason . . . We acknowledge that the spirit of broad humanity of our age is our ally in the fulfillment of our mission, and therefore extend the hand of fellowship to all who cooperate with us in the establishment of the reign of truth and righteousness among men.

Seventh— . . . We reassert the doctrine of Judaism, that the soul of men is immortal.

Eighth— . . . In full accordance with the spirit of Mosaic Legislation which strives to regulate the relation between rich and poor, we deem it our duty to participate in the great task of modern times, to solve on the basis of justice and righteousness the problems presented by the contrasts and evils of the present day organization of society.[10]

In sum, the Platform is a statement to the America of that time that Judaism fits most comfortably into the American religious establishment, and the Jewish religious community has its contribution to make to the common weal. The third and fourth planks are addressed to American Jews. It makes them feel comfortable, even virtuous in their nonobservance. The casting off of ritual law and custom was part of their "Americanization." Now, it was given religious sanction.

Isaac M. Wise presided at the conference, and his students and disciples, Rabbis Joseph Krauskopf and David Philipson, served respectively as vice-president and secretary. The Platform was the work of Kaufmann Kohler, but Wise welcomed it as if it were his own. He called it "this Declaration of Independence," thus giving it hallowed American associations. Wise hailed the conference as opening "a new chapter in the history of American Judaism," claiming that, as a result of the conference, "we are the orthodox Jews of America" as they "were the orthodox of former days in other countries." Wise thus sees the Platform as essentially an *American* document.

The Pittsburgh Platform separated the Reform camp from the "half-civilized orthodoxy" of the East European immigrant; it presented

Judaism's best foot forward to "the enlightened world"; it propounded a Judaism for "American Israelites." Isaac Mayer Wise accepted it with enthusiasm and made it his own, for it was he who fashioned the component *American,* in *American Reform* Judaism.

SOURCE
Reform in a Congregation

Conferences issued ideological pronouncements of Reform. The practical changes took place within the growing number of congregations that identified with the movement. A leader of Radical Reform was Dr. Emil G. Hirsch of Chicago's Sinai Congregation, son of Philadelphia's Rabbi Samuel Hirsch and son-in-law of David Einhorn.

In the year of the Pittsburgh Conference, the annual meeting of the Sinai Congregation addressed itself to ritual questions, turning to its rabbi for his views.

From Proceedings of Chicago Sinai Congregation at Its Annual Meeting, March 26, 1885 and Special Meeting, April 9, 1885

First Recommendation of the President:

The rite of circumcision to which even the most radical among us cling with such tenacity, has frequently been denounced from our pulpit as *a disgusting relic of barbarism.* If this assertion is true, as most of us concede it to be, why is it not our duty to declare in unmistakable language that the practice of the rite of circumcision is sacrilegious and should be discontinued, and also make known the fact by resolution?

Reply of Dr. Hirsch:

On the first point, I am glad to find myself sharing the views of the President. *Milah* was never considered the *conditio sine qua non* of membership in Judaism. That, according to all Talmudical authorities, was a *birth* right. The child of a Jewish mother is *natu* a Jew, whether circumcised or not . . . If the resolution has reference to the admittance or so-called non-Jews, I still can have no objections. . . .

Resolution of the Congregation:

Resolved, that the Abrahamitic Rite is not an essential condition, the compliance with which must precede or follow admittance to membership in Sinai Congregation.

Second Recommendation of the President:

It has frequently been stated from our pulpit that stereotyped forms of prayer are no indication of true devotion. That this statement finds an echo in the hearts of our members can be readily observed on those holidays when long prayers are the rule. Few are interested enough to take up the prayerbook. Nevertheless in spite of this fact, we continue to insist on having read, for us and to us, prayers and chapters from the bible in a language understood by few of our members and not at all by the younger generation. . . . Such praying or reading has no more effect than Chinese prayer machines or Latin mass. Both of these methods of devotion do seem very ridiculous to us, and yet we substantially go through similar exercises. Let us then be consistent and abolish at the earliest moment practicable, all Hebrew reading and prayers.

Reply of Dr. Hirsch:

That any and every prayer might be recited in any language is also an old Jewish principle. . . According to *Kol-Bo*, the Kaddish was written in Aramaic for the purpose of rendering it intelligible for Jews and non-Jews. . . . The question is thus not one of principle. I have anticipated any official action, by reading, with the exception of some of the prominent watch words all our prayers in modern tongue. The "Thora" is still read in Hebrew. If you desire to change that, I have no objection!

Resolution of the Congregation:

That the recommendation of the President in regard to the use of "Hebrew in our service" be referred to the Committee on Public Worship, with power to act.[11]

THE BEGINNINGS OF CONSERVATIVE JUDAISM

The "positive-historical school" in Judaism, which came into being in Central and Western Europe in the second half of the nineteenth century, maintained that it had looked at Judaism through the totality of Jewish experience, and found it to be a dynamic, and therefore changing, expression of the Jewish people's commitment to God and Torah. Its emphasis was on the continuing religious experience of the *Jewish people;* on the authority of tradition, but freedom of research.

The spiritual center of the positive-historical school was the Jewish Theological Seminary at Breslau; its leaders, President Zechariah Frankel and the faculty. There were no conferences, no pronouncements, but an ideology developed which was brought to America by such rabbis as Benjamin Szold, Marcus Jastrow and Alexander Kohut.

In 1882, American Reform rabbi Sigmund Hecht discerned a distinctive pattern in the religious group known as Conservatives.

> Conservatism seeks to reconcile the differences of opinion, to harmonize the written law [Torah] and the oral law [Tradition] with the claims of this advanced age; to maintain venerable institutions, although purified and rendered more attractive, and to impart more sanctity and devotion to the divine service, not by discarding the traditional mode entirely, but by retaining it in the main and only removing those features that are antagonistic to its purpose.[12]

At the founding in 1913 of the United Synagogue of America, the federation of Conservative congregations, Dr. Solomon Schechter paid tribute to the central influence of "such men as Isaac Leeser, Sabato Morais, Marcus Jastrow, Benjamin Szold, Alexander Kohut."

"To progress with the age, to adopt all the improvements which have been proved lawful . . ." is what Leeser espoused for those "who really love their religion." He thus presages the Conservative doctrine of the permissibility of change in conformity to the law. Sabato Morais, first president of the Jewish Theological Seminary, established in New York in 1886, proclaimed,

> Our seminary has created itself a church militant, so to say, to fight skepticism arrayed against the history and tradition that have rendered Israel deathless. Well meaning and unwise orthodoxy tells us that by keeping altogether aloof from "Reformers" . . . we will guard our children from the effects of teachings subversive to Holy Writ. Isolation is an impossibility. It would be inadvisable if it were possible.[13]

Although their congregations opted for Reform, Szold, Jastrow and Kohut were ideologists of the positive historical school. In personal life, they tended to Traditionalism and attempted, without success, to turn their congregations in that direction. No doubt they hoped that a seminary modeled on that of Breslau would produce religious leaders who would succeed in accomplishing what they failed to do. Szold upheld the obligatory nature of putting on *tefillin* (phylacteries) observing *kashrut*, placing the *mezuzah* on the doorpost, wearing the *tallit* (prayer shawl), observing the second day of festivals, reciting grace after meals and other rituals. Jastrow's farewell sermon, "On the Occasion of His Retirement," which is his testament, is instructive.

> What was this congregation's position heretofore? It stood before the world as representative of progress, of due regard for the demands of time, combined with a faithful adherence to Israel's truths and to those forms which tradition and time have sanctioned as

visible expressions of these truths. . . . So we stood before the country, a type of conservative Judaism.[14]

The preeminent scholar of the group was Alexander Kohut, who had the most pronounced influence on shaping the program of the seminary.

His vision is of

> a new Seminary [where] a different spirit will prevail . . . This spirit shall be that of *Conservative Judaism,* the *conserving* Jewish impulse which will create in the pupils of the Seminary the tendency to recognize the dual nature of Judaism and the Law; which unites theory with practice, indentifies body and the soul, realizes the importance of both matter and spirit, and acknowledges the necessity of observing the Law as well as studying it.[15]

Kohut was hoping that rabbis trained by the seminary would be able to accomplish what he and his colleagues had been unable to do, to fashion a Judaism which would be committed both to freedom of ideological expression and loyalty to traditional observance. The seminary graduates added American pragmatism to European emphasis on ideology.

In the vestry room of Congregation Shearith Israel, New York, the preparatory class of the newly founded Jewish Theological Seminary of America held its first session on Monday, January 3, 1887. "Ten pupils were enrolled in the class," the Honorable Joseph Blumenthal, president of the Jewish Theological Seminary Association, reported to its First Biennial Convention, "and the tuition was for time imparted by various members of the Advisory Board."[16]

The composition of both the Advisory Board of Ministers and the "congregations entitled to representation" point to the coalition nature of the constituency which founded the Jewish Theological Seminary as a

> seminary where the Bible shall be impartially taught and rabbinical literature faithfully expounded, and more especially where youths, desirous of entering the ministry, may be thoroughly grounded in Jewish knowledge and inspired by the precept and the example of their instructors with the love of the Hebrew language, and a spirit of fidelity and devotion to the Jewish law.[17]

Of the rabbis, five—Sabato Morais (president of the faculty), Henry Pereira Mendes, Bernard Drachman, Henry W. Schneeberger and Abraham P. Mendes—were Traditionalists who comfortably termed themselves Orthodox; and five, Alexander Kohut, Marcus Jastrow, Henry S. Jacobs, Frederic de Sola Mendes and Aaron Wise, had broken

with traditional Judaism and were considered at the border of Reform
Judaism. The congregations ranged all the way from the Beth Hamidrash Hagadol of New York, the first and leading East European Orthodox synagogue, and Shearith Israel of New York, officially Orthodox,
formally Traditional, to Ahawath Chesed, Rodeph Sholom and Shaarey
Tefila of New York, then as now in the Reform camp.

What influenced these disparate individuals and congregations
to join together to establish a new seminary?

The immediate impetus came from a recognition of the radical
nature of American Reform and the conviction that the Hebrew Union
College would not produce a rabbinate which would be "reverent,
thoughtful, and ready to tend its aid to the moral elevation of millions
among our co-religionists who do need refining influences and a soul-
inspiring example," as Morais expressed it. Nor did Morais think that
these coreligionists could do it for themselves. Responding to an in-
quiring reporter of the *New York Herald* about Rabbi Jacob Joseph of
Vilna, who was being brought to serve as chief rabbi of the Association
of the American Orthodox Congregations, he stated:

> I am familiar with the manner in which the Hebrews in the place
> whence he comes are educated, and I know he is not a cultured
> man. He does not possess the knowledge nor the literary attain-
> ments which a rabbi should possess.[18]

The coalition was based on a dissociation from both radical
Reform and East European Orthodoxy. The former was viewed as
dangerous to Judaism, the latter inimical to America. The rapidly growing American Jewish community would need rabbis who would be
true to the traditions of Judaism and fully at home in the culture of
America. The new seminary was founded to fashion such a rabbinate.

Of the fourteen founding students only one remained till ordination, Joseph Herman Hertz, who rose to the position of chief rabbi
of the British Empire. One reason for the wide defection was the nature
of rabbinic positions which awaited a seminary-ordained rabbi, described by Joseph Blumenthal in his presidential address:

> This . . . is more urgent than the training of silver-tongued and
> golden-priced orators for city pulpits. In little places where the
> congregations are supported by only a handful of members, but
> one congregational officer can be afforded, and that is usually and
> naturally a *chazan*. We hope to give these places in one person a
> reader and as well—a preacher. . . .[19]

President Morais had a more challenging vision:

> This is the laboratory in which we try to mould the minds of men
> who will thus mightily battle for the religion hallowed by the

suffering of ages. . . . Pulpits now converted into a nursery for the propagation of heresies, will become strongholds of the written and oral law.[20]

Of the members of the Advisory Board of Ministers (to which Rabbis Benjamin Szold and Aaron Bettelheim were added), not one was succeeded by a graduate of the seminary he had helped found and maintain. It is surprising that the seminary survived into the twentieth century. It lacked the ingredients which gave life and strength to its elder sister institution, the Hebrew Union College: a natural constituency, an ideology acceptable to that constituency and a charismatic leader.

The group which would become its natural constituency, composed of acculturated East European immigrants and their children, had not yet come into being. The immigrants came, transplanted their *shtiblach* (small one-room synagogues) and appointed cantors and traditionally ordained rabbis who eked out a living largely through *kashrut* supervision. English-speaking rabbis were viewed as a threat to the sanctity of the synagogue which was a fortress against an America bent on the destruction of the ancestral faith. Nor did the seminary have the appropriate leaders to appeal to the East European immigrant, who would hardly respond to a Sephardic *hazzan* or a Central European-trained moderate Reform rabbi. As for ideology, Morais felt the need to plead in his report as the president of the faculty in 1888, "The opponents of the Jewish Theological Seminary still clamor for a definition of that purpose, ignoring the fact that the institution has set it forth unequivocally."[21]

Morais recognized the need for a charismatic leader, and as early as 1890 he chose the man. Dr. Solomon Solis-Cohen of Philadelphia reports that

> in the year 1890, I had the privilege of bearing a message from Sabato Morais and his colleagues of the Jewish Theological Seminary . . . asking Schechter to consider the possibility of joining the teaching staff of that institution.[22]

For a dozen years thereafter, sporadic attempts were made to bring to America Dr. Solomon Schechter, Reader in Rabbinics at Cambridge University, author of scholarly works in a readable, elegant English, and a man of great energy and unmistakable charisma.

FOCUS
Solomon Schechter Comes to America

Philadelphia provided the intellectual leadership in the persons of Dr. Cyrus Adler, Judge Mayer Sulzberger and Dr. Solomon Solis-

Cohen. New York's contribution was the philanthropic generosity of Jacob H. Schiff, the Lewisohns and Guggenheims. The former provided the persuasion and the latter the possibility of plucking Dr. Schechter from Cambridge and placing him at the head of a reorganized, endowed Jewish Theological Seminary of America.

In the early nineties both Dr. Adler and Judge Sulzberger visited Schechter in England and came away impressed with the man, convinced that America must be his field of activity.

A product of Romanian and Galician yeshivot, he had continued his studies in Vienna and Berlin. The West added scientific order and method to the knowledge he had amassed in the East. A position had been created for him at Cambridge University. His unearthing of the Cairo Genizah and his discovery of a Hebrew text of the Book of Ecclesiasticus not only increased his scholarly reputation, but gave him international popularity. In 1897 when Sabato Morais died, the quest for a successor turned to a scholar deciphering manuscript fragments in Cambridge.[23]

At the time, the seminary was under the direction of a Rabbinical Board, which, as Sulzberger put it, "may be properly orthodox in belief or expression, but they do not command the financial support of the only people to be relied upon to maintain the Institution in permanence." The judge knew to whom to turn. "I have discussed the matter with Schiff, who is *the* Yehudi of New York."[24] Cyrus Adler describes the reorganization of the seminary:

> In 1901, I . . . was invited to a man's party at the house of Mr. [Isidor] Straus . . . I said that the Jewish community of New York, which was destined to be the largest community in the world, was allowing its only institution of higher Jewish learning to perish, and I told them something of the precarious situation of the Seminary. Mr. Schiff, who was a man of quick decisions, said to the men standing around, "Dr. Adler is right," and a few weeks later I received a letter from him, asking me when I was coming to New York next time, so that he might invite a few men to meet with us. Among the men, I remember, were Leonard Lewisohn and Mayer Sulzberger, joined the next day by Daniel and Simon Guggenheim. . . . Within a few months an Endowment Fund of over one-half million dollars had been secured . . . which rendered it possible to invite Doctor Solomon Schechter . . . to come to America, as head of the Seminary.[25]

American "pioneer pride," that pride which caused other men of wealth to bring to America Europe's finest art and rarest books, moved Jewish men of substance to choose Schechter. Jacob H. Schiff put it in his own direct manner: "We in the United States, who are ever striving to secure the best, were not long in the discovery [of] Solomon Schechter . . ."[26]

Schechter summed up his desire for America in a letter to Adler on the first day of 1900:

America has thus only *ideal* attractions for me, offering as it does a large field of activity which may become a source of blessing to future generations. I also feel that I shall be more happy living among Jews. I want my . . . children brought up among Jews, which is the only guarantee for the acquiring of a real heartfelt Judaism. . . .[27]

To Sulzberger he wrote, "In your country I can hope to 'make school' and leave students . . . useful to the cause of Judaism. . . . The future of Judaism is in America."[28]

What promise did Solis-Cohen, Sulzberger and Adler see in Schechter's coming to America? The first saw in him the leader needed to give direction to American Jewry, "striving vaguely, not knowing what they want, but knowing that they want something. . . ." Sulzberger, ever the scholar, thought the time propitious for laying the foundations for a cultured Jewry. "He who has scholarship, talent and enthusiasm may be more appreciated for the first time in our history than he who leads a party." Anxious for the future of the seminary, Adler saw in acquiring Schechter an opportunity to enlist in the seminary's support the resources of Schiff and his friends, the one possibility to establish an institution which would initially stay and eventually turn the tide of Reform.

Schiff, the Lewisohns, the Guggenheims and their group were much concerned about the children of the East European immigrants. The poverty of the immigrants moved many to Socialism and Anarchism. The social flux, the breakdown of the family unit, the bewildering difference in social patterns sometimes led to crime. These uptown Jews saw in the seminary-ordained rabbi and his teachings a force to bring moderation, stability and order into the community and help in the Americanization of the East European immigrants and their children. In June 1899, Mrs. Henry Pereira Mendes, wife of Shearith Israel's minister, and chairman of the Committee on Religion of the National Council of Jewish Women, reported:

I have urged a plan for the religious betterment of our poorer brethren, by employing our English-speaking Seminary graduates, who are so eminently qualified for that work.[29]

Leonard Lewisohn contributed $50,000 to the reorganized seminary, because it would "afford the surest and safest means of handling

the down-town problems of Americanizing the foreign element by
sending among them trained and well-equipped Rabbinical teachers."[30]

"Positive historical Judaism," which provided the philosophic
cornerstone of Conservative ideology, viewed Judaism as the product
of historical development, and called for a positive attitude toward
traditional Judaism. The traditional complex of Jewish values, practices
and ideals were not lightly to be surrendered. The specifically Jewish
elements in Judaism, as, for example, the Hebrew language, were considered essential to preserve its character and vitality. Conservative
Judaism was a "threefold cord" whose strands were: the scientific study
of Judaism of the "positive historical" school; the congregational manner and mode of Sephardic and West European synagogues; and the
piety and zeal of East European Orthodoxy. Indeed, the leaders of the
seminary looked to the dramatically emerging East European Jewish
community in America as a source of students and of congregations
for its graduates.

THE EMERGENCE OF ORTHODOX JUDAISM

The East European Orthodox community did not respond with
support for the seminary. Its members would not accept religious leadership from a Sephardic *hazzan* like Morais, or from a moderate reformer like Kohut. It had a plan and a project of its own. For a quarter
of a century since 1860, its leading rabbinical figure had been Rabbi
Joseph Asch. With his death in 1887, an association of American Orthodox Congregations was formed to seek a chief rabbi, who would
"be the leader in the battle which must be waged to keep the next
generation faithful to Judaism in spite of the educational, social and
business influences which in America are so powerful to make our sons
and daughters forget their duty to . . . their religion." Rabbi Jacob
Joseph of Vilna was brought as chief rabbi to a community fired with
great hope. Though the venture proved to be ill-fated, arousing antag-
onisms and rivalries in the community, it also marked the emergence
of Orthodoxy in America as an independent, self-conscious religious
force.

FOCUS
A Chief Rabbi for America[31]

It is not surprising that the first attempt at a union of East
European Orthodox Jewry in New York had as its purpose the election
of a chief rabbi. The Russian Jew, who feared the negative effects of
the American milieu upon his faith, and also aware of his inferior status
in the eyes of the Americanized German-Jewish community, hoped that

a chief rabbi renowned for scholarship and spirituality could remove both disabilities, as England's chief rabbi apparently had done in Britain.

In the period 1880–85, more than 50,000 Jews had migrated to the United States from East European countries. The European rabbis were becoming increasingly concerned with the American Jewish immigrant community and its religious problems. In 1887, Jacob Halevi Lipschitz, secretary of Rabbi Isaac Elchanan Spektor, the leading rabbi of East European Jewry, wrote from Kovno:

> For some years now, leading rabbis have turned their attention to their brethren in America. Since the material and spiritual lives of American Israel are so intertwined with our brethren here, in matters of aid and support, in matters of family purity, marriage and divorce, which are officiated over by improper men, in matters of kashrut . . . [To deal with these problems] the leading rabbis advise their brethren to invite an outstanding rabbinical leader to America.[32]

The advice was taken and in the spring of 1887, Beth Hamidrash Hagadol, as the first and largest congregation, obligated itself to contribute $500 per annum for five years toward the support of a chief rabbi. Within a month, $2500 was pledged by sixteen congregations and four individuals who to pursue their object organized themselves into the Association of American Orthodox Hebrew Congregations. Announcements were placed in Russian Hebrew periodicals, and the secretary was instructed to write to eight leading European rabbis to recommend candidates. It was found that no "outstanding rabbinical leader" was eager to come to America. In the eyes of the learned and pious European Jew, the new land was suspect. A rabbi of status would not immigrate to a land where, it was felt, scholarship was not respected, religion was abused.

One distinguished candidate, however, seemed responsive. Heavily in debt because of family mishap, Rabbi Jacob Joseph expressed his willingness to accept, stating that other leading European rabbis had urged this action. The association acted quickly. A state charter was notarized on December 2, 1887, including the following in its statement of purpose: "to encourage, foster and promote the observances of the Orthodox Jewish religion, . . . to improve and elevate the moral, social and spiritual condition of the Jewish people, to designate, support and maintain a Chief Rabbi. . . ."[33] At the association's meeting the following day, Rabbi Jacob Joseph was elected chief rabbi for a period of six years. His salary was to be $2500 per annum and he was to be provided with a suitable apartment.

Rabbi Jacob Joseph was at that time the communal preacher and religious judge in Vilna, known as "the Jerusalem of Lithuania." He had previously served as rabbi in various communities and, although he was a recognized scholar, it was his preaching that had brought him to Vilna and spread his fame to the New World. The love and esteem in which Rabbi Jacob Joseph was held is expressed in a letter from a resident of Vilna to his nephew, Abraham Cahan, in New York:

> He is very dear to us. He is both brilliant and unusually pious. It pains us deeply that we had to bid him farewell. We did not want to lose such a precious possession. See to it that New York Jewry knows that they took from us a rare jewel. See to it that he is properly appreciated. I know that you do not go to the synagogue, but you do have a Jewish heart. Therefore, won't you tell everyone that Vilna gloried in him and that New York must recognize that it now wears a precious crown.[34]

A call dated April 1888 was issued in English and Hebrew to all Orthodox congregations to join the Association of the American Orthodox Hebrew Congregations. It announced that in order to keep the next generation faithful to Judaism, Rabbi Jacob Joseph of Vilna had been chosen as chief rabbi. A *Beth Din* (religious court) under his leadership would be formed to meet the religious and judicial needs of the Jewish community. An appeal was made for proper support, and organizations and congregations were summoned to organize, to contribute financially and "show the world that Orthodox Judaism has zealous followers."

On early Saturday morning, July 7, 1888, the ship *Aller* docked at the port of Hoboken, New Jersey. Rabbi Jacob Joseph remained aboard until sundown. After evening services were over, delegates of the Association crossed the river by ferry to welcome their rabbi with symbolic offerings of bread and salt, reciting the traditional benediction upon seeing a great sage. The chief rabbi responded in a brief address calling for unity and cooperation to carry on the holy work. The procession set out from Hoboken to the rabbi's residence, and when it reached the house at Henry and Jefferson streets, thousands of Jews were waiting to welcome the rabbi.

An article on the chief rabbi's arrival appeared in the *New York Herald* of July 8, while the Anglo-Jewish press, which had heretofore reflected the uptown Jew's view of his East European coreligionist as an uncouth product of a barbaric state, now spoke off these Jews and their rabbi with respect. "The rabbi will find his uptown brethren eager to welcome him and to co-operate with him," the *Jewish Messenger* commented editorially, but added a warning: "providing he remembers that with all our freedom the law of the land is supreme over rabbinical interpretations, that in marriages and divorces the courts of the State must be sought for redress, not the rabbinical court that he is reported to favor."[35]

Criticism which had begun with the promulgation of the plan soon became more intense. The New York correspondent of the *American Israelite* advised his Orthodox brethren that "a man who can speak neither German nor English, and whose vernacular is an unintelligible jargon, cannot be a fitting representative of Orthodox Judaism to the world at large." The Reform periodical *Jewish Tidings* of Rochester, New York, suggested that Rabbi Jacob Joseph "go back to the land that gave him birth," adding:

> Rabbi Joseph is unfamiliar with the language of this country and is therefore unfitted to exercise authority or influence over American Jews. The Jews of this country do not need a Grand Rabbi and one from a foreign country; one who is reared among the prejudices and bigotries of the Eastern countries will certainly prove an obstacle to the people over whom he is expected to exercise control.[36]

Dr. Henry Pereira Mendes was also disturbed by the diversion of funds to the project. He issued a circular criticizing downtown Jewry for not supporting the newly established seminary. He argued that the money spent in importing rabbis was largely wasted, for only graduates of an American seminary, speaking the language of the land, would appeal to the younger generation. Dr. Mendes even carried this message to a meeting of the association. "Will he be able to take up the fight against the encroaching steps of Reform in America?" he challenged. "Do not give way to false hopes. Those who come after you will be Americans, full-blooded Americans like your brethren in faith uptown."[37]

The bitterest opponents of the chief rabbi were Jewish radicals, Socialists and Anarchists. To them religion was the "opiate of the masses"; the institutions fostering Orthodoxy were creations of the exploiters, designed to keep the suffering masses oblivious to social ills and inert to social action. The chief rabbinate became the symbol of what they despised. The *Judische Volkszeitung* and *Der Volksadvokat* carried on a continuous stream of acrimonious and satirical attacks on the office and person of the chief rabbi. Such criticism was not confined only to the Yiddish press. A lengthy article appeared in the *New York Sun,* headlined, OPPOSED TO THE NEW RABBI.[38] It extolled the Americanization of immigrants accomplished by the radical societies and labeled Orthodoxy an anti-intellectual force hindering the progress of Americanization.

Within the Orthodox group there was opposition to the chief rabbi based on monetary considerations. A salary of $2500 a year, further exaggerated by the press (a headline in the *New York Sun* read: A $10,000 RABBI FROM RUSSIA ON HIS WAY TO THIS CITY), aroused the envy of other Orthodox rabbis, and there were complaints that Rabbi Jacob Joseph lived in luxury through the sweat of the workingman.

The Beth Hamidrash Hagadol was packed beyond capacity on Saturday, July 31, 1888, and a vast crowd gathered at the synagogue's entrance on Norfolk Street. Soon a vanguard of four policemen cleared a narrow path and Rabbi Joseph, accompanied by four leaders of the association, made his way to the synagogue. The police had to send for reinforcements to keep the enthusiastic crowd under control. This was the event that all the East Side had awaited, the chief rabbi's first sermon, to be delivered on "The Sabbath of Consolation." The sermon was generally acclaimed. The New York correspondent for the *American Israelite* reported, "The favorable impression which he made on me at our first interview, I now find strengthened after his first discourse."[39] The *Tageblatt,* a strong supporter of the rabbi, proudly announced that all now agreed that the right man had been chosen. An English translation was published in the general press, and the *Sun* devoted a column and a half to it. Dr. Felix Adler, respected in the Jewish community, was sent a copy, and he replied: "If such is to be the tenor of the new rabbi's teaching, we must all, no matter what our opinions, welcome his advent to this country and congratulate the congregations over which he presides."[40]

The personality, character and manner of Rabbi Jacob Joseph won over even his critics. The New York correspondent of the *Jewish Exponent* wrote, "Rabbi Jacob Joseph . . . is a conundrum . . . [his] orthodoxy is genuine and sincere; [he] just came from the very hot bed of Jewish learning and piety; and yet he makes the impression of a broadly tolerant and liberal-minded gentleman."[41] The chief rabbi apparently did not fit the preconceived stereotype of an East European Orthodox rabbi. An editorial in the sympathetic *The American Hebrew* best describes the initial impact made upon New York Jewry by Rabbi Joseph:

> "They who came to scoff, remained to praise," is a proper paraphrase expressive of the disappointment awaiting those who were to disparage and ridicule the Grand Rabbi. Everyone who has heard him or who has conversed with him, . . . testifies to his great abilities, to his strength of mind, and most particularly to the breadth of view and liberality of thought that characterizes him.[42]

The rabbi's acceptance by uptown Jewry found concrete expression when Dr. H. Pereira Mendes and Judge Philip J. Joachimsen invited the chief rabbi to accompany them on a tour of inspection of the Hebrew Orphan Asylum. It meant much to the Russian Jews, who had previously been tolerated at best, to have their rabbi accorded respect by the spiritual leader of New York's oldest congregation, and by one of New York Jewry's most prominent communal leaders.

Guided by the association's energetic and ambitious secretary, Judah Buchhalter, Rabbi Jacob Joseph acted the role of a chief rabbi. His appearance at the funeral of victims of a fire on the Bowery, his vigorous appeal in behalf of widows and orphans, were acclaimed as public-spirited. On the day before Rosh Hashanah, his request to the civil authorities that Jewish prisoners be permitted to rest from labor on the holidays was received courteously and granted. Before Election Day, the chief rabbi, at the request of the Political Reform Club, issued a proclamation to his constituents emphasizing that the laws of the country must be obeyed even as religious laws. "Hence it is our duty to admonish all our brethren who are not legally entitled to vote, to keep away from the voting places."

Rabbi Jacob Joseph was beginning to fulfill the hopes of those who had looked to a chief rabbi to raise the status of the Russian Jew in the eyes of the Jewish and general community.

One of the chief reasons for engaging a chief rabbi was to bring order to the religious life of Lower East Side Jewry. Rabbi Joseph now set about organizing and supervising the kosher meat business. Time and again, the Jewish community of New York had witnessed squabbles between butchers and *shohatim,* and their joint abuse of the rabbis who tried to impose on them some system of supervision. Disregard for both Jewish law and Board of Health ordinances was flagrant.

The leaders of the association argued that proper supervision cost money, and those who benefited from it should pay for it. The chief rabbi was opposed to any direct charge for such supervision, and maintained that *kashrut* was in the interest of the entire community and the costs of administering it should be borne by the Association of American Orthodox Hebrew Congregations. But the rabbi had to surrender to the superior wisdom and experience of the "American business men" who had brought him to this country. He was, however, able to exact the compromise that the tax for supervision be placed not upon meat but upon poultry, because it was believed that meat was the staple of the poor, while poultry was, for the most part, bought by the wealthier Jew. If a tax must be levied, let it at least fall upon those who could best afford it.

The matter having been thus agreed upon, it was formally announced on September 18, 1888, through a circular in Yiddish and English.

Announcement from the chief rabbi:

Herewith I make known to all our brethren, the children of Israel, who tremble at the word of the Lord, that inspectors have already been appointed in the poultry slaughter houses to test the knives and to have supervision of everything in their care. From this day forward every bird slaughtered in the abattoir under our supervision will be stamped with a *plumbe* [lead seal] . . . we make it known to you that if you find any butcher's chicken not so stamped, that it was not killed under our supervision and we cannot guarantee it to be kosher. . . .

Saith: Jacob Joseph, Chief Rabbi
of New York[43]

One cent was to be charged for the metal tag attached to the leg of the chicken to certify its *kashrut*. In the English announcement a footnote was added: "The fowl bearing seals should not be sold for any higher price than others, except one cent on each fowl for the seal."

The attack against the *plumbe* and the charge began even before the office of the chief rabbi issued the circular. The butchers resented any control, the other Orthodox rabbis saw a source of income taken from them, and housewives protested the extra charge. The radical press defended the poor housewives against price gouging and attacked organized religion at the same time. "*Karobka*" became the battle cry. *Karobka* was a tax imposed by the Russian government on kosher meat. The Russian Jew knew its meaning well; the very mention of the word conjured up all the disabilities and persecutions he had suffered in the land of the czars. The butchers who opposed supervision, and the rabbis who resented the power and were envious of the salary of Rabbi Joseph, joined forces to fight the *plumbe* and the poultry tax. At a meeting of the anti–chief rabbi forces, a resolution was adopted which stated:

> The *karobka plumbe* on chickens which evil men wish to import from the old country to the New World is an insult to Judaism and an affront to Mosaic law, because these men mean only to flay the skin off our backs through this despicable tax and put us to shame in our city, New York. Therefore, at this assemblage in the presence of three rabbis, we declare as *terefah* all meats sold by the butchers who have made common cause with the charlatans who impose the *karobka*. . . . Down with the shameful *karobka*![44]

These attacks took heavy toll of the position and authority of the chief rabbi, but Rabbi Joseph answered vituperation with mildness and continued his labors.

Kashrut supervision was expanded. In early December, the office of the chief rabbi invited flour merchants who planned to sell flour for the baking of *matzoth* (unleavened bread) to submit to the supervision and receive the approval of the chief rabbi. This action again loosed a tide of criticism. Even heretofore friendly *The American Hebrew* now declared: "The first and greatest mistake was to use him as a source of revenue. This was a profanation, a sacrilege. . . . Such a shameless outrage as bringing here a learned man to act as Grand Rabbi and then setting him to collecting money for them."[45]

The radical element among the East European Jews stepped up their attacks on the chief rabbi. Flagrant violations of the Sabbath were organized in the streets of the Lower East Side, to mock his authority. Wagons were rented, and young men and young women smoking cigarettes (some for the first time in their lives) paraded past the synagogues of downtown New York on the Sabbath. When tempers grew hot, fists, bricks and sticks flew. The "religious war" was climaxed by a Yom Kippur Ball, arranged by the anarchist youth organization, Pioneers of Freedom. While father and mother walked solemnly to the synagogue to recite the Kol Nidre, son and daughter marched mockingly to the dance hall to dance and feast.

Rabbi Joseph's urging the purchase of *matzoth* and wine bearing the seal of his approval was proclaimed evidence that he was a tool in the hands of ambitious men who were interested only in the aggrandizement of their names or the welfare of their pocketbooks. Joshua Rothstein, a leader of the Association, sent letters to the leading rabbis of Eastern Europe requesting their support of the chief rabbi. Letters came back expressing sympathy for the rabbi, and shock and anger at the accusations. Rabbi Joseph was urged to take courage and wage the "battle of the Lord," but it was of no avail. The opposition defied Rabbi Joseph's defenders as they had defied him. The Association began to totter. Congregations began to skip payments and gradually withdrew their support entirely. Leading butchers undertook to pay the salary of the rabbi and his aids. To all practical purposes, the chief rabbi and his staff became the employees of the butchers whom they were to supervise.

Conditions took a serious turn for the worse in the spring of 1895. The retail butchers banded together, rejected Rabbi Joseph's authority and dispensed with his supervision. The rabbi was left without any income. To his financial distress was added physical illness. The community that had once hailed him now completely neglected him. At the end of July 1902, the chief rabbi once again became the topic of discussion. On the twenty-eighth of the month he died at the age of fifty-nine, after a five-year confinement to his bed because of paralysis.

The obituaries spoke with respect for the man. The then militantly antireligious *Jewish Daily Forward* called Rabbi Joseph a fine and honest man, but declared: "The socialists and freethinkers may with pure hearts throw in the face of the hypocrites this story of a man who

lived and died in America as a sacrificial offering to business-Judaism."[46]
The *Jewish Gazette,* reflecting the view of Orthodoxy, editorialized:
"Against the man himself, even his most bitter opponents never dared
breathe a word, though it must be admitted, and with deep regret, that
many of his unscrupulous opponents linked his name, unjustifiably and
without the slightest reason, with the scandals that arose from time to
time in the kosher meat affairs."[47] As if in atonement for the abuse and
neglect of Rabbi Joseph during his lifetime, downtown Jewry turned
out a hundred thousand strong to pay him final respect, in the largest
funeral the East Side had witnessed.

It was unrealistic to expect that a rabbi like Jacob Joseph could
"be the leader in the battle . . . to keep the next generation faithful to
Judaism." Rabbi Joseph did not speak the language of the immigrants'
children, either literally or figuratively. To the generations of the sons
and daughters, trying desperately to be fully accepted as Americans,
the bearded, Yiddish-speaking rabbi represented the Europe they were
attempting to forget. To place upon such an individual the responsibility
of securing the new generation for Orthodoxy was to doom him to
failure from the start. It was not the rabbi's ineptness but the impos-
sibility of the whole situation that brought the "noble experiment" to
an end.

But the enterprise had its lasting positive effect. East European
Jews demonstrated to uptown German Jews, and to themselves, that
they possessed an awareness of the problems confronting their community, a willingness to plan their solution and the ability to implement
the plans with action. The organization of the Association and the
enthusiasm it evoked demonstrated the latent vitality of Orthodoxy. A
decade later it led to the organization of the Union of Orthodox Jewish
Congregations in America. Choosing a chief rabbi, flawed experiment
that it was, gave to American Judaism its third component: Orthodoxy.

Within the brief span of half a decade, the division of American
religious Jewry into Orthodox, Reform and Conservative movements
had been established. Each group had undertaken to express the nature
of its philosophy. Reform Judaism, which had rejected the binding
authority of received tradition, recognized that it nonetheless required
a declaration of commonly accepted principles and adopted a platform
stating its ideological position. Accepting the authority of the received
legal tradition, Orthodoxy sought a rabbinic figure of stature to transmit
and enforce that authority. The Historical School (called Conservative
Judaism), committed to the relevance of the entire Jewish historical
experience and the evolutionary character of Jewish law, established a
rabbinical school to educate young American men in the tradition and
to train them to expound it in a contemporary fashion. By 1890, the
institutionalized pattern was set for American Judaism.

5.

The Great Wave

JEWS IN RUSSIA

FEW EVENTS HAD GREATER INFLUENCE ON THE COURSE OF AMERICAN JEW-
ish history than the assassination of Alexander II, "Czar of all the
Russias," in March 1881. The government and the populace, seeking
a scapegoat, turned upon the Jews, touching off pogroms in more than
a hundred communities. These were followed by restrictive laws against
the Jews aimed at eliminating them from economic and civic life. Physical persecution, political oppression, and economic disabilities set in
motion a wave of immigration which brought more than two and one
half million Jews from Eastern Europe to American shores in the next
half century.

The story of the Jews of Russia begins with the Jews of Poland.
Until the annexations of Poland, there were but few scattered Jews in
Holy Russia. The third and final partition of Poland in 1795 added to
the Russian Empire over half a million Jews. In the first decade of the
new century attempts were made to integrate the Jew into the economy
and the social order.

Czar Alexander I's reign began with expectation but ended with
dashed hopes. Expulsion of Jews from the villages was resumed and
attempts at their conversion were officially encouraged. His successor,
Nicholas I, was appropriately called "the new Haman." Oppression,
coercion and brutality marked his reign. In 1827, the notorious cantonist
system (young Jewish boys pressed into army service) was decreed.
Service in the Russian army was for twenty-five years, beginning at
eighteen, but Jewish boys were taken as young as twelve to be trained

for military service. The Jewish communities were given quotas of recruits, and it fell upon the community leaders to fulfill this demoralizing task. In its program to assimilate the Jew, the government undertook the establishment of Jewish secular schools, founded two modern rabbinical seminaries, and engaged Dr. Max Lilienthal, a German-born and educated rabbi in Riga, as a special emissary of the Ministry of Education. In 1841, Lilienthal visited leading Jewish communities, but his assurances that the government's intentions were honorable and benevolent were met with suspicion and derision. When, at last, he became convinced that the skeptics were right, he fled to America, where he had a distinguished rabbinic career as a leader of Reform Judaism.

Alexander II (ruled 1855–81) was a "good czar." A man of liberal tendencies, he liberated the serfs before Lincoln emancipated the slaves. Changes were made in military service; the cantonist system was abolished; local self-government was established. New opportunities were opened to the Jews. A number of Jews became doctors or lawyers, and others took advantage of the opportunity to enter business and finance, some amassing fortunes in banking or in railroad holdings, and as tea and sugar merchants.

Emancipation of the serfs created a volatile, impoverished class, anxious and restive. Many crowded the cities, ready material for revolutionary agitators. The plight of the uprooted peasants was blamed by Russian nationalists on Jewish exploitation, and the Jews bore the brunt of the seething discontent. The first pogrom under Alexander II erupted in 1871, and what made it all the more ominous is that it occurred in Odessa, the most cosmopolitan of all Russian cities.

Pent-up emotions were loosed in the wake of the assassination of "good Czar" Alexander. Pogroms broke out in Russia and Poland in 1881 and continued into the twentieth century. In order to "shield the Russian population against harmful Jewish activity," the "Temporary Laws" of May 31, 1882 (known as the "May Laws") were passed. These forbade the Jews to settle in villages; gave villages the right to drive out Jews already living in them; expelled Jews from such cities as St. Petersburg, Moscow, Kiev; limited the number of Jews in secondary schools and universities; prohibited Jews from entering the legal profession and from participating in local government.

The "strong man" of Russian politics at the time was Konstantin Pobedonostsev, who advocated a police state guided by the Church. He had a formula for the solution of the Jewish problem in Russia: one-third of the Jews would be permitted to die, one-third to convert to Christianity and one-third to emigrate. The Jews of Russia took the third plank of his platform seriously. Emigration, which had begun in significant numbers in the 1870s, accelerated; it grew in geometric progression, doubling in each of the last two decades of the nineteenth century and in the first of the twentieth. The mother country was glad to see the beginnings of a solution to the long vexing "Jewish problem." Those who were deemed to be a problem sought a solution of their own in more hospitable surroundings, as rapid expansion and industrialization made the United States a receptive host country.

Russian Jewish immigrants brought with them an ingrained capacity to cope, to improvise, to survive. Their experiences with government and populace taught them to be wary of both, caused them to seek security within their own group and the comfort of their own way of life. Some who had witnessed or partaken of revolutionary activity in the Old World, where it was fraught with danger, found it easy to take it up in the New, under a relatively tolerant government.

THE EMIGRANTS

The migration from the German states which made for the hundredfold increase of American Jewry in the first eight decades of the nineteenth century had by 1880 virtually ceased. In the next three decades, only 20,454 German Jews came to the United States. The German Jews had come as part of a large-scale migration from Germany in the nineteenth century, which constituted the single largest immigrant group into the United States. Being part of a larger group of German emigrants made leaving, journey and integration into the host country much easier for the German Jew.

The Jews of the Russian Empire and Galicia were generally the first of their region to undertake large-scale migration westward. The endeavor was, therefore, fraught with all the anxieties and difficulties which beset any pioneering effort. The first to leave were those who had least to lose. One who could not make a living at home left to try to elsewhere. Those whose religious or political views were suspect were encouraged to leave to spare their parents pain and their families embarrassment. America was haven for those who sought escape from military conscription, release from the burden of debt and relief from those who had real or imagined grievances against them. When Sarah Yetta Reznikoff's family tried to dissuade her from setting out for America, they argued: "Who goes there but bankrupts, embezzlers, and those who have wrecked their lives here?"[1] In a society organized as a network of extended families, to leave the family homestead weakened a social order where the older took care of the younger until the younger could take care of the older.

The first to leave were almost always the young, depleting the community of its most productive element and weakening its physical security. In that hostile environment the presence of the young and strong tended to discourage persecution and pogroms. The trauma of leaving was greatest for the first to depart. On the way to America, Benjamin L. Gordon remembered his thoughts as a wanderer about the streets of Hamburg waiting for the *Bohemia* to sail.

> I knew I was going to the Land of the Free, but I also was cognizant of the fact that no one expected or awaited me there. I did not have the slightest idea as to how I was going to make a living: I had no trade and was physically unfit for hard manual labor. Then, too, the fact that I was leaving the continent where my ancestors had lived for so many centuries weighed heavily on my mind.[2]

Once begun, migration generates a dynamic of its own. Economic problems in depleted communities precipitate more departures. The trauma of uprooting and the uncertainty of reception by the host community are offset by the knowledge that outposts of family in the country of destination are ready to welcome kin and absorb *landsleit* (persons from the same town). Routes have already been laid out. The conveyers of the immigrants, railroads and steamship companies, have acquired the necessary expertise. For Jewish emigrants, the journey was eased by agencies set up in Europe and America to aid them. In the twentieth century, they were emboldened to undertake the journey by the reports that those who preceded them had already established those cultural, religious and social institutions which their life demanded. The religious heard of synagogues, rabbis, schools. The Freethinkers read of an atmosphere free of societal constraints and of governmental surveillance. So the East European migration to America, which began with thousands in the 1880s, grew to hundreds of thousands in the latter years of the nineteenth century and millions in the first decades of the twentieth. Until 1890, the immigrants arriving in New York disembarked at Castle Garden; then Ellis Island served as their doorway to America.

It was to the metropolitan cities that the East European Jewish immigrants flocked. The port cities of New York, Philadelphia, Baltimore and Boston (and for a later group, Galveston) were first to receive them, and a majority settled in these cities and their environs. In 1925, more than 40 percent of America's Jews lived in the greater New York area and more than 80 percent were concentrated in six states: New York, Pennsylvania, Illinois, Massachusetts, New Jersey and Ohio. Such concentration made possible the rapid establishment of Jewish institutions, the proliferation of organizations and some degree of political presence, if not power; but it also subjected the immigrant Jew to urban slum conditions, the uncertainty and oppressiveness of sweatshop labor and the tensions which mark congested urban living.

Above all other immigrant groups, the Jews came to stay. Others may have come to test the New World, or to "make their fortune" and return home; for the Jews, America was to be both haven and home. Planning to remain, they came as family units as these comparative figures indicate.

	Jewish	Non-Jewish
Women	45.8%	32.9%
Children	25.3%	12.3%

The selective memories of their descendants portray the immigrant group as composed of pious, learned Jews and cultured, idealistic radicals. A great number were, but it must be also noted that some 20 percent of the men and 40 percent of the women were illiterate. While these figures were far below the illiteracy level of other East European immigrant groups, their number is nonetheless significant. Labor leader Bernard Weinstein recalls that those who came with a trade quickly found employment, but that "the great majority of the Jewish immigrants consisted of non-workers." They did not remain nonworkers for long. Relatives and *landsleit* took them into the sweatshops where they were taught a trade and became part of the vast army of "Columbus's tailors."

With the beginning of mass emigration, established Jews came to the aid of the Jewish immigrants. The Jews of Western Europe formed a network of organizations to help the Jews of Eastern Europe emigrate to America. While the main motivation was to come to the aid of brethen in distress, self-interest was a not insignificant factor. The Jewish communities of Germany, France and England preferred to serve as bridge and conduit rather than as final residence for the growing emigration from the Russian and Austro-Hungarian empires. Historian Elias Tcherikower observes that the Jews of Western Europe were

> anxious on the one hand to help the victims of the pogroms, and, on the other, afraid that they might engulf their countries. They therefore seized upon America as an ideal solution and resolved to direct the stream of immigrants to that "vast free and rich country, where all who want to work can and will find a place."[3]

A tripartite division of responsibility was arranged. The journey westward across Europe became the responsibility of the German Jews; the London Manor House Committee was to get the immigrants to their destination, America. On arrival, their settlement and integration were the responsibility of American Jewry. The Jews of America were no more anxious to have a mass of Russian Jews settle among them than were the Jews of Western Europe. A spokesman for the United Jewish Charities of Rochester expressed the fears of many, calling the

Russian Jews "a bane to the country and a curse to all Jews. The Jews have earned an enviable reputation in the United States, but this has been undermined by the influx of thousands who are not ripe for the enjoyment of liberty and equal rights, and all who mean well for the Jewish name should prevent them as much as possible from coming here."[4]

Nonetheless, American Jewry began to organize philanthropic aid for its persecuted brethren. The Board of Delegates of American Israelites and the Russian Emigrant Relief Fund in cooperation with the more permanent and inclusive Hebrew Emigrant Aid Society gave extensive help in the 1880s. But even the organizations formed to aid the newcomer urged that immigration be selective and controlled.

A letter from the Russian Emigrant Relief Fund in New York, dated October 31, 1881, addressed to the Alliance Israélite Universelle, sums up American Jewry's concerns with the increasing number of Jewish immigrants:

> The recital of the outrages in Russia, of which our unfortunate brethren have been the victims, have excited in us the deepest sympathy, and an earnest desire to alleviate their condition as far as lies in our power. . . .
>
> It was understood that you were to send us only the strong and able-bodied, willing to work and possessing a knowledge of some handicraft; . . .
>
> You will doubtless share our disappointment and vexation when you learn that fully one-third of those who have arrived thus far possess none of the requisite qualifications, . . .
>
> Most that we have seen are clerks or tradesmen; they know no handicraft and wish to peddle. We are overrun with peddlers already, who have become a source of much annoyance to us. . . . It is impossible to find positions here for clerks or tradesmen who are ignorant of our language, of our methods of conducting business, . . . Many of the clerks and tradesmen who have arrived are too old to learn any trade, and not a few of them are burdened with large families. . . .
>
> The great bulk settle in this city and crowd the filthy tenements in a certain section on the East Side. . . .
>
> Many are sent over here purposely, merely to relieve the European Communities; there are constantly arriving widows with small children, and also deserted wives and children seeking their husbands and fathers, but without any definite idea where to find them. . . .
>
> Local Committees have been formed in Philadelphia, New Orleans, Houston (for the State of Texas), Milwaukee (for the

State of Wisconsin), Louisville, Albany, Rochester, Quincy and other cities. . . . These Committees are sending us orders for mechanics, farmers and laborers, but they have had their patience sorely tried by some of the emigrants refusing to accept employment.

The American Jews reminded their European coreligionists:

Please bear constantly in mind that the position of the Jews in America is not such that they can well afford to run any risk of incurring the ill-feeling of their fellow citizens.

The Relief Fund sent word to Europe that immigration must be limited because "the number of persons whose condition can be bettered in this way is comparatively small."

The selection of emigrants must be systematic, and must be controlled by the European Committee. . . . The shipments must be regulated according to the ability of the American Committee to receive and distribute emigrants. Only those having a trade, or able and willing to settle on the lands of the Society, or to work as laborers on railways and otherwise, should be selected for emigration. The aged and helpless should remain in Europe, . . .[5]

A year later the Aid Society sent an even sharper warning: "We will not receive another refugee . . . Emigration must cease."

Emigration not only did not cease but the trickle of the 1880s grew into giant waves in the 1890s and the decades beyond. And as the immigration increased, so too did the scope and intensity of the organized efforts to aid.

Ultimately the Russian Jewish immigrants themselves took the leadership in organizing aid for the new arrivals. One of the first organizations offering direct aid to the arriving immigrant was the Association of Jewish Immigrants of Philadelphia. The nature of its activities is described in the president's report offered at its third annual meeting on November 7, 1886:

We have assisted immigrants to reach other points to which they were destined, and have provided them with food on their route. We have lodged and fed those who remained in the city until their friends were found. . . . We have hunted up lost baggage, rescued some from the thieves who frequent the wharves, and redeemed it when held for unpaid freight.

We have guarded their rights so that they would not suffer through ignorance or the bad advice or evil designs of others. We have protected them against thieving innkeepers, imposters under the guise of co-religionists, agents of haunts of vice, and others

whose vocation it is to rob, swindle and mislead ignorant and
unsuspecting foreigners. We have procured employment for many,
homes for some and have aided in furnishing rooms and in starting
others in business suited to their abilities.[6]

In this and subsequent reports concrete illustrations of work done
were cited under the following headings: Telegrams and Letters, Advertisements (for lost relatives), Reshipments, Distribution, Baggage,
Rooms Rented, Care of the Sick and so on. The Miscellaneous category
in the 1887 report suggests the range of personal problems with which
the association had to cope:

> A girl of 12 years, with frozen feet, so much swollen as to be
> unable to wear her shoes, could not proceed with her father to
> their destination, although their tickets were already changed and
> the train about ready to start. Our Agent's attention was called to
> the case, and with some trouble he induced the dispatcher to detain
> the train a few minutes until he could procure a pair of shoes for
> the sufferer. This was reluctantly done and the shoes were pur-
> chased to the delight of the poor family, who feared they would
> be separated.
>
> A family consisting of a husband, a wife and four children,
> arrived on the 28th of July. Even in their downcast and wretched
> state, traces of a noble, honest and charitable life could be seen.
> For fourteen years they had lived peacefully and happily together,
> the husband cultivating the soil, and dwelling in perfect harmony
> with his Christian neighbors. . . . Suddenly the decree of *expulsion*
> reached him, forcing him to leave his happy home and beloved
> soil, and with his wife and little ones to endeavor to begin life
> anew in a strange land. "Do not despair, my friend, take my advice
> and go west, where you must learn tailoring through which to
> earn a livelihood. This trade you will pursue for a year or two,
> until you have acquainted yourself with American life and the
> English language. Then you can again return to your former vo-
> cation. May Israel's Redeemer, for whose religion you suffer, lead
> you in the path of comfort and prosperity." Thus spoke the
> Agent. . . . Two tickets were purchased for him and his wife at a
> low rate for Indianapolis. It was arranged that the children should
> go free.[7]

SOURCE
Joining Father in America

First the father came. He worked hard, scrimped, saved the
precious dollars which would enable him to bring his dear ones. In the
old country, the mother told idyllic tales of the Golden Land and drew

idealized pictures of the departed husband. The children waited the day of joyous reunion with father in the New World.

Mary Antin in her *From Plotzk to Boston*,[8] and Ephraim E. Lisitsky in his autobiography, *In the Grip of Cross-Currents*,[9] recount their experiences of reunion with father.

Mary Antin: "The Climax of Our Joy . . ."

Before the ship had fully stopped, the climax of our joy was reached. One of us espied the figure and face we had longed to see for three long years. In a moment five passengers on the "Polynesia" were crying, "Papa," and gesticulating, and laughing, and hugging one another, and going wild altogether. All the rest were roused by our excitement, and came to see our father. He recognized us as soon as we him, and stood apart on the wharf not knowing what to do, I thought. . . .

Oh, dear! Why can't we get off the hateful ship? Why can't papa come to us? Why so many ceremonies at the landing? . . .

Still the ceremonies went on. Each person was asked a hundred or so stupid questions, and all their answers were written down by a very slow man. The baggage had to be examined, the tickets, and a hundred other things done before anyone was allowed to step ashore, all to keep us back as long as possible.

Now imagine yourself parting with all you love, believing it to be a parting for life; breaking up your home, selling the things that years have made dear to you; starting on a journey without the least experience in travelling, in the face of many inconveniences on account of the want of sufficient money; being met with disappointment where it was not to be expected; with rough treatment everywhere, till you are forced to go and make friends for yourself among strangers; being obliged to sell some of your most necessary things to pay bills you did not willingly incur; being mistrusted and searched, then half starved, and lodged in common with a multitude of strangers; suffering the miseries of seasickness, the disturbances and alarms of a stormy sea for sixteen days; and then stand within a few yards of him for whom you did all this, unable to even speak to him easily. How do you feel?

Oh, it's our turn at last! We are questioned, examined and dismissed! A rush over the planks on one side, over the ground on the other, six wild beings cling to each other, bound by a common bond of tender joy, and the long parting is at an END.

Ephraim E. Lisitsky: "In the Dusk My Father's Face . . ."

During all of my trip to America my imagination kept conjuring up a picture of my encounter with my father. The image of my father's face, which had dimmed in my memory, shone through a haze of eight and a half years as it had registered in it the night before his departure, as I lay at his side holding him in tight desperation. Only now, his melancholy look of compassion had brightened. Anticipation of reunion softened the trials of the journey—stealing across the border, wandering through thick forests in the dark of night, the ship tossed about by storm for three consecutive days.

The picture of our reunion became sharper when, in New York, I boarded the train for Boston. The entire trip I visualized my father at the station, waiting for the train to pull in. When the train arrived and I got off, he would rush over and embrace me. I could see him standing there and hear the clatter of the train wheels bringing his greetings to me: "Welcome, my son!" And my heart responded in joyful tones: "Papa! Papa!"

The train slowed down to enter the station and my heart beat faster, as though to prod the train to hurry. Through the coach window I could see faces and eyes happy, trembling with anticipation. I searched for my father but he wasn't there! I descended from the coach, still looking and my heart scrutinizing every face in the crowd. But my father was nowhere in the crowd! I trudged to my father's home stopping passers-by on the street to show them the crumpled address transcribed in my strange tongue. When I finally got there he was not in—he had gone to work early, as he did every day, for the telegram from New York announcing the time of our arrival in Boston had been misaddressed and had not reached him.

At the entrance to the hall of a house populated with poor tenants, with one of whom my father roomed, I stood tense with anticipation. My eyes scrutinized every passer-by; perhaps father would be there, for his landlord had gone to look for him in the street to tell him of our arrival . . . Many tedious hours I waited. . . .

Suddenly, a figure came towards me through a rosy mist. As it approached, the mist lifted and I saw it, radiant and compassionate. I leaped up—it was my father.

In the dusk my father's face loomed up from the street. He walked heavily bent under a sack full of rags and bottles. His face was dark and hard, with an expression of mingled humiliation and forgiveness. I shrank back, offended and silenced.

At midnight, lying on the bedding they had laid out for me in a corner of the kitchen floor in the apartment where my father roomed, I cried in silence over the alienation that screened me from my father.

AMERICA, THE HAVEN

Economically, America was ready to receive them. The depression of the early seventies had come to an end, and the country was again expanding, geographically and economically. Industry needed additional laborers, and the new laboring class needed purveyors of food and clothing. Recognizing these needs, the Jewish immigrants became the small merchants and clothing workers. In towns across the country they opened stores; in the cities they entered the sweatshops. Some immigrants brought needed skills, but most arrived without a craft or trade and had to begin anew.

A greenhorn who had a relative awaiting him in the New World, a *landsman* who could stake him to a minimal inventory, became an itinerant peddler, carrying his stock on his back. But it was the burgeoning mass-produced clothing industry, in the main, that swallowed up the immigrants, no matter what their status in the old country. Dr. B. Hoffman, in *Fufzig yahr klockmacher union*, states, "Former Yeshiva students, sales clerks, insurance agents, semi-intellectuals, teachers, bookkeepers, sons-in-law of the well-to-do, storekeepers, merchants, etc., became cloak operators."[10]

In his popular *Sunshine and Shadow in New York*, Matthew Hale Smith writes:

> The people of Israel are very numerous. A portion of them are intelligent, respectable and wealthy. The leading bankers are Jews of this class; so are the importers. . . . But the Jews of the lower class are disagreeable, and their presence a nuisance to any Christian neighborhood. . . . When they get into a neighborhood, in any numbers, it is deserted by all others . . .[11]

He makes a distinction between the wealthy uptown and the poor downtown Jews, a distinction and division that grew with the increased number of new immigrants of the downtown variety. But lest we think that discrimination is directed only against the poor "lower class" Jews, Smith notes:

> A new hotel, erected two years ago, was occupied by leading families from this and other cities, on the express condition that Jewish women and children should not be allowed in the house. . . . Every means has been resorted to by the people of Israel to get rooms in this hotel, and fabulous prices offered.[12]

He offers an early description of the Lower East Side.

> Chatham Street is the bazaar of the lower Jews. It is crowded with their places of trade, and over their stores they generally live. Noisy

and turbulent, they assail all who pass, solicit trade, and secure general attention and general contempt. They know no Sabbath. On Saturday, their national Sabbath, they keep open stores because they live in a Christian country. On Sunday they trade because they are Jews. . . .[13]

A more sympathetic account is that of James Parton in *Topics of the Times.* He speaks of the Jews as good and loyal citizens, devoted to the liberal principles of the nation; they "are rising in the esteem of the people among whom they dwell."[14]

Arrival is described by Israel Kasovich, of the Am Olam movement, organized in Russia to "return [Jews] to the land." Some members, highly motivated idealists, came to America to found and settle in agricultural colonies. They were not fleeing from persecution but journeying to a life's ideal, the life on the soil.

> We lined up on deck in expectation of a warm welcome. . . . Our leaders unfurled our large flag. . . . But no sooner had the flag begun to wave . . . displaying the large golden words *Am Olam* than a man ran up and ordered us to lower the flag. We told him . . . that this was a free country, whereupon he became furious, snatched up the flag and hurled it straight into the sea. We felt as though our faces had been slapped.

This was but the first of a series of disillusioning and embittering experiences suffered by the Am Olam group. Exhausted, patronized by petty officials, let down by inept leaders, the group disbanded and scattered. Kasovich later described his introduction to American life.

> I set out for the office of the Immigrant Aid Committee. I saw a line of people. . . . At the door stood a policeman who behaved anything but gently. Near him stood a Russian Jew employed by the Committee, and he behaved even worse than the policeman. . . .
> My brothers-in-law found work . . . one stripped tobacco leaves for three dollars a week; he would come home from work all wan and waxen, and keep on vomiting. The older one was employed at turning a heavy wheel; he would return home all dirty like a chimney-sweep and too weak to eat. . . . On Saturday, when the children had to go to work, the house was filled with wailing . . . I . . . agreed to become a peddler . . . stockings, socks, combs, buttons, handkerchiefs, towels, scissors, pocket knives, etc. . . . My portable shop was pulling me down to the ground . . . my feet were staggering . . . I was ashamed to look people in the face . . . Presently a gang of Gentile street urchins began to pelt me with stones and lumps of coal. . . .

Some did buy a couple of cents' worth of goods . . . giving alms . . . they took pity on a poor immigrant. My face burned with shame. . . .

My father-in-law . . . decided to try his hand at peddling. . . . A couple of hours later he returned. . . . He had been assailed by loafers, who ran after him, pulled his beard, kicked him, and showered him with refuse. . . .

Kasovich, the idealistic dreamer, the man who yearned for the good life on the good earth in the land of the free, took stock:

We had uprooted our home and traveled to a distant land overseas in order to lead a quiet, honest, independent life as tillers of the soil, as Jews and as free citizens, and instead of this we had to live amid noise and dirt, and to eke out a livelihood by engaging in a contemptible business that smacked of begging or else by hiring ourselves out as wage slaves. . . . Nor was there any evidence of a particular love for us here; we were stoned in the streets, and many refused to rent their houses to Jews. . . . It was impossible to observe the Jewish religion here . . . compelled to work on the Jewish Sabbath and holidays. Where, then, was the freedom, where the human equality?[15]

This was a typical plaint found in the immigrant literature of the day. The dreams of freedom, equality and prosperity turned to ashes, endless toil engaged in by the whole family in suffocating surroundings. Jacob A. Riis describes the life:

In a dimly lighted room with a big red-hot stove to keep the pressing irons ready for use, is a family of man, wife, three children, and a boarder. "Knee-pants" are made there too, of a still lower grade. Three cents and a half is all he clears, says the man, and lies probably out of at least two cents. The wife makes a dollar and a half finishing, the man about nine dollars at the machine. The boarder pays sixty-five cents a week. He is really only a lodger, getting his meals outside. The rent is two dollars and twenty-five cents a week, cost of living five dollars. Every floor has at least two, sometimes four, such shops. Here is one with a young family for which life is bright with promise. Husband and wife work together; just now the latter, a comely young woman, is eating her dinner of dry bread and green pickles. Pickles are favorite food in Jewtown. They are filling, and keep the children from crying with hunger. . . .

In this room a suspender-maker sleeps and works with his family of wife and four children . . . a little coop of a bedroom

where the old folks sleep. The girl makes her bed on the lounge . . .
the big boys and the children sleep on the floor.[16]

It was early recognized by leaders in the organized immigration
aid effort that one of the chief problems was the concentration of the
immigrant population in the port cities of the Eastern seaboard, particularly in New York. This presented a twofold evil: It was a hindrance
in the social integration of the resident population, and it worked unusual hardships, economic, social and moral, on the immigrants. A
constantly increasing population made for job competition which kept
wages low and production expectancy high. Sweatshop workers were
driven by the fear of loss of their jobs to a newcomer ready to work
maximum hours for minimum pay. The crowded ghetto environment
was a health hazard, physically and morally. Unventilated sweatshops
and dark tenements brought the incidence of tuberculosis to epidemic
proportions. Life in crowded cities made prostitution and crime not
only prevalent but also highly visible. The concentration of the immigrant population in self-contained communities prevented a more
rapid rate of acculturation and integration, driving a wedge between
the immigrants and their Americanized children.

One suggested solution was dispersal of population and diver-
sification of occupations. The largesse of the Baron de Hirsch Fund was
used to establish training schools and agricultural settlements. Efforts
in these directions had been anticipated in the Russian Jewish community. Schools to teach a trade were set up by the fund in Russia,
and young Russian Jewish idealists, influenced by the back-to-the-soil
movements in Russia, organized the Am Olam. Members of Am Olam
did found cooperative colonies in the South and in the West, but because
of the lack of practical experience in agriculture these were short-lived.
The Baron de Hirsch Fund colonies fared better, but large-scale colonization of the immigrant Jew on the land in America was never realized.

Efforts at dispersal were more successful. The Jewish Alliance
of America undertook to promote the resettlement of immigrants in
the American hinterland. In 1891, at the First Convention, its goals
were spelled out by President Dr. C. D. Spivak:

> What do we want to accomplish by this Alliance? We want to
> secure for those of our brethren who overflood the market of hands
> some honest work. We desire that the Jewish immigrant shall not
> crowd into the large seacoast cities; we want to exterminate ped-
> dling and petty trading; we purpose, in short, to give a possibility
> to the immigrant to make a living for himself and his family—not
> to fall a burden upon the various Jewish charitable institutions—
> and to become an independent, self-supporting citizen of this re-
> public.

How are we to accomplish this? By directing and leading the immigrant in the way of acquiring new trades apart from the needle that has pierced many a heart, and outside of the basket under whose burden so many have succumbed.

Agriculture, in the opinion of my co-laborers and myself, ought to be the mainspring of the future activity of the Alliance.[17]

By the end of the nineteenth century, after attempts at colonization had failed, it was decided that a more determined effort for the dispersal of Jewish immigrants had to be made, particularly to divert or remove them from New York City. For this purpose, the Industrial Removal Office was created in 1900. New York was ready to send the newcomers, but some "host" cities refused to accept them. Immigrants, once arrived in New York, were loath to leave. Nonetheless in the first five years, some forty thousand immigrants were relocated.

The structured, religiously ordered life which Jews had experienced in the European *shtetl* (Jewish town) was replaced by the socially fluid, economically pressured and religiously lax life of the American urban center. The change brought disorientation and disintegration in its wake. Life was difficult in Eastern Europe, but it had a degree of security and status which gave the individual a sense of personal worth. Each man had his recognized role in the family, his place in the community, his seat in the synagogue. In America he was depersonalized, dehumanized—bereft of extended family, devoid of status.

Morris Rosenfeld, "Poet of the Ghetto," sang the immigrant's plaint:

Oh, here in the shop the machines roar so wildly,
That oft, unaware that I am, or have been,
I sink and am lost in the terrible tumult;
And void is my soul . . . I am but a machine.[18]

The Jew in Russia dreamed of the Golden Land. The folk poet, Eliakim Zunser, sang of this land. He believed his songs and came to America. Here he again sang of the Golden Land:

I came to the land, saw it and lo!
Tears and suffering and tales of woe . . .
Poverty, misery, darkness, cold—
Everywhere in this "Land of Gold!"[19]

Yet immigrant Jews proved equal to the dehumanizing challenge of America. They persisted, in the faith that this was but a temporary situation, that work and will would make an easier life in better surroundings, that their children's lot would be better still.

Jacob A. Riis, chronicler of American social conditions, appreciated the armor which Jewish religious laws and values had fashioned, and which the ghetto Jews could now use in their struggle for physical survival.

> They [the Jews] do not rot in their slum, but, rising, pull it up after them . . . they brought temperate habits and a redeeming love of home. Their strange customs proved the strongest ally of the Gentile health officer in his warfare upon the slum.[20]

James B. Reynolds, of the University Settlement House of New York, spoke of the qualities of the immigrant Jew which impressed him most: "intellectual avidity . . . intensity of feeling, high imagination . . . the extremest idealism, with an utter disregard of the restraining power of circumstance and conditions . . . a character often full of imagination, aspiration and appreciation."

The qualities of imagination, aspiration and appreciation fashioned cultural institutions and created cultural values. Sociologist-demographer Jacob Lestschinsky writes of the character of this first immigration wave from Eastern Europe, 1880–1900:

> The East European Jewish immigration was made up of an enormous vocationless lower middle-class mass, of approximately twenty-five percent handworkers, and of altogether common people, porters, wagoners, peddlers, and the like. The percentage of intellectuals was negligible; its influence, however, was great . . . there were quite a few who had attended not only a good *heder* . . . but also a *Yeshiva* . . . this group . . . adjusted itself quickly to the new environment and culture. . . . And this group of educated Jews, with Talmudic acuteness and Jewish energy, soon began to produce modern intellectuals who became the leaders of Jewish movements and the founders of Jewish institutions. Not a few . . . quit the ghetto to take their place in the general cultural life of America.[21]

In the *shtetl* culture which had shaped the Old World Jew, learning was the vehicle for social mobility, desirable marriage partners, community status, influence. The same obtained in the immigrant ghetto, with some variations. *Heder* learning gave way to public-school education; the *yeshiva bochur* of Europe became the college student in America.

Immigrant Jews kept dawn-to-dark hours in their grocery or candy stores, or coughed out their lungs in sweatshops, to afford the schooling for their sons that would free them from store counter and shop bench. Their children took to public school and college with a passion; these institutions for Americanization were the means to improve economic opportunity and social status. The education the public school provided liberated the offspring from the immigrant status of their foreign-born parents. The *New York Tribune* on September 18, 1898, reported on the "East Side Love of Learning."

> The people of the East Side are again confronted with the problem of how to educate their children, and the limited capacity of the city schools, which is evident again this fall, is once more a cause for keen disappointment and unfulfilled hopes.
>
> There were several cases brought to public notice last fall where the boys who had been denied school advantages committed suicide. In other cases similar disappointments resulted in insanity. . . . It will astonish many people to learn that the average small boy of the ghetto has none of the commercial instinct which is ordinarily taken as a sign and heritage of his race. There, boys want to become doctors and lawyers. It is a peculiar fact, too, that the fathers of these boys, who spend their days in the ill-smelling fish market of Hester Street or live their lives haggling over the price of pushcart wares, encourage the younger generation in their desire for knowledge.

CULTURAL ROOTS

The immigrants were not only intent on educating their children; they also eagerly sought schooling for themselves, attending evening school and classes in settlement houses to learn English, civics and related subjects that would better equip them for life in the new country. In *The Atlantic Monthly* of July 1898, Abraham Cahan, writing of "The Russian Jew in America," describes a vast informal adult-education network in which those who had acquired rudimentary skills in the new language were initiating the neophytes into the baffling rules of English grammar and spelling. Many aspiring hearts were broken, many valiant warriors in the classrooms were defeated by the mysteries of the *th* and the *w*, but the struggle went on. Cahan's picture of "A tenement house kitchen turned, after a scanty supper, into a classroom, with the head of family and his boarder bent over an English school reader," was more the usual case than the exception. His boast, "I know many Jewish workmen who before they came here knew not a word of Russian . . . whose range of English reading places them on a level with the average college-bred American,"[22] sounds like the exaggeration of an advocate, but is borne out by the witness of more objective observers.

The easy accessibility of secular education inevitably led to lessening, if not actual forsaking, of strictly Jewish studies. The rabbi and Hebrew teacher could hardly compete with the public schoolteacher.

The former represented a past which the Jew sought to escape; the latter offered the key which unlocked the gates of the "Golden Land of Opportunity." Yet religious education was not neglected. Those who left the land of the czars did not do so to become the last generation of their people. A long, obstinate, difficult and costly enterprise was undertaken to retain in the new generation the ancient faith. Here, too, the key was education. Private Hebrew teachers were legion. Time and again, we hear of the immigrant Jew having failed in job or business turning to give "Hebrew lessons." But schools of quality were established as well. At the end of the century the Machzikay Talmud Torah on East Broadway had a student body of eleven hundred pupils ranging in age from six to fifteen years; it had been established fifteen years earlier with twenty-five students. A reporter for the *New York Tribune* reports on November 12, 1899:

> The pupils are for the most part children of poor parents . . . they display an earnestness in their work which shows that they share, even in a childish way, the sentiments of their parents. . . . In order . . . not to interfere with their regular school duties, the sessions are from four to seven o'clock on weekdays and from nine to one o'clock on Sunday. "We take no pupils," said Mr. Robinson, the head of the school, "who do not attend public schools."

Even in the best circumstance the Hebrew schools were supplementary to the public schools and had to compete for the student's time, interest and devotion. Generally, the financial conditions were shaky, the faculty beleaguered, the students sullen if not rebellious. But the effort never ceased.

For the immigrant generation, a rich and varied cultural life was available. The religious could attend a wide variety of synagogues featuring "star" cantors; the "enlightened" had their lectures in popular culture and meetings of a bewildering variety of Socialist and Anarchist groups. Most popular of all was the Yiddish theater, which offered escape and provided social activity. It gave the ghetto heroes and heroines to adore and idolize; their romantic exploits provided delectable gossip. Historical musical dramas were popular because they not only offered entertainment but also lifted the immigrant out of everday fears and frustrations. *Shulamit* reminded him of Jewish sovereignty, and *Bar Kochba* recalled Jewish victories. Contemporary melodrama brought the release that free-flowing tears often provide. And what better topic for discussion and argument than the quality of the writing and the success of the acting?

Hutchins Hapgood reports in his *The Spirit of the Ghetto*:

> In the Yiddish theatres . . . crowd the Jews of all the Ghetto classes—

the sweatshop woman with her baby, the day-laborer, the small Hester Street shopkeeper, the Russian-Jewish anarchist and socialist, the Ghetto rabbi and scholar, the poet, the journalist. The poor and ignorant are in the great majority, but the learned, the intellectuals and the progressive are also represented . . .

On Friday, Saturday and Sunday nights . . . poor workingmen and women with their babies of all ages fill the theatre. Great enthusiasm is manifested, sincere laughter and tears accompany the sincere acting on the stage. Pedlars of soda-water, candy, of fantastic gewgaws of many kinds, mix freely with the audience between the acts.[23]

In the words of Cahan the sons and daughters of the People of the Book mounted "A feverish literary activity unknown among the Jews in Russia, Roumania and Austria." He boasts that the periodical literature created in the last decade of the century by the Russian Jew in America "furnishes intellectual food not only to themselves, but also to their brethren in Europe." To document this assertion, he points out:

The five million Jews living under the Czar had not a single Yiddish daily paper even when the government allowed such publication, while their fellow countrymen who have taken up abode in America publish six dailies . . . not to mention the countless Yiddish weeklies and monthlies, and the pamphlets and books which today make New York the largest Yiddish book market in the world. . . .[24]

In addition to Yiddish cultural activity, which was to achieve great importance after the turn of the century, a Hebrew press began to develop. The East European immigration produced a Hebrew reading public of such size as to encourage the establishment of three Hebrew weeklies in New York. Michael L. Rodkinson, who later translated the Talmud into English, published *Ha-Kol* (1889–90); Ephraim Deinard, bibliographer, who helped establish the major Jewish libraries in America, put out thirty-two issues of *Ha Leumi* (1888–89), and Wolf Schur published *Ha-Pisgah* (1890–99). Schur continued his publication efforts in Chicago, Boston and Baltimore, undaunted by financial difficulties and undiscouraged by indifference and rebuff. His was a voice promoting early Zionism and combating assimilatory tendencies in American Jewish life.

Menahem Mendel Dolitsky, a known Hebrew poet in Russia, eked out a living in America by producing Hebrew and Yiddish potboilers as well as verse of quality. Gerson Rosenzweig eased the difficulties of his adjustment to the New World by utilizing the Talmudic form to poke bitter fun at Jewish life in America. Naphtali Herz Imber led a picaresque existence as a pamphleteer and poet, and gained immortality as author of "Hatikvah," the Jewish national anthem.

ILLUSIONS AND REALITY

Jews in the Russian and Austro-Hungarian empires heard about America from relatives who had gone there and sent letters, or returned for a visit.

In an article in the Russian Hebrew periodical *Hamelitz* in 1889, Nahum Wolf Goldin, a recent immigrant, warned against believing every rosy description of America, and paints a dark picture of lives of peddler and laborer:

> For every customer there are seventy-seven peddlers, who wander about hungry, crying out in a hoarse voice, "Lady look in the basket." But the lady does not even turn their way. She has had her fill of peddlers and their wild cry. The hour doesn't pass that someone doesn't knock at her door and beg for mercy—pleading for her to buy something, because he hasn't eaten all day. . . . On many doors is the sign, "Peddlers are prohibited to enter," and when a peddler ignores such a sign he courts a beating. So the peddler wanders about all day long, and if he has been able to put together a few cents from selling or begging, he rents a night's lodgings; if not, he sleeps in the open air.

Goldin declares that the fate of the factory worker is no better, because forced to work twelve to fifteen hours a day "with a haste never asked of workers in Europe . . . Pressed one against the other, they toil in cellars without fresh air. The smoke of the kerosene lamp doesn't let them breathe. For twelve hours of labor, the workers receive five dollars a week." True, he admits, there are workers who earn ten or twelve dollars a week, but theirs is seasonal labor, which lasts no more than three or four months a year. "The little strength one brings from the old country is soon dissipated. The face grows pale, the limbs lose their healthy roundness and the eyes become sunken."

He turns his wrath on the immigrants who paint a false picture for those they left behind.

> Do they warn their dear ones . . . No! they are ashamed to do so. Before they left they boasted that they would soon attain great wealth. . . . Now they are ashamed to disclose the bitter truth, and fill their letters with lies. They triple their earnings, and hide their problems. It doesn't even occur to them that in hiding their troubles, they will inflict the same on their relatives, who reading such glowing letters . . . will sell all they have and set out for America.[25]

Goldin understood that the prospective emigrant in Europe does not want to hear the truth. He knew that his closing plea, "Pay no attention to those who picture America as a Garden of Eden. Don't waste your last few *groschen* in vain fantasies," would fall on deaf ears, that it is precisely these fantasies which would draw them to the land in which, in their imaginations, they already felt at home and prospering. When the Jew of the *shtetl* read Sholom Aleichem's account of Berl-Isaac's report on America, he knew it to be fiction, but no factual truth spoke to him more tellingly. Said Berl-Isaac:

> First, the country itself. A land flowing with milk and honey. Money you scoop up with both hands; gold, by the shovel full. And business you can have as much as you like. It turns the head. You want a factory—you can have a factory; a store—you open a store. If you want you push a pushcart, or go out to peddle or work in a shop. What you want you do. It's a free country! . . . The Jews, what honor they enjoy there! No other people is so respected, so revered as the Jews. The Jew is made to feel important. In America it is a great honor to be a Jew. . . . In America they love the Jews. . . .

The monologue continues, and one reads, "I go for a walk. Two boys accost me. I put down my bundle, take off my coat and blows began to fall on me. It's a miracle I escaped with my life . . . when they see a Jew with a beard, they pull on his beard so long, that to get rid of them, he must shave it off. . . ."[26] But the East European Jews who read Berl-Isaac's account chose to believe the picture of a land where you scoop up gold by the shovelful.

In her *Hungry Hearts*, Anzia Yezierska recalled her expectations of America, and the reality as well:

> In America you can say what you feel. . . .
>
> In America is a home for everybody. The land is your land, not, as in Russia, where you feel yourself a stranger in the village where you were born and reared, the village in which your father and grandfather lie buried.
>
> Everybody is with everybody alike in America. Christians and Jews are brothers together.
>
> An end to the worry for bread. . . . Everybody can do what he wants with his life in America.
>
> There are no high or low in America. Even the President holds hands with Gedalyah Mindel.
>
> Plenty for all. Learning flows free, like milk and honey. Age-old visions sang themselves in me—songs of freedom, of an oppressed people.
>
> America! America![27]

Journey over, little Anzia looks out at her America:

> narrow streets of squeezed-in stones and houses, ragged clothes,
> dirty bedding oozing out of the windows, ash-cans and garbage
> cans cluttering the sidewalks. . . . "Where are the green fields and
> open spaces in America? . . . Where is the golden country of my
> dreams?" . . . All about me was the hardness of brick and stone,
> the smells of crowded poverty. . . . I looked out into the alley
> below, and saw pale-faced children scrambling in the gutter. "Where
> is America?" cried my heart.[28]

Even the popular lullabies of the day resonate with the conflicting
themes of America the Ideal, America the Real. In 1892, Sholem Aleichem published "Sleep My Child" where a mother sings to her little
boy:

> Sleep my child, my consolation, my lovely,
> Sleep my little son,
> Sleep my crown, my only *kaddish*
> So sleep, so sleep *lyu, lyu.*

"Your father is in America," she tells her son, "a land which is a place
of happiness for everyone; for the Jew, a veritable Garden of Eden.
Why, it's a place where one can afford to eat *hallah* even on week days!"

Two stanzas describing this Garden of Eden the author thought
best not to publish in Russia, but they were known and sung:

> There one does not know of troubles
> Evil decrees, my son,
> Knows not of pogroms or terrors,
> So sleep my little one.
>
> They say that Jews are rich there,
> May no evil eye be cast,
> Each one lives there in contentment
> Equal with the rest.[29]

There is a note of apprehension, however. "I long since would
have joined him," she sighs, "but I do not know where." Still she
refuses to despair. "God willing he will send us a letter, send us twenty
dollars, his portrait—and take us to him." Her musings raise her hopes:
"He will come to greet us, take you and kiss you, glow with joy. And
I will shed tears of joy, silent tears of joy. . . . But until then my son,
sleep, sleep my little one."

Most men did send for their wives and families, but some, as
Sholem Aleichem implies, did not. The Russian Jewish periodical press
at the turn of the century carried heartrending pleas of wives searching

for husbands who had gone off to the New World and were not heard from again. Among those who brought wife and family, there were those who found that the husband's few years in America had so removed him from the ways of the Old Country, so "Americanized" him that he felt estranged from his newly arrived greenhorn wife. Some deserted wives and families. For many years, the *Jewish Daily Forward* published "A Gallery of Vanished Men," with descriptions, pictures and pleas for information about them. For some, like Yekl (Jake, in America) in Abraham Cahan's novel of that name, the solution was divorce.

The great majority remained with wife and family, all joining in a long (and, for some, never-ending) struggle for the bare necessities. Morris Rosenfeld wrote a lullaby for the immigrant father. One needs not stretch one's imagination too far, to see Sholem Aleichem's mother and son reach America to be welcomed by husband and father, and then hear his mournful song about the America which mother had described as a "place of happiness for everyone."

> I have a little boy,
> A lovely little son;
> When I see him,
> The whole world is mine, my own.

But, the father explains, he seldom, seldom sees his son, for his work takes him from home at dawn, when the boy is still asleep, and when he returns late at night, the boy is already asleep. Father and son remain strangers to one another. The son asks, "When will Poppa come and give me a penny, when?" The father looks down upon his sleeping child:

> And I—I think in bitterness
> And disappointment sore;
> "Someday you will awake, my child,
> To find me nevermore."[30]

Lullabies express disappointment in personal, tender words and tone; not so folk doggerel and street rhymes. Theirs is a more strident voice punctuated with social protest. Eliakim Zunser was the most popular bard of the East European Jewish community. In the cities and towns of the Russian Pale his songs were sung, his verses recited. He recorded and commented upon the more dramatic features of Russian Jewish life: the cantonists, the early Zionist movement and the colonization of the Holy Land, and the mass exodus to America. He himself became part of that migration, settling in New York's Lower East Side to open a print shop, and in the New World as in the Old, he continued to publish topical songs in Yiddish. *For Whom Is the Gold Country?*

appeared in 1894, five years after his arrival. By the end of the century, it was widely sung by the immigrant generation, for it expressed their experiences in, and perception of America.

> While yet a child
> Of America, I was told:
> "How happy its people,
> It is a Land of Gold!"

> I came to the land, saw it and Lo!
> Pain and suffering and tears of woe.
> > In its narrow streets, on square and place,
> > With gloom and poverty writ on each face
> > Stand from morn till night
> > Huddled masses. A frightful sight!

> One will sacrifice his child for a cent,
> Or drive a man from his flat for rent.
> > Here a greenhorn hungering for bread
> > Falls in the street, starved, dead!

Zunser sings of the dehumanization of the worker, "a brother to the horse," displaced by the machine, discarded by his employer. The immigrant is fair game for everyone, unprotected by the law or its officers.

> Justice here is bought and sold,
> In this golden land, this Land of Gold!

The worker is exposed to all sorts of hazards, mutilation in factory and mine, fire in his tenement flat. Life is cheap.

> Oh, how many times has the death knell tolled
> In this golden land, this Land of Gold!

The lot of the woman is no better. The sacred bond of marriage has become a chain which fetters the wife to a house filled with children and boarders.

> A woman's lot—too dread to be told
> In this golden land, this Land of Gold!

The air is heavy and vile, the filthy tenements oppress and depress people as fathers cough out their lives and sons give up education and sacrifice future to "keep the family from the throes of starvation."

> But happy the man who has money,
> His years filled with laughter, his day
> > always sunny.

Power and pleasure his wealth does bring,
The millionaire is America's King! . . .
America is his to have and to hold,
His golden land. *His* Land of Gold![31]

Zunser, and those who sang his words, bridled at the injustice of the
few having so much and the many so little, at the devastation of the
dream expressed by mother singing to her son:

Each one lives here in contentment.
Equal with the rest.

Or Yezierska's imaginings: "There are no high or low in America." The immigrant Jew found that "the high" in America were very
high indeed, and the low, "a brother to the horse." Anticipating Louis
D. Brandeis's perception of "the contrast between our political liberty
and our industrial absolutism," the turn-of-the-century immigrant could
ask: "Did I exchange political repression for economic oppression—one
tyranny for another? And if so, then what have I gained—sacrificing
so much in the process?" Having gazed on the dark side of the coin,
his driving optimism veered to the brighter side. In Russia, he could
not rise to the nobility, certainly not to the throne, but in America he
could reign as king—America's king, the millionaire. A hundred generations who believed in "perfect faith" that the Messiah would come,
could produce a generation which believed that "a millionaire, I can
become."

The children of that generation growing up in America, filled
with the knowledge public schools were providing, sopping up the
wisdom of the streets, joined in the belligerent patriotism following
the Spanish-American War. Being heirs to generations which had looked
with apprehension on pious proclamations of patriotism they sang this
street rhyme in a mixture of Yiddish and English to the tune of "There'll
Be a Hot Time in the Old Town Tonight":

Marsch Onkel Sam
Die krieg iz shoin ferbai
In moil a chew *tabak, a fulle hant mit* pie
Zingt er a lied, un whistles *zu derbai*
'Zis schwindel, 'zis humbug
'Zis boom, tara-ra-ra!

March Uncle Sam!
The war has now gone by.
Mouth filled with chew tobacco
Hands all filled with pie
Singing a song,

And whistling along:
It's swindle, it's humbug
It's boom tara-ra-ra.[32]

All America was caught up in the heady excitement of becoming a world power, but the streetwise boys and girls of the Lower East Side cast a jaundiced glance at marching Uncle Sam. America at the turn of the century was a nation grown big and strong, but it was a nation marred by a social system distorted by discrimination and exploitation. East European immigrants saw through the attempt to identify national power with national well-being. The boom tara-ra-ra of the chauvinist drum could not drown out the cries heard in the sweatshops and the vile tenements. Their outrage was not only against the personal economic deprivation but against a system which shattered their dreams of a golden land.

The East European immigrant Jew had a vision of and for America which flowed out of the concepts of social justice which he found in the words of the ancient Prophets or in the writings of a nineteenth-century apostate Jew, Karl Marx. A member of that generation, Hebrew poet, editor and educator Gershon Rosenzweig, in an English preface to his Hebrew translations of "The Star-Spangled Banner" and "America," wrote in 1898: "the youngest nation is heir to the oldest, and all that was best in the Jewish nation is now in possession of the American nation to be developed and cultivated for all humanity." The immigrant Jew provided both leaders and foot soldiers for the most radical movements for social betterment, the Socialists and Anarchists. That they did so as Jewish Socialists and Jewish Anarchists was due to the high sense of ethnic consciousness which pervaded the immigrant community, to the perception that as Jews they had the most at stake. Other immigrants could make America their home or return to their native land; for the Jew, return was not an option. It did not take long for some to perceive that political freedom conferred political power, and that this power could be used to oppose social discrimination and economic oppression.

Among the first to sound the call was Eliakim Zunser. Four years after his satirical "For Whom Is the Gold Country?" he published "Overlooked—Lost!" "Jews are coming to America," he wrote, "from Russia, Austria, from the whole world. They form their congregations, lodges, clubs. But they do not perceive what it is that they really need— political power." When others form political clubs, he pointed out, we readily give them our support, but he warned

We dare not rely too much on others
Two thousand years of experience instruct us in this.

"Germans and Irish form their political clubs, and all officials respect them. How can we expect to be respected if we do not do the same?" he argued. Our enemies are all about us, he warned. How often has it been our lot to be the chief sufferers when the world has lost its way and wandered off . . .? So

> Be patriots—be Americans . . .
> Become citizens—organize! . . .
> Use your vote—vote your interest!
> The Jew will no longer be attacked
> He will be protected in court
> He will not need to complain
> The judge will listen to his words . . .
> Only then will you be able to say:
> "This land is for the Jew, a secure, serene place."[33]

SOURCE
America Speaks to the Immigrant Jew: A Plea for the Jewish Vote

As the century was drawing to a close, late in October of 1899, the Lower East Side of New York was flooded by Yiddish handbills signed by "Jewish Members of the Republican State Committee," appealing to Jews to vote for Theodore Roosevelt for governor of the State of New York. The appeal, directed to Jewish parochial interests and emotions, asked: can a Jew dare vote against the man who was so instrumental in fashioning the defeat of Spain in the Spanish-American War?

Who Takes Vengeance for Us?

Every respectable citizen, every good American and every true Jew, must and will vote for the Republican gubernatorial candidate—*Theodore Roosevelt.*

As citizens who are concerned with the welfare of their city and state, and as Jews, we direct this message to you. We will take for our text the verse in our Psalms: "Oh you murderous Babylonia, may it be done to you, what you have done to us!"

Babylonia sinned against the Jewish people. But how small is Babylonia's sins in comparison with the untold crimes which Spain committed against us! Babylonia came as an enemy and took us into exile. Spain did much worse. In Spain our ancestors were good and useful citizens. They made rich Spain's treasury; outfitted the ships which discovered America and gave Spain the power which made her a mighty nation. How did Spain reward them?

Spain took away everything her Jews had, and she sent her Jews
to the dungeons of the Inquisition and to the fires of the auto da
fe. When Jews left Spain they were murdered on the road, as sheep
are slaughtered by wolves. Those who remained as disguised
Christians were slowly persecuted.

The cruelty and tyranny which Spain set loose, did not
remain in its own land. Spain brought it to the new world—Brazil,
Mexico, Cuba—Santiago, where Theodore Roosevelt met the
Spanish face to face, were long stained by Spain's murderous and
bestial methods. And until Theodore Roosevelt charged up San
Juan hill, there still rang in our ears the cries and screams of Spain's
brutality.

The long felt Jewish desire to see Spain fall was finally
fulfilled. The Republican Party through its president gave the word
that Spain should move out of the New World and the Republican
gubernatorial candidate for New York State *Theodore Roosevelt* was
one of the chief instruments of the late war. He worked day and
night till he worked out all the plans for our navy, and when
Admirals Dewey, Sampson and Schley chased the enemy, Theodore Roosevelt, at his own expense organized a Regiment of Rough
Riders and went to the Battle Field to meet the foe.

Under Roosevelt's command there were many Jewish Rough
Riders. Roosevelt was like a brother to them. He recommended
them to the president for promotions, and sang their praises to the
world.

Spain now lies punished and beaten for all her sins. But the
Party which brought Spain her defeat, and the *man* who fought
against her, now stand before the citizens of this State and ask
whether they are satisfied with their work.

The decision about President McKinley and the late war
with Spain lies now in the hands of the citizens of this State in this
present election. Every vote for the COLONEL OF THE ROUGH
RIDERS is approval of McKinley and the war. Every vote for
Roosevelt's opponent, who is also McKinley's opponent, is a vote
for Spain, for Generals Weiler and Blanco . . .

Can any Jew afford to vote against Theodore Roosevelt and
thereby express his disapproval of the war against Spain? Can any
Jew thus deny the joy of his nation in the entire world? . . .

Vote for Theodore Roosevelt . . .

Vote to express your approval of Spain's defeat.

Jewish Members of the Republican State Committee.[34]

To the immigrant Jew, the campaign handbill said many things.
In this country, each male Jewish citizen had something of great value,

his vote. Those in power valued and wanted it. Not only the neighborhood Tammany lackey sought it, but so, too, did the patrician Republican State Committee.

This appeal for his vote suggested to him that it was legitimate to vote one's own ethnic self-interests. The citizen in America had the right to determine not only for whom to cast his ballot, but also for what reasons. If Jewish pride was important to him, it was proper to permit it to determine his choice. The immigrant community might well conclude that its integration into the American social and cultural fabric would be permitted in accordance with its own perceptions of America and in response to its own particular needs.

Part Two

From Haven to Home

6.

Americanization

THE WORLD LOOKED TO THE NEW CENTURY WITH EAGER ANTICIPATION, and none more so than Americans, and among them, most notably, American Jews.

Post-Civil War America had been engaged not so much in Reconstruction as in construction and expansion. The latter was rapidly making the United States the major breadbasket of the Western world; the former promised to place it in first rank of industrial nations. Emerging industrial complexes invited workers to man the mines, build the railroads, fill the assembly lines, to make clothing for and distribute food to the rapidly growing laboring class.

During the nineteenth century, world Jewry had grown fourfold from some two and one-half million to over ten million. The American Jewish community had multiplied more than five hundredfold from two thousand to more than a million; from one-twelfth of one percent of world Jewry to over ten percent. In the preceding centuries, America had been a haven for Jews who reached its shores. In the century now dawning, the children of the immigrants were confronted with the challenge of turning that haven into a home.

"The year 1899," a lead editorial in *The New York Times* of Monday, January 1, 1900, summed up, "was a year of wonders; a veritable *annus mirabilis*, in business and production. . . . To paraphrase a celebrated epitaph, prosperity left scarcely any of our industries untouched, and touched nothing it did not enrich. It would be easy and natural to speak of the twelve months just passed as the banner year, were we not already confident that the distinction of highest records must presently pass to the year 1900."

The American Jewish Year Book, reviewing the year 5661 (1900–1901), echoed the assessment of *The New York Times,* but with a sobering reservation. "The United States has witnessed an exceptional year in its history, politically and commercially, and seems at a bound to have taken its place among the greatest nations of the earth. The Jewish community has participated in the fever of expansion, and, like the rest of the nation, is suffering from an attack of overconfidence." The article stated that publication of the first volume of the *Jewish Encyclopedia* was a "capital event in the history of Jewish learning in America," but notes that it "can hardly be called an American work . . . having its collaborators in all parts of the world." It reported that the two theological seminaries "have been seeking funds" with some success; that the convention of the Orthodox Union and the meeting of the Central Conference of American Rabbis "were without unusual incident, save that both were the subject of unfavorable criticism from their friends. Lewis N. Dembitz declared the Orthodox Union ineffectual, and both the *American Israelite* and the *Reform Advocate* were dissatisfied with portions of the proceedings of the Central Conference." Particularly disturbing to the reporter were the following: "In the Legislature of the State of Massachusetts a bill was presented to allow observers of the Seventh Day Sabbath to work on Sunday, but it was finally defeated," and "the attempt to secure the removal of the word 'Christian,' as a qualifying benevolence, from the Bill of Rights of the State of Virginia, was also unsuccessful."[1]

Lights and shadows bathed the American Jewish landscape in the first years of the new century. Whether one was dazzled by the sunshine or cast into gloom by the shadows depended in large measure on whether the observer was a member of the established, affluent, Americanized "old" community, or a part of the rapidly growing "new" community, grudgingly welcomed, bewildered by strange ways of an alien world, struggling for a living.

George E. Barnett of Johns Hopkins University noted in 1902, "a sharp differentiation, both in economic condition and in age configuration," between "the Jews of Portuguese and German descent—the longer settled class, and the new immigrant of Russian and Polish origin."[2] Henrietta Szold recognized a threefold Jewish community at the birth of the century, "the Spanish-Portuguese, the German, and the Russian." In the introductory article, "Elements of the Jewish Population in the United States," in Charles S. Bernheimer's *The Russian Jew in the United States,*[3] Szold argued that each group was not homogeneous at first, differing in origin, local customs and the like, but circumstance had welded the "various elements" into united communities. "The Russian Jewish element," she writes, defies analysis. "With its Lithuanian, Volhynian, Bessarabian . . . its Galician, Polish and Roumanian tributary streams, it is more complex than either of the other two. . . . To say what the Russian Jew is and can be in America is to prophesy the course of the twentieth century." Szold seems to suggest that just as the eighteenth century was the era of the Spanish and Portuguese Jew, the nineteenth of the German, the twentieth-century American Jewish community would be fashioned by the Russian Jew.

> The time is not distant when the Russian Jew will have solved the elementary problems of American existence. . . . His spiritual energies will flow in quieter channels without abating a jot of their force and fervor. . . . They will soon reach the point at which they will turn for guidance to the history of the Germans and of their Sephardic predecessors. Eschewing the foolish pride of both, they will emulate the dignity and self-respect of the latter, and the sobriety and the steadiness of purpose of the former. They will use the institutions created by them as the stock upon which to engraft their intenser fervor, their broader Jewish scholarship, a more enlightened conception of Jewish ideals, and a more inclusive interest in Jewish world questions.

THE SEPHARDI JEW: "DIGNITY AND SELF-RESPECT"

The dignity which Szold perceived in the Sephardic community was based on the security and serenity which old wealth and social acceptance provided. The Hendrickses, the Nathans, the Cardozos and Lazaruses (who became Sephardim by choice and marriage) mixed freely with the social elite of New York. Stephen Birmingham, author of *The Grandees,* reports, "the men decorated the boards of directors of the proper corporations, and the correct hospitals, museums, charities. Women engaged in daintier pastimes—painting, reading, letter writing, going to concerts, operas, and ballets."[4] Their congregation, the Spanish and Portuguese synagogue, Shearith Israel, which they were proud to remind others was almost two and a half centuries old, in 1897, built a magnificent building on fashionable Central Park West. The solemn dignity of the traditional Sephardic service was retained in all its purity. The old rite suited old families and old money. True, Ashkenazim had outnumbered Sephardim in membership since the early eighteenth century, but the Ashkenazim in Shearith Israel often outdid the descendants of Iberian families in their allegiance to the Sephardic rite. As early as 1872, W. M. Rosenblatt, writing on "The Jews: What They Are Coming To" in *The Galaxy* magazine, noted that the younger Sephardic Jews "entertain no reverence for the antiquated usages of their people."[5]

The congregation's bridge to the larger Jewish community was its rabbi, Henry Pereira Mendes. Scion of a long and distinguished line of Sephardic rabbis, he had come to Shearith Israel from England and soon took leadership in all avenues of Jewish life. He was a founder of the Jewish Theological Seminary (as noted earlier), the Union of Orthodox Jewish Congregations and the New York Board of Jewish Ministers. In the days when Zionism was anathema to the majority of "proper" Jews, Mendes responded to a request from Theodor Herzl to help organize the movement in America, and he served as a member of the Actions Committee of the World Zionist Organization and vice-president of the Federation of American Zionists. His congregants indulged him in such activities, in which they had little interest, for his activism also gave him positions of honor and respect in the general community. He was vice-president of the Guild for Crippled Children; a member of the Mayor's Committee on the Hudson-Fulton celebration; a speaker at the celebration marking the 250th anniversary of the establishment of municipal government in New Amsterdam; and the first Jew to be grand chaplain of the Masonic Grand Lodge of the State of New York.

In 1870 the close-knit congregation was shaken by the brutal murder of Benjamin Seixas Nathan, scion of American Jewry's premier families. Nathan was a banker, philanthropist, congregational president and communal leader. At the time of his murder he was a member of the Union League Club and the Saint Nicholas Society, president of Mount Sinai Hospital and a vice-president of the New York Stock Exchange—which on the day of his funeral closed down as a mark of respect and offered a $10,000 reward—never claimed—for the capture of the murderer. The resignation of brother-in-law Judge Albert J. Cardozo from the New York State Supreme Court bench two years later cast a deeper pall over all the congregational family. The New York State Bar ordered an investigation into the judge's activities in awarding refereeships, a majority of which had been granted to political boss William M. Tweed's son and nephews. To avoid investigation, the judge resigned. His son, Benjamin Nathan Cardozo, lived to vindicate the family name and to become one of the most respected justices to serve on the United States Supreme Court.

The community preserved memories it cherished as well: recollections of distinguished sons and daughters in public service, accepting civic and communal responsibilities from a sense of noblesse oblige, and providing the general and Jewish communities with institutions of healing and culture, Mount Sinai Hospital and the Jewish Theological Seminary of America, to name two of many.

And there was Emma Lazarus whose sonnet "The New Colossus" inscribed on the base of the Statue of Liberty welcomed America's immigrants. The Lazarus family had for four generations been associated with Shearith Israel, and through her mother, a Nathan, Emma was related to the Seixas, Hendricks, Solis, Judah and Lyons families. Great-grandfather Samuel Lazarus had joined with Gershom Mendes Seixas in organizing Kalfe Sedakah for relief of those stricken by the yellow fever epidemic in 1798, and had himself fallen victim to it. His son, Eleazar S., American-born son of German Ashkenazic immigrants, become the leading authority on Sephardic liturgy in the first half of the nineteenth century. He was one of two members of Shearith Israel "who took over the duties of the *hazzan*" on the death of Gershom Mendes Seixas. The first Hebrew prayer book published in America had its "Text Carefully Revised and Corrected by E. S. Lazarus." He also served as *Parnas* (president) of the Shearith Israel Congregation, as did his eldest son, Samuel, who, like his father, would on occasion lead the service in the synagogue.

The second son, Moses, added to the family fortune through the sugar refining business and married Esther, the sister of Benjamin Nathan. They raised six daughters. The lives of three of these, Emma, Josephine and Annie, illustrate what was happening to socially elite, acculturated, wealthy Jews in late nineteenth- and early twentieth-century America.

Private tutorial education, stressing literature and languages, was provided for the Lazarus children; Hebrew education was not. Like others in their group, the Lazarus family relegated their Jewish life to the formal, occasional expression that good social manners required.

Emma early displayed literary gifts, and her proud father in 1866 published for her "for private circulation," *Poems and Translations,* "written between the ages of fourteen and sixteen." She dutifully dedicated the 207-page volume of thirty "original pieces" and translations from Heine, Dumas and Hugo, to her father. A long review in a leading New York newspaper hailed the new poet: "It is seldom, nay, we do not remember ever having had a volume of poems in our hands written by one of immature years, which gave such promise of future greatness." Ralph Waldo Emerson befriended her and became guide and mentor. She dedicated her *Admetus* to him. Turgenev wrote of his admiration for her prose romance *Alide:* "I feel proud of the approbation you give my works, and of the influence you kindly attribute to them on your own talent; an author who writes as you do is not a pupil in art anymore; he is not far from being himself a master."

For all the praise, spiritual unease troubled the young poet, an emptiness which the Judaism of her father and her uncle could not fill. The uncle, the Reverend Jacques Lyons, *hazzan*-minister of Shearith Israel, dispensed a proper, decorous, liturgy-centered religion which neither stirred her soul nor satisfied her heart.

She needed an audience which would be stirred, and a cause which would challenge. When friend Edmund C. Stedman, poet and critic, suggested that she turn to the Jewish tradition as a source of inspiration, she replied, as Stedman later remembered, that "although proud of her blood and lineage, the Hebrew ideals did not appeal to her." When Rabbi Gustav Gottheil invited her to contribute to a hymn book he was compiling, she replied: "I will gladly assist you as far as I am able; but that will not be much. I shall always be loyal to my race, but I feel no religious fervor in my soul."

Her fervor was aroused by the plight of her people. The Russian pogroms of 1881, which followed on the assassination of Czar Alexander II, brought terror-stricken survivors to America. Emma Lazarus's first response was to go to Ward's Island to see what might be done for the hapless men, women and children who crowded its facilities. The "loyalty to race" was not so much a kinship with preceding generations, but a bond with those of her generation who needed her—and her gifts.[6]

She began to read the literature of her people, to study the Hebrew language and to associate more and more with Jews. In an article in *The Century Magazine*, entitled "Russian Jews and Gentiles," the author, Madame Ragozin, justified the pogroms, blaming the victims and defending the czarist government. In the May 1882 issue, Lazarus published a scholarly essay, "Russian Christianity versus Modern Judaism,"[7] exposing the volume by the apostate Jacob Brafman upon which Madame Ragozin had based her accusations. The essay was an impassioned defense of Judaism and of the Russian Jew and a skillful plea to the American public, concluding with a quotation from former Secretary of State William M. Evarts: "It is not that it is the oppression of Jews by Russians—it is that it is the oppression of men and women by men and women; and we are men and women."

A half year later *The Century* published her "The Jewish Problem,"[8] which is particularly noteworthy for her Zionist stance more than a dozen years before Herzl published his *Judenstaat*. In a milieu in which Jewish national aspirations were denounced as contrary to the highest expression of Judaism, and suppressed because of the fear of dual-loyalty accusation, she hailed the Zionism espoused in George Eliot's *Daniel Deronda*. With high anticipation she greeted the colonies being planted in the Holy Land, and took seriously English writer and traveler Laurence Oliphant's formulation of the Jewish problem as a choice before the Jew of: "race-extinction by marriage in countries which are too civilized to attempt massacre, or of separation in a young nationality."

She closes her article with the view of "a young Russian Jew on this subject, for they sum up the desires and ambitions of the nation":

what they [the Jews] need is to be once more consolidated as a nation. . . . Let them organize with sufficient strength under a competent leader, and establish their central government. . . . In their present wretched condition the Jews have grown old. . . . But a new life will be instilled in them by such an achievement; and once more incorporated as a fresh and active nation, they will regain youthful vigor and power.

In devoting the rest of her brief life to the cause of a nation revived, Emma Lazarus found herself possessed of a new inspiration. She now wrote her poems for *The American Hebrew*, such as "The Banner of the Jew."

With Moses' law and David's lyre,
    Your ancient strength remains unbent.
Let but an Ezra rise anew
To lift the *Banner of the Jew*!

"The New Ezekiel" sang of dead bones which "twenty scorching centuries of wrong" produced, but:

The Spirit is not dead, proclaim the word,
    Where lay dead bones, a host of armed men stand!
I ope your graves, my people, saith the Lord,
    And I shall place you living in your land.

The credo of her newfound faith was also expressed in a series of articles in *The American Hebrew,* which bore the title "An Epistle to the Hebrews."[9] Earlier, she had lamented that there was "nothing to stir, nothing to awaken"; now she felt confident that she could make her contribution "towards rousing that spirit of Jewish enthusiasm which might manifest itself":

First, in a return to the varied pursuits and broad system of physical and intellectual education adopted by our ancestors; Second, in a more fraternal and practical movement towards alleviating the sufferings of oppressed Jews in countries less favored than our own; Third, in a closer and wider study of Hebrew literature and history; and finally in a truer recognition of the large principles of religion, liberty, and law upon which Judaism is founded, and which should draw into harmonious unity Jews of every shade and opinion.

We have here a comprehensive program for a revitalized American Jewry.

Emma's sister, Josephine, was her senior by three years, but deferred to her younger sister's greater gifts and during Emma's lifetime did not take up the pen. Josephine apparently shared her sister's Zionist sentiments. In an article in *The Century*, January 1892, on "The Jewish Question," she wrote:

> Of all the schemes of colonisation, the one that appeals most to the imagination is the return to Palestine. On the spot where they once were a great nation, and amid surroundings that seem better suited to their traditions and highest destiny than our Western conditions, they might again put forth some great spiritual idea, some new blossoming of the genius which is surely theirs.

Other causes stirred her more. At first, it was an impassioned argument that the world needs both Christianity and Judaism. "Judaism gives the Ten Commandments, and Christianity the Beatitudes; but only the two together can yield the perfect ideal,—the love that is simply the highest duty, and the duty that is lost in love." A year later, in a paper, "The Outlook of Judaism," read at the World's Parliament of Religions in Chicago, Josephine speaks to her fellow Jews of their responsibility toward their coreligionists. "This exodus from Russia, from Poland, these long black lines like funeral lines, crossing the frontiers."

> Let us not think our duty ended when we have taken in the wanderers, given them food and shelter, and initiated them into the sharp daily struggle to exist.
> What is it that the enlightened Jews of free America owe to the benighted refugees from ghetto and persecution, and to themselves? The Jew must change his attitude before the world, and come into spiritual fellowship with those around him. We must cross the Rubicon, the blank page that separates the Old Testament from the New, and read with fresh eyes, fresh hearts, the life and teachings of the one whom the world calls Master. We shall not thereby leave our own soil. John, Paul, Jesus himself,—we can claim them all for our own.[10]

She continued her argument on the pages of the *Jewish Messenger*. It is not conversion she espouses; what she asks for is religious assimilation. To save Judaism, she contends, the Jews must "lose it, by merging and adding to it that which will make it no longer Judaism, in other words by entering into the larger, spiritual life which . . . draws no boundary lines; sets up no barriers between man and man. . . ." It is the plea of a religiously emancipated, culturally integrated American Jew denied entry into the dominant Christian society. She perceived this "lurking discontent, a sense of personal grievance and disadvantage" in others of her generation, a generation alienated from a world they would not have, and a world which would not have them. She urged the Jews to rise above "race or sect or narrow creed," rise above the "aloofness which is the basis of our own existence."

She cites British Jewish leader Claude G. Montefiore's view: "The doctrine of Jesus may be regarded as pure Christianity or pure Judaism. Either way contains the truth." And she adds: "Teach us thus to know God, O teachers of Israel who starve us on dry husks and formulas!"

Her call went beyond religious assimilation to total assimilation. By 1895, the year in which she wrote "The Task of Judaism," some four hundred thousand East European Jews had come to America. It may well be that this mass immigration of coreligionists so different from the community that had become integrated into the American social scene made her despair of the acceptance of the Jews by American society at large. Of the new immigrants she wrote:

> We do not say to these bewildered and belated wanderers from other climes and times: "Keep your jargon and your uncouth ways and customs. Insist upon being Russian, Poles, Roumanians, for on no account must you lose your nationality and identity." On the contrary, we bid them welcome only on condition that they *shall* lose it, that they shall become Americans as we are. . . . And so too with our Jewish nationality. We cannot expect to become citizens of the world while we remain citizens of Judaea, bound by local ties, local prejudices and interests; so long as we insist upon perpetuating a race-tie that separates us from the people around us.

The essays were published in 1895 as a volume entitled *The Spirit of Judaism*.[11] It is a plea to the Christian to become more Christlike and to the Jew to become most fully a Jew through Jesus, whose message of Love will unite both in love.

Emma's was a passionate call for Jewish affirmation; Josephine's was a pain-laden plea for assimilation. Then there was Annie.

Annie, the youngest of the Lazarus children, ten years Emma's junior, married a popular though minor artist of the romantic school, a Christian named John Humphrey Johnston. She owned the copyright to the works of sister Emma. In 1926, Bernard Richards, planning to publish an edition of the complete works of Emma Lazarus, requested her permission and Annie, then living in Palazzo Contarini in Venice, refused and explained:

> While her politico-religious poems are technically as fine as anything she ever wrote, they were nevertheless composed in a moment of emotional excitement, which would seem to make their theme of questionable appropriateness today.

There has been, moreover, a tendency, I think, on the part
of some of her public, to overemphasize the Hebraic strain of her
work . . . I understand this to be merely a phase in my sister's
development, called forth by righteous indignation at the tragic
happenings of those days. . . . If my sister were here today I feel
that she might prefer to be remembered by the verses written in
her more serene mood.

Annie's reply is not surprising; she had long since become a devout
Catholic.

Affirmation, assimilation, apostasy. Three sisters, in the same
Lazarus-Nathan household, in a community marked, as Henrietta Szold
phrased it, by "dignity and self-respect." At the turn of the century,
one contemplating the fate of the fourth generation living in American
freedom and affluence might recall Rebecca Samuel's perception a century earlier, that for the Jew, America was the land of freedom, of
economic well-being, but also of spiritual peril.

THE GERMAN JEW: "SOBRIETY AND STEADINESS OF PURPOSE"

The new century saw the marshaling of forces in the American
Jewish community to come to the aid of the European. Two decades
earlier, European Jewry, through the French Alliance Israélite, the German Central Committee and the London Manor House Committee,
had come to the aid of the American Jewish community burdened by
the task of receiving an ever-growing influx of refugees from czarist
oppression. In 1882, American civil servant, B'nai B'rith leader and
editor Moritz Ellinger was sent by the Hebrew Emigrant Aid Society
to Europe, "directed to ask for advice and suggestions of the European
Committees as to methods of operation" and to "obtain aid from all
Hebrews wherever resident."[12] Advice was freely offered and monetary
aid as well. Over $112,000 was sent by the European committees to
the United States. A decade later, two delegates represented American
Jewry at a conference called by the European agencies, which met in
Berlin in 1891. Dr. Julius Goldman of the American United Hebrew
Charities arranged a sharing of financial responsibilities by the American
and European societies.

Early in 1901, Nissim Behar, representing the Alliance, came to
Jacob H. Schiff, head of Kuhn, Loeb and Co., the leading Jewish banking house, and acknowledged head of the American Jewish "establishment," urging a mass meeting to coalesce forces in the Jewish community
in behalf of the needs of Jews abroad. Schiff was at first reluctant,
believing that the burden of helping the new Jewish immigrants in

America was so great that "my brethren could not listen to the woes abroad." "Go to our tenements," said Schiff, "our asylums, and you will see how much we already have to do." The meeting of the Alliance was called nonetheless, Jacob Schiff presiding; and it was held in Temple Emanu-El, the cathedral synagogue of the German Jewish elite.

No one had anticipated the response to the call. The ties to European Jewry and concern for the well-being of fellow Jews abroad forced a move from the overcrowded vestry to the more spacious temple, but "even there," the press noted, "the main floor and the gallery were filled almost immediately." The main speaker was Louis Marshall, constitutional lawyer, and architect and arbiter of Jewish communal endeavor. He spoke of unity, but his remarks suggested division within the community.

> The conscience of the world must be aroused. Unity of voice will be heard even by tyrants. Solidarity of purpose on the part of the Jewish people will bring freedom even to the Jew of Russia and darkest Roumania. Some believe in the virtues of Zionism. God speed Zionism. [Applause] Others believe in building up in every country a citizenship.

The plight of brethren abroad united New York Jewry. Sephardic Orthodox Rabbi Henry Pereira Mendes opened with a prayer; Reform Rabbi Samuel Schulman and the Reverend Zvi Hirsh Maslian-sky, the "Orator of Zionism" in the East European Jewish community, were among the speakers. To demonstrate that the welfare of Jews everywhere and their civil and religious liberty were the concern of all Americans, Bishop Henry Codman Potter, Protestant Episcopal bishop of New York and the city's leading churchman, spoke for the community at large. He concluded with the comment:

> I feel it will grieve you very much if I say that I am not a Zionist. If I understand the term, it means one who would go away and live alone with his own nation. We don't want you to do that. You are a very valuable part of our nation. Make America your Zion.[13]

None were more elated than Schiff and Marshall, and the elite of the German-Jewish community they represented. They did mean to make America their Zion; indeed, they felt they had already done so. They had become a valuable part of the nation and felt pleased to be told so. They represented the responsible, prudent element of the community. Concern for the well-being of coreligionists everywhere was a duty of the Jewish tradition. It was also an expression of their Americanism, their duty as citizens of a nation becoming a world power. For two decades, Schiff and Marshall presided over American Jewry.

The German Jewish elite exercised communal power because they had the wherewithal to purchase that power and the will to maintain it. It demanded the expenditure of significant sums of money, but even more of time and energy and patience.

If there was cause for a sense of security and well-being for the German Jews, there was reason for unease and discomfort as well. They had established Jewish communities across the continent. Their economic presence was felt in communities large and small, not only along the Atlantic seaboard, but in the Midwest. In Chicago and Rochester as well as in New York City, the men's ready-to-wear clothing industry was largely in Jewish hands; in Cincinnati, St. Louis, Milwaukee, Cleveland, Louisville, Memphis and Kansas City, leading mercantile establishments bore their names. In many Midwestern cities, Jews had become integrated with the community as part of the larger German immigrant group. Their rabbis, as "Reverend Drs.," took their place side by side with Christian clergymen. The congregations they established were the leading synagogues. Their mother organization, the Union of American Hebrew Congregations, often acted as the representative body of American Israel, and its Hebrew Union College provided rabbis for its expanding network of congregations. The names Seligman, Guggenheim, Schiff, Lewisohn, Straus, Loeb and Lehman were names that evoked admiration and envy.

But social ostracism was pervasive and galling. It did not spare the wealthiest in the Jewish community, and it reminded all that even in the land of limitless economic opportunities, there were social barriers. This was dramatized in the experiences of two generations of the first Jewish family of great wealth in America, the Seligmans.

The grandest of America's resorts in the latter part of the nineteenth century was Saratoga, New York, and its grandest hotel was the Grand Union. In the summer of 1877, Joseph Seligman, a leading financier, confidant of presidents, member of the Union League Club, and employer of Horatio Alger as private tutor of his sons, was refused accommodation at the Grand Union Hotel because the hotel had a policy not to accept "Israelites." By 1893, Joseph's brother Jesse had risen to the office of vice-presidency of the Union League. His son, Theodore, recently graduated from Harvard and practicing law, naturally applied for membership. The list of his sponsors included some of the most prestigious names in New York society, Elihu Root and Joseph Choate among them. His application was rejected, the membership committee explaining the reason as "not a personal matter in any way . . . the objection is purely racial."[14]

This attitude was publicly expressed by Austin Corbin, president of the Long Island Railroad and of the Manhattan Beach Company, then developing Coney Island into a fashionable summer resort:

We do not like the Jews as a class. There are some well-behaved people among them, but as a rule they make themselves offensive to the kind of people who principally patronize our road and hotel, and I am satisfied we should be better off without than with their custom.[15]

Doors remained closed, entire neighborhoods off limits, to men who conferred with presidents, captains of industries. This form of social exclusion intensified in the new century. The exclusion of the elite of New York Jewry from New York society had more to do with the psychosocial needs of the discriminators than the character or "race" of the excluded. Unlike Boston Brahmin, Philadelphia Main Line, or New York Knickerbocker society, in which aristocracy was based on ancestry and wealth, the would-be aristocrats of the late nineteenth and early twentieth century New York were distinguished by wealth alone. A society, to retain its exclusiveness, must exclude others. The Jewish millionaire families served that purpose.

The German Jews, who had successfully leaped every hurdle on the road to financial success, and who felt certain that success would open every portal in America, now found that something stood in their way to full acceptance. Many blamed the newly arrived Russian Jews. Their dress, language, and manner were an embarrassment. The political radicalism of a vocal segment outraged them. To change, to Americanize downtown immigrant Jews—more correctly their children—became a passion of uptown Jews. Vocational training institutes, and classes in hygiene, home economics and the "privileges and duties of citizenship" were organized for the young. The Hebrew Institute, later renamed the Educational Alliance, became the chief means of Americanization. Its founders described it as a "center of sweetness and light, an oasis in the desert of degradation and despair," hardly a description which would be taken kindly by those who lived in that "desert." The adults kept away from it, but their children flocked to its clubs, led by gifted and devoted volunteers, and to its classes in art, music, literature and physical education. Similar institutions were established in cities across the continent.

Uptown unease would from time to time be heightened when the public press reported on the "foreign district" of the city, such as an article which appeared in the *New York Tribune,* November 25, 1900:

the squalor, the poverty, the hopeless drudgery, and the queer features of this foreign district are evident to the visitor . . . but the crime with which that part of the city is infested has been concealed from the general public . . . the police say, and the records show, that there is less drunkenness there than in other parts of the East Side tenement-house district, that there are not many

cases of assault, and that street fights are of rare occurrence. But
the big tenement houses in Chrystie Alley, Stanton and Forsyth
Streets shelter crime in its worst form, and the inmates of these
apartments contaminate their neighbors and create an atmosphere
in which good morals cannot exist. For years these places have
been known by the red lamps which shone in the windows or
hallways."

German Jews faced problems within their own community as
well. One was the crisis of identity for them and their children. They
had chosen Reform Judaism, a theologically liberal, ritually lax definition of Judaism which emphasized its religioethical teachings over its
national/cultural component. Such an identity made them comfortable
in America as religious liberals who had made America their Zion. But
challenges to their definition of Jewishness shook them, particularly
those launched by the sons of two rabbis of Reform Temple Emanu-
El, two gifted young men who the congregation had hoped would
succeed their fathers in the pulpit. Felix Adler, son of Rabbi Samuel
Adler, challenged them to extend their religious liberalism beyond the
bonds of Judaism to an ethical universalism which he called Ethical
Culture; Richard J. H. Gottheil, son of Rabbi Gustav Gottheil, urged
them to incorporate Zionism in their Jewish identity.

Six-year-old Felix accompanied his father when in 1857 Dr.
Samuel Adler was called to America by Temple Emanu-El to serve as
its rabbi. Felix was a brilliant student at Columbia University, and the
congregation sent him to Germany in 1870 to study for the rabbinate
at the Hochschule für die Wissenschaft des Judenthums. At the age of
twenty-three he received a doctorate in philosophy from the University
of Heidelberg. On his return to New York, it became obvious to all
that his religious liberalism had taken him outside the bounds of Judaism. Instead of the pulpit, he took to the classroom, accepting the
chair of Hebrew and Oriental literature established for him by his friends
at Cornell University. In 1876, he returned to New York and established
the New York Society for Ethical Culture, its motto "Deed not Creed."
It took the organizational form of a congregation, meeting on Sunday
morning for a lecture, but eschewing theology, doctrine, prayer and
ritual.

Adler challenged the Reform rabbis of America to draw the
radical conclusions of the liberalism of the Pittsburgh Platform of 1885,
arguing that: "a logical consequence from the position of the Reformers,
is the wiping out the lines of separation . . . between Reformed Jews
and Unitarians."[16] What he was advocating was not that Jews unite
with Unitarians (though a leading Reform rabbi of St. Louis traveled
to Boston to explore such a possibility), but that the old separations be

wiped out by Jews through his Ethical Culture movement. The first president of the Society for Ethical Culture was Joseph Seligman, who had formerly served as president of Temple Emanu-El.

Rabbi Gustav Gottheil, the incumbent in Emanu-El's pulpit, answered Adler's challenge in four sermons which attracted wide attention, but which did not stem the steady trickle of wealthy, acculturated Jews, who found in Ethical Culture a comfortable vehicle for total assimilation. What caused discomfort to the loyal German Jew was not the intellectual criticism or ideological challenge laid down by Felix Adler, but the fact that, as the *Jewish Encyclopedia* noted in its article on Ethical Culture in 1903, "though the society does not in any degree bear the stamp of Judaism . . . its chief supporters . . . are Jews, as is its founder and leader."

Like Felix Adler, Richard J. H. Gottheil also studied at Columbia, at German universities and the Hochschule in Berlin. Both men had long academic careers as members of the faculty of Columbia University. But in their approach to Judaism and the Jewish people, their paths diverged. Adler urged eradication of Jewish particularism; Gottheil advocated intensification of Jewish distinctiveness through Zionism.

Gustav Gottheil was the most prominent of the handful of Reform rabbis who at the turn of the century identified with Zionism. His son Richard was among the first leaders of American Zionism, served as president of the American Federation of Zionists from 1898 to 1904, and was a co-worker of Theodor Herzl in world Zionist endeavors. His *Zionism* became the textbook of the American movement. To Reform spokesmen who pointed to the incompatibility between the Reform ideal of mission and Zionism, he argued that Zionism would keep many Jews in the fold of Judaism who might otherwise depart: "The closer Jews are kept within the fold, the greater their interest in Jewish life and Jewish thought, the more propagators there will be for that mission."[17] To those who raised the specter of dual loyalty, he pointed out that German-Americans and Irish-Americans managed to retain their ethnic identity and their ties to the mother country, yet no one accused them of lacking of American patriotism. He argued that just as the state cannot "demand that the individual shall relinquish his peculiarities, his traditions, his family relationship," so too it cannot "ask of any group to give up its historic associations, its connections with other groups of the same race or of the same religion living elsewhere." If ever there should arise a conflict between "the duties towards the state the Jew lives in and his responsibility to the reconstructed Jewish home," then the Jew will have to face it in the same manner that the German-American or Irish-American in similar circumstances would have to do. But he saw no possibility of such a dilemma ever confronting

American Jews, for "the Jewish home is not to be founded for territorial
or other aggrandizement."

It is hardly likely that the discomfort of the German Jews with
Zionism was lessened by Gottheil's arguments. They would have preferred silence on the whole matter. More disturbing was having one
who grew up in their own midst voice such views, for it denied them
the argument that Zionism appealed only to immigrant Jews living
with memories of Czarist oppression.

The turn-of-the-century Reform Jew preferred Bishop Potter's
statement of the meaning of Zionism, or the closing words in *Justice
to the Jew, the Story of What He Has Done for the World* (1899), by
Madison C. Peters, pastor of the Bloomingdale Church of New York:

> America is the Zion from which goes forth the law. Here is liberty
> enlightening the world. America and not Palestine is the Jewish
> Mecca. America peerless, unrivalled, unapproached and unap-
> proachable America, has become the Jewish Canaan. America is
> the refuge of the oppressed of all the nations. Take your harps
> down from the willows and sing the song of Zion. Here you have
> found not only liberties, but Liberty![18]

Such words could lift the "Jews of German descent" from "sobriety"
to high enthusiasm as they looked to life in the new century in their
new Zion.

THE RUSSIAN JEW: "INTENSER FERVOR"

"The Russian Jews," Miss Szold wrote, "are looked upon by
their patrons and by their own leaders as the most unorganizable material among the Jews." She, however, saw this characteristic as a "manifestation of reserve energy that cannot yet find an outlet in the scholarly
life, a reaction from the work-a-day struggles and anxieties, with a just
admixture of desire to show self-reliance and initiative."

A walk through the East Side of New York, through South
Philadelphia, Chicago's West Side, Boston's North End, Rochester's
Joseph Avenue section, and similar neighborhoods in other American
cities would disclose the variety and vitality of the East European Jewish
immigrant community. The more perceptive observer would note that
both were the outward manifestations of a rich cultural life rooted in
a heritage which the immigrant had brought with him to the New
World. Synagogues of every variety abounded, filled with worshipers
on Sabbaths and holidays, and weekdays as well. The leading congregations vied in luring the star cantors of Europe to their pulpits. Newly-
arrived immigrants, whether they came from the Polish provinces, the
cities of Russia or the towns of Lithuania, could find a place in a syn-

agogue whose rite, liturgy and worshipers provided them with a spiritual home and a welcoming community. If they sought a Hasidic prayer room, that too was available. Many could meet their own townfolk in a *landsmanschaft* (organization based on place of origin) congregation which re-created the ambiance of their *shtetl*.

On the newsstands, one could find newspapers and journals in Yiddish and Hebrew. Six Yiddish dailies appeared, four in New York, two in Chicago; and weekly journals in Chicago, Philadelphia and Baltimore. Hutchins Hapgood noted that "Yiddish newspapers have, as compared with their contemporaries in the English language, the strong interest of great freedom of expression. They are controlled rather by passion than by capital."[19] Orthodox readers would take the *Tageblatt*, or, if their politics favored the Republican party, the *Morgen Zhurnal*. Socialists would choose either the *Abendblatt* or the *Forwerts*, depending on which faction of the Yiddish section of the Socialist party they favored. Anarchists read and supported the weekly *Freie Arbeiter Shtimme*. The *Abend Post* claimed that its purpose was "to Americanize the ghetto," and those who wanted their news straight, without ideological slant or bias, could get it from the *Herald*. For readers of Hebrew, there was the weekly *Ha-Ivri*, the monthly *Modia L' chadashim*, and fugitive publications which folded when the publisher ran out of money or enthusiasm. Ch. Enowitz, for example, published a Hebrew monthly, *Ha-Emes*, to promote atheism.

Books, serious tomes and penny dreadfuls, translations from the classics and original works, sermons in Hebrew and Socialist tracts in Yiddish daily came off the press. Almanacs and calendars published by newspapers, organizations and individuals were important means of education. *The Jewish-American People's Calendar: A Yearly Literary Review*, edited by Alexander Harkavy, contained the calendar for the year 5658 (1897–98), and 120 pages of articles on the political scene, on the government of the United States, on the split in the Socialist party, on the history of soap and on Mark Twain, with a section on the basic documents and the history, laws and government of the United States, the state and the city, all in Yiddish.

In the 1902 edition of the *Vorwerts Calendar and Almanach*, an advertisement of the Hebrew Publishing Co. announced its recent Yiddish publications: fourteen works of Leo Tolstoy, sixteen of Émile Zola and eight of Mendele Mocher S'forim, ranging in price from three cents to fifty (for *War and Peace*).

The leading magazines and the daily press informed their readers about the Lower East Side. "No part of New York," Hutchins Hapgood wrote, "has a more intense and varied life than the colony of Russian and Galician Jews who live on the East Side and who form the largest Jewish city in the world." In *The Atlantic Monthly* and other leading journals, he wrote about the life and the people of this community. His readers read about the three Yiddish theaters flourishing in the first year of the new century; about popular playwrights Joseph Latteiner and Moses Horowitz, and serious dramatist Jacob Gordin; about dramatic star Jacob Adler, and matinee idol Boris Tomashevsky; and about the audience which formed an integral part of the enterprise called "The Yiddish Stage." The reader was introduced to scholars—"submerged scholars," Hapgood called them—Moses Reicherson, "probably the finest Hebrew grammarian in New York, and one of the finest in the world"; S. B. Schwartzberg, "the apostle of a lost cause—the regeneration in New York of the old Hebrew language and literature"; and the Reverend H. Rosenberg, "waiting for an opportunity to publish his *magnum opus,* a cyclopedia of biblical literature." The bard Eliakim Zunser, the acclaimed Hebrew poet Menahem Dolitzki, the Poet of the Ghetto, Morris Rosenfeld; and Socialist Abraham Wald Liessin, "the youngest and least known of the four poets, and yet in some respects the most interesting," are described with surprising insight. Essays on the woman "old and new," a covey of writers, the novelist Abraham Cahan, artists and "odd characters," their lives, and their work, their exotic ways, and their vitality captivated the readers. In 1902, the articles appeared as a book, *The Spirit of the Ghetto,* with illustrations by a young ghetto artist, Jacob Epstein, who upon receipt of payment for his sketches, went off to Paris to study art—and to eventual world fame and knighthood. "Well-to-do persons visit the ghetto merely from motives of curiosity or philanthropy," Hapgood wrote in the foreword, "writers treat of it sociologically, as a place in crying need of improvement. . . . I was led to spend much time in . . . Yiddish New York . . . simply by virtue of the charm I felt in men and things there."[20]

Newspaperman Lincoln Steffens became "infatuated with the Ghetto." He found there "a queer mixture of comedy, tragedy, orthodoxy and revelation" which interested the Christian reader. He reported that the uptown Jews complained now and then that too much space was being given "to the ridiculous performances of the ignorant, foreign East Side Jews. . . ." To one socially prominent Jewish lady, Steffens "had the satisfaction of telling her about the comparative beauty, significance, and characters of the uptown and downtown Jews."[21]

"The Jewish quarter of New York," Hapgood observed in the first year of the new century, "is generally supposed to be a place of poverty, dirt, ignorance and immorality—the seat of the sweatshop, the tenement house, where the people are queer and repulsive." He found it to be also a community pulsating with cultural life and creativity, peopled by men and women possessed of social concern and human sensitivity.

Jacob A. Riis describes the debilitating effects of the sweatshop on men, women and children, and the social problems and disease festering in the tenements, in his *How the Other Half Lives*. He also saw the other side of the coin (as he writes in his *Children of the Poor*):

> It happened once that I came in on a Friday evening at the breaking of bread, just as the four candles on the table had been lit, with the Sabbath blessing upon the home and all it sheltered. Their light fell on little else than empty plates and anxious faces; but in the patriarchal host who arose, and bade the guests welcome with a dignity a king might have envied, I recognized with difficulty the humble peddler I had known only from the street.[22]

It must be stressed that at the turn of the century, the majority of the East European Jewish community in America had arrived within the last ten years, and been thrust into the world of sweatshop and tenement. Economic necessity often demanded jettisoning religious disciplines which had given stability to the communal and personal life of the Jew in Europe. It was a trauma of shattering magnitude for many to have to work on the Sabbath so that there would be bread on the table. To have children look at their parents as obstacles on their road toward Americanization caused many to question the whole uprooting and relocation, for it was tearing up of roots deep in a nourishing tradition, a relocation from a world of social stability and religious certainty to a land which welcomed you for what it could get out of you and to a community of Jews to whom you were a source of embarrassment. It offered a way of life which made for "heartbreaking comedies of tragic conflict between the old and the new . . . in many matters, all at once," as Lincoln Steffens observed it, "religion, class, clothes, manners, customs, language and culture . . . between parents of the Middle Ages . . . and children of the streets of New York today."

There were those who despaired of the future. Zev Schur, publisher of the Hebrew periodical *Ha-Pisgah,* after visiting Rochester, New York, at the end of the century and meeting Jewish Socialists and Anarchists there, felt impelled to publish a small volume pleading for Jewish survival, *Nezah Yisrael* (The Eternity of Israel). S. B. Schwartzberg's pamphlet in Hebrew bore the title *Tikatev Zot L'dor Ho-acharon* (Let This Be Written for the Last Generation). But the very great majority shared the optimism of Miss Szold that a vital, viable, creative Jewish community would be established in America and that the chief actor in this drama of creation would be the Russian Jew, whose life is informed by "intenser fervor, broader Jewish scholarship, a more enlightened conception of Jewish ideals, and a more inclusive interest in Jewish world questions."

Writer Mary Antin's father "left home in search for bread for his hungry family" and more "to test his own fate" in a land "unhindered by political or religious tyranny." But the land defeated him. "He was not prepared to make a living even in America . . . the American flag could not protect him against the pursuing nemesis of his limitations. . . . In business, nothing prospered with him. Some fault of hand or mind or temperament led him to failure where other men found success. . . . So in his primary quest he had failed."

America made it possible, however, for him to snatch the promise of success from inexorable failure.

> He could send his children to school, to learn all those things that he knew to be desirable . . . the common school . . . perhaps high school . . . perhaps even college.
>
> So it was with a heart full of longing and hope that my father led us to school on that first day. . . .
>
> I think Miss Nixon guessed what my father's best English could not convey. I think she divined that by the simple act of delivering our school certificates to her he took possession of America.[23]

Mary Antin called her immigrant autobiography *The Promised Land*.

SOURCE
Dear Mr. Editor . . .

The conflict between the religious and Socialist sectors of the immigrant society is depicted in the query to the editor and his answer in the "Bintel Brief" (Sheaf of Letters) column of the *Jewish Daily Forward* of December 23, 1910.

Dear Mr. Editor,

> A member of our branch of the *Arbeiter Ring* [Workmen's Circle] got married. We sent a large delegation to the wedding. One of the members spoke on the aims and purpose of the *Arbeiter Ring*. At the wedding dinner, a member of our delegation made an appeal for the strikers in Chicago, who are suffering hunger—they, their wives and their children—and asked for contributions.
>
> The groom rose to protest against "shnorring" [asking for money] at his wedding. So all the members, forty-five in number, rose and left. Only two members, one claiming to be a Russian revolutionary and the other a strong trade unionist refused to leave.
>
> Mr. Editor, what is your opinion of the conduct of the groom and the two members? We want to point out that the groom was seated next to his boss. Perhaps his enslaved soul forced him to do what he did. The two members claim they did not want to disturb the joy of the celebration. . . .

Answer:

It is an ancient custom to take up collections for good causes at weddings and other happy occasions. Others consider a good cause a *Talmud Torah* [Hebrew School] or *Hachnosas Kallah* [dowering the bride], we consider helping and supporting strikers a good cause. "Shnorring"? By the Orthodox they "shnorr" at almost every wedding, when the cantor recites the "He who blesses . . ." benediction. And the wealthier the guest the louder the singing. What else is that but "shnorring"? When they take up a collection for the rabbi, the "shamash" [sexton], the "badhan" [bard], the waiters . . . Is this not "shnorring"? Such "shnorring" is for individuals, who did nothing to earn it. But a collection for thousands of strikers—to call that "shnorring" is an insult to the proven fighters who are suffering for the whole laboring class! The *simhah* [joyous celebration] of a worker cannot be more worthily graced than by such a collection.

At a worker's *simhah* it is a duty to remember the plight of the thousands sacrificing for our class . . . The Orthodox break a glass at a wedding, so that in the midst of joy, the destruction of the Temple in Jerusalem be not forgotten. In the same spirit progressive workers should remember their brothers locked in strife and struggle.

Naturally, if the worker wants to curry favor with his boss who is at the wedding, he is in an uncomfortable position. The whole incident points out that even at a private affair like a wedding, sharp class distinction is present. Workers can only be comfortable with themselves, and be true to their conscience only in the company of their comrades. The groom was, therefore, wrong. However, this was not the time and place to mount a protest demonstration. The friends should not have left. They should have postponed the protest for another occasion. For everything there is a time and place. The two who remained did not act wrongly. They had the right to maintain that a celebration should not be disturbed.[24]

SOURCE
Jews and Judaism in America: Three Views at the Beginning of the Century

Rabbi Solomon Schindler came to the pulpit of Boston's leading congregation, Temple Adath Israel, in 1874, from a small Orthodox *shul* in Hoboken. In the next two decades, he led his congregation from Traditionalism to radical Reform. Rabbi Jacob David Willowsky, known by his acronym "Ridbaz," visited America in 1900. He was accorded

a royal welcome by the Orthodox Jewish community. Within five
months, he had obtained a sufficient number of subscriptions for his
classic commentary on the Palestinian Talmud and set sail for home.
He returned from Russia in 1903, and made his home in Chicago. The
organization of Orthodox rabbis, the Agudas Harabonim, conferred
upon him the title *Z'kan Harabonim* (senior rabbi). Elected chief rabbi
of Chicago, he nevertheless called himself "Jacob David, of the City
of Slutsk, a guest in Chicago." Dr. Israel Friedlaender, born in Poland,
educated in the Universities of Berlin and Strasbourg, served as professor of Biblical literature and exegesis at the Jewish Theological Seminary of America. He introduced to the American Jew the concepts of
Diaspora Nationalism of Simon Dubnow, and the Cultural Zionism of
Ahad Ha-am. Each of the three wrote perceptive comments on American Jewry. The first two reacted to America, the melting pot, Schindler
yielding to it, the Ridbaz rejecting it. Friedlaender's vision for America
was as a land of cultural pluralism, in which the Jewish community
could flourish.

Arthur Mann, biographer of Temple Adath Israel's rabbis, wrote:

> It is doubtful that Solomon Schindler's aspirations were ever iden-
> tical to those of his congregants. The latter wished to retain their
> Jewish identity; Schindler wished to destroy it. For him, Re-
> form . . . was a first step toward a non-sectarian religion that would
> include the highest ethics in the Jewish Christian tradition . . .
> Twenty-five years after his arrival in Boston, Solomon Schindler
> was a confessed Socialist and agnostic. . . . In September 1893 he
> and his congregants agreed to part, he to continue in free thought
> and socialism but later to return to Orthodoxy, they to hold fast
> to humanist Judaism.[25]

Schindler's successor, Charles Fleischer, continued in the ways
of his predecessor, and went beyond them. He called for an ethical
humanism based on democracy to replace the traditional faiths, a new
religion to be proclaimed by a new prophet like "Jesus, Isaiah." By
1908, he advocated intermarriage for America's Jews to build "a new
nation to emerge from the melting pot." As Fleischer was moving from
his ancestral faith toward a "free and natural religion" that would replace
both Judaism and Christianity, Schindler was returning to the ways of
his ancestors, to traditional Judaism, a return which in March 1911 he
explained to his former congregation in a sermon entitled:

Mistakes I Have Made

> When I came to Boston I was confronted with one great problem
> which I was expected to solve; namely, how to get people into the
> synagogue . . .

I tried reform . . . Neither the family pew, nor the choir and the organ, nor the abolishment of rites and rituals would fetch the neighbor . . .

I tried sensationalism—sensational lectures which the newspapers would publish. I went to the very verge of a yellow pulpit . . . Christians came to hear me. They praised me for what I said. But while they filled the temple, my congregation remained absent. . . .

I fell into an atmosphere of rationalism which then was spreading all over the world. It was the time of Ingersoll; it was the time when every one swore by Darwin, Huxley, and Spencer . . . I, too, . . . wanted to solve everything by reasoning. I forgot one thing—that religion does not rest upon reason. Religion rests on man's emotions . . . As a rabbi I should have appealed to that very emotion. The beginning of wisdom is the fear of God.

Reform should have meant merely a change of form, but not the destruction of the form. But in my shortsightedness . . . I did away with rituals and ceremonies . . . I took away whatever symbolism there was.

I believed in making the Jew like the Gentile. He was to be like [the] Gentile in appearance, in thoughts, in ceremonials, in everything. The more he became near to that ideal being like his Gentile fellowmen, the more I believed success would crown my work. It was a great mistake. There must be a difference . . . The Jew we shall have in years to come will be something different. The melting pot will not melt him. Assimilation, in which I believed, is a failure.

Fifty years ago we seemed near assimilation. Then a cloud out of the East brought here to us two millions of people . . . different from us in appearance and habits . . . and they brought a new spirit amongst us . . . This great army strong in the old ideals acting upon and changing our mode of thought, demanding from us change—this was the hand of God.

The Jew should differ from his neighbour. He can be on the same terms with him in politics, can be socially his friend, and he can do business with him from morning to night, but he must be, in his religion, a different person.

. . . We can never unite mankind into one great body. We can only unite them into groups.

That was something I have learned, only too late.

You may take a lesson from my experiences, and I pray to you to avoid the mistakes, which I made.[26]

Fleischer answered with a sermon in which he proclaimed: "I have gladly made the seeming mistake of encouraging assimilation."

Before a half century had passed, the congregation of Temple Israel
was far closer in spirit to the repentant Schindler than to the assimi-
lationist Fleischer.

In 1904, Rabbi Willowsky (Ridbaz), in the introduction to *Nimukei Ridbaz,*[27] a commentary on the first two books of the Pentateuch,
wrote about the Jews in America:

> . . . The Jews came to the United States, a land blessed with
> prosperity. Here they have prospered, and are honored among
> peoples. But the ways and customs of this land militate against the
> observance of the laws of the Torah and the Jewish way of life.
> For example, the rule that boys and girls must attend public school.
> A boy will spend most of his day in the public school where he
> learns the ways of the gentiles and becomes estranged from Ju-
> daism. Even when his father hires a tutor to teach him for an hour,
> all he will be able to learn is the prayers, and no more. Most boys
> of 13 and 14 don't even know to say their prayers.
>
> Sabbath observance is very difficult for one who is not truly
> pious, for by violating the Sabbath he can earn more money. . . .
>
> There are many God-fearing Jews in this land. When they
> see what is happening to their children, they curse the day they
> came to this land. I have also seen many Jews, who violate the
> Sabbath, yet whose hearts still ache, and who would flee if only
> they could.
>
> In matters of *kashrut,* many have fallen away. To this land
> have come people from all corners of the earth. Many who were
> unworthy in their own native lands, coming here displayed or-
> dination certificates as rabbis. Similarly, there were those of evil
> ways in their native lands, who came here and became butchers.
> They joined with the above-mentioned rabbis and now feed the
> public non-kosher meat. Many *shohatim* are no better.
>
> And the people care not who is the *shohet,* who is the butcher
> and who is the rabbi who gives supervision to both.
>
> When the Jews first settled this land, they did not have
> rabbis, . . . but were served by *shohatim-mohalim,* who did not
> know the laws pertaining to marriage and divorce. Even after
> qualified rabbis came to this country, matters did not change. The
> people had become accustomed to the *Mohel-Shohet-Marriage Per-
> formers,* who advertise their trade on signs outside their homes.
> These self-styled *Marriage Performers* have led many people to sin,
> officiating at the wedding of a man who had not properly divorced
> his first wife.
>
> Another evil which I found here is that anyone can be a
> publisher or an editor. Wicked men buy type and establish a pe-
> riodical which violates, desecrates and vilifies both Torah and

scholars. If a scholar or preacher exhorts his people to return to the Heavenly Father, he will be laughed to scorn in the jargon press.

Brothers and friends! When I came to this land to visit my brethren . . . I responded to their pleas . . . and decided to settle among them, to try to remedy the situation. I felt moved to accept their entreaties, for I saw that they were strong and sincere in this desire. So I said to myself, perhaps I'll be able to establish here a great Yeshiva, and bring here fine students from Europe. American Israel will be built only through the study of Torah. It has happened often in our history that Torah was introduced into a land by but a few scholars.

If I do not succeed in my hopes for Torah, why remain a rabbi here?

My advice and urging is:

Even though the laws of this land make it obligatory for the father to send his son to school, permission is granted to a Jewish community or a congregation to establish its own school, where the boys can study Torah, as well as those subjects which are taught by "teachers." The Poles who have come to this country have done so. They have established schools in their churches, to preserve and foster their faith. Why should we not do the same for our children?

If we do not bestir ourselves now, I am sore afraid that there will be no Jew left in the next generation.[28]

To the Zionists of America, assembled in Pittsburgh in 1903, he urged the establishment of day schools as the answer to the dangers of assimilation:

Give your attention to the education of your sons, for most of them have so assimilated among the population . . . that in twenty years there may not be Jews or Judaism left in this land. . . . Establish a school in every synagogue, in which half the time will be for God [religious studies] and half for you [secular studies]. . . . Dear brothers: This letter is written with heart's blood and not with ink.[29]

Despairing of a future for Jews and Judaism in America, the Ridbaz left for the Holy Land in 1905, settling in Safed. It took more than a half-century for the network of day schools that he urged to become a reality.

As a disciple of both Ahad Ha-am and Simon Dubnow, Israel Friedlaender labored for national and spiritual rebirth in Palestine and for fashioning a vital Jewish community in America, but he went further, emphasizing the *religious* component of Jewish nationalism and culture. "Judaism was essentially a *national* religion," he maintained; "the Jewish people was, first and foremost, a religious nation." Such a Judaism, stressing both its national and religious character, is possible in America as nowhere else in the Diaspora. Friedlaender set forth this thesis in "The Problem of Judaism in America," a lecture delivered before the Mikveh Israel Association of Philadelphia, on December 8, 1907.[30]

> It was the fatal mistake of the Jews of emancipation, . . . that, in order to facilitate their fight for political equality they introduced Judaism not as a culture, as the full expression of the inner life of the Jewish people, but as a creed, as a summary of a few abstract articles of faith, similar in its character to the religion of the surrounding nations. . . . Judaism became a church, the rabbis became priests and the Jews became a flock . . . Jewish education dwindled down to Sunday School experiments . . . The modern Jew satisfied his highest tastes and desires outside the Jewish camp, while in Judaism he only perceived a few colorless doctrines, which could be had elsewhere, and a few cold liturgical ceremonies, which did not always appeal to him. . . .
>
> If Judaism is to be preserved amidst the new condition . . . it must break the narrow frame of a creed and resume its original function as a culture, as the expression of the Jewish spirit and the whole life of the Jews . . .
>
> It will have to take in and digest the elements of other cultures. . . . while it will endeavor to preserve all those features of Jewish practice which give shape and vigor to Judaism. . . . It will give full scope to our religious genius. . . . It will develop our literature, create or preserve Jewish art in all its functions, stimulate and further Jewish scholarship. . . .
>
> The only place where such a Judaism has a chance of realization is America. For America . . . is fast becoming the center of the Jewish people of the Diaspora. . . . America has every chance of also becoming the center of Judaism, of the spiritual life of the Jewish people in the dispersion. Those who are on the spot may be slow or even reluctant to recognize it. But there is no thinking Jew outside of America whose eyes are not turned towards this country as the center of Judaism in the nearest future. America has the numbers which are necessary for the creation of a cultural center. It possesses the economic prosperity indispensable to a successful spiritual development. The freedom enjoyed by the Jews is not the outcome of emancipation, purchased at the cost of national suicide, but the natural product of American civilization. . . . The true American spirit understands and respects the traditions and

associations of other nationalities, and on its vast area numerous races live peaceably together, equally devoted to the interests of the land.

. . . He who feels the pulse of American-Jewish life can detect, amidst numerous indications to the contrary, the beginnings of a Jewish renaissance . . . The American Jews are fully alive to the future of their country as a center of Jewish culture. They build not only hospitals and infirmaries, but also schools and colleges; they welcome not only immigrants, but also libraries; not only tradesmen and laborers, but also scholars and writers.

But will a Judaism that endeavors to embrace the breadth and depth of modern life, leave sufficient room in the heart of the Jew for the interests and demands of his country? . . . A full and successful participation in all phases of American life is reconcilable with a deep attachment to Judaism in all its aspects. . . . Compromises will be unavoidable . . . But these compromises will never be such as to obliterate or mutilate the character of either. In the great palace of American civilization we shall occupy our own corner, which we will decorate and beautify to the best of our taste and ability, and make not only a center of attraction for the members of our family, but also an object of admiration for all the dwellers of the palace.

Friedlaender did not live to see the renaissance he predicted. While on a mission of mercy to the Jewish communities of the war-devastated Ukraine, he died a martyr's death in 1920.

7.

New Arrivals

THE DRAMATIC GROWTH OF THE JEWISH POPULATION OF THE UNITED STATES
during the last two decades of the nineteenth century continued in the
first two of the twentieth. America's population grew from 50 million
in 1880 to some 115 million in 1925. From some 250,000 in 1880 to
over 1 million in 1900, by 1925 American Jewry grew to more than 4
million. The sixteenfold increase was due to the massive migration
which transplanted one-third of East European Jewry to the New World.
At the beginning of the new century, only the Russian and Austro-
Hungarian empires had larger Jewish populations; a quarter of a century
later American Jewry had become the largest in the world. New York's
1.6 million Jews outnumbered those of the world's second-largest Jewish community, Warsaw, by more than five to one; and Chicago's
285,000 and Philadelphia's 240,000 ranked these American cities as third
and fourth largest in the Jewish world, outstripping such major Jewish
centers as Vienna, Budapest, London, Berlin, Paris, Lodz and Kiev.

In 1900, only six American cities had total populations greater
than the 400,000 Jews of New York. Twenty-five years later, New
York Jewry was America's "fourth city," surpassed in numbers only
by New York, Chicago and Philadelphia. In the four decades, 1877–
1916, the increase in the Jewish population was at a pace five times
greater than that of the general population.

The more than 2.5 million Jews who came to the United States
from 1830 to 1930 constituted one of the largest ethnic groups to immigrate in that period, exceeded only by the Germans (5.9 million),
the Italians (4.6 million) and the Irish (4.5 million). In the last two

decades of the nineteenth century almost 600,000 Jews arrived and three times that many, 1,800,415, came in the first quarter of the twentieth. From 1908 to 1924 (for which statistical data are available) Jews constituted 9.4 percent of the total number of immigrants admitted. The percentage of non-Jews who left the country during those years was 33.54 percent, while the percentage of Jews who left was only 5.18 percent of those admitted, bringing the net (number admitted less those departed) to 13.4 percent. In short, *one of every seven* immigrants who arrived and remained in the United States was a Jew.

The number of immigrants arriving annually fluctuated, depending on conditions in the lands of emigration and the host country. Thus, the Kishinev pogrom of 1903, which had a traumatic effect on Russian and world Jewry, caused a spurt in numbers from 76,203 in 1903 to 106,236 in 1904. The Russian revolution of 1905 and the widespread pogroms of that year produced annual increases: 1905: 129,910; 1906: 153,748. The economic crisis of 1907 in America caused a decrease from an annual average of 130,000 immigrants during the five-year period 1904–8 to an average of 80,000 in the four succeeding years. A temporary increase in 1913 and 1914 was followed by a precipitous decline in the war and postwar years 1915–20, to an average of less than 14,000 per year. Almost 120,000 arrived in 1921, but in that year the first of the restrictive immigration laws was enacted, followed by the Reed Johnson Act in 1924, when only 10,292 entered. The average to the end of the decade was about 11,000 annually, falling to 2372 in 1933.

The great immigrant wave which had made American Jewry the largest in the world came to an end, partly because emigration was shut off by the newly created Soviet Union, but chiefly because of the immigration laws enacted in the isolationist climate in America in the postwar years.

FROM OPEN DOOR TO RESTRICTED IMMIGRATION

The National Association of Manufacturers and local chambers of commerce favored an open-door policy of immigration. Not only did the immigrant mass provide low-cost labor; its availability could be counted on by the employers to stem the growing strength of the unions. Free and unrestricted immigration was also favored by immigrant groups themselves. Such organizations as the German American Alliance and the Ancient Order of Hibernians worked hard to keep the nation's doors open wide. They were supported in their efforts by the Democratic party, which saw the new arrivals as potential supporters, and they were protected by social reformers who saw the immigrants as victims of, rather than the cause of, social evils.

Organized labor, however, led by the American Federation of Labor, advocated restriction of the numbers admitted. The advocates of an Anglo-Saxon America argued for restricted and *selective* immigration. New England Brahmins, through their Immigration Restriction League, founded in 1894, warned against "mongrelization" of America. The racist prejudices of Western Americans against Asians, and Southern Americans against Blacks, turned them to the camp of the restrictionists. By the end of the nineteenth century, the contending forces had joined in battle; in the twentieth century, battle escalated into warfare.

The issue was as old as the nation itself. What was to be the character of the new nation: an extension of Anglo-Saxon civilization in the New World, or a new creation forged of the best creations and energies of the Old World? In the year of the Declaration of Independence, Thomas Paine declared for the latter: "Europe not England is the parent country of America." Less than a quarter of a century later, a political spokesman in the new republic, Harrison Gray Otis, pleaded: "If some means are not adopted to prevent the indiscriminate admission of wild Irishmen and others to the right of suffrage, there will soon be an end to liberty and property."

The restrictive tendencies in nativist sentiments in nineteenth-century America were countered by the economic needs for an ever-growing labor force, which only massive immigration could provide. Thus, a serious decrease in the number of immigrants during the Civil War years impelled Congress in July 1864 to enact the first national immigration law, the purpose of which was to encourage immigration. Although the law was repealed four years later, it had had its effects. Immigrants came in ever-increasing numbers: 5,246,613 in the 1880–90 decade.

The large number of immigrants and the change in their places of origin from northwestern Europe to the south and the east of the continent forced the issue of open door versus restriction to open debate. As the number of immigrants continued to increase and as the majority of arrivals came from Italy and Russia (i.e., Jews), the debate turned into argument, propaganda, lobbying. Those favoring restriction of immigration and selectivity of immigrants began to win victories, at first minor, then of consequence.

A law enacted on March 3, 1891, provided for exclusion of physically and mentally handicapped, of the morally undesirable and of "paupers or persons likely to become a public charge . . . any person whose ticket or passage is paid for with the money of another or who is assisted by others to come . . ."

The staid language of the law hid the anti-alien, and more specifically the anti-Jewish and anti-Italian prejudices which caused its enactment. An American correspondent to the Hebrew periodical *Ha-Magid* perceived its danger. His report from America, published July 3, 1891, warns:

> The United States of America is not what once it was: a land of fullest freedom . . . a land of one law for the native-born and the stranger . . . the hundreds of thousands of immigrants who came to America's shores are no longer welcomed with open arms . . . The day is near when the gates of the United States will be closed to immigrants. . . . The American legislature is already studying the question of immigration . . . to determine what kinds of immigrants America should accept. As soon as they finish with the Chinese, they will turn to the Jews and the Italians and find all kind of reasons for their exclusion. . . . The agitation against Jewish immigration has already taken on serious proportion. Who knows where it will end?[1]

The leaders of American Jewry were no less disturbed than *Ha-Magid's* correspondent by this ominous development. Esther Panitz wrote:

> From 1870 to 1891, when America as a whole was pro-immigrant, American Jewry was restrictionist in approach. . . . From 1891 to 1924 . . . a complete reversal of attitudes prevailed.
>
> . . .Acknowledged Jewish spokesmen such as Simon Wolf, Max J. Kohler, Abram Elkus and Louis Marshall . . . tried to demolish, or at best modify, every piece of restrictive legislation as it arose.[2]

Leading Jewish organizations rallied to take joint action in defense of Russian Jewish immigration. They did so out of fraternal concern for the welfare of their Russian brethren in need of the asylum America could provide, and out of understanding that an attack on any segment of the Jewish community threatened the larger community as well. On July 27, 1891, Simon Wolf, as spokesman for four national Jewish bodies which joined in protest against the restriction of immigration—the Independent Order of B'nai B'rith, the Jewish Alliance of America, the Baron de Hirsch Fund Trustees and the Union of American Hebrew Congregations—wrote to the secretary of the treasury:

> To close the avenues of this fine and liberty-loving country, that has always opened its gates to the down-trodden and unjustly persecuted, would be against the underlying genius and theory of our glorious and beloved constitution.
>
> Neither the letter nor the spirit of the laws of our country require us to "close the gates of mercy on mankind . . ."A very large number of Russian Hebrews sought this land of liberty as a

haven of rest. They have been assimilated in the mass of citizenship . . .

The Russian Hebrews are wrecked on their voyage of life; cast out on tempestuous oceans by inhuman machinations. National and international law should not interfere when humanity throws them life preservers.[3]

As if anticipating American Jewry's protest and plea, British-Canadian historian and restrictionist Goldwin Smith published an article on the Russian persecution of the Jews, in the *North American Review* (August 1891), in which he argued that it had been greatly exaggerated, and that if indeed persecution existed, one should look to the Jew as its cause. What begins as an examination of the anti-Jewish prejudice in Russia ends as an attack on the character of the Jew in general, and an accusation against the American Jew.

[The Jew] changes his country more easily than others. When the southern confederacy fell, its leaders generally stood by the wreck and did the best for those whom they had led; but Judah Benjamin went off to pastures new . . . The Jew in America . . . has not much reason to complain . . . his financial skill, sharpened by immemorial practice and aided by the confederacy of his kinsmen, makes him the master of wealth . . . The press is rapidly falling under his influence, and becoming the organ of his interests and his enmities.[4]

The article raised a storm of protest; rejoinders were many. Its net effect was to aid the forces advocating restrictive and selective immigration, and to alert the Jewish community to the anti-Semitic component of restriction advocacy.

The Immigration Restriction League, which led the battle for restriction and selection, made the distinction between the "old" desirable immigrants and the undesirable "new" immigrants. The league's founder, Boston Brahmin lawyer Prescott F. Hall, urged: "Let us continue the benefits of that selection which took place in the early days of the nation by sifting the immigration of today, so that no discordant elements shall enter to imperil the ideals and institutions of our nation . . ." To him and his colleagues the issue was clear. Will America "be peopled by the British, German and Scandinavian stock, historically free, energetic, progressive; or by Slav, Latin, and Asian races, historically down-trodden, atavistic, stagnant."[5]

The arguments of the league were bolstered by a forty-two-volume report of a study conducted in 1907–11 by the United States Immigration Commission, which contrasted northwestern and south-eastern Europeans. The former were characterized as stable components of the economy, scattered across the continent, skilled in trades and industry. The latter were portrayed as a temporary, installed labor force, concentrated in disease-ridden slums, marred by a high incidence of crime and insanity.

As a practical means of selecting desirable immigrants, the league proposed literacy tests. Senator Henry Cabot Lodge led the enactment of a law in 1896 which required that the adult immigrant be able to read forty words in any language. Such a requirement would have excluded one-fourth of the Jewish and far more of other immigrants then arriving. The law was vetoed by President Grover Cleveland, but attempts were made again in 1898, 1902, 1906, 1913 and 1915; the first three were defeated in Congress and the latter two vetoed by Presidents William Howard Taft and Woodrow Wilson.

Louis Marshall's argument against a literacy test is both practical and personal. In a letter to Governor Carrol S. Page of Vermont he wrote:

> An educated immigrant is not ordinarily the most beneficial. The ranks of the anarchists and the violent socialists are recruited from the educated classes. . . . It is the illiterate immigrants who are now building our railroads, and canals and subways. The native American shrinks from such labor . . . Personally, I know a great deal concerning the immigrant, because my parents were both of that class . . . The entire wealth of my father when he landed consisted of a five-franc piece. While he was able to read and write, I am sure that he would not have been able to read fluently the Constitution of the United States in German, the only language he could read, and that he would not have understood it; and yet you are able to say whether or not he has become a good citizen. What is true of him is true of millions who have come to this country from abroad.[6]

What added poignancy to Marshall's argument was the fact that the father who could not read nor understand the Constitution of the United States on his arrival begat a son who became one of America's leading constitutional lawyers.

As immigration increased, so did the agitation against it. In his *The Old World in New York* (1914), sociologist Edward Alsworth Ross speaks of "The East European Hebrew":

> east European immigrants lower standards wherever they enter . . . Most alarming is the great increase of criminality among Jewish young men and the growth of prostitution among Jewish girls . . . With his clear brain sharpened in the American school, the egoistic, conscienceless young Jew constitutes a menace.

The German Jew could take little solace in the fact that the subject of this venom was the East European Jew, knowing that while the author might make such distinctions, most readers would not.

Two years later, Madison Grant, in his widely read and influential *The Passing of the Great Race,* pictured the Nordics valiantly holding out against the engulfing hordes from the south and east of Europe.

World War I kept immigration low, a mere 110,618 immigrants (3627 Jews) in 1918. The war over, immigration surged to over 800,000 in 1921, and again anti-immigration sentiment came to the fore. In postwar, isolationist, xenophobic America, the restrictive/selective forces became dominant. On May 7, 1921, Congress enacted a law which limited "the number of aliens of any nationality who may be admitted . . . in any fiscal year . . . to 3 percentum of the number of foreign born persons of such nationality resident in the United States as determined by the . . . census of 1910 . . ."

The Immigration Act of 1924 provided that the following three years the percentage was to be cut from 3 to 2, and that the base year for calculation be moved back to 1890 when the north Europeans predominated in even greater numbers. After 1927, the maximum number of immigrants was to be 150,000 per annum. It was a law to do away with any sizable immigration from Eastern and southern Europe; such immigration as was permitted would favor immigrants from northern and Western Europe. Immigration decreased from over 700,000 in 1924 to less than 300,000 in 1925, Jewish immigrants declining from 50,000 to 10,000.

Laws reflect national sentiment. The 1921 law expressed America's desire that its doors no longer be open wide to "the homeless, tempest-tossed." As Congressman Albert Johnson phrased it, "the idea of asylum is played out forever." The 1924 enactment declared that it was proper for America to choose some as more desirable than others, and that that choice might justly and legally be based on racial or ethnic grounds.

Both laws also spoke to the Jews, the former to the prospective immigrant, saying to him that the welcoming "lamp beside the golden door" had grown dim, the latter reminding the American Jew, once again, that in the land which proclaimed to the world "that all men are created equal," some were considered "more equal than others."

THE MAKING OF AMERICANS

Congressman John Cable of Ohio in an article which argued for selective immigration in the January 24, 1924, issue of *The Outlook,* stated:

On the whole, our duty lies first with the alien now in our land. Give him the privilege of an education, teach him the history and ideals of our country, the duties and obligations of citizenship. This is the highest of duties—the making of Americans for a bigger, better America.

The message is clear. America needs the immigrants in order to grow. But the immigrant must quickly become an American. It calls upon "native Americans" to foster the Americanization of the immigrant as "the highest of duties."

Two decades earlier, in 1903, in a letter to *The American Hebrew*, Professor Morris Loeb of New York University, son of Solomon Loeb, a founder of Kuhn, Loeb & Co., and brother-in-law of Jacob H. Schiff, placed the matter of Americanization in the context of the relationship of the German and Russian Jewish communities. "The struggle with which we are faced," he writes, "is one between Eastern and Western civilization. Russian civilization is diametrically opposed to Western ideals."

It is our duty to care for his [the Russian Jew's] speedy Americanization even more than for his physical welfare. Experience has shown that the Jewish immigrant, once he was able to leave [Russia], could prosper without any outside help, particularly outside of the ghetto; but the entry to the land will be forbidden, if it becomes clear that they want to eat American bread, without acquiring American ways.[7]

Isaac Max Rubinow, an immigrant physician who turned to social work, attacked Professor Loeb in "The Jewish Question in New York City," an article about the German Jewish and Russian Jewish confrontation, which was published in the Russian Jewish monthly *Voskhod*. "You should be ashamed of yourself, Professor Loeb. . . . It is true that the Russian Jew eats bread, but it is also true that the American wears Jewish clothes. Doesn't this even up the score?" Rubinow saw the inevitability of Americanization—"Spiritually and socially the Russian Jewish immigrant will undoubtedly undergo a metamorphosis"—but he wanted this to be a natural process, not dependent upon the whims of others. He contended that uptown Jews were eager to Americanize their downtown brethren because of their own problems.

The wealthy Jew who suffers a great deal from social ostracism tries his best to erase his individuality and to compel the public to forget that he is a Jew. And when he imagines that he has succeeded, his Russian cousins shatter this idyll by the outward appearance of the latter.[8]

The motives were far more complex, however, ranging from self-serving to truly altruistic; complex also were the relationships between the communities, as the life and interests of Morris Loeb will indicate. His biography is a history of his time and his class, a generation born into the new wealth which post–Civil War America made attainable. Raised in a home which retained Jewish loyalties and accepted Jewish civic responsibilities, he became a leading member of a community of German Jews who took full advantage of the opportunities which America offered, and felt a sense of noblesse oblige toward their people. An extraordinary number of Loeb's contemporaries, removed by social, economic and religious distinctions from the mass of their Russian-born coreligionists, felt it their obligation to establish institutions which served the others. In part, it was a Jewish expression of the "Social Gospel" emphasis in the Protestantism of the time, and thus the American thing to do. But it was also a sincere desire to Americanize the immigrants for their own benefit. American Jews of German origin had done well, and they attributed their success not only to their native abilities and enterprise but also to the opportunities America provided. "To eat American bread," as Loeb phrased it, one had to acquire "American ways." This meant knowledge and use of the language of the land, participation in the institutions of the nation, and conformity to the way of life of its people. The radicals among the new immigrants were urged to alter their views. Why change an economic and social system which had so benefited those who had come before? The East European Orthodox Jews were encouraged to modify their ways. Why not take on a way of life which had brought acceptance to those who had arrived earlier?

Morris Loeb was among the first American Jews who turned from the family business to a career in academia. A professor of chemistry at New York University, he was active in the organizations of his profession, serving as president of the Chemists Club of New York. No less important to him was his career of Jewish service, which, in his day, was largely the maintenance of institutions that served the immigrant community. He is an example of the German Jewish elite who took their philanthropic mandate seriously. He assumed a position of leadership in the Americanization projects discussed below.

ON THE LAND

The Americanization of the East European immigrants demanded that they become part of the American community spread across the continent. To remain dwellers in self-created ghettos in the metropolises of the Northeast was not in the interest of America, the Jewish community or the immigrant himself. At the end of the nine-

teenth century, the independent farmer was looked upon as the quint-
essential American, the backbone of the nation. It was not lost on the
leaders of the American Jewish community that very few Jews were
among these respected stalwarts. There were those in the immigrant
mass, as we have noted, who aspired to a life on the land. Members
of the Am Olam movement, for example, came to the New World to
colonize it with cooperative, Socialist settlements. Thirty-two families
established a colony at Sicily Island, Louisiana, in the spring of 1882,
which a Mississippi River flood wiped out. A dozen regrouped under
their leader, Herman Rosenthal, to found Crimea in South Dakota in
the fall of the same year. The settlement Bethlehem of Judea was established nearby, but both were liquidated three years later because of
debts and the lack of preparedness for farm life. New Odessa, near
Portland, Oregon, survived five years of physical problems and social
stresses, but had to give up in 1887. Most immigrants, however, never
got beyond the port city of New York.

To this problem leaders of American Jewry addressed themselves
at the beginning of the century. In February 1900, Morris Loeb was
one of seven representatives of the Baron de Hirsch Fund and the Jewish
Colonization Association who founded the Jewish Agricultural and
Industrial Aid Society, to promote "agriculture among Jews in America
and the removal of those working in crowded metropolitan sections to
agricultural and industrial districts."[9] The Jewish Colonization Association had been established in 1891 by the greatest of Jewish philan-
thropists, Baron Maurice de Hirsch, the Franco-German railroad magnate.
His gift of $10 million was to be used to assist emigration of Jews from
those parts of Europe and Asia where governmental restrictions made
life untenable, and to have Jews settle in agricultural colonies in the
New World, chiefly Argentina. The stated purposes of the Baron De
Hirsch Fund included loans to immigrants from Russia and Romania;
transportation of immigrants to places where they might find work;
instruction in the English language and the duties of American citizenship; technical and trade education in special schools and workshops;
and instruction in agricultural work and improved methods of farming.
The first and last expressed the wishes of the baron; the others reflected
the views of the designated American trustees. Their essence can be
summed up as dispersal, technical training and Americanization.

THE INDUSTRIAL REMOVAL OFFICE

Throughout the era of mass immigration dispersion continued
as a goal. To realize it, two imaginative and, to some degree, successful
projects were launched. In 1901, the Jewish Agricultural and Industrial
Aid Society, in order to relocate the workers congesting the already

crowded East Side ghetto, engaged Louis Kahn to seek out places in which immigrants might be encouraged to settle, and to secure the cooperation of Jewish communities in receiving these newcomers. A store was rented on the Lower East Side, the sign above it reading INDUSTRIAL REMOVAL OFFICE, and the IRO was launched. Professor Morris Loeb was one of the two designated to take charge.

In the local communities, B'nai B'rith chapters assumed the task of arrangements and reception. The problems were formidable. Many communities resisted an influx of new immigrants who might become a burden and whose Old World ways might prove an embarrassment. One Midwestern city responded that it was ready to return two for every immigrant sent. Often, when the newcomer lost or failed to keep his job, the local charity administrators were quick to protest to the IRO headquarters.

The New York office was overrun by eager prospects, and registering and investigating them were far more demanding than had been anticipated. But the work went forward and by the end of the first year, over 1500 persons had been relocated at the modest per capita cost of $12. In the next year, the number doubled. That only 100 of the almost 3000 dispersed returned to New York is an indication of the success of the project.

In his annual report for the year 1904, Cyrus L. Sulzberger, chairman of the Removal Committee, reported that the endeavor not only removed "meager earners" from the densely populated seaboard cities to the interior, but also recast the occupational patterns of the workers. He noted that those immigrants who remained in New York tended to the needle trades, but those sent to inland communities entered a variety of occupations which "range alphabetically from baker to wood carver."

By 1910, at the end of a decade of activity, the IRO could report the relocation of 54,000 persons to more than 1300 cities and towns in all the 46 states and territories and Canada. The effective work of the organization came to an end with the outbreak of the war and the subsequent diminution of Jewish immigration. It remained in existence until 1922, when the restrictive immigration laws removed the need for it, and it was formally dissolved. Overall, it had sponsored the relocation of 79,000 persons, about 6 percent of the 1.5 million immigrants who arrived in that period.

What the IRO did for one far-Western Jewish community is recorded in the *History of the Jews of Los Angeles*:

> From its inception in 1900 . . . somewhat less than 5,000 moved to California, of whom perhaps 2200 to 2300 arrived in Los Angeles. . . . The Hebrew Benevolent Society took responsibility for receiving the removals and for helping them to settle. Summarizing

its activities for 1912, the society reported: "We have had 160 applications from the Removal Office for families and single persons to be sent to Los Angeles this winter. We gave our permission to 117 and refused 43. . . . Most of the persons were single men. . . . Once established . . . the emigrant worker sent for his family . . . A satisfied 'removal' served as a magnet for his larger family and acquaintances."[10]

What its activities did for individuals is attested to by one of many hundreds of letters in its files:

Gentlemen:

I shall never forget the favor you have done me in sending me to Milwaukee. In New York I suffered for fully seven years. I always worried where to find the next day's job, where to get money to pay my rent and from whom to borrow money.

Regarding Mr. G. to whom you have sent me . . . you cannot realize how hard he tried for us. He gave us some money and brought our baggage from the depot. The first week I earned $12 which actually delighted me. The coming week I shall make $18.00. I hope to be able to earn a livelihood for me and my family.[11]

THE GALVESTON PLAN

On October 25, 1906, Jacob H. Schiff wrote to Israel Zangwill, head of the Jewish Territorial Organization (ITO), in London,

I had a conference yesterday with Messrs. Cyrus Sulzberger, Oscar Straus and Professor Loeb upon the project about which we have been recently corresponding and we have reached the conclusion that the Removal Office at New York, with the experience and connections it has already secured, would be well in position to undertake the carrying out of my project, as far as the labor on this side is concerned.[12]

The letter spells out the scheme which Schiff called "my project." The ITO, together with the German Hilfsverein, would gather proposed emigrants in Russia, arrange steamship routes and finance their journey to America, directing them to Galveston. There, they would be met by representatives of the Removal Office, who would guide them and finance their journey to towns and cities west of the Mississippi. United States immigration laws forbade the encouragement and financing of immigration, so European Jewish philanthropic organizations would have to assume the costs of the operation till the immigrant set foot on American soil. Once here, American Jewry would take over, and Schiff pledged a sum of $500,000 "to the initiation of the project," which "should suffice to place from 20,000 to 25,000 people in the American 'Hinterland.' "

The motivation for what came to be known as the Galveston Movement was twofold. Overcrowded conditions in the ghettos of New York, Philadelphia and Boston were creating problems for both the German and Russian Jewish communities. The former was discomfited by sensational articles in the daily and periodical press about poverty, crime and disease in the immigrant community, the latter experienced the economic and social problems—cutthroat job competition, unsafe work conditions, inadequate housing, filthy streets and intergroup tensions—which beset the rapidly expanding immigrant mass cooped up in nonexpanding neighborhoods. For the sake of both, it would be wise to locate new arrivals beyond the port cities. As David M. Bressler, a leading social worker and manager of the IRO, explained it:

> The Galveston Movement, [was] organized with the purpose of popularizing the West and Southwest as objective points for Jewish immigration. . . . The immigrant, in throwing in his destiny with the newer sections of the United States, will reap the benefit of a growing country where the struggle for a livelihood is not so intense, and where the environment is more favorable.[13]

Historian Zosa Szajkowski saw a larger purpose:

> The disperson of immigrants throughout the United States was only one of Schiff's goals. His main desire was to effect the removal of as many Jews from Russia as possible because he did not believe that Russia would ever emancipate her subjects. In 1910 Schiff wrote to Israel Zangwill that in Galveston "we have an immediate outlet in the next few decades for 2,000,000 of our co-religionists."[14]

Schiff recalled a conversation in 1906 with Frank P. Sargeant, United States commissioner of immigration, in which the latter suggested that "it would be wise on the part of those having the weal of Jewish immigrants at heart to make an effort to deflect the constant and large stream of Jewish emigrants from Russia, from New York and other North Atlantic seaports to . . . the Gulf ports."[15]

The movement for restrictive immigration had gained enough adherents and influence so that some immigrants themselves were expressing anti-immigration sentiments. A letter to the editor of the *Forward* of March 24, 1906, argued:

> You want to convince me that the rush to America of so many foreigners is good for the American worker? . . . If it will continue the American worker will not be able to make a living. The Russian

Jew deserves pity; but does America have to worry for the entire world?

The immigrant arriving through less busy ports and settling in less crowded cities would become less "visible" to those who would keep him out. The purpose of the Galveston Movement was to alleviate the plight of those who arrived and to keep the doors open to those yet to come.

The problems were formidable. The depression of 1907 made the economic absorption of immigrants more difficult. The ITO was not the most reliable of partners. The Jewish Colonization Association, despite a personal presentation to it by Morris Loeb at a meeting at its headquarters in Paris, kept aloof. Only one steamship line carried passengers to Galveston. For the great majority of Russian emigrants, New York City was the America of their dreams; land beyond the Eastern seaboard was terra incognita, a place where Jews would no longer be Jews. The most formidable obstacle, however, was the United States Bureau of Immigration.

At its inception the project was not only suggested by the commissioner of immigration, but hailed by the secretary of commerce and labor, Oscar S. Straus, and President Theodore Roosevelt was reported to be particularly happy about the "effort to open a new door to immigration to the United States." By 1910, the Immigration Bureau, urged on by organized labor, began to curtail the project's work by ruling that it was violating the contract labor law, which forbade encouragement of immigration through the promise of employment. Through legal briefs and the marshaling of public opinion, Schiff and his co-workers waged a valiant battle, until the outbreak of the war, when the decline in immigration effectively put an end to the Galveston Movement.

In its eight years of activity, the Jewish Immigrants' Information Bureau of Galveston received and sent into the "hinterland" over 10,000 men, women and children. Many Midwestern and Western communities were strengthened and enriched by the newcomers. In 1910, Rabbi Ephraim Frisch of Pine Bluff, Arkansas, reported:

> 21 people were sent to us—15 men, 4 women and 2 children; 3 children have been born. . . . There were sixteen wage-earners; of these all but one had occupations—6 being tailors, 2 shoemakers, 2 blacksmiths, 1 iron moulder, 1 ring maker, 1 tinner, 1 carpenter and 1 barber. . . . They average between $13 and $15 a week now. . . . We have had some very gratifying experiences. We have also had some trouble, chiefly in connection with securing work at the beginning. . . . The native Jewish people are very friendly to them. . . . The Orthodox Jews, except the tailors and shoe-

makers, with whom the newcomers compete, are delighted to
receive them. . . .

The immigrants become Americanized very rapidly. They learn
to speak English quickly, even the older ones. . . . One little girl
was on the honor roll of the public schools in her first month after
landing.[16]

Americanization was far more rapid in Pine Bluff, Arkansas,
than on Pike Street, in the Lower East Side of New York. Dispersion,
then, was in the service of "The Making of Americans."

"TO TEACH THEM 'AMERICAN' TRADES"

"He was repeatedly president of the Hebrew Technical Institute," Cyrus L. Sulzberger wrote of Morris Loeb, "a form of philanthropy which, because of its educational features, particularly appealed
to him."[17] The institute was founded in 1884 by the United Hebrew
Charities of New York, the Hebrew Orphan Asylum and the Hebrew
Free School Association "for promoting industrial education among
Jewish boys." The three organizations were founded by German Jews;
the "Jewish boys" were the sons of Russian immigrants.

The turnover of students in the early days was high. The first
roll book notes various reasons for leaving:

Left, because his father does not want him to be a carpenter.
Left, as his parents want him to follow a "gentlemanly calling."
Left, because a pistol was taken from him.

A report on the institute's twenty-fifth anniversary records:

In Russia the work of a carpenter is looked down upon as one of
the lowest, and so it was not easy to induce these early immigrant
parents to send their boys to a school to learn "carpentry" . . .

Miss Annie S. Kantrowitz . . . went from house to house
to visit parents, to induce them to send their boys to a school where
they might learn use of tools and the beginnings of a trade.

It was at once recognized that pupils must be kept the full
day if the proper influence over them was to be gained.[18]

The course of study included the public-school subjects of English, mathematics, history and geography as well as the technical-
school curriculum, mechanical drawing, freehand drawing, wood-
working, wood carving, metal working, instrument making and applied electricity and physics. Lunches were served to students and faculty,
summer tramping tours were organized, and "when the new school
building was erected in 1896, shower baths were provided, and from
that time bathing has formed a regular part of the school program."

"The proper influence over them" was "Americanization," which would temper the immigrant dream of striking it rich in the Golden Land with the sober reality that hard, skilled work in service of the American economy is what America expects from those to whom it has opened its doors. The East European mother sang lullabies to a future scholar; the father labored long hours to produce a doctor, a lawyer; the German Jewish patrons built institutions to train carpenters, metal workers, electricians. On the list of ninety-four officers and directors who served the institute during its first twenty-five years, not a single one was from the immigrant community which the institute was founded to serve.

The Technical Institute was a venture in the "economic assimilation of the Jewish immigrant in the New World." Its purpose, as conceived by the officers and trustees, was described by Samuel Joseph, a professor of sociology at the College of the City of New York, whom the trustees of the Baron de Hirsch Fund selected to prepare an "account of their stewardship."

> They desired to wean away the immigrants from the needle industries and to make it possible for them to enter non-Jewish trades. To teach them "American" trades, American technical processes and methods, was to open the door for positions with American firms, non-Jewish unions, and, for the more able, to create opportunities for advancement in their field, through business or the professions. [19]

FOR BODY AND SOUL

From its founding in 1906, Morris Loeb served as president of the Solomon and Betty Loeb Home for Convalescents, in Westchester County, New York. The home was one in a remarkable network of hospitals, orphan asylums, homes for the aged, day-care centers, settlement houses and relief societies established by the German Jewish community, but in a spirit of philanthropy which often catered more to the wishes of the donors than to the needs of the patrons. The newcomer was expected to conform to the ways of these "American" institutions, many of which made little accommodation to the religious sensitivities of the immigrants. Thus, the Beth Israel Hospital was founded in New York City in 1890 by East European Jews "to meet the peculiar needs of sick poor among the Jewish immigrant population," the older German Jewish Mount Sinai Hospital being unable or unwilling to do so. "The strictly kosher dietary maintained for the patients" was listed as one of the *unique* features of Beth Israel.

From its reorganization in 1902 to his death, Professor Loeb served on the board of the Jewish Theological Seminary of America.

He joined other German Jews of Reform persuasion in maintaining an institution which would train the kind of rabbi who would aid in the Americanization of the children of the East European immigrants, and keep them from political and social radicalism.

"THE BENEFACTORS OF THE EAST SIDE"

Three thousand East European Jews met at the annual ball of their Educational League in 1903. The league was the Russian Jews' answer to the Educational Alliance sponsored and directed by the leaders of the German Jewish community. The Russian Jews wanted their own cultural institution, whose programs they could determine, whose policies they could control.

The announcement of the league's annual ball proclaimed, "We do not need any one's pity and benevolence," and the ball became a protest meeting by residents of the Lower East Side against their uptown benefactors. The dramatic form the protest took was a play—a satire written by the leading dramatist of the immigrant community, Jacob Gordin. *The Benefactors of the East Side* portrays a meeting in the home of a Jewish millionaire, called to discuss ways and means of raising the economic, physical, intellectual and moral level of the Jewish East Side. Isaac Max Rubinow described the contents of the play:

> Among those present at the meeting are the philanthropic ladies, a Christian to whom the Jewish aristocrats are catering, the Reverend Dr. Knobel [garlic in Yiddish], and, for the sake of contrast, Goldberg, the Jewish labor leader from the East Side, whose attire evokes sarcastic smiles. The Reverend Dr. Knobel outlines to Goldberg the main points of his philosophy, namely, the importance of living in peace with their benefactors and of concealing their Russian extraction, because the German Jews despise the Russian, et cetera. A series of rather humorous resolutions are adopted: 1. To open classes for cooking; 2. To cultivate music appreciation, whereby they will be enabled to improve their social status. The third points to the unsanitary conditions prevailing on the East Side and it recommends that model bathhouses be established, where the immigrants would be taught to take baths, etc. One of the lawyers present at the meeting stresses the need of introducing all sorts of sports, such as boxing and wrestling, because the inhabitants of the East Side devote too much time to reading and thinking. . . . All these proposals are interspersed with expressions of contempt for the Jews of the East Side . . . schnorrers and paupers. Goldberg makes a heated speech which is interrupted from time to time by the chairman's gavel, but the labor leader manages

to tell the wealthy people what he thinks of them and their attitude. . . . The public applauded enthusiastically.[20]

What the public applauded was an attack on the Educational Alliance, on whose board Loeb served. Its program was summarized by its superintendent, David Blaustein, in a paper read before the New York State Conference of Charities on November 19, 1903, titled, "The Making of Americans":

The plan of which I speak is the plan we have devised and which I have personally applied in dealing with the Jews who come from Eastern Europe, people who spoke one language of their own— Yiddish. We must teach them:
The language of America: The children in the public schools; the older people in evening classes. Many . . . were residents of an absolute monarchy so we teach them civics . . . the spirit as well as the law and history of the American Republic. It is part of our work to make the immigrant understand and feel a victory at Concord and Lexington, the Declaration of Independence, that he may feel his share in the glory of America, of which he is a part. We are striving to make a physically strong American, and physical culture is by no means one of the minor branches of our work. To give him social life, we have our roof concerts, our entertainments, our receptions, our dances. In Europe, religion is the fundamental fact of the Jews' existence. In America children [are] separated by a gulf from their parents. In our system we teach progress to the older, and the value of religious tradition to the younger. In Eastern Europe he learns the value of bribery, the absolute necessity of corruption. In America we teach him whence comes the authority of the court. American schools and American traditions bring the woman from the nonentity to a powerful factor. If we take her from the house, in reaction against the old semibondage, we tend to create a neglect of those domestic sciences, . . . To meet this, our system embraces classes in Domestic Art and Science in practical problems of home life.[21]

David Blaustein, who had come to America in 1886, at age twenty, from the Lithuanian provinces of the Russian Empire, was sensitive to the psychological needs of the immigrants to retain in the New World the cultural support system of language, folkways and religious rites, which they brought with them from the Old World. He stated that "evening schools should teach not merely the three R's but should develop the latent talents of the nationalities with which they deal."

Louis Marshall described Blaustein:

> He appreciated as few have, the moral and intellectual excellencies of the Jewish immigrant; the idealism and poetry of the Jew of Eastern Europe. . . .
>
> He believed in the establishment of a religious service, which, while adhering to the tenets of orthodoxy, conformed to the ethics of the country. . . . He felt to the very marrow of his bones the importance of a Yiddish press, which would not corrupt and contaminate, but would be made the vehicle for converting the Yiddish-speaking immigrant into a self-respecting Jew and an American.[22]

The last was the key phrase. East European Jews resented a juxtaposition which made "the Yiddish-speaking immigrant" and "self-respecting Jew" mutually exclusive. Indeed, they often expressed the conviction that when it came to Jewish self-respect, the English-speaking German had much to learn from the Yiddish-speaking immigrant.

German Jews could not understand the reluctance of their coreligionist to undergo rapid Americanization, and the latter could not accept their brother-Jews' insistence on Americanization as the panacea for all ills. America did not treat them kindly, why hasten to succumb to its ways? Corrupt politicians used them, police terrorized them, neighbors attacked them, the boss and landlord took advantage of them, their children were embarrassed by them and their German Jewish benefactors strove hard to change them.

East European Jews were necessarily ambivalent about Americanization. They realized that to retain their children they had, to some degree at least, to enter their world, for they would not remain in theirs. But the process of imposed Americanization demanded of them too sudden an alteration of their life. They preferred a slow, evolutionary acculturation which would permit them to live in the security of the old and known ways, even as they were taking on the new.

The Americanization of the East European Jews was far more rapid than that of other immigrants who arrived at the same time. Historian Thomas Kessner contrasts the rate of Americanization of Italian and Jewish immigrants, who arrived and settled in New York between 1880 and 1915.

The Italians:

The persistence of the Italian attitude among the offspring is evident from a number of indications: The second generation's occupational similarity with their elders, especially in the concentration of Italian sons in unskilled jobs; the persistence of Italian offspring in first-generation neighborhoods. . . . American-born Italian offspring did not differ much from their Italian-born brothers in occupational interests . . . attendance in American schools made no noticeable difference in occupational outlook.

The Jews:
Jewish offspring did not follow their parents so closely. They were reared to exceed their parents' achievements . . . created tremendous tensions. . . . They must succeed. They must be ambitious. . . . Thus by 1905 Jewish offspring were moving into white-collar positions as professionals, sales people, clerical workers, shopkeepers. Unlike the Italian, place of birth did make a difference. Jewish offspring born in America, open to its training and schools, did better than their European born brethren . . . moved up the ladder more quickly.[23]

At the beginning of the century, newspaper articles marveled at the progress made by the sons and daughters of the immigrants in the public schools: EAST SIDE LOVE OF LEARNING, a headline in the September 18, 1898, issue of the *New York Tribune* declared. Eight years later the same newspaper wrote about "The Largest Public School in the World," P.S. 188 on the Lower East Side, with "seats enough for the students of Yale, Brown, Amherst, and Bowdoin combined." By 1914, thirty colleges and universities had chapters of the national Jewish students' organization, the Intercollegiate Menorah Association. By the end of World War I, 85 percent of the students at the College of the City of New York, 29 percent of Hunter College (New York), 21 percent of New York University, 18.5 percent of Temple (Philadelphia), 15.7 percent of Columbia (New York) and 15.3 percent of Johns Hopkins (Baltimore) were Jewish.

Americanization was as rapid as it was inevitable. To some degree, it was speeded up and refined by the institutions which the German Jews set up for that purpose, but largely it was accomplished rapidly and successfully by the desire of the immigrants to afford their children those opportunities which had been denied them in the Old World.

8.

Making a Living

"ECONOMICALLY, THE RUSSIAN JEWISH IMMIGRANT MASSES ARE NOT FARING badly at all," Isaac Max Rubinow reported in 1903. He attributed this well-being to economic progress of the country as a whole and proudly notes that "we did not lag behind in this economic advance."

> Jews have in their midst an appreciable number of millionaires . . . There are Jewish bankers and factory owners in all branches of industry, but the unique Jewish branch is the garment industry, both retail and wholesale. In the manufacture of men's and ladies' garments and undergarments the Jews of New York play an important role. Clothing in America has become much cheaper, and there is no doubt that the neatly dressed American public is indebted to the tattered, sometimes soiled, Jewish masses.[1]

At the apex of the American Jewish socioeconomic triangle stood a small coterie of investment bankers, mining and metals entrepreneurs and "merchant princes." They were more visible than powerful. Jewish wealth was concentrated mainly in New York City. "It is estimated that within the radius of fifteen miles from New York City Hall there are more Jews than in the whole of Germany," Beckless Willson reported in 1903 in his *The New America: A Study of the Imperial Republic.*[2] "Slowly but surely, the Jew is permeating the whole commercial life of New York, and getting the control of many trades within his fingers. . . ." Newspapers found the "new Rothschilds" made good copy. Readers welcomed stories which bolstered their view of America as the land of limitless opportunities for all, and which, at the same time, justified their inherited prejudices that the Jews, in manner fair or foul, take fuller advantage of opportunities available than any other part of the population. Willson complained that, while the Jews were only about one-eightieth of the population, "yet they claim 115 out of the 4,000 millionaires of the country—about two and a half times as many as they are entitled to."

The Jewish millionaires were almost all in the German Jewish community and had risen from humble beginnings in the post–Civil War American geographic and economic expansion. The Seligmans began as peddlers in Pennsylvania, Alabama and Missouri, became wholesale clothiers in New York and then gold merchants in San Francisco. With the capital accumulated they formed the banking firm of J. & W. Seligman and Co. which established offices in leading American and European cities. The company helped finance railroads, the Panama Canal, public utilities and the variety of industrial enterprises that investment banks help underwrite.

The prolific and public-minded Guggenheims began as horse-and-buggy peddlers in the coal fields of Pennsylvania, expanded into the manufacture of lye and stove polish, entered the embroidery business and used the monies realized to move into mining, smelting and refining which established their great fortune. The anthracite fields of Pennsylvania also provided a peddling livelihood for recent immigrant Marcus Goldman, who later joined fellow immigrant Joseph Sachs to form Goldman-Sachs.

The Lewisohn brothers' fortune was made in copper mining which was made possible by their ostrich-feather import business. The Lehmans, sons of a Bavarian cattle dealer, were cotton brokers in Montgomery, Alabama, before coming to New York and establishing Lehman Bros., which in time became one of America's largest investment banking houses.

Julius Rosenwald, born in Springfield, Illinois, went to New York to work in an uncle's clothing store, opened his own, established a clothing manufacturing firm which he moved to Chicago, and bought into the Sears, Roebuck mail-order firm. Under his leadership it became the largest merchandising firm in the United States. Its catalogs brought uniformity to American styles in clothing, furnishings and notions, and to the family one of America's great fortunes. The Strauses of Macy's began their American activities in Talbotton, Georgia, came to New York after the Civil War, sold china and glassware, leased the basement of R. H. Macy and Co. for a crockery display and, in 1887, became owners of the business, which later could boast itself the "largest department store in the world." Adam Gimbel came from Bavaria in 1835. Like so many fellow immigrants, he peddled in the Mississippi Valley and opened a store in Vincennes, Indiana. His sons, Jacob, Isaac and Charles, followed the father's example, opening department stores in Milwaukee and Philadelphia, and the flagship store in New York.

Solomon Loeb and Abraham Kuhn (who had started as a peddler) prospered as dry-goods retailers and boys' pants manufacturers in Cincinnatti. Kuhn returned to Frankfort, Germany; Loeb moved on to New York and became a private banker. In Frankfurt, Kuhn found Jacob Schiff, and suggested to him that Loeb might have a position for him. Schiff wrote, Loeb responded, and in 1873 Schiff was off to New York. Two years later, he married Solomon Loeb's daughter, and ten years after that, he became head of Kuhn, Loeb & Co. Railroad financing made the firm second only to J. P. Morgan in private investment banking. Edward H. Harriman's Union Pacific and James J. Hill's Great Northern Railway, as well as the Pennsylvania, the Baltimore and Ohio and other roads were financed, for Schiff early recognized that a rail network serves as the arteries of a thriving industrial society.

The lives and careers of the turn-of-the-century Jewish millionaires were success stories in the best American "rags to riches" tradition. To their credit, they undertook leadership in Jewish as well as general philanthropic endeavor. The names of Schiff, Guggenheim, Lewisohn, Straus, Rosenwald, Seligman, Lehman graced the letterheads of the major Jewish charitable institutions and led the lists of contributors to causes Jewish and general. Their fortunes were considerable, the Guggenheims and Julius Rosenwald being listed as among the thirty richest men in America in 1909 by Gustavus Myers in his *History of the Great American Fortunes*.

Rich and influential as the American Jewish economic elite were, they did not compare to the Jewish bankers and entrepreneurs of Europe, nor did their wealth begin to match that of America's wealthiest families—the Morgans, Mellons, Rockefellers, Vanderbilts, Du Ponts, Harrimans, Carnegies. Jacob Lestchinsky argued:

> the place occupied by Jews, including the German Jews, in the economic life of America remains the same as formerly in Europe, with one exception: in Europe Jews played a dominant role in banking and on the stock exchange . . . the bankers Kuhn Loeb & Co., Lehman Bros., Speyer & Co., J. W. Seligman and Co. . . . do not have and never had nearly as much importance here as Jewish bankers in England, let alone Germany and Austria, Russia and Poland, Hungary and Roumania, where Jews pioneered and dominated in these branches of the economy throughout the nineteenth century and until the first World War.

And he explains why:

> In central, and partly in Western Europe, Jews stood at the cradle of infant capitalism. They were the possessors of liquid capital and

for this reason, as well as for others, they were the pioneers and innovators in many fields of capitalist development, particularly in banking and credit, railroad building, export and import, etc.[3]

But as for the American experience:

> German Jews came to America when the native capitalists already had important and firmly entrenched positions in these branches of the economy. They came here without capital, with the natural consequence that they have remained . . . outside the top positions of the economic life of the country.[4]

The Russian Jew came to America later, with even less capital. But Abraham Bisno, deputy inspector of workshops and factories for the state of Illinois, observed at the beginning of the century that the change in the economic condition was most rapid among the Russian Jews in the United States. "The transition period from the junk peddler to the iron yard owner, from the dry goods peddler to the retail or wholesale drygoods merchant, from the cloak maker to the cloak manufacturer is comparatively short." He noted that these immigrants "seem able to develop business methods of their own, which in many instances successfully defy or modify well-established economic laws." They launched and carried on their businesses with little or no capital, and competed successfully against larger factories and well-established mercantile establishments. Bisno also reports that he met "few wage-earners among Russian Jewish people who regard it as their permanent lot in life to remain in the condition of laborers for a wage."[5]

Despite all aspirations, the great majority did remain laborers, and in the first decade of the century, because of the steady stream of cheap labor which mass immigration supplied, their condition did not improve. The wealth of the nation was increasing at a ratio twice that of the wages earned by its workers. Skilled workers did make a good living, but the unskilled labor crowding the tenements had little to justify the trauma of uprooting and relocation. A New York correspondent of the journal for prospective emigrants, published in St. Petersburg, *Der Jüdischer Emigrant* (Yiddish), warned in 1911:

> It is remarkable that so many are of the opinion that the American worker earns the best wages in the world. The naive belief is deeply rooted on the other side of the ocean, that the worker in New York "lives like a count": he has a fine and comfortable dwelling, eats the finest foods and can afford all luxuries. If one examines the condition with open eyes, one perceives a completely different picture. The dwelling is neither nice nor comfortable, the food is not too tasty, and the pleasures are few. . . . A professor of economics . . . in a recently published work demonstrates . . . that

the American worker does not earn enough to adequately provide for his family.

He also reported that a recent conference on child labor disclosed that thousands of young children labored in their tenement apartments on work brought home from the shop by their parents. Worst of all was unemployment. The director of one of the leading charities reported that of five thousand families who turned to the charity, 69 percent did so because of unemployment.

> The smallest ad asking for a "hand" attracts hundreds of the un-employed. . . . A middle-aged, unskilled laborer has little chance to find employment. . . . Of 400,000 union members, 62,851 were unemployed in 1910. One hundred and ninety labor unions re-ported to the Bureau of Statistics an unemployment rate of 24 percent for the first half of 1911.[6]

Despite such warnings, the mass migration continued, bringing to America the labor force which produced its clothing, which, as Abraham Cahan's David Levinsky states it, made the average American woman the average best-dressed woman in the world.

Rubinow reported on the visible presence of Jews in the retail trade in dry goods, clothing and furniture. "The signs: Silberstein, Goldstein, and Cohen testify to that . . ." He also maintained that the Jewish masses of New York were better off economically than other immigrants; "extreme poverty . . . is not prevalent in the Jewish sec-tion." He was less sanguine about the condition of the Jews in the interior ("and by interior I mean the whole country"), whom he divides into four economic groups: persons of the free professions, the large merchants, the small businessmen and the peddlers.

> The members of the first group . . . are in the minority and have no difficulty in adjusting. . . .
> The important merchants are for the most part German Jews who are Americanized, speak English fluently and have the poise and bearing to be able to become integrated into the community.
> . . . The small shopkeepers are for the most part Russian Jews . . . most of them speak broken English . . . earn a living but are isolated from the rest of the community which look upon them with contempt . . . they live in hope of returning to New York or to another large city. Finally, the peddlers are total out-casts.[7]

There was a time when peddling was a respectable source of livelihood. In rapidly expanding nineteenth-century America, the ped-dler served the highly useful function of being a portable country store for the farmers and ranchers pushing back the frontier. Many immigrant peddlers used the money earned to open stores, and a few of the most enterprising among them, to expand their stores into lucrative department stores. By the twentieth century, all this had changed. Improved means of transportation and the growth of towns and the country stores within them erased the need for "portable stores." Free rural postal delivery and mail-order purchasing made peddling expendable. The mass immigration of men without skills increased the number who turned to peddling. The cutthroat competition which resulted made peddling at best a marginal economic pursuit, and made the peddler a figure bordering on the itinerant pauper. In the cities, some took to customer peddling, the peddler providing his customers with goods which they were seeking. Serving as a broker, he became a respected member of the immigrant community.

The generalization that, in the nineteenth century, the Jewish immigrant took to peddling while in the twentieth he entered a shop, is essentially true. In both, he was entering a chink of the economy which needed filling; in both, the choice of occupation was dictated. The desire of most was a mercantile establishment or small factory. For a considerable number, the imposed occupation eventually provided the means to establish the desired one.

Abraham Bisno found Jews at the beginning of the century "scattered through the industries" of Chicago.

> I find them employed as iron molders, machinists, locomotive engineers, sailors, farm helpers, boilermakers, butchers at the stock yards, street sweepers, section hands on railroads, motormen and conductors on the street cars . . . brick layers, carpenters, steam-fitters, plumbers; in bicycle plating shops; in manufactories of electrical appliances, of iron beds and springs, of shoes, of wood work and of upholstery; in tin, mattress and picture frame factories; and in bakeries. But the industries in which they are employed in the greatest numbers are the sewing and cigar trades. . . . A very large number speculate on the notion of opening, in course of time, a shop for themselves or going into business of some kind, or educating themselves out of the condition of the working class.[8]

Though he discovered a number of doctors, lawyers and teachers, he found far greater numbers employed in stores and offices "to obtain business training." He also noted that a new form of peddler, the rag peddler, was ubiquitous, as many as two thousand in Chicago. Their more established business colleagues dealt in old clothes, furniture and produce. Of the latter, "some develop into grocery storekeepers."

Grocery stores, candy stores, soda water stands, newspaper kiosks and neighborhood stores selling cheap clothing, dry goods and notions

were the immigrants' main business enterprises. The *Want Ads* section
of the *Yiddisches Tageblatt,* New York, December 25, 1910, offered
among other "business opportunities":

> Delicatessen near big shops . . . Good established seltzer busi-
> ness . . .
> Grocery store: Rent $25 with five rooms, business to $200 a week . . .
> Grocery, Butter & Egg corner store . . . Jewish, Christian trade,
> large stock weekly trade: $400, all cash. . . .

The history of the Los Angeles Jewish community shows that
businesses tended to be family firms "taking in brothers and brothers-
in-law . . . sons and sons-in-law."

> Moritz, with his cousin Eugene Meyberg . . . established the Los
> Angeles Gas and Electric Fixture Manufacturing Company. Max
> joined his brother and cousin . . . staying until 1919. The firm . . .
> continued until the death of the founders, after which it was liq-
> uidated in 1935. Simon Nordlinger, veteran jeweler, passed his
> business on to his sons, who . . . stayed in business until they
> sold out in 1923. S. Marshutz, an optician . . . established the
> Marshutz Optical Company in 1916. His sons Stephen and Her-
> bert, each possessing an optometric degree, entered the business
> during the 1920's.[9]

Immigrant Jews who later became leaders of their industries
remembered their first jobs in America. Harry Germanow, who became
one of the world's largest manufacturers of watch crystals and crystal
machines, recalled long hours, dangerous working conditions and discrimination in hiring in the first decade of the century:

> I accepted a job at Baldwin Locomotive Works for $9.00 per
> week. . . . The building was eight or ten stories high. The ceilings
> were very low. The machines were very crowded and dangerous.
> People were getting hurt every day, so I quit and got a job at Crane
> Shipyards. . . .
>   One morning at 10 o'clock I met with an accident. . . . My
> second finger of my right hand caught in open gears and chopped
> a piece of my finger off . . . I was taken to a hospital where my
> finger was trimmed and bandaged. I was paid for the day's work
> till 10 o'clock only. . . .
>   We worked overtime everyday until 10 o'clock except Sat-
> urdays. . . . I . . . went to Elizabeth trying to get a job with the
> Singer Sewing Machine Co. . . . It was not easy. The Singer Co.
> did not care to hire Jewish people.[10]

Oscar Handlin observed:

The unrestrained flow of people across the Atlantic . . . relieved every American entrepreneur of concern about this [labor] element in the production system. Docility compensated for the immigrants' lack of skill. . . . Satisfied with a meager level of consumption, they left their employers a substantial surplus of profits that could flow back into economic expansion.[11]

This was true of the Jewish immigrants who came at the end of the nineteenth century, but became increasingly less true of those who arrived in the twentieth. Jacob Lestchinsky writes, "with the turn of the twentieth century, we already encounter a Jewish immigrant mass with a majority of workers, but having a unique character." It was a working class in its first generation, having but recently acquired labor skills in the textile factories of Lodz and Bialystok or in the workshops of Warsaw. It came to America, not with the docility of a labor force looking for work, but rather with the enterprise of petite bourgeoisie seeking opportunities "to transact business." The work skills they brought were a recent acquisition. What they also brought was "a business tradition of many centuries . . . where the artisans . . . had to purchase their raw materials and enter into combination and competition with others."[12] The labor skills they brought were in themselves a commodity which had market value, and after a brief period of adjustment they set about to "enter into combination" which would secure for them greatest return for the sale of this commodity. It did not take them long to recognize that in the clothing industry into which they were thrust, managerial skill and daring were more essential than capital; labor skills—designing, cutting, sewing—were more important than the raw material. The employer sought workers who were docile and satisfied with meager compensation; the immigrant worker responded with mass organization and united action. For the workers their presence in the labor force was a temporary expedient (which most often lasted a lifetime) during which they had to preserve their strength and stamina, and build up sufficient capital to leave the labor force for middle-class economic pursuits. Jewish immigrant workers were not only a member of a *first*-generation labor class, they were a *one*-generation labor class. They did not want their sons to join them in the shop, nor did small storekeepers expect to turn the grocery store (unless it became a supermarket chain) over to their descendants.

THE GARMENT INDUSTRY

German-born Meyer Greentree arrived in America as a young man in 1840, and like many of his fellow immigrants, he took to peddling. Beginning in New England he followed the westward migration of Yankees and in 1843 reached Rochester, New York, where he went to work in the dry-goods store of Sigmund Rosenberg. A year later he married the lady who had established the first clothing-manufacturing concern in the city. Within two years, he took over the shop located on Front Street, which produced children's clothing. Joseph and Gabriel Wile joined Greentree to form Greentree and Wile in 1848, and laid the foundation for the largely Jewish garment industry in Rochester, an industry which dominated the economy of the city to the end of the century. In the 1860s, of the thirteen leading firms, twelve were all or in part Jewish-owned. By 1870, the industry employed a greater number of workers than any other. In the 1880s over two hundred traveling salesmen placed the manufactured men's clothing in stores (generally Jewish-owned) throughout the country. A chronicler of the Jewish community of Rochester wrote in 1911:

> Little could [Greentree] have imagined that in a city of 225,000 inhabitants, more than one-fifth . . . would derive their sustenance from the manufacture of men's, boys' and children's clothing. . . . From the little Front Street pant shop have sprung about 40 commercial houses and most of them are in themselves "Little Cities of Industry." . . . A conservative figure from an inside source, places the total amount of business done at approximately $22,000,000 annually. . . . Rochester, twenty-second among the Cities of the United States in population, is third in the amount of its clothing output. [13]

First in clothing output was, of course, New York City. In 1885, Jews owned 234 of its 241 garment factories. From 1880 to 1920, the value of the output of the industry increased fifteenfold from $60 million to $900 million. By 1950, the figure was over $4 billion. An industry founded largely by Jews, it has remained largely in Jewish hands, but the number of Jews in the labor force diminished with increasing rapidity in the interwar era.

The main reasons for Jewish entrepreneurs entering the soft-goods industry was that it was a low capitalization, labor-intensive, high-risk enterprise. Jews had come to America with little or no capital, nor were they in a position to borrow. Investors preferred enterprises which promised greater security and greater return, industries which would take fullest advantage of the abundant natural resources. It was easier to contend with the earth ready to yield up its bounties than with a volatile labor force clamoring for higher wages. Jews who arrived late on the American scene had to seek out economic opportunities in the crevices of an already established economy. To provide clothing for those furnishing the muscle for the industrialization of America was an opportunity which they quickly seized.

Little capital is needed when the parlor or back room of a tenement apartment can serve as workshop, and when the tools of production—needle, sewing machine, flatirons and shears—are supplied by the workers. Wife, children and other members of the family were the initial labor force. When an expanded labor force was needed, it was provided by the steamships disgorging their cargoes of immigrants seeking jobs. This constant source of cheap labor kept wages low and labor force docile. Raw material could be obtained from wholesalers at little carrying cost because of the quick turnover, the time span from raw material to finished product being so brief. Because sales depended more on the ever-changing whims of fashion rather than on product loyalty, newcomers to the trade had a relatively high chance for success. Organization, improvisation and a keen sense of the market receptivity were more important than capitalization, and the control of raw material and the markets.

The first branches of the needle trades Jews entered were the manufacture and sale of women's wear and material, and household fabrics. These were soon joined by ready-to-wear men's clothing, which after the Civil War gained wide acceptance. Wearing of uniforms removed the stigma of uniformity of dress, and the comparatively low price of a ready-to-wear suit made customers of middle-class Americans and of the laboring class as well. Ready-to-wear clothing brought a uniformity of dress which in turn added to American egalitarianism, and clothes became less and less a means to distinguish between social classes.

Because the needle trades are labor-intensive, and the flow of cheap labor was constant, mechanization did not render the small shop impractical. The tools of production which "mechanized" tailoring—the sewing machine and the cutting and ironing machines—were relatively simple and inexpensive. Where savings could be effected was in keeping wages low and hours long. This was accomplished by the contractor, who received goods from manufacturer or jobber, then organized a labor force to turn them into the finished product. Because he worked with his laborers, and could therefore use newly arrived, relatively unskilled labor, he was able to keep wages lower and working hours longer than those of workers in the factories. Such enterprises, called "outside shops," were useful to large manufacturers not only because they could produce at lower capital investment, but also because they served to keep a lid on the demands of the more skilled workers in their factories, the "inside shops." The mobile work force of the "outside shops" was difficult to identify and organize. They were often, as we noted, members of the family or *landsleit* of the employer, looking upon themselves less as workers and more as potential employers. The industry rested on a complicated, delicately balanced relationship among manufacturer, contractor and worker. When the balance was upset, through the desire to exploit or the pressure of competition, unrest developed which escalated into strike and lockout.

Many newly arrived immigrants chose (or were forced by circumstance to choose) employment in the "outside shops," where wages were lower, hours longer and working conditions palpably worse. But they provided unskilled immigrants with a more homelike atmosphere: they could arrange not to work on the Sabbath, and they could escape the hostility which skilled factory workers expressed toward new arrivals. But work in the "outside shop" ("sweatshop" was its more descriptive name) was fraught with dangers: unsanitary conditions, which made many a laborer susceptible to the dread plague of the New York East Side or Chicago West Side ghettos, tuberculosis (or consumption as they called it); seasonal employment ("We have five seasons here: summer, fall, winter, spring and slack," the garment worker would lament); irregularity in payment of wages; and the possible bankruptcy of the contractor which left the worker without any pay. Bernard Weinstein recalled: "The life of the green immigrants in the Eighties was a veritable hell. . . . Today it is difficult to imagine how people could exist in such conditions." Jacob Riis described a sweatshop in his *How the Other Half Lives*:

> Five men and a woman, two young girls, not fifteen, and a boy who says unasked that he is fifteen, and lies in saying it, are at a machine sewing "kneepants" . . . The floor is littered ankle-deep with half sewn garments. . . . The faces, hands, and arms to the elbows of everyone in the room are black with the color of the cloth on which they are working . . . How much do they as "learners" earn? "From two to five dollars" [a week].
>
> . . . They work . . . to nine o'clock at night, from daybreak.
>
> . . . We stumble upon a nest of cloakmakers in their busy season. Six months of the year the cloakmaker is idle, or nearly so. Now is his harvest. . . . Seven dollars is the weekly wage of this man with his wife and two children . . . There was a time he made ten dollars a week and thought himself rich . . . The other cloakmakers aver that they can make as much as twelve dollars a week, when they are employed, by taking their work home and sewing till midnight.[14]

Edwin Markham, author of "The Man With the Hoe," alerted the readers of *Cosmopolitan* magazine (January 1907) that in New York City alone there were 60,000 children "shut up in the home sweatshops."

> You can see them—pallid boy or spindling girl—their faces dulled, the backs bent under a heavy load of garments piled on head and shoulder . . .

. . .The little worker sits close to the inadequate window, struggling with the snarls of thread or shoving the needle through unyielding cloth . . . a child may add to the family purse from 50 cents to $1.50 a week . . . In the rush times of the year . . . there are no idle fingers in the sweatshops.

. . .Many of this immense host will never sit on a school bench.

Markham rises to righteous indignation against the elite of a society which forces such conditions upon its immigrant population: "Is it not a cruel civilization that allows little hearts and little shoulders to strain under these grown-up responsibilities, while in the same city a pet cur is jeweled and pampered and aired on a fine lady's velvet lap on the beautiful boulevards?"

The haphazardly organized, economically irrational and socially deleterious sweatshop could not long survive. Under twin pressures from labor and capital, it gave way to a renewed factory system. Manufacturers preferred the new system because it permitted greater use of machinery which made for lower unit costs. Workers preferred it, because it enabled them to effect industrywide unionization, which was accomplished by the two great clothing unions, the Amalgamated Clothing Workers and the International Ladies' Garment Workers Union.

An observer writing in *The Outlook* (November 21, 1903) sees the change as a mixed blessing for the worker. True, in the sweatshop, "positions are tense, their eyes strained, their movements quick and nervous . . . Among operators twenty years is an active lifetime. Forty-five is old age. They make but half a living. . . ." But the system cannot last, for "in these days of machine invention, a process to live must not only be swift and cheap; it must be able, by saving labor, to grow forever swifter and cheaper." So, the factory system of "endless saving, dividing, narrowing labor . . . forty operators bend over machines, and each one sews the twentieth part of a coat." The factory offered better working conditions, more light, more air, steadier work and higher wages for the skilled, but lower wages for the unskilled, whose numbers increased because machines were replacing human skill. The work was also "more minute, more intense, more monotonous." So, though hours were shorter in the factory than they were in the sweatshop, "the pocketmaker is often as exhausted at 6:00 P.M. as the coatmaker was at 10:00 P.M."

LABOR ORGANIZES

The long struggle between Jewish workers and employers began in 1888 with the organization of the United Hebrew Trades. Formed by three unions, four years later it claimed forty affiliates. In Chicago,

the Jewish Workers Educational Society was formed and later became
a labor union. Philadelphia's Jewish Federation of Labor and similar
organizations in other cities impressed upon the Jewish laborer the need
to organize, but it was not education but confrontation which led to
unionization. In 1890, a strike in New York in support of workers fired
for their union activity proved widely popular. A lockout was the
response to the strike and in response to the lockout of the operators,
the cutters (the elite of the work force) struck. This, again, was met
by a lockout. An Amalgamated Board of Delegates representing an
alliance of cutters, operators and contractors sought union recognition.
The first step was to seek an injunction against the Manufacturers Association, but the courts refused to grant it. The employers then fired
all the striking workers.

Sympathy in the Jewish community was with the workers. Strike
funds were raised. One congregation offered five-cent dinners to hold-
ers of union cards. Each Friday, on the eve of the Sabbath, the strikers
met to renew their resolve. Mass meetings, parades, agitation lasted for
six weeks. The Manufacturers Association at last agreed to meet with
the Amalgamated Board. In itself this was hailed as a historic victory.
A speaker at the mass rally spoke the workers' spirit: "The day has
come when the manufacturer will no longer dare to trample underfoot
the ignorant, poor Jewish workingman. The Jews have ceased to be a
patient creature who allowed himself to be driven."[15] The cause of the
garment worker was expanded into a Jewish cause, a matter of rights
and dignity. New Jews in the New World would not allow themselves
to be treated as they were in the Old. The manufacturers agreed to
recognize the union and accept a system of arbitration, but they would
not relinquish their strikebreakers, or their system of piece rates. At a
mass meeting addressed by Abraham Cahan and brought to a high pitch
of righteous indignation by their charismatic leader, Joseph Barondess,
the strikers voted 1536 to 20 to reject the agreement. A participant (A.
Rosenberg) describes the wild enthusiasm of the occasion:

> Men and women jumped on the tables. Their voices could be heard
> ten blocks away . . . The chairman . . . declared . . . that the thing
> most needed was money . . . one of the people walked up . . . and
> taking the ring off his finger handed it over to the chairman . . .
> the chairman's table became covered with rings, watches, earrings,
> brooches . . . Many cried. Others yelled and argued.[16]

The strike continued. The support of the public cooled. Police
threatened. But the workers persisted. The agreement finally signed on
July 25, 1890, was a clear victory, granting higher wages, better conditions and union recognition.

Labor historian John R. Commons couldn't quite understand the Jewish workers' attitude to their union:

> In the manufacture of clothing, whenever any real abuse arises among the Jewish workmen they all come together and form a giant union and at once engage in a strike. They bring in ninety percent of the trade. They are energetic and determined. . . . They stay out a long time, even under the greatest of suffering. . . . with almost nothing to live on . . . insisting that their great cause must be won.
>
> But once the strike is settled . . . that usually ends the union, since they do not see any practical cause for a union when there is no cause to fight for.[17]

Jews saw the union as a weapon against injustice, to be used when needed, to be held in quiet readiness for future battles. Their alertness to danger and ability to unite quickly in the face of injustice had been fashioned by a bimillennial experience of being beset by enemies and joining to resist them, and by an ingrained concept of a mutual responsibility for each other's welfare.

This reflex response to injustice and disciplined pursuit of justice came into play in the general strikes in the ladies' wear and menswear garment industries in 1909–12, which made a major union of the International Ladies' Garment Workers Union (ILGWU) and established the Amalgamated Clothing Workers of America. In 1900 eleven delegates from seven locals in four cities launched the ILGWU. It struggled on during its first decade, contending with rival unions for power and battling with manufacturers for better working conditions, higher wages and union recognition. Two strikes, the "Uprising of the Twenty Thousand" in 1909 and the "Great Revolt" in 1910, which ended with a "Protocol of Peace," brought order and rationality to the ladies' garment trade.

The "Uprising" was just that, an angry, impassioned protest against the social injustice of an industry which existed on long hours and low wages, where workers were charged for the needles they sewed with and the electricity they used, and were at the mercy of bosses who leveled excessive fines for lateness and "spoiled work." Three-quarters of the labor force of 20,000 which rose in protest were young women between the ages of sixteen and twenty-five. Their passion fueled the struggle, and their willingness to brave all hardships—marching in the picket lines during three cold wintry months, braving threats, taunts and arrest—won the support of the larger public, especially some leading uptown ladies who made the cause their own. Only a partial victory was gained by these young women who were the labor force of one segment of the ladies' garment industry, the waist makers and dress-makers. The larger segment, the women's garment workers, had from the summer of 1908 been preparing for a general strike. The strike of young women workers with no strike experience and the public support it elicited gave heart to the seasoned union men to launch their "Great Revolt," against "low wages, long hours, homework, irregularity of pay, unreasonable fines and charges, inside subcontracting, and inse-curity of employment." This strike was well organized and financed. The union demanded a "closed shop" where only union members would be employed. The manufacturers felt that this would give the union control of the industry and opposed it with all vigor. The battle was joined, and a bitter battle it was! Workers were battling for what they saw as justice itself; the manufacturers were protecting not only their property, but what they conceived to be the essence of the American promise, the right to success.

Leaders of the Jewish community were deeply disturbed by the "scandal" of Jews warring against Jews in public before the unfriendly eyes of the community at large. Unfriendly tongues called the manu-facturers conscienceless exploiters, modern-day pharaohs crushing the enslaved; or labeled the workers as dangerous Anarchist-Socialists threatening the social order. The leaders pointed out that conflict was not the traditional Jewish way of settling disputes. Mediation was wiser and more prudent. Louis D. Brandeis, the "People's Attorney," was called in to preside over the attempts at conciliation. "Schiff, Marshall & Co." used their persuasion to help bring about a peaceful solution, an agreement called the "Protocol of Peace." It abolished the hated charges and fines, forbade subcontracting and home work, granted a substantial increase in wages and lowered the work week to fifty hours. On the issue of the union shop, Brandeis permitted both sides to save face by offering a new concept—the "preferential shop"—that is, pref-erence in employment was to be given to union members.

Other provisions in the protocol were of greater consequence. Its basic philosophy was that the welfare of industry is the responsibility of both labor and capital; both benefit from its well-being, and both should therefore contribute to it. The relationship between capital and labor should be cooperation rather than confrontation. The protocol, unlike other agreements, which had terminating dates, was a treaty of peace permanent in its duration and containing dispute-settling ma-chinery to assure its continuation, though either party could end it at its will. The union gave up the weapon of the strike; the manufacturers surrendered the lockout. The machinery of peaceful adjudication in-cluded a permanent Committee of Grievances to settle minor disputes; a permanent Board of Arbitration, composed of one representative of the employers, one of the union and one from the public, to decide major issues; a Joint Board of Sanitary Control to establish and supervise decent working conditions. Strife was not eliminated, but the machinery which had been set up for conciliation was used.

The greatest beneficiary of the agreement was the ILGWU. By 1912, it became the fifth largest union in the American Federation of Labor (AFL). In New York City, its Joint Board had contracts with 1796 out of the 1829 shops in the industry. In 1914 the ILGWU had risen to become the third largest union in the AFL and had an income of $362,000 annually.[18]

THE AMALGAMATED

New York was the center for the manufacture of men's clothing, but a strike in Chicago laid the foundation for establishment of the Amalgamated Clothing Workers of America. At the end of September 1910, three weeks after the "Great Revolt" had been settled, 1000 workers left their work to protest a pay cut given 17 young women in the pants shop of Hart, Schaffner and Marx, the giant manufacturer in the men's clothing industry. Within three weeks, their number had increased to 38,000. The conservative, American-born leadership of the United Garment Workers Union signed an agreement which accepted nonrecognition of the union and the open shop. It was angrily rejected by the striking workers, consisting mainly of East European immigrant Jews; they were fighting not only against long hours and low wages, but also against a system which violated their standards of justice and decency. "In many factories workers were required to pay the full retail price for damaged garments or for lost materials, and in some shops they were fined the equivalent of fifteen minutes of working time for punching the time clock one minute late." Joseph Schaffner, secretary-treasurer of the firm against which the strike was first called, acknowledged, "When I found out later of the conditions that had prevailed, I concluded that the strike should have occurred much sooner."

Public pressure, as well as economic considerations, brought the strike to an end. The employees of Hart, Schaffner and Marx emerged victorious from the ordeal, and their victory had ramifications beyond their shop and the garment industry. Because an arbitration committee brought the conflict to an end, machinery for arbitration of conflicts was set up. Inside the shops, grievances were dealt with by labor and management representatives working together. Conciliation was sought before confrontation might occur. "This arbitration machinery," wrote Joel Seidman, a chronicler of the needle trades, "grew into one of the most significant experiments in industrial relations, not only in the garment trades, but in American industry as a whole." [19] Eventually it developed into the "impartial chairman" system, which recognized that manufacturers and workers both had a stake in the health of the industry, that this mutual interest would be served by a system of agreements, rules and regulations binding on both. It was not the American leadership of the United Garment Workers who worked out this system of arbitration and "common law of the job," but the Chicago and New York Jewish tailors who, under the leadership of Sidney Hillman, broke away to form the Amalgamated Clothing Workers of America.

Will Herberg has argued:

> Trade unionism helped very materially to obtain acceptance for the immigrant Jewish worker in the United States, for it was trade unionism, along with the public school, that constituted for the mass of immigrant Jews their first real initiation into American institutional life. As a trade unionist, the immigrant Jew began to speak a "language" that Americans could understand . . . as a trade unionist, he was behaving in a familiar way, behaving like an American: it was the visible sign of his Americanization, as authentic as speaking English.[20]

If Americans noticed this, they also noticed that the unions through which the Jewish immigrants were becoming integrated into the American scene were unions largely Jewish in membership and leadership, and with a Socialist orientation. Thus the composition and the political-economic orientation caused a cleavage between the needle trade unions and the American labor movement. This cleavage became more pronounced during World War I, when these unions lagged behind the general labor movement in commitment to the Wilsonian program of, first, preparedness for, and, later, involvement in the war. Samuel Gompers (a Jew, but not associated with the Jewish labor movement) and the leadership of the AFL were uneasy about the influence these separatist, Socialist unions exerted, especially in New York. That unease turned to serious concern during the war years, lest the garment unions' Socialist pacifism cause the loyalty of the labor movement to be called into question.

The garment unions, in turn, were equally concerned about the widening cleavage between themselves and the national labor movement. They began to turn from pacifism to supporting participation in the war effort, demonstrating this reorientation by heavy purchases of Liberty Bonds. Some union leaders began to suppress the Socialist influence in favor of "unionism pure and simple." This was also part of Americanization, an accommodation to American sentiment which viewed labor unions as organizations solely for economic betterment rather than as movements for social change.

The anti-Bolshevist atmosphere which pervaded America after the Russian Revolution "hardened the hearts" of manufacturers and intensified their attempts to wipe out the gains won by labor. In Rochester, in 1919, Michaels, Stern & Co. sued the Amalgamated for $100,000 damages, one of five such suits against the union during this period. In Philadelphia, in the same year, the newspapers refused to sell space to the union to publicize its case during a strike. The most serious challenge was in New York, where the manufacturers demanded lower wages, the right to install production goals and piecework, and greater freedom in hiring and disciplining workers. The Amalgamated resisted, and in December 1920, 50,000 union members were locked out, a lockout which spread to other cities as well. The conflict reached the floor of the Senate, one senator urging an investigation of the union, another proposing an investigation of the whole industry. The acrimonious battle finally ended with the union forced to make concessions.

THE POSTWAR YEARS

In the postwar years, the ILGWU led by David Dubinsky was also beset by a challenge from within. Some former doctrinaire Socialists now became militant Communists and launched a decade-long effort to control the union. The battle between Left and Right was fierce, with victories and defeats on both sides, and it almost shattered the union. The internal strife sapped the energies for action against the employers, and long-fought-for and sacrificially bought trade-union gains were lost with hardly a battle. This war was waged in other "Jewish" unions, as well. "Though losses were suffered in membership, in standards and in funds," Seidman writes, "by far the most serious loss was in morale. The bitter hatreds that had developed during the long period of civil strife hampered union activities for years to come."

During the decade 1920–30, the "Jewish" unions became increasingly less Jewish in membership. Looking back in 1927, author and editor Samuel M. Melamed reports that:

> Only five or six years ago 95% of all manufacturers were Jews and the Unions of the needle industry were considered Jewish unions, the overwhelming majority of the membership having been Jewish. Today this is no longer the case . . . The decline is both steady and rapid. . . . In the course of the next five years, the unions of the needle trades will cease to be Jewish unions, because the majority of the membership will consist of Gentiles. The Jewish garment and cloak manufacturer . . . will still keep on, but it is more than doubtful if his children will continue the tradition.

Melamed attributes the de-Judaization of the needle industry in part to the stoppage of emigration from Eastern Europe, but mainly to "the temperamental attitude of the Jewish laborer to his trade." "Since he is not a tailor by choice but by chance, he not only gets out of the trade himself as soon as he can, but he never teaches his son his trade." He looked at this phenomenon with sadness and apprehension.

> To some it may matter little whether the needle industry of America is controlled by Jews or not. But to those who are concerned with the future of the American Jew it matters a great deal. It is not necessary that all American Jews become businessmen or professional men. It will be a sad day for American Jewry when the last Jewish workingman will leave his shop and his tools.
>
> In the tailor shop the Jewish workingman competed with no one else. When he will leave the shop and invade the field of the retailer, the peddler, the promoter or the real estate man, he will tread upon somebody's corn. The result can only be an intensified anti-Jewish *stimmung*.[21]

Making a living in the garment trade was difficult and trying for workers and manufacturers alike. Work was seasonal, wages low, hours long; cheap labor was plentiful, and recurrent strikes and lockouts quickly eroded whatever savings one was able to amass. Entrepreneurs were plagued by the uncertainties of fashion, by new competitors who could launch a business with little capital and overhead, and by industry-wide unions which could supervise an established factory but had little control over "outlaw shops." The same volatile, exasperating industry also gave wealth and social status to a not inconsiderable number of immigrants who had arrived on these shores with little more than ambition and enterprise; it provided many workers with the wherewithal to leave the ranks of labor, and enabled many more to afford their children the education which would permit them to enter the professions.

The transition from worker to businessman, from "cloak maker to cloak manufacturer" was already noted by Abraham Bisno at the beginning of the century. Entry of Jews into the professions in appreciable numbers came a generation later. In both, the American experience followed upon the European. European Jewry was already well represented in the middle class at the time when American Jews began to enter it in large numbers. As for the professions, a few statistics will suffice: In 1925, in Prussia, 26.6 percent of the lawyers, 15.5 percent of the physicians and 14.8 percent of the dentists were Jewish, though Jews constituted 2/3 of 1 percent of the population; in 1930, in Poland, Jews constituted 10 percent of the population, but accounted for 62.2 percent of the doctors and 53 percent of the lawyers. A similar situation obtained in Hungary also, 54.5 percent of the doctors and 49.2 percent of the lawyers being Jews.

From 1901 to 1925 in the ten leading American cities, there were only 5212 Jewish graduates of medical schools, but during that time the number had increased at three times the general population increase. By 1937, 65.7 percent of the lawyers and judges, 64 percent of the dentists and 55.7 percent of the physicians of New York were Jewish.

In the mercantile sector there was a significant Jewish presence, most visible in ownership of America's great department stores. The list is long and notable: Gimbel's, Macy's (the Straus family), B. Altman, Abraham & Straus, Bloomingdale's and Saks Fifth Avenue in New York; Filene's in Boston; Gimbel's and Lit Bros. in Philadelphia; Kaufmann's in Pittsburgh; Goldsmith's in Memphis; Rich's in Atlanta; Nieman-Marcus in Dallas; Magnin's in San Francisco; Meier and Frank in Portland, Oregon. Across the continent Jewish names on department-store buildings proclaimed the accomplishments of Jews in American retail trade. Later some of these were amalgamated into the largest department-store chain, the Federated Department Stores, created and controlled by the Lazarus family, whose merchandising career began in Columbus, Ohio, in 1851, when Simon Lazarus opened a men's clothing shop.

In America, Jacob Lestchinsky noted, the integration of the Jew into the economy was not only in line with "age-old . . . economic traditions of the Jews," but also fully coincided "with the developmental trends of the American economy." Jews became more like their neighbors, but some pronounced differences in the occupational pattern persisted. They were not represented in the lowest-income brackets—farmers and unskilled workers—and, in small towns, "the whole Jewish population is engaged in trade and very often in particular lines of business, in which it constitutes the great majority."[22] By the end of the first quarter of the twentieth century, Jews were moving increasingly into the service sector of the economy, a vanguard in the direction in which the American economy was moving.

SCHOLARS AND SCHOLARSHIP

While intent on making a living, the American Jews did not neglect the life of the spirit. The foundations for scholarship were laid, books were published, periodicals proliferated and a significant literature in Yiddish and Hebrew was created.

In 1901, a work which boasted of itself that "for the first time the claims to recognition of a whole race and its ancient religion are put forth in a form approaching completeness," began to be published in New York City. The boast was not an overstatement, for the twelve-volume *Jewish Encyclopedia*[23] remains a landmark of Jewish scholarship.

Preparation and publication of the *Encyclopedia* stimulated scholarly activity in America and turned the attention of world Jewish scholarship to America. Though leading European Jewish scholars were co-opted for the enterprise, the great bulk of the work fell on Americans. To be sure, almost all those were European-born and European-trained, but it is important to note that scholarship accompanied Jewish immigration to the New World. On the editorial board one finds such names as Cyrus Adler, Arkansas-born, who served as president of both Dropsie College (the Philadelphia institution for graduate studies in Hebrew and cognate studies) and the Jewish Theological Seminary of America; Richard Gottheil, professor of Semitic languages at Columbia University and president of the Federation of American Zionists; Marcus Jastrow, pulpit rabbi in Philadelphia and author of the scholarly *A Dictionary of the Targumim, the Talmud Babli and Yerushalmi and the Midrashic Literature;* and Kaufmann Kohler, New York rabbi, author of works on various aspects of Jewish thought who later headed the Hebrew Union College. The youngest editor was Louis Ginzberg, a product of the Lithuanian yeshiva and the German university, who became the acknowledged doyen of American Jewish scholarship. His *The Legends of the Jews,* a multivolume collection of Biblical Aggadic material, demonstrates his mastery of Jewish sources and cognate material and disciplines. The three-volume *Perushim ve-Hiddushim bi-Yerushalmi* (A Commentary on the Palestinian Talmud) deals only with the first four chapters of Berakot, but in so ample a manner as to constitute a work on Jewish law, theology, history and culture.

A year after the publication of the *Jewish Encyclopedia,* Solomon Schechter was brought from Cambridge University to head the Jewish Theological Seminary. Himself a scholar in theology, Aggadah and liturgy, he brought to the seminary a faculty unsurpassed by any other institution of Jewish learning. Chief among them was Louis Ginzberg, joined by colleagues Alexander Marx, historian and bibliographer, who made the seminary library the greatest repository of Jewish books and manuscripts ever assembled; Israel Friedlaender, scholar of the Bible and Judeo-Arabic and ideologist of American Judaism; Israel Davidson, whose four-volume *Otzar ha-Shirah ve-ha-Piyut* (The Treasury of Medieval Hebrew Poetry) is the basic work on Hebrew poetry and liturgy; and Mordecai M. Kaplan, American-trained rabbi, educator, theologian and religious leader, who has had a dominant influence on American Jewish religious life and thought.

In 1917, the Jewish Publication Society issued a new translation of the Bible done by a group of American Jewish scholars, replacing Isaac Leeser's translation published sixty years earlier. The Board of Editors contained "an equal representation of the Jewish Theological Seminary, the Hebrew Union College, and Dropsie College," but most of the translation was done by men associated with Hebrew Union College. The HUC faculty has made important contributions to Jewish scholarship. Jacob Z. Lauterbach wrote with authority on the Talmudic age, David Newmark, on the history of Jewish philosophy. Max L. Margolis and Julian Morgenstern have enriched Biblical study. Jacob R. Marcus, who has done pioneering work in American Jewish history, founded and headed the American Jewish Archives.

Talmudic study and scholarship in the East European tradition was carried on in the third great institution of higher Jewish learning, Yeshiva University in New York City. Dr. Bernard Revel, its first president, succeeded in shaping a school which blended sacred and secular studies.

Scholars of originality and accomplishment must be noted. Brilliant linguistic insight and daring conjecture mark the work of the Biblical scholar, Arnold B. Ehrlich. Originality was the hallmark of historian Solomon Zeitlin, of Dropsie College. Alexander Kohut completed his monumental *Aruch Hashalem* in America. Meyer Waxman's five-volume *A History of Jewish Literature,* and Menahem M. Kasher's twenty-volume compendium of *midrashim* (Rabbinic commentaries) on the Bible, *Torah Shelemah,* are works of monumental scope.

HEBREW LITERATURE

The new century also witnessed a new birth of Hebrew literary creativity in America. Among the million Jews who arrived in the first decade were men of literary achievement and enterprise. A new Hebrew literary society bore the name of Mefizeh Sfat Ever (Disseminators of the Hebrew Language). The mood was optimistic, the goal not merely to preserve a bit of Hebrew, but to establish Hebrew creativity. In 1909, and again in 1913, a Hebrew daily, appropriately titled *Ha-Yom* (Today), was launched. Though short-lived, it gives evidence of the optimistic mood. The excellent Hebrew periodical *Ha-Toren* (The Mast), which fostered creative Hebrew writing, began publication in 1913 and continued for a dozen years. It brought together leading Hebraists, and encouraged Hebraic literary expression by a growing group of young writers.

These young Hebrew writers were in and of America. They had received their general cultural education in America. In turn, many took American themes for their poetry. The first among them was Benjamin N. Silkiner, who, in 1910, published an epic poem of American Indian life, *Mul Ohel Timorah* (Facing Timorah's Tent). Ephraim E. Lisitsky's *Medurot Doakot* (Dying Campfires) deals with the same theme. Black folklore and suffering is found in Lisitsky's *B'Ohale Kush* (In Negro Tents). Poet and philosopher Israel Efros wrote of the tragedy of the red man, and treated the California gold rush, in an epic poem *Zahav* (Gold). The poets identify the American Jews' fight for spiritual survival in America with the Indians' struggle to preserve life on their soil and the Blacks' endeavor to establish a sense of proud identity.

In the poetry of Simon Ginsburg, Hillel Bavli and Simon Halkin there are also American themes. Halkin translated Walt Whitman's *Leaves of Grass*, Bavli wrote about Mormons and New Englanders and Ginsburg about New York. Their American orientation is also indicated by their appreciation of English language and literature. Silkiner, Lisitsky, Efros, Bavli and Halkin each undertook to translate Shakespeare plays.

Jacob Kabakoff states:

> They felt at home in the natural beauties of America and in its literature. And they wished to transmit their appreciation of the American spirit as their contribution to modern Hebrew letters. In so doing, they helped free American Hebrew writing from the dominance of the Russian Jewish center and to give it character of its own.[24]

Prose followed poetry. Simon Halkin wrote a trilogy on American Jewish life. The novels of Reuben Wallenrod dealt with the problems of adjustment to America. *Ki Fanah Yom* (The Day Wanes) is the sad story of Jewish farmers in the Catskills forced to turn to hotel-keeping. Chayim Abramowitz deals with life in the Brownsville section of Brooklyn in his *Al Ha-Lechem Levado* (By Bread Alone).

Poet, educator and literary critic Eisig Silberschlag speaks of three periods of Hebrew literature in America. Up to 1860, it was a period of "oddities." The "period of belated beginnings" lasted till World War I. The third, starting with publication of the monthly *Miklat* (Haven) in 1919, may be called the "period of emerging achievement."

> It was in this last phase of Hebrew literature that various strata of Americans burst into Hebrew poetry and fiction: the Indian, the Negro, the white gentile and the Jew. The great events in recent Jewish history—the slaughter of millions in Nazi-dominated Europe and the establishment of the State of Israel—have not yet been properly realized in the works of Hebrew writers in this country.[25]

Menahem Ribalow made the weekly *Hadoar* (The Post) the major organ of American Hebrew literature. He added supplements for the younger readers, edited the annual *Sefer Hashanah L'Yhudei Amerika*, and founded the publishing house Ogen. Mention should be made of *Bitzaron*, a monthly journal, edited for many years by Hayim Tchernowitz (Rav Zair), and the scholarly quarterly, *Talpiot*, which Rabbi Samuel K. Mirsky edited.

A sizable Hebrew religious literature has been produced in America, books of Responsa, volumes of sermons, tomes on Jewish philosophy and theology. Suffice it to mention three rabbinic periodicals. In 1903, Rabbi Dov Ber Abramowitz began to publish the monthly *Bet Vaad Lachachamim,* which printed articles on Jewish law by Orthodox rabbis and religious functionaries, as well as commentaries on traditional texts, and observations on the current religious scene. *Hamizpeh,* a monthly edited by Rabbi J. Eskolsky, listed in its first issue (1910), thirty-one rabbis—twenty-five American and six European—who promised to contribute. Six years later, Rabbi Moses Benjamin Tomashoff continued to publish in America his *Yagdil Torah,* which he had begun in Russia seven years earlier. This periodical was devoted entirely to traditional rabbinic scholarship.

THE YIDDISH PRESS

Interest in the Franco-Prussian War of 1870 and the Russo-Turkish War in 1877 became the impetus for establishing a Yiddish press in America. In 1870 the lithographed *Yiddische Zeitung* began to appear, and a year later, *Die Post.* A half-dozen years later the *Israelitische Presse* of Chicago began its brief career. The language of this early press was Germanized Yiddish; the social view, conservative and favorable to religion. Its existence was precarious, its appearance, weekly, monthly or "on occasion." Ezekiel Sarasohn, whose father, Kasriel Zvi Sarasohn, established the Yiddish press on a firm foundation, described the early struggles:

> Most Polish and Lithuanian Jews came from small towns. The older ones among them did not have the slightest need for a newspaper . . . The younger ones, those who had some education, read German newspapers and gradually English newspapers . . . The very young were ashamed of a newspaper with Hebrew characters.[26]

The East European immigration in the 1880s enabled Sarasohn to establish the daily *Yiddisches Tageblatt* in 1885. It attained wide readership and influence and was published till 1928, when it merged with the *Morgen-Zhurnal.* Newspapers of the day were also journals of opinion: the *Tageblatt* represented the Orthodox religious viewpoint; its competitors, *Der Volksadvocat* and *Die Volkzeitung,* were critical of the religious establishment; the *New Yorker Yiddische Folkzeitung* attempted to speak for both Socialism and the nascent Jewish nationalism represented by the Hibat Zion (Lovers of Zion) movement. The 1890s saw the beginning of the *Forverts* (Jewish Daily Forward), which, under the editorship of Abraham Cahan, became the largest Yiddish newspaper in the world. The outstanding Yiddish journal of literature and thought, *Die Zukunft* (The Future), began its life in 1892 and attained preeminence under its distinguished editor, the poet Abraham Liessin.

At the turn of the century, the reader of Yiddish could choose among four dailies: the Orthodox *Tageblatt,* the right-wing Socialist *Forverts,* the left-wing Socialist *Abend-Blatt* and the nonpartisan *Yiddisher Kurier* of Chicago. These were soon joined by another Orthodox daily, the *Morgen-Zhurnal,* and later by the *Varheit,* and in 1915 by the non-partisan, cultural *Tog.*

In the early years of the century, periodicals proliferated. The ideologically oriented included the Zionist *Dos Yiddishe Folk* (1909); the Socialist and nationalist cultural, *Der Arbeter* (1904); the Territorialist *Dos Folk* (1905); and the Socialist-Zionist, *Der Yiddisher Kemfer* (1906). There were journals of literature and thought, notably Dr. Chaim Zhitlowsky's *Dos Naie Leben* (The New Life) (1908); Abraham Reisen's *Dos Naie Land* (The New Land) (1911); and his *Literatur und Leben* (1915). The *Zukunft's* Liessin summed up the goal of the Yiddish periodical press to be to place before the reader "the entire radiant world of science and progress, as well as the intellectual world of art and esthetic enjoyment."

Yiddish publications attained their widest circulation and greatest influence in the 1920s and 1930s, but the restrictive immigration laws dealt a death blow to the Yiddish press. Young American Jews may no longer be ashamed of "Hebrew characters," but very few have the ability to read Yiddish.

THE YIDDISH THEATER

The Yiddish theater in America had its beginnings in the early 1880s when members of Abraham Goldfaden's troupe arrived as immigrants and presented from memory some of the plays of "The Father of Yiddish Theatre." In 1891, the gifted playwright Jacob Gordin, and the leading actor of the Yiddish stage, Jacob P. Adler, joined forces to present the first play "worthy of serious consideration," *Siberia.* The early Yiddish theater came to be dominated by the folk operettas of Goldfaden and by Gordin's serious plays.

At the turn of the century Hutchins Hapgood wrote:

> In the three Yiddish theatres on the Bowery is expressed the world of the Ghetto—that New York City of Russian Jews, large, complex, with a full life and civilization. In the midst of the frivolous Bowery, devoted to tinsel variety shows, "dive" music halls, fake museums . . . the theatres of the chosen people alone present the serious as well as the trivial interests of an entire community.[27]

The theater began to attract literary figures of high talent who made the Yiddish stage a cultural force in the Jewish community. Among them were Leon Kobrin, who wrote realistic plays on American themes, and David Pinski, whose plays expressed his labor Zionist passion for social justice and love for the Jewish people. The works of Sholem Aleichem and I. L. Peretz attracted large audiences, and outstandingly popular were the dramas of Sholem Asch. The best plays of European dramatists were adapted for the Yiddish stage so that the Jewish audience came to know Shakespeare, Ibsen, Strindberg, Molière, Zola, Zangwill and Tolstoy.

Through his Yiddish Art Theater, Maurice Schwartz brought the Jewish stage to its triumphant heights. Dramatists of high quality,' Asch, Pinski, Peretz Hirschbein, H. Leivick, I. J. Singer and others wrote the plays, which were produced with artistic dedication and competence. Schwartz gathered about him a gifted group, who made the Yiddish Art Theater into one of the greatest of repertory companies. From this group Muni Weisenfreund went on to movie stardom under the name of Paul Muni.

The stars of the Yiddish stage were the heroes of the ghetto. Jacob P. Adler, David Kessler, Zelig Mogolescu, Bertha Kalisch and Madame Liptzin—each had loyal adherents who formed spirited, partisan claques. None had more devoted fans than Boris Tomashefsky, the idol of the working girl, and Molly Picon, the gamine musical comedy star.

In 1918 there were twenty-four Yiddish theaters in America, no less than eleven in New York City, and the others in Chicago, Philadelphia, Boston and Detroit.

The theater reached its heights in the 1920s and early thirties. Its decline since has been rapid, although there has been a revived interest in the Yiddish stage in recent years.

POETS AND NOVELISTS

American Yiddish poetry had its origins in plaint and protest, in the immigrant's golden dreams turned to dross. Freedom and wealth were the promise America held out; reality was a dingy tenement, backbreaking sweatshop labor, grinding poverty which oppressed body and soul. Morris Rosenfeld expressed the plight of the immigrant in a series of simple, sentimental, bitter poems.

A contemporary, David Edelstadt, was the poet of angry protests and cry of rebellion. He died a poet's early death of the immigrant's affliction, tuberculosis. Morris Winchefsky's poetic cry is classic: "You can kill only our body, our flesh; but not our holy spirit." The most gifted American Jewish poet was Yehoash (Solomon Bloomgarden). His poetry, universal and spiritual in theme, draws upon Jewish sources and uses Jewish imagery. His poems exude deep national feelings, and some rise to Psalm-like passion. His major work was the translation of the Bible into Yiddish "in a style that purified and enriched the Yiddish language itself."

Die Yunge (The Young) was a name given a group of writers whose work began to appear before World War I. One of the group, Joseph Opatoshu, described its creed: "Yiddish literature ceased to be an educational tool and became an end in itself. It assumed artistic standards . . ." It was an "art for art's sake" movement, and its poets and writers turned away from themes of tears and struggle, of social protest and upheaval, to impressionism, mysticism, individualism. Among them were Moshe Leib Halpern, H. Leivick, I. J. Schwartz and Menahem Boraisha, whose epic poem, *Der Geher,* is one of the great creations of American Yiddish literature.

Sholem Aleichem spent his last years in America and incorporated the immigrant experience in his works. Sholem Asch, who lived for many years in America, wrote powerful novels of American Jewish life. I. J. Singer, a novelist and playwright of rare power, is best known for his *The Brothers Ashkenazi.*

A survey of the "Fate of Yiddish in America" published in the July 1928 issue of *The Menorah Journal* disclosed a "pronounced tendency for English to supplant Yiddish" as the language spoken in immigrant homes. Although 575,053 Yiddish-speaking immigrants arrived in the decade 1910–20, the number of foreign-born Jews who listed Yiddish as their "mother tongue" to the U.S. census takers rose by only 40,053, from 1,051,767 to 1,091,820. The author, Uriah Z. Engelman, concluded that "soon only arithmetic and mortality tables will be needed to reveal the point at which the language will disappear."

He argued that although a number of Yiddish newspapers were showing "great prosperity," circulation figures led to pessimistic projections for the future. More than a half-million Jewish immigrants entered the United States in 1913–27, but the aggregate circulation of the twelve major Yiddish newspapers and journals in New York (comprising more than 85 percent of the total) decreased by almost 25 percent from 676,349 in 1914 to 536,346 in 1927. Engelman also reported that such Yiddish trade papers as *The Butcher's Trade Journal* and *Waste Materials, Junk and Metals* had ceased publication, and that the Yiddish-English newspaper was beginning to intrude upon the purely Yiddish. In the decade 1917–37, the number of all-Yiddish publications declined from thirty to twenty, the number of Yiddish-English rose from one to thirteen.

Publication of Yiddish books rose dramatically with the spurt of immigration following the pogroms of 1905. It increased even more during the war years when importation of books came to a halt and immigrants' wages rose, providing more money for the purchase of books. The Yiddish newspapers and journals began to publish books on a large scale, the works of Heine in eight volumes, of Abraham Raisin in twelve, and multivolume editions of the works of Dr. Chaim

Zhitlowsky and Sholem Aleichem. But the postwar years saw a drastic decline in book production. Engelman's explanation was: "the assimilation of the immigrant and the de-proletarianization of the Jewish masses, both of which processes began long before the war, were intensified and quickened by it and its aftermath." He also noted that of the 286 Yiddish writers in America, half were over forty-four years of age, only six were in their twenties and that "America has failed to produce a single Yiddish writer of its own."

The Yiddish theater, of which there were twenty-four in the United States, half in New York and half in the "provinces," seemed to be doing well. Membership in the Yiddish Actors Union had grown to 345 from its 40 in 1905. In twenty years theatergoers had quadrupled to 120,000 a week, and the minimum wage during that time had risen from $18 to $70 per week. The average salary was in the range of $150 to $200 per week, some stars getting as much as $600. But while the Yiddish stage was progressing financially, it was deteriorating in quality. The theater, once a vehicle for culture, was now mainly a place of entertainment. The literary plays of the Yiddish Art Theater were abandoned in favor of "mawkish, bloody melodramas of the People's Theater and the senseless operettas of the Second Avenue Theater."

Some 16,000 children were enrolled in more than 200 Yiddish elementary schools, 6 high schools and 2 teacher-preparation institutions. All the schools were "secular and radical, and ignore religion and Biblical history." The Socialist fraternal order, the Workmen's Circle, sponsored about 100 schools (of which 21 were in New York), and other schools and summer camps were sponsored by the Communist Independent Workers' Order, the Labor-Zionist Jewish National Workers' Alliance, and the independent Yiddishist Sholem Aleichem Institution. All the schools were small, averaging some seventy students each. Over 95 percent were one-teacher establishments. Engelman estimates that the "Yiddish school system can reach between 2 and 2.5 percent of all American-Jewish children of school age, and many of these are touched only for a moment." "Yiddish teachers are, for the most part," wrote Engelman, "drawn from the Yiddish socialist-radical group, for whom Yiddish is only a convenient vehicle for revolutionary propaganda. When Yiddish passes away in America, these Yiddishists will neither mourn it nor attempt to revive it. They will take up their work in English." He concludes his appraisal:

> With its old strongholds disintegrating as population shifts, the decline of Yiddish has already set in. This decline bids within another generation to wipe out Yiddish as a common medium of speech in the United States . . .[28]

9.

The Shaping of the Jewish Community

SIX CONFRONTATIONS IN THE FIRST HALF OF THE TWENTIETH CENTURY helped determine the character of the emerging Jewish community.

The American Jewish Committee tested the ability of the organized Jewish community to affect national policy in a confrontation with the national administration. The oligarchic ways of the American Jewish Committee were challenged by the more democratic ways of the American Jewish Congress. New York Jewry confronted the challenges—cultural, spiritual and moral—which beset the world's largest Jewish community, adapting the Old World communal structure, the *kehillah,* to the New World. The needs of fellow Jews in war-torn Europe tested the will and the ability of the American Jew to rise above social, economic and religious divisiveness to cooperative efforts to aid brethren abroad through the Joint Distribution Committee. Zionism forced American Jews to confront their identity as both Jews and Americans. Anti-Semitism, native and imported, challenged Jews' sense of security in America.

In each instance the Jewish community experienced the opportunities which free, democratic America afforded, and also the limitations which it imposed. The organized Jewish community learned to live with the limitations, and to avail itself of opportunities in pursuit of its self-defined interests.

THE AMERICAN JEWISH COMMITTEE

President Theodore Roosevelt's response to the memorandum presented to him on June 15, 1903, by the Executive Committee of the

Independent Order of B'nai B'rith echoed the sentiments of the American people.

I need not dwell upon the fact so patent as the widespread indignation with which the American people heard of the dreadful outrages upon the Jews in Kishineff. I have never in my experience in this country known of a more immediate or a deeper expression of sympathy for the victims and of horror over the appalling calamity that has occurred.[1]

The "appalling calamity" was a pogrom on Easter, 1903, in the city of Kishinev, which took the lives of 49 Jews, wounded some 500 more, looted 700 homes and destroyed 600 business establishments. Overnight "Kishinev" became a catchword for anti-Jewish excesses aided and abetted by the czarist government. What aroused American public opinion was that official Russian spokesmen justified the pogrom as the understandable reaction of the Russian peasants against Jewish exploitation.

The response was immediate. Protest meetings were held in twenty-seven states, in fifty cities from Boston to San Francisco, at which 363 addresses were delivered, "among them by one ex-president of the United States, two United States senators, nine members of Congress, and three governors of states."

The purpose of the meetings, organized by the ad hoc Jewish bodies, was to raise funds to aid victims and arouse public indignation, which would demand United States government intercession on behalf of Russian Jews. Editorials appeared in the nation's leading newspapers pointing to this dual goal.

American, Baltimore, Md., May 9, 1903

Details of the massacres in Russia which have reached this country . . . tell a story of horror and bloodshed which must shock the whole world. . . . The United States has taken the lead in this matter [to supply the needs of the poor sufferers of Kishineff], and already several thousands of dollars have been forwarded to Russia . . .[2]

Globe, Boston, Mass., May 28, 1903

The terrible destruction of life and property in the city of Kishineff naturally has aroused the deepest sympathy and indignation among all the advocates of tolerance, peace and liberty in America. . . . The present sympathetic movement in America . . . is certain to have a powerful influence on the Czar. . . .[3]

American and Journal, New York, May 28, 1903

Let the president of the United States, through his Secretary of State, address Russia . . . and the civilized world would applaud . . . The American Republic has a right to cry out against the persecution of the Jews in Russia, and it will be false to its spirit and duty if it shall not do so.[4]

The United States government did not issue a condemnation; instead, the secretary of state transmitted to the American chargé d'affaires in St. Petersburg a petition drawn up by B'nai B'rith, signed by 12,544 leading citizens of the United States, with instructions that he transmit it to "His Imperial Majesty the Emperor of Russia." The Imperial Government of Russia declined to accept the petition. For consolation, "By permission of President Roosevelt, the separate sheets of the petition, suitably bound and enclosed in a case provided for the purpose, have been placed in the archives of the Department of State." Secretary of State John Hay commended the petition for "language so earnest and eloquent and yet so dignified, so moderate and decorous," and assured Leo N. Levi, Esq., president of the Executive Committee of the Independent Order of B'nai B'rith, that "It will be a valuable addition to public literature, and will be sacredly cherished among the treasures of this department."[5] American diplomacy had found a way of placating public opinion and retaining a cordial relationship with the czarist government.

A month earlier, President Roosevelt had reminded representatives of American Jewry that "the United States is that country in which from the beginning of its national career most has been done in the way of acknowledging the debt due to the Jewish race," assuring them that "In any proper way by which beneficial action may be taken, it will be taken . . ."[6] Apparently, no proper way other than to attempt to serve as a conduit of a citizens' petition, known to have been framed and circulated by Jews, could be found. It was not lost on the leadership of American Jewry that, while it had the skills to arouse public opinion and evoke sympathy for the plight of its fellow Jews abroad, it still lacked the numbers, organization and power to call forth governmental action. Discreet discussion about the need for a national body which could speak for Jewish interests began.

The group best fitted by influence and affluence, the Jewish "establishment"—Jacob Schiff, Oscar Straus, Mayer Sulzberger, Louis Marshall, Cyrus Adler, the Lewisohns, the Guggenheims, et al.—was galvanized into action by the pogroms which erupted in Russia, climaxed by a second in Kishinev in August 1905. Louis Marshall, who was to be chief architect of such an organization, wrote to Adolf Kraus, the president of B'nai B'rith, the largest and oldest of Jewish organizations in America:

We all recognize that there is in the air a general desire for the formation of some central organization. . . . It has . . . occurred to some of us, that a number of leading Jews, say twenty or twenty-five . . . should be invited quietly to confer . . . whether or not it is desirable to form such a body . . .[7]

Those who were called together, men "who for some time past dealt with the serious problems which confront the Jewish people," formed the American Jewish Committee in 1906. It was to be a body of the elite, limited to sixty American citizens, directed by a tightly knit Executive Committee. It was hoped that this "prudent" group would work quietly through discreet intercession with government authorities in behalf of Jews abroad and in the service of Jewish interests at home.

The Jewish situation in the Russian Empire was growing more ominous; racism was expressing itself through anti-Semitism in Germany; France, land of "Liberty, Fraternity and Equality," had demonstrated its festering latent anti-Semitism in the Dreyfus Affair.

At home the Jewish immigrant newcomers were beginning to show a political awareness which they were expressing in radical political and social activities. It was feared that if leaders of the immigrant community spoke out on matters of Jewish interest, they would do so in a manner which might jeopardize the status and security which the established Jewish community had thus far achieved. The time had arrived for the establishment to institutionalize the leadership which it had assumed; to do so through an organization which would comport itself not as a quasi-political, self-serving ethnic group taking advantage of American freedom, but as a religiocultural body which worked within the American democratic process, and in its service.

The founders of the American Jewish Committee were politically sophisticated men who knew that what they constituted was indeed an ethnic lobby, but they were also astute enough to know the importance of appearances in domestic diplomacy. They were also wise enough to perceive that the committee they formed would need at least the acceptance of the larger segment of the Jewish community, i.e., the East European Jews, who would not be represented in the composition and the deliberations of this body.

What was needed was a cause which would mandate the organization of such a body, and which would be of such crucial concern to the larger Jewish community as to win its grateful approval. The pogroms of 1905 and 1906 provided the cause and created the mandate. That the agenda of the committee would extend beyond concern for massacre victims is evident from the concept of Judge Mayer Sulzberger, who was to serve as its first president:

he would favor a prominent Russo-Jewish relief organization, with the idea that the union . . . having once been formed and brought into working order, would evolve automatically on a safe and practical basis to act in subjects other than in relieving the Russian situation.[8]

Most East European Jews initially applauded the formation of the committee because the plight of their families and *landsleit* in the Old World was the stated purpose for its coming into being. Though vigorously attacked by Socialists and Zionists the committee continued to merit Jewish acceptance because of its forceful opposition to restriction of immigration; its successful fight for abrogation of the discriminatory Russo-American treaty of 1832; and because of the leadership it provided during World War I in organizing the American Jewish Relief Committee and the American Jewish Joint Distribution Committee, whose chief beneficiaries were the Jews in war-torn Eastern Europe.

The historic experience of European Jews had prepared them for accepting leadership whose chief virtue was its real or apparent influence with governmental authorities. These American *shtadlanim* (men of influence with governmental officials) had organized themselves to aid Jews abroad, and to preserve and expand rights at home. Time and again, these self-appointed leaders of the American Jewish community demonstrated that the doors of power were open to them, that men of influence responded to their invitations to grace a platform, sign a petition, deliver a statement.

The program of the American Jewish Committee in its first decades may be perceived from the summary of its activities for the year 1913:

> The Committee, which was organized to prevent the infraction of the civil and religious rights of Jews, and to alleviate the consequences of persecution, has occupied itself with a number of problems of Jewish interest. It has raised funds for the relief of the Jewish sufferers during the Balkan War; it interested our State Department in securing for those Jews who were formerly Turkish subjects and now subjects of the Balkan Allies, guarantees of civil, political and religious equality; it has interested itself in the problems of the Jews in Roumania and Russia; it has opposed the restriction of immigration to this country by a literacy test, which would have barred thousands of Jews who are emigrating from Russia and Roumania because of the impossible conditions under which they live in those countries; and it has been active in a number of other ways.[9]

It was the kind of program which could be hailed by most segments of the Jewish community. Even the leaders of the radical segment of the community who decried the political stance, the social views and the economic interests of Schiff, Marshall et al., grudgingly accepted their leadership of the larger Jewish community. President Roosevelt responded once and again to the Committee's requests. President Taft's door was open to their visit. It was reported that, at one such visit, Jacob H. Schiff refused to shake the proffered hand of President Taft because of Taft's negative response to a representation on the Russian treaty.

THE RUSSO-AMERICAN TREATY CONFLICT

The Schiff-Taft confrontation took place in February 1911 at the height of an American Jewish Committee-led campaign for abrogation of the Russo-American treaty of 1832, a commercial treaty guaranteeing freedom of commerce and navigation, and the free entry of residents of the signatory states. In the latter half of the nineteenth century, the czarist regime began to use clauses of the treaty to exclude Catholic priests and Protestant missionaries and to subject American Jews visiting Russia to the restrictions under which their Russian coreligionists lived. Despite repeated objections from the American government, notably the interposition of Secretary of State James C. Blaine in 1881, the Russian government remained adamant. It even suggested that the American government consider refusing passports to Jews intending to travel to Russia, thereby sparing itself the embarrassment of having its citizens discriminated against by a "friendly" foreign power.

Czarist authorities believed that according foreign Jews freedoms like those of any other visitors would undermine its policy of discrimination against its native Jews. Jacob H. Schiff explained to Adolph S. Ochs, publisher of *The New York Times:*

> The moment Russia is compelled to live up to its treaties and admit the foreign Jew into its dominion on a basis of equality with other citizens of foreign countries, the Russian government will not be able to maintain the Pale of Settlement against its own Jews.[10]

To the leaders of American Jewry U.S. governmental acquiescence to restrictions upon American Jews by a foreign nation relegated American Jews to second-class citizenship. Louis Marshall was astute enough to demonstrate that the issue was an affront against all citizens.

> If Russia should announce that it would not honor the passport of the United States when held by an Episcopalian or a Presbyterian . . . our country would not look upon this breach of treaty obligation as a mere insult to the Episcopalians or the Presbyterians . . . but would justly treat it as a blow inflicted upon every man who holds dear the title of American citizen.[11]

The response of the U.S. government through its various branches was correct. The State Department issued formal protests in appropriate diplomatic language; Congress passed the proper resolutions denouncing discrimination against American citizens by foreign powers; and President Roosevelt (at the insistance of Oscar S. Straus) wrote to Count Sergei Witte that relaxation of its passport restrictions by the Russian government would aid Russo-American friendship. But in the era of expanding American political and economic imperialism, the government believed that other American interests outweighed moral considerations. Japanese expansionism in the Far East was threatening American interests in China, and Russia was a power which might contain that expansion. American economic interests would suffer through any rupture in relationship with a trading partner that had the potential of becoming a major market for American manufactured goods. That these considerations were paramount in the determination of American policy became clear when on May 28, 1907, the State Department issued a letter which informed applicants for passports that:

> this Department will not issue passports to former Russian subjects or to Jews who intend going to Russian territory, unless it has the assurance that the Russian government will consent to their admission.[12]

The American Jewish Committee's charge of "an unconstitutional religious test . . . condoning [Russia's] contemptuous disregard of the American passport," led to a change in the directive, but it had become clear that appeals to the self-interest of Russia by the American government would be of no avail. Only the radical alteration of the treaty or its abrogation could solve the problem. American policy, Secretary of State Elihu Root stated, was "for a complete revision and amendment of the Treaty of 1832." Before any action could take place, Roosevelt was replaced by William Howard Taft, and Root by Philander C. Knox as secretary of state.

Because President Taft had spoken out forcefully on the issue during the campaign and at his inaugural, a positive policy was expected, but the new administration chose prudent silence. Schiff sensed that all was not well. "Four years more will pass and nothing will have been accomplished. . . . We do not respect ourselves sufficiently to come out boldly and demand our rights,"[13] he challenged early in 1910. A meeting with the secretary of state in May of that year disclosed to the American Jewish leadership that the administration was unwilling to press Russia for revision of the Treaty of 1832. When discreet appeals to President Taft were answered with a promise to study the subject, it became clear that only the most forceful action might accomplish abrogation.

Louis Marshall opened the campaign for abrogation on January 19, 1911 with a strong and reasoned address. He argued that in the Russian discrimination against American Jews, "It is not the Jew who is insulted; it is the American people. . . . Finding a proper remedy against this degradation is not a Jewish, but an American question." Secretary Knox countered that the abrogation of the treaty "would be an act of unprecedented disdain towards a friendly nation, which could scarcely fail to arouse antagonism and challenge retaliation." It would serve only "the interests of the Jewish population of the United States."[14]

In February a delegation of representatives of the American Jewish Committee, the Union of American Hebrew Congregations and the B'nai B'rith called on President Taft. They soon found that he was adamant in support of the State Department position. The delegation left in anger. Later, Schiff recalled:

> I told the President: The question will not be downed. Mr. President, we had hoped you would see that justice was done us, but you have decided otherwise; we shall go to the American people.

President Taft's reaction, stated privately, is reported to have been: "I am president of the whole United States, and the vote of the Jews, important as it is, cannot frighten me in this matter."[15]

Schiff made good his promise. A wide-ranging proabrogation campaign was launched. First, a climate of opinion would be built, and then a congressional resolution would be sought.

Marshall's address and a speech of Herbert Parsons of New York in the House of Representatives, "which had the advantage of non-Jewish authorship," were widely distributed. Pertinent data were supplied to newspapers, and popular articles were prepared for leading magazines. State legislatures were solicited for resolutions; special committees were organized and public meetings sponsored throughout the country. A New York rally was addressed by Woodrow Wilson and William Randolph Hearst. With public opinion properly prepared, effort was now directed to persuade Congress to pass a joint resolution calling for abrogation of the treaty. The wooing of key members of both houses is a case study of the lobbying a representative democracy permits. Friends were armed with expertly prepared studies pointing to legal precedents, to the wide popular support for abrogation and to the practical advantages which might accrue. The noncommitted were addressed by political supporters, friends and constituents. Those in opposition were reminded of political realities—the undesirable consequences of voting "wrong" on a popular issue.

The administration did not remain idle. The president, in private, and the secretary of state, in appearances at committee hearings, urged restraint, and pointed to the political and economic consequences of

terminating an agreement with a friendly nation. There were those in
the Jewish community, Simon Wolf and Oscar S. Straus among them,
who, though favoring the cause, were apprehensive about the tactics.
The former had been practicing quiet diplomacy on behalf of Jewish
causes for many years; the latter had risen to the post of secretary of
commerce. They thought their personal careers bore evidence to the
efficacy of quiet persuasion. Why change tactics now?

The American Jewish Committee had chosen to "go public,"
and its initial successes caused it to pursue its campaign with vigor.
Prodded by Schiff and led by Marshall, gathering support in both houses
of Congress continued despite conciliatory offers by the president and
secretary of state. Taft received a delegation of Jews and agreed to abide
by a congressional resolution for abrogation. Knox promised to pursue
vigorously negotiations with Russia. Clearly, the administration was
asking for time, but the Committee pressed its efforts in Congress,
which seemed rewarded by the friendly reception their spokesmen received from the House Committee on Foreign Affairs, and by consideration of the resolution in the full house where, as Naomi W. Cohen
states in her history of the Committee:

> most members could not wait to express their horror of Russian
> barbaric practices, their eulogies of the Jewish people and of the
> American Jews in particular, and their insistence on the inviolability
> of the rights of American citizens.[16]

By a vote of 301 to 1 the House resolved "that in the judgment
of Congress the said treaty . . . ought to be terminated at the earliest
possible time. . . ." The vote in the Senate was unanimous, and a treaty
of commerce and navigation between the United States and Russia
which had lasted 80 years was brought to an end on January 1, 1913.

The leaders of the Committee exulted. Schiff hailed the termination as "of greater importance than anything that has happened, since
civil rights were granted Jews under the first Napoleon, or since English
Jews were admitted to Parliament . . ."[17] It was considered a victory
not alone for the Jews but for America itself. A great nation had risen
to its historic mission to act for human rights.

Cohen concludes:

> As the months passed, the earlier predictions of the executive branch
> seemed to come true: a bitter and unfriendly Russia, a decline in
> trade, anti-Semitic and anti-American reprisals in Russia. Foreign
> countries did not follow America's action but sought rather to reap
> the benefits of her rift with Russia. In the United States abrogation
> brought adverse reaction for American Jews in some quarters . . .

From their pulpits rabbis were declaiming that the United States had scored a victory against bigotry and intolerance, but America and the Jews, not Russia had lost out.[18]

The newly organized American Jewish Committee chose "The Passport Question" as its first great cause, committing to it all its resources and daring a confrontation with an angered State Department and a piqued president as well. Should not the leaders of the Committee, such outstanding men of affairs, have foreseen the dangers to Russian Jewry of a thwarted czarist regime, and the consequences to American Jewish interests of an aroused American administration? Yet they pressed on, spurred by the conviction that as patriotic Americans and proud Jews they could do no other than to battle for American principle and Jewish dignity. Was this not the obligation they assumed when they launched the *American Jewish* Committee? Schiff really did believe that Russia could be brought to heel. If European nations could determine the destiny of Asia and Africa, why could not the growing power of America influence one aspect of Russian policy? Had he not frustrated Russia's efforts to float loans in the United States during the Russo-Japanese War, while he himself was organizer of a $200-million Japanese loan!

Schiff and his colleagues soon learned that to cause America embarrassment in its relations with other nations was a perilous enterprise, that one pays a price for victory when the vanquished retains all the power.

Louis Marshall, astute statesman though he was, realized too late that while America would permit minority groups to influence opinion, it would not tolerate minority attempts to determine policy. Freedom to exercise the democratic right to speak and to influence is accorded to groups as to individuals, but they must not forget that there is a firm hand at the other end of the leash. This limitation on minorities is a limitation which democracy imposes.

"The Passport Question" campaign also illustrated that rights may be fought for within the system, by groups as well as by individuals, that so long as free expression exists, so long as groups mount public campaigns, so long are those in power vulnerable to those who would oppose them.

"The Passport Question" enterprise taught the American Jewish establishment much about possibilities and limitations in America. Within the newly perceived parameters of possibilities, the American Jewish Committee continued to serve what it identified as the best interests of Jews and of America. But henceforth it would do so quietly, with such propriety and discretion that it was often accused of timidity.

THE CONGRESS MOVEMENT

The American Jewish Committee was elitist in composition, oligarchic in organization, "prudent" in operation and anti-Zionist in ideology. All of these were opposed by a number of elements and interests in the newly emerging Jewish community. At the outbreak of World War I, American Jewry numbered some three million, 80 percent of East European origin. Though they applauded the committee's campaigns against restriction of immigration and for abrogation of the Russo-American treaties, they would not long suffer an organization which ostensibly worked for their interests but which resisted their participation. "A Congress for and from all Jews" was urged by publicist and communal functionary, Bernard G. Richards, in an article in the *Jewish Daily News*, May 14, 1914, and joined by Labor Zionist leaders Dr. Nachman Syrkin and Baruch Zuckerman, he proposed it to a conference of Zionists meeting in New York, March 25, 1915. The proposal was enthusiastically adopted, and the Jewish Congress Organization Committee was set up, headed by Religious Zionist leader Gedaliah Bublick. Its purpose was the creation of a democratically elected body to serve as a single representative of the American Jewish community, to deal with all matters affecting it and to give high priority to aiding overseas communities in securing civil and political rights in the reconstituted Europe which would follow the war. The East European Jews in America were demanding a role in that enterprise, which would so affect the future of their brethren in Europe. The Zionists, who took the lead in promoting the congress movement, naturally expected that it would especially serve their cause, the establishment of a Jewish commonwealth in Palestine.

The American Jewish Committee recognized the challenge to its hegemony. It could not publicly oppose democratic expression, so Marshall warned against "a debate with respect to the holding of a Jewish congress . . . the very holding of which will give aid and comfort to Germany, a potential enemy of our government," expressing his opposition as though on a patriotic basis. To Adolf Kraus, Marshall wrote:

> Referring to the "Jewish Congress," . . . I would consider the holding of one deplorable . . . positively detrimental to all that we hold dear. The agitation . . . is that of a body of noisy, blatant, demagogues, principally nationalists and radical socialists. . . . They live on notoriety, and if they can make a speech in which they can denounce everybody and everything they will be perfectly happy, even though the destruction of our European brethren might immediately follow.[19]

One such "noisy, blatant demagogue" was Louis Lipsky, then serving as executive chairman of the Federation of American Zionists. Of the confrontation between the forces vying for control of the American Jewish community, he wrote:

> The American Jewish Committee has acted as the Ministry for Foreign Affairs ever since the Kishinev pogroms. At its annual meetings, pretentious claims were made as to its participation in Jewish events, but it never made an effort to enlarge the sphere of interest and to bring in the forces of the people . . . It had no faith in the competence of the Jewish people, and no confidence in the judgment of the rank and file. It treated the enthusiasms of the general run of Jews with disdain and contempt . . . It did not believe in Jewish nationality not because the symptoms of nationality were not present, but because in its opinion such symptoms should be eradicated . . . Not only did the self-elected leadership insist on doing what it pleased, but it insisted that American Jewry must conform to its thinking.[20]

The indictment is the protest of a talented, American-born and educated young Jew who feels denied entry into the decision-making apparatus of American Jewry because his parents happened to come from a town near the River Niemen in Poland, rather than from a city on the banks of the Main in Germany. He expresses disdain for the radical element in the East European Jewish immigrant community which permitted itself to be "absorbed and then smothered" by the Committee. The National Workmen's Committee on Jewish Rights which sided with the Committee in its confrontation with the pro-congress forces, had among its leaders a former Socialist congressman, a future Socialist judge and the future editor of the Communist Yiddish daily, *Die Freiheit*. Anti-Zionism forged strange alliances.

For Lipsky and those who read his indictment in *The Maccabean*, the official publication of American Zionism, the immediate issue was a struggle for leadership of the Jewish community. He declared that "the self-appointed leaders had two forces to contend with," one American, the other Jewish, which would eventually defeat them.

> First, such a form of life could not endure in an American atmosphere, where freedom and democracy are ingredients of every phase of social life. . . . Second, such a policy excluded from consideration the large, predominant element of Jews coming from Eastern Europe. A policy that refused to take them into account was doomed to failure. . . .[21]

The concept of a democratically elected representative body had wide appeal. Its leaders were popular and able figures. Louis D. Brandeis served as ideologist, Rabbi Stephen S. Wise roused the masses, Louis Lipsky was an able bureaucrat and polemicist. At a rally on January 24, 1916, Brandeis argued that only an American Jewry united in a democratic representative body would have the power to obtain equal rights for their brethren in postwar Europe. (Four days later he was appointed to the Supreme Court of the United States.) Compromises proposed by the Committee were rejected. A conference to create a Congress, meeting in Philadelphia March 27 and 28, heard Stephen S. Wise proclaim that the people

> are resolved to be free of their masters whether these be malevolent tyrants without, or benevolent despots within the life of Israel . . . the time is come for a leadership to be chosen, a leadership that shall democratically and wisely lead rather than autocratically command.[22]

The Congress forces had won the allegiance of the majority of American Jewry; the Committee used its established hegemony. Both realized that American Jewry would not long tolerate continued bickering—the plight of Jews in war-torn Europe demanded unity—and agreement was reached. The "honest broker" role was accorded the National Workmen's Committee on Jewish Rights, which had a constituency in the immigrant community and which had earned credit with the American Jewish Committee by siding with it. For its participation, the American Jewish Committee was able to obtain the following conditions: that the Congress limit its agenda to Jewish rights abroad; that it refrain from ideological pronouncements; that the autonomy of all existing Jewish organizations remain inviolate; that its mandate extend only to one year past the signing of the peace treaty; and that, in addition to democratically elected delegates, there also be representatives of the national Jewish organizations.

Elections were duly held in which some 335,000 ballots were cast. On December 15, 1918, 367 delegates representing 83 cities and 33 organizations, with a combined membership of over a million, convened in Philadelphia and by acclamation elected Judge Julian W. Mack of Chicago as president. A founding member of the American Jewish Committee, he had served for twelve years on its executive board. A close associate of Justice Brandeis in Zionist matters, he was then serving as president of the Zionist Organization of America. As a leader in both groups, Committee and Congress, he could thus serve as a symbol of their unity in commitment to their brethren abroad.

The main order of business was election of a delegation to represent American Jewry at the Peace Conference with a view to securing legally recognized rights for Jews in the "new or enlarged states of Europe." It was in due course to ask the Peace Conference for recog-

nition of the aspirations and historic claims of the Jewish people and
of the Balfour Declaration's promise that "His Majesty's Government
views with favor the establishment in Palestine of a national home for
the Jewish people." The delegation chosen was representative of all
elements of the American Jewish community. Chairman Mack, Reform
Rabbi Dr. Stephen S. Wise and Jacob de Haas represented Zionist forces,
as did Labor Zionist leader Dr. Nachman Syrkin; Louis Marshall and
Harry Cutler were leaders of the American Jewish Committee; Rabbi
Bernard L. Levinthal of Philadelphia was a leading Orthodox rabbi and
a founder of the religious Zionist organization, Mizrachi; Joseph Barondess, charismatic labor leader, and Morris Winchefsky, proletarian
poet and Socialist leader, were from the East European immigrant
community. Bernard G. Richards served as secretary to the delegation.
German and Russian Jews, Zionists and non-Zionists, Orthodox and
Reform and leaders of the labor movement were joined in common
purpose.

The American Jewish Committee nonetheless sent a delegation
of its own, and both delegations cooperated with European Jewish
bodies through the umbrella organization, Comité des Délégations Juives.
They faced a formidable task. New nations did not take kindly to great
powers determining their national policy, and even more so to special
interest groups influencing that determination. Arab interests opposed
a legally recognized Jewish presence in Palestine. Representatives of old
established European Jewries looked with some resentment upon those
who had come from America. Conflicting views as to the order of
priorities vis-à-vis minority rights in Europe and Zionist aspirations in
Palestine threatened to weaken whatever influence a united world Jewry
might be able to exert. It took all the skill of Louis Marshall (who
headed the delegation after Judge Mack returned to the States) to maintain the unity and the discipline that successful negotiations demanded.
Negotiations brought good results: minority rights were guaranteed to
Jews in the new countries of Eastern Europe, and the mandate over
Palestine was granted to Great Britain, which had issued the Balfour
Declaration.

Its work done, the delegation returned to report to the Congress,
scheduled to meet in Philadelphia, May 30–31, 1920. Appropriately, it
was Marshall who presented the report. Once the session was concluded, the American Jewish Congress, as per agreement, was ad-
journed and dissolved.

A number of delegates, mainly from the Zionist and Orthodox
groups and from the *landsmanshaften*, reassembled the next day, and
under the leadership of Stephen S. Wise called for a reconstituted congress as a permanent organization. Two years later, the American Jewish
Congress became a fixture on the American Jewish landscape. Its stated

purpose was little different from that of the American Jewish Committee, "to further and promote Jewish rights . . . generally to deal with all matters relating to and affecting specific Jewish interests." More democratically constituted than the Committee, its leadership was more representative of the larger Jewish community. In two matters it diverged radically from the Committee: the nature of Jewish peoplehood and Jewish destiny. The Congress's constitution committed it "To further the development of the Jewish National Homeland in Palestine. To cooperate with Jews of other lands through the World Jewish Congress to defend Jewish rights and maintain the Jewish status."

This commitment to Zionism and to the international character of the Jewish people was opposed by the Committee which also looked askance on the more militant way in which the Congress pursued its goals.

In the post–World War I world, neither Committee nor Congress became *the* national representative body of the American Jewish community; each remained a national Jewish organization with an agenda limited to Jewish rights at home and abroad. In the 1930s, both did effective work in alerting the Jewish and American communities to the growing danger of Nazism; and in the 1940s and 1950s they were in the vanguard of forces laboring to expand democracy and extend freedom, fighting bigotry in American society and discrimination in the economy, education and social relations.

The Committee, elitist, anti–Zionist, prudent; the Congress, democratic, Zionist, activist—became expressions of the diversity which marked the Jewish community. The unity which did exist was of shared concerns, particularly touching upon the plight of Jewish communities abroad.

A KEHILLAH FOR NEW YORK

Prior to the congress movement, New York Jewry experimented with building a united community on the local level. The enterprise had its beginnings in a response to a charge of high incidence of criminality in the immigrant community.

The immediate response was unbridled anger and the accusation "Anti-Semite!" The Yiddish press of New York called it an attack worthy of the czar's own Black Hundreds. It besmirched the fair name of a decent and moral community, it threatened the very future of the Jew in America, Jewish spokesmen accused, and, what's more, it was an outright fabrication. What caused this outburst of righteous indignation was an article by New York City Police Commissioner Theodore A. Bingham in the September 1908 issue of the prestigious *North*

American Review, "Foreign Criminals in New York." About the Jews, he wrote:

> It is not astonishing that with a million of Hebrews, mostly Russian, in the city (one-quarter of the population) perhaps half of the criminals should be of that race when we consider that ignorance of the language, more particularly among men not physically fit for hard labor, is conducive to crime . . . They are burglars, firebugs, pickpockets and highway robbers . . . pocket-picking is the one [crime] to which they take most naturally.[23]

What hurt more was his observation, "Among the most expert of all the street thieves are Hebrew boys under sixteen who are brought up to lives of crime."

"Jews constitute six percent of the total population of New York State," Abraham Cahan had claimed in *The Atlantic Monthly* in 1898, yet "furnish only three percent of the prisoners of that state . . . The ratio of foreign-born Jews to the total immigrant population is fifteen percent, yet less than five percent of foreign-born prisoners are of the Hebrew race."[24] In 1893, Dr. Adolph M. Radin, rabbi of Congregation Shaarei Tikvah and Jewish chaplain at New York's correctional institutions, boasted that Jews had the lowest proportion of prisoners: 72 of 1600 at Sing Sing; 25 of 900 at Clinton; 81 of 1000 at Blackwells Island. He was particularly proud that, of 1475 "students" at the Elmira Reformatory, only 99 were Jewish.[25]

What heightened the anger was the knowledge that, though exaggerated, Bingham's claim nevertheless touched upon the most disturbing aspect of Jewish life in New York, Jewish criminality, particularly among the young. Dr. Radin reported that most Jewish prisoners were men aged sixteen to thirty. Who did not know that gang leaders Kid Twist, Big Jack Zelig, Kid Dropper were Max Zweiback, William Albert, Nathan Kaplan? That strong-arm men Dopey Benny and Gyp the Blood were Benjamin Fine and Harry Horowitz, and that the "King of the horse poisoners," Yuski Nigger, was Joseph Toblinsky? Prostitution was endemic in this immigrant community, as in all immigrant communities. What was disturbing was the visible presence of traffickers in "white slavery," "Cadets" who enticed young women into lives of shame and owners of houses of prostitution and madams— "Mother" Rosie Hertz and her ilk. Shunned by the Jewish community at large and excluded from communal services, they established their own community, even including a mutual-aid society and a cemetery.

Leaders of the downtown Jews, notably Joseph Barondess, labor leader turned Zionist, and David Blaustein, superintendent of the Educational Alliance, began to lay the foundation for a permanent organization which would deal with problems affecting the community, through an East Side Committee they formed. Louis Marshall, eschewing the "sensational methods" threatened by downtown Jewry, quietly arranged for retraction of the statement by Bingham. The East Side Committee considered the incident closed. Through a letter to the *Tageblatt* Marshall took the occasion to remind the community that, though a dignified solution of an unpleasant episode had been reached, the underlying problems remained.

> What has the great east side, with all of its protests, done to obviate and cure the existing evils, and to eradicate the causes which have led to juvenile delinquency? . . . We have cried because a corn has been trodden on, and we are entirely indifferent to the cancer which is gnawing at our vitals.[26]

An organization to address itself to removal of the cancer was urged by voices downtown and uptown. The "Jewish Council" (as *The New York Times* labeled the East Side Committee) proposed that representative Jews of the city form a "permanent organization to foster the interests of the Jews in every proper way." Dr. Judah Magnes stated: "The one million of Jews of New York . . . need a permanent and representative organization that may speak on their behalf, that may defend their rights and liberties and that may also cope with the problems of criminality."[27] Magnes was then rabbi of Reform Temple Emanu-El, whose membership included New York's Jewish elite, the Schiffs, the Lewisohns, the Guggenheims, the Warburgs; and he was the brother-in-law of the temple's president, Louis Marshall. At the same time, he served as secretary of the Federation of American Zionists, made his spiritual home with the Zionistic-oriented faculty of the Conservative Jewish Theological Seminary, was a friend of Yiddishist spokesman Dr. Chaim Zhitlowsky, and from time to time appeared at the services of one or another East Side Orthodox synagogue. Because his associations and interests were as wide as the Jewish community, he would be the ideal person to lead an organization of all elements, and this leadership he was ready to assume. To the editor of the *Tageblatt,* who had chided Marshall for his attack, Magnes proposed:

> Mr. Marshall represents, in some measure, that section of the community with leadership and wealth. You, Mr. Editor, represent in some measure, that section of the community with our masses, our hopes. An army without leaders is almost as absurd as leaders without an army. The opportunity is now at hand for leaders and soldiers to recognize the need they have of each other and to join ranks.[28]

Both uptown and downtown Jews recognized who would be the captains and the generals and who would serve as foot soldiers.

Deliberations by the American Jewish Committee with elements of the "Great East Side" followed. Meetings were followed by a founding convention, and officially The Kehillah of New York City came into being in March 1909. Leaders of the American Jewish Committee were elected to its first executive committee along with leaders of the Orthodox Jewish Community, downtown and uptown sections. Committee leaders remained dominant in the affairs of the Kehillah, which became the New York arm of the Committee. The Socialists, who had charged that such an organization would be forged through an alliance of the "dark forces" of religion and exploiting capitalists, felt their fears confirmed and remained aloof.

In its fourteen years of existence, all under the chairmanship of Magnes, the Kehillah concentrated on four areas of Jewish communal concern: Jewish education, order and discipline in organized Orthodox religious life, control of crime in the community and harmonious relationships within the "Jewish" clothing industry. It operated on the principle of full confidence in the ability of an enlightened public to reach just decisions and to subordinate special interests to the public good.

JEWISH EDUCATION

At the first convention, February 27, 1910, Mordecai M. Kaplan, head of the Teachers Institute of the Jewish Theological Seminary, and Bernard Cronson, a public-school principal, reported on the "First Community Survey of Jewish Education in New York," which they had conducted. They found that education was conveyed by six agencies: Talmud Torah schools, publicly supported, attended mainly by boys in the congested neighborhoods; institutional schools for girls, attached to orphan asylums; congregational schools for boys and girls, sponsored by synagogues; Sunday schools; the *heder,* a private enterprise teaching rote prayer-book reading to boys; and Private Instruction by itinerant teachers in private homes. Of 170,000 Jewish children of school age, only 40,000 were receiving some kind of Jewish education. The conclusions reached were: (1) the demand for Jewish education was comparatively small; (2) small as demand was, means and equipment were too inadequate to meet it; (3) whenever demand is met, there is lack either of system or content.

Jewish education in New York was one of the most painful problems confronting the community; to have the magnitude of the problem documented by a "scientific study" raised it to top priority on the communal agenda. The challenge was formidable. Less than one-quarter of the eligible children were receiving any form of Jewish instruction. Of these, one-third were in the educationally inadequate (and often personally repulsive) *hedorim*. Only 10 percent, at most, were receiving a Jewish education which might be termed acceptable.

The immigrant community accepted with alacrity an educational system totally new to their experience. High school and college were the doorways to economic opportunity and social status. Small wonder that the religious schools fared as they did. They were meant only to supplement the American public school, the primary educational establishment. In Europe, mother's lullaby urged the son to study Torah; father and son both knew that it was the best students in the *yeshiva* who reaped the rewards of a desirable marriage, a wealthy father-in-law and status. In America, the road to the good life led through the public school, high school and college. A reporter on the *New York Tribune* was told by "a long-gabardined peddler" in 1898: "My boy shall be a lawyer, learned and respected of men . . . My boy shall have knowledge. He shall go to college." The reporter observed:

> College! That is the aim and ambition of hundreds of them. The father . . . instills into his children's minds the necessity for knowledge. He points to his own life—how meager, sordid, and poor it is—and he tells them to avoid it they must study hard and learn much. [29]

Yet the same fathers, "bent beneath the load of coats he is carrying to the factory or trudging along with his pushcart," spent their hard-earned dollars to send their sons to heder and Talmud Torah, their daughters to religious school; and mothers skimped and saved for tuition money, and continued to sing the Old World lullabies, adding a sad sigh. The education their sons were receiving was far different from that which their husbands or brothers had received in the Old World. (Excepting only the five hundred boys studying in the Rabbi Jacob Joseph Yeshivah, an all-day school, which the Kaplan report did not even mention.) The public schools might be preparing the young for their future occupations, but they were not assuring their future as Jews. The supplementary Jewish schools' record was at best spotty, and the great majority of Jewish children were receiving no Jewish education at all. It was widely believed that better schools would attract more pupils. Magnes concluded that the most needed and popular contribution the Kehillah could make to the quality of Jewish life was in Jewish education.

Large funds would be required to accomplish such improvement, and it was natural to turn to Schiff to take leadership. This Magnes did. The direct appeal was to Schiff's overriding interest: the good name of the Jew. The environment of the New York ghetto, Magnes argued, pulled children away from "the anchorage which the religion of their fathers might have given them." The public school could not, of course, provide the religious teaching which could make the children of the immigrants, "pure, clean and honorable." Only a vastly improved, modern, appealing supplementary school system could make them "American men and women who will prove not a menace to the Republic but a blessing to it." Schiff could not resist such a prospect, nor be unmoved by Magnes's conviction that "Judaism in this country is largely dependent for its strength upon the education this generation is able to give its children." Eventually, he and his associates at Kuhn, Loeb and Co. provided $35,000 annually for the Kehillah's Bureau of Education. In 1915, of the Kehillah's total budget of $108,493.18, the bureau was receiving $68,064.40, well over 60 percent. In 1917, the communal responsibility for Jewish education was formalized, when the bureau became affiliated with the Federation for the Support of Jewish Philanthropic Societies, the central charitable fund of New York Jewry.

Magnes called for creation of a board of Jewish education and appointment of a superintendent of instruction. Palestinian-born Samson Benderly, a Johns Hopkins–trained M.D., who abandoned medicine for a career in Jewish education, was brought from Baltimore, where he had already made a reputation for fashioning a modern, effective Jewish educational system and in 1910 was appointed head of the newly created Bureau of Jewish Education. Benderly was devoted to Jewish culture, to American democracy and to the most modern educational methods. "The great public school system," he wrote, "is the rock bottom upon which this country is rearing its institutions, so we Jews much evolve here a system of Jewish education that shall be complementary to and harmonious with the public school system." The curriculum of the Jewish educational system he would fashion would not only create Jews who would be comfortable and happy in their Jewishness, but would also demonstrate that the principles of Judaism "are perfectly compatible with and essential to the fundamental principles upon which the American nation is building a wonderful structure of human liberty and happiness."[30]

For half a century Jewish education reflected Benderly's philosophy. The methods he introduced have lasted even longer. In time, every major Jewish community established a Bureau of Jewish Education to coordinate, stimulate, instruct and service its educational institutions. Benderly established model schools and carried on far-reaching experimentation in them. He urged the use of modern visual aids. Classes for in-service training of teachers, a council of principals, parents' groups and a leadership training program were organized. Textbooks were commissioned and published, curricula were built and tested.

He brought to Jewish education the best and latest techniques. The insights of John Dewey and his co-workers were utilized to teach the Torah of Moses and his disciples.

No matter how great the vision, how perfect the system, in the end education depends on the skill and devotion of the men and women in the bureaus and classrooms. "Benderly's Boys," as his disciples referred to themselves, A. M. Dushkin, I. B. Berkson, Israel Chipkin, Leo Honor, Emanuel Gamoran and many others, were attracted to the field by Benderly's enthusiasm. For content he had them study at the Teachers Institute of the Jewish Theological Seminary; he urged them to complete their doctorates at Teachers College of Columbia University for methodology. In time, they headed the bureaus of the major cities, directed the leading teacher-training schools and prestigious commissions of education. Through them and those they trained, the influence of Benderly pervaded the Jewish educational enterprise.

ORGANIZED RELIGIOUS LIFE

The rabbis of America were organized into two bodies, the Reform Central Conference of American Rabbis and the Orthodox Agudas Harabonim. The Reform were congregational rabbis, preaching, teaching, dispensing pastoral services for their congregations, maintaining their roles as spiritual leaders in the Jewish and the larger community. The Orthodox, engaged by a congregation or an Orthodox communal body, assumed the title of *Rav Ho-Ir* (rabbi of the city), derived their income from salary, fees for rabbinical services and *kashrut* supervision. To the last mentioned the Kehillah now turned its attention.

In 1917 it was estimated that one million of New York's one and a half million Jews bought kosher meat, consuming each week about three million pounds. Kosher meat was big business, and the abattoir owners, meat wholesalers and retail butchers were a powerful force in the Orthodox community. Unlike the European setting, where income from kosher slaughter was used by the organized community to help finance its activities, in America laissez-faire obtained both in distribution of kosher products and in supervision of *kashrut*. The ritual slaughterers were in the employ of slaughterhouse owners and butchers, and so too were the supervising rabbis. Room for abuse was ample and scandals abounded. There was hardly a community whose religious life was unstained by vituperative dispute between rabbinic colleagues as a consequence of the competition between their employers.

The Kehillah attempted to bring some order to this chaotic scene. The situation was complicated by the fact that there were so many functionaries, "reverends," "marriage performers," who dabbled in religious matters for which they had neither the knowledge nor the authority. "There was no authoritative body to lay down the rule or to enforce it," a contemporary rabbi observed. To supply this communal deficiency, the Vaad Harabonim (Board of Orthodox Rabbis) of New York was organized. Ten leading rabbis were invited by the Kehillah to form the group and authorized to augment the membership. They, in turn, invited twenty more whose credentials and standing were unassailable. More members were added, and a procedure for the orderly supervision of *kashrut* and *gittin* (divorces) was established.

As in similar attempts, the good intentions and good work were vitiated by a consortium of butchers who would not accept independent supervision, and who were able to employ a rabbi who would subvert his organized colleagues. It had been hoped that a board of Orthodox rabbis would supply the base for the organization of the Orthodox community into a disciplined and self-disciplining body, "a strong and unified section of the community," but competing social and economic forces within the community did not even permit an organized rabbinate. As in the Biblical description of chaotic conditions in the time of the Judges, "Each man did what was right in his own eyes."

The same freedom permitted Jewish religious life in New York a richness and variety which has not as yet been fully recognized. *The Jewish Communal Register of New York City, 1917–1918,* published by the Kehillah, records that 42 percent of the "communal budget" went to synagogues, religious school and religious affairs. New York City had no less than 1127 synagogues. Of these 784 were permanent, with a seating capacity of 217,725, and 343 temporary (meeting mainly on the High Holy Days) houses of worship with 163,638 seats, for a total of 381,363 seats. They ranged from Reform Temple Emanu-El, with a membership of 920 families, a synagogue building with a seating capacity of 1600 on Fifth Avenue, two rabbis and a school, a sisterhood, a brotherhood and cemetery grounds, through Conservative Temple Petach Tikvah in Brooklyn where Rabbi Israel H. Levinthal delivered sermons in English to a membership of 275 in a synagogue seating 1200, and supervised a Hebrew School and a junior congregation, to Chevrah Achei Grodno V'anshei Staputkin, an Orthodox congregation on the Lower East Side, which claimed 80 members, to whom it offered the facilities of a synagogue seating 350, a free loan society and a cemetery.

Only 25 percent of the permanent synagogues had rabbis. 93.9 percent (730) were Orthodox conducting their services wholly in Hebrew, 4 percent (32) were Conservative and 2 percent (16) Reform, but the congregations of the latter two groups were far larger in membership and their synagogues far greater in seating capacity.

Almost half the synagogues were organized before 1902, but over one-fifth were less than five years old. While only 13 percent had schools, 28 percent had free loan societies, 24 percent extended sick

benefits, and 77 percent had their own cemeteries. The smaller Orthodox congregations provided their memberships the benefits of a fraternal order, so important to immigrants who had left the care of the
extended family and the sheltering services of a closely knit community.

Commenting on the gathered statistics, Mordecai M. Kaplan
pointed to the negative disclosures:

> The synagogue has lost hold on more than one-half of the largest
> Jewish Community in the world . . . It is evident from . . . the
> unevenness of the percent of the population affiliated with the
> synagogue, when judged by districts . . . that density of popula-
> tion, economic conditions, and length of stay in this country have
> so rapid an effect upon synagogue affiliation that we cannot but
> infer that the synagogue owes its existence more to the momentum
> of the past, than to any new forces created in this country that
> make for its conservation and development.[31]

He noted that less than one-fifth of the permanent synagogues "have
reckoned with the environment and have to some extent, at least, taken
root in American life" by introducing the English sermon. His concern
for the future of Judaism in America is heightened by the recognition
that "in this country . . . the synagogue is the principal means of keeping alive the Jewish consciousness . . . and is the only institution that
can define our aims to a world that would otherwise be at a loss to
understand why we persist in retaining our corporate individuality."
Kaplan maintained that a new type of synagogue, a *synagogue center*
whose activities would reflect the entire *religious civilization* of the Jewish
people, would have to replace the Reform temple and the Orthodox
shtibl. Only such a reconstituted synagogue, reflecting the "new forces
created in this country," would be able to keep "Jewish consciousness"
alive. The Jewish religious establishment might be serving some of the
needs of the older generation, but it had little appeal to and less influence
on the younger.

BUREAU OF SOCIAL MORALS

Sober, deliberate Louis Marshall could contain himself no longer.
On July 23, 1912, in a fury of indignation he scribbled an epistle (which
he never sent) to the "Organization of Orthodox Rabbis, whatever the
name may be . . .":

> You have closed your eyes to the departure of the children of a
> race, that justly prided itself on the purity of its moral life, to adopt
> the career of gamblers, thugs, gangsters, thieves, and prosti-
> tutes . . . You have remained silent witnesses to the degradation
> of Judaism, to the alienation from it of the new generation.[32]

What had kindled Marshall's ire was the murder a week earlier of gambler Herman Rosenthal after he had publicly accused Lieutenant Charles Becker of the Police Department's antigambling squad of corruption and had offered to disclose other police involvement in crime and graft. The sensation the accusation and the murder caused brought to public attention the presence of crime on the Lower East Side, which four years earlier Marshall had warned was "a cancer . . . gnawing at our vitals."

Yiddish dailies blamed criminality on the American environment which tore children away from the moral influences of the religion of their parents. The Socialist newspaper, the *Forward,* pointing to crime among Jews in large industrial cities of Europe, argued that its cause was economic exploitation and the social problems it created. Uptown Jews accused the Orthodox establishment of failing to make religion attractive to the young, permitting them, in a phrase of Marshall's, to turn to "an orgy of materialism, license and indifference."

Five days after the Marshall outburst, the Executive Committee of the Kehillah acted favorably on a Magnes recommendation to form a "vigilance committee" and a "bureau of information and investigation." In early August 1912, the Bureau of Social Morals was established. The biographer of the Kehillah, Arthur A. Goren, describes it as "a secret service which fought crime and vice in the Jewish quarter." For five years, a small staff of investigators working in cooperation with the city administration and the police department sought out and disclosed houses of prostitution, gambling houses and gathering places of known criminals.

In this self-policing action, the Kehillah was able to enlist the cooperation of that segment of the East Side which had avoided affiliation with it, the secularist, labor, Socialist groups. To fight the "cancer," Meyer London, labor lawyer and first Socialist to serve in Congress, Henry Moskowitz, a social worker and leader of the Downtown Ethical Culture Society and communal worker Belle Moskowitz joined the Kehillah initiative.

The Bureau of Social Morals was accepted as an "unfortunate" necessity, the need to keep one's house in order being a communal responsibility.

BUREAU OF INDUSTRY

The adoption of the Protocol of Peace which settled the cloakmakers' strike of 1910 was hastened by the recognition that the great preponderance of Jews among employers and employees had made the strike a matter of Jewish communal concern. Henry Moskowitz, A. Lincoln Filene, the Boston department-store owner, and social worker

Meyer Bloomfield persuaded the contending parties to bring in Louis Brandeis to mediate. Shortly thereafter, Jacob Schiff and Louis Marshall interceded, using their considerable influence to force the merchants' association to return to the negotiating table as a matter of Jewish responsibility. Julius Henry Cohen, attorney for the manufacturers, saw the system for arbitration set up by the protocol as an application of the traditional Jewish mode of settling disputes.

> These immigrants came from parts of Europe where arbitration was an accepted method of settling disputes . . . The early success for development of arbitration boards in the needle trades can be traced directly to this experience.[33]

In 1912 Magnes was instrumental in mediating a fur workers' strike. It gained him credit in the labor community and enabled him to establish communication with some of its leaders, particularly Meyer London. Early the following year he attempted to utilize this contact to incorporate the radical elements into the Kehillah. Though his approaches were ignored, the attempts continued. The involvement of the Kehillah in labor arbitration served its basic purpose of lessening tension and furthering harmony in the Jewish community.

In 1914, the Bureau of Industry was formed with Drs. Paul Abelson and Leo Mannheimer as arbitrators. During the next five years, it mediated labor disputes and strengthened the network of boards of arbitration, and served the fur, embroidery, bakers, leather bag and men's clothing industries. Its mediators were invited to intervene in labor-industry disputes in Boston, Philadelphia, Rochester and Chicago.

At the Ninth Annual Convention of the Kehillah on June 1, 1918, Magnes spoke of the promise of the Kehillah to America's Jews, and its meaning to America:

> The Kehillah in America must be that instrumentality through which the Jews of America exercise self-determination, exercise the right and the privilege of every group to determine what they want to become in this country, what their relationship shall be with one another . . . The organization in America of such Kehillahs, upon a democratic basis, is a distinct contribution by the Jews to community life in America. Rightly used it will come to be regarded . . . as one of the many group endeavors which may be of aid to the American people in understanding and furthering the development of so complex a unit as America.

Arthur A. Goren, in his masterly study of the Kehillah, *New York Jews and the Quest for Community,* comments on its decline:

> In the early days of the Kehillah movement . . . Magnes had assumed the existence of an ethnic solidarity which, grounded in the

group's minority experience and the national-religious quality of Judaism, led to collective responses to outside threats . . . But in the declining period of the Kehillah, Magnes came to understand that under the free conditions of American life, ethnicity was but one of many attachments shared by group and individual . . . Most Jews remained interested in the minimum separation from the larger society for maintaining Jewish identity. They would be content with a more modest vision of community.[34]

Magnes's search for community took him to Palestine in 1922. What he planned as a visit for a year or two, became a lifetime of leadership in cultural and communal life as president of the Hebrew University and worker in the cause of Jewish-Arab amity. Without Magnes, the Kehillah to which he had given life and spirit remained with neither. Three years after his departure, it came to an end.

FOR BRETHREN ABROAD

In September 1914, twenty-eight-year-old Maurice Wertheim debarked in Palestine's port city, Jaffa, from the U.S.S. cruiser, *North Carolina,* carrying a suitcase filled with "the equivalent of fifty thousand dollars." He had brought the money from Constantinople at the request of his father-in-law, the Honorable Henry Morgenthau, United States ambassador to Turkey. In a letter to "Messrs. Jacob H. Schiff, Louis Marshall, Nathan Straus, and Members of the American Jewish Committee, New York City," dated October 21, 1914, Wertheim reported: "the relief sent so promptly by American Jews and on an American warship produced a tremendous impression throughout all Palestine, and has, I think, done a great deal for the prestige of the Jews of Palestine."[35]

Louis Marshall, president, pointed out to the members of the committee, met for the eighth annual meeting, "Among the earliest victims of the war were the Jews of Palestine." He reminded his colleagues that most Jewish residents of the Holy Land were dependent on the benevolence of their coreligionists in Europe and America. Because with the outbreak of the war, all aid from Europe had come to an end, everything now depended on the Jews of America.

Toward the end of August of that fateful year, Ambassador Morgenthau had sent "urgent cablegrams" to the American Jewish Committee alerting it to the desperate plight of Palestinian Jewry and requesting an immediate grant of fifty thousand dollars. The Committee responded at once. As was his wont, Jacob H. Schiff took leadership, pledging one-quarter of the amount. The Committee appropriated $25,000 from its Emergency Trust Fund, and it invited the Federation of American Zionists to complete the sum required. That organization promptly responded.

Marshall pointed out that "the amounts thus far forwarded will afford only temporary relief" for the Jews of Palestine and predicted that "as soon as they can communicate . . . the Jews of Russia, Belgium, Austria-Hungary . . . will [also] appeal to their brethren in America."

The first to hear the "appeal" was the Orthodox Jewish Community. On September 28, the Reverend Dr. Bernard Drachman, president of the Union of Orthodox Jewish Congregations, sent telegrams to eighty congregations: "Our unfortunate brethren abroad are suffering the terrors of a frightful war. Your congregation is requested to make offerings on Kol Nidre Eve . . ." A month later the union, Mizrachi, the Agudas Harabonim and the Central Committee of Palestine Institutions joined to form the Central Committee for the Relief of the Jews Suffering Through the War. The Orthodox community was the first to organize for relief, because it had both the immediate motivation and a ready means for solicitation and collection. To the recently arrived immigrant community from what was now the war zone in Eastern Europe, the suffering there was not only of fellow Jews but often of members of one's own family. The "First Official War Relief Appeal Addressed to American Jewry October 14, by the Central Relief Committee" stressed: "Remember—No one can tell, today, whether his own relatives are not refugees far from their own home. Remember—You cannot know where your own father or mother, sister or brother is. Your help, through us, may help them."[36] A network of synagogues in which charitable contributions were a daily occurrence, and rabbis who engaged in solicitation for all manner of worthy causes, provided the site and manpower for raising "an enormous amount of money at once . . . and to continue the effort . . . possibly even through the next few years to come!"

It soon became apparent that to raise the "enormous" sum the situation demanded would require an unprecedented effort of a community united, under the leadership of Schiff, Marshall, and Warburg. To launch such an effort, a conference was convened by the American Jewish Committee on October 25. The national organizations represented reached across the entire gamut of the American Jewish community. The Orthodox Agudas Harabonim and Union of Orthodox Jewish Congregations joined with the Reform Central Conference of American Rabbis and Union of American Hebrew Congregations and the Conservative United Synagogue of America; the Federation of American Zionists sat with the anti-Zionist Arbeiter Ring; Jewish fraternal orders came to express fraternal concern. A crisis abroad, the plight of fellow Jews and the enterprise of coming to their aid "to accomplish the largest measure of relief" brought unity to an American Jewry divided still by ethnic and religious differences, as well as by economic and social antagonism. The conference appointed a committee of five: Oscar Straus; the Honorable Julian W. Mack and Louis D. Brandeis, American-born establishment Jews become Zionists; Orthodox leader Harry Fischel; and Meyer London. A group representative of and respected by all elements of the community, it was charged with selecting one hundred leading American Jews to constitute an American Jewish Relief Committee. Louis Marshall was to be president, Felix M. Warburg, treasurer.

The relief committee set to work at once, organizing a campaign to extend through the entire community. It soon became obvious that, though overseas needs called for unity, realities at home made for the retention of diversity. Different groups had different modes of operation; their constituents lived in different areas and spoke different languages. So long as such differences obtained it would be easier and more effective to permit the campaign to reflect the diversity in the community.

THE JOINT DISTRIBUTION COMMITTEE

The Central Relief Committee remained the campaign apparatus of the Orthodox community, and the American Jewish Relief Committee that of the German Jewish establishment. They organized the Joint Distribution Committee of American Funds for the Relief of Jewish War Sufferers on November 27, 1914, and chose Felix M. Warburg chairman. A few months later the East European Labor-Socialist groups formed the People's Relief Committee under the chairmanship of Meyer London and joined the other two.

Though each committee carried on its campaigns in its own manner, the American Jewish Relief Committee set the tone. Its mass meetings inaugurated the campaigns. The large gifts announced set the standards for giving. In 1915, $1.5 million was raised for the Joint Distribution Committee. In 1916, Nathan Straus pledged $100,000 and urged a target of $5 million. President Woodrow Wilson declared a Jewish War Sufferers Relief Day, the Red Cross aided in collections, and before the year was out, the goal urged by Straus was nearly met. The following year, Dr. Judah Magnes returned from the war zone demanding a goal of $10 million. At a great rally in Carnegie Hall which he addressed, the first million was raised. Julius Rosenwald made the first of his great pledges, $1 million, conditional on the goal being met. It was.

The Central Relief Committee sold War Relief Stamps and War Relief Certificates, conducted appeals in synagogues, sponsored cantorial concerts and a tour by the most renowned cantorial artist of the time, Yossele Rosenblatt, which opened in New York's Hippodrome and brought in $70,000. A Tag Day, collections in the garment district, pledges of days of labor and newspaper solicitations raised funds for the People's Relief Committee. The gathered funds were entrusted to the Joint Distribution Committee, which, during the war years, distributed some $20 million.

In Russia the funds were disbursed by the Jewish Committee for Relief of Sufferers from the War in Petrograd. In German-occupied Poland, Das Judisches Hilfskomite für Polen administered the aid, and the Israelitische Allianz aus Wien did the same for Jews in Austria-Hungary and in territories occupied by its armies. The American embassy at Constantinople conveyed JDC funds "for distribution through committees accredited to it." In Palestine, the consul of the United States in Jerusalem aided the committee in its work.

During the war years and in the years which followed, German Jews in America learned to respect the ardor and selflessness of Russian immigrant Jews, and they, in turn, grew to appreciate the concern and generosity of this elite group toward all Jews everywhere. Anti-Zionists and non-Zionists began to understand the single-minded passion of the Zionists; Zionists, in turn, learned that what divided them from others were perceptions of nationalism and political loyalties, not devotion to the welfare of fellow Jews. Socialists laboring for the social revolution turned their attention to the immediate needs of sorely beset brethren and, finding their "class antagonists" and "exploiters" engaged in similar labors, joined hands with them.

The postwar years 1919 and 1920 posed the challenge of a million homeless Jews, of mass pogroms in the Ukraine, of devastated Jewish communities attempting to reestablish themselves in a chaotic, hostile Europe. "Bread for the Hungry—Shrouds for the Dead" was the chilling call to American Jewry. Some $27 million were contributed in these years and some $20 million more by 1924. JDC workers moved through the war-torn landscape, organizing self-help committees, distributing food, clothing and medicine, setting up small loan societies. The cooperation of the United States government and America's great relief agencies was sought and obtained. Generosity and skillful use of resources made the term "Joint" synonymous with hope and rescue to the Jews of ravaged Europe.

Herbert Hoover, who headed the major American relief projects in war-shattered Europe, stated in 1923: "There is no brighter chapter in the whole history of philanthropy than that which could be written of the work of the American Jews in the last nine years."[37]

10.

After the Armistice

THE FIRST WORLD WAR PRESENTED NEW CHALLENGES FOR THE AMERICAN Jewish community. It reoriented itself from a prewar pro-German stance to wartime patriotism, except for the Socialists who espoused neutrality, and a small group of pacifists. Jewish men went into the army, and the Jewish press hailed their exploits. The National Jewish Welfare Board was established to care for their Jewish needs. War Bond rallies were held in Jewish neighborhoods and their results were announced with pride.

The community rallied to the aid of overseas brethren, and pressed their claim for rights in the postwar, politically restructured Europe. Because the hated czarist monarchy had come to an end, the Russian Revolution was welcomed; a new era of freedom and equality seemed to be opening for that long persecuted Jewish community in Russia. The Balfour Declaration was hailed by the majority of American Jews as the harbinger of Jewish nationhood in their ancient homeland.

Whatever euphoria existed at the signing of the peace treaty was soon dissipated. A wave of anti-Semitism swept through America. A new generation of American Jews, the children of the mass immigration, ready to enter the middle class, found door after door shut to them. Zionism marshaled latent energies and evoked loyalties, but also caused division within the community. The emergence of Communism split the Jewish labor community into two warring camps. And the perennial challenge remained. How to retain the loyalty of the American Jew for Judaism, how to win the commitment of the young? Organized American Jewry took to the challenge at once, initiating new projects, improvising on old solutions, restructuring inherited institutions. Often, however, promising enterprises yielded meager results. The community was sustained throughout this period by the faith that America— despite temporary aberrations—was hospitable to the Jew and Judaism.

ZIONISM: THE BRANDEIS ERA AND BEYOND

"The end of the war," Melvin I. Urofsky writes in *American Zionism from Herzl to the Holocaust,* "found Zionism greatly changed from the puny movement it had been five years earlier. Its membership stood at nearly two hundred thousand, its budget involved millions, and its leaders dealt with the world's statesmen on the establishment of a Jewish homeland."[1] Nonetheless, in early June 1921, the Zionist Organization of America, assembled in Cleveland, Ohio, repudiated the leadership that had elevated American Zionism to the powerful force it had only recently become.

In the 1880s and 1890s many East European immigrants brought with them Zionist loyalties and established a whole network of Hovevei Zion (Lovers of Zion) clubs. They supported the recently established colonies in Palestine and laid the foundations for a Hebrew culture in America. The Zionist idea also found adherents among "native" Americans, even in the ideologically anti-Zionist Reform rabbinate, notably Rabbis Bernhard Felsenthal of Chicago and Gustav Gottheil of New York's Temple Emanu-El. Dr. Richard Gottheil of Columbia University, son of Gustav, served as first president of the Federation of American Zionists (FAZ), established in 1898 in the wake of the Zionist Congress in Basel. Rabbi Stephen S. Wise, who was to give leadership to the Zionist cause for the next half century, was named secretary. At the turn of the century, the appeal of Zionism was weak, but opposition to it vigorous. There were those who warned about potential accusations of dual loyalty: "Is not America our Zion, Washington our Jerusalem?" they proclaimed. Others argued that it was Israel's destiny to be dispersed so that it could fulfill its divine mission to "be a light unto the nations," bringing to them the meaning of ethical monotheism. Fired by Herzl's vision and seeing in Zionism a powerful antidote to indifference in Jewish life, the small band of Zionist adherents persisted. Dr. Harry Friedenwald, a respected ophthalmologist and scholarly Jewish leader of Baltimore, succeeded Gottheil to the presidency of the FAZ. In 1903, the American religious Zionist Mizrachi was founded, two years later, the Socialist Labor Zionists, Poale-Zion. Both drew their membership from the East European Jewish immigrant community, while the leadership and much of the constituency of FAZ was of the more Americanized Jews.

As a working-class movement American Poale-Zion gave priority to Socialism as its program adopted in 1909 indicates:

1. The Jewish Socialist Labor Party Poale-Zion, aims, together with the working classes of all nations, to overthrow capitalism and to establish the Socialist system of Society . . .
2. . . . aims to concentrate the Jewish people in Palestine and to establish there an autonomous Jewish commonwealth.

As the movement developed, the emphasis on Socialism yielded to devotion to Zionism. The survival of the Jewish people took precedence to the victory of the proletariat.

The Jewish national consciousness, aroused by the Kishinev pogrom in 1903 and by the pogroms which swept Russia in 1905, caused a dramatic rise in membership in Zionist organizations, but the immediate impact over, membership fell. The FAZ saw Zionism as a cultural force that could infuse new spirit and would create new Jews proud of their heritage and proud of their people. The home of the FAZ Zionist leadership—Friedenwald, Magnes, Friedlaender—was the Jewish Theological Seminary, whose president Solomon Schechter saw Zionism as "the great bulwark against assimilation. . . . I belong to that class of Zionists that lay more stress on the religious–national aspects of Zionism. . . . The activity of Zionism must not be judged by what it has accomplished *in* Zion and Jerusalem but *for* Zion and Jerusalem, by awakening the national Jewish consciousness. Our synagogues and homes show plainly the effect."[2]

The emphasis is clearly on what Zionism can do for the American Jew, not on what the American Jew must do for Zionism; this remained the view of Zionist leadership till the outbreak of World War I. In 1909 when Magnes and Friedlaender, the most articulate proponents of Zionism, turned their energies to New York's Kehillah, it had marked effect on Zionist vitality. From 1911 to the outbreak of hostilities, FAZ was led by Louis Lipsky and a group of hardworking East Side luminaries, who could not appeal to the "classes" and whose call to the "masses" found little response. In 1914, there were fewer than 15,000 members in the FAZ. Poale-Zion's primary loyalty was still to Socialism, and Mizrachi consisted of a small group of enlightened Orthodox rabbis and laymen. Such was organized Zionism on the eve of World War I.

Louis D. Brandeis first met East European immigrants when he helped settle the cloakmakers' strike in 1910. Soon after, he met Jacob de Haas, whom Theodor Herzl had sent to America in 1902 to strengthen the Zionist enterprise there, and was converted by him to the cause. "My approach to Zionism," Brandeis later explained, "was through Americanism. Practical experience and observation convinced me that Jews were by reason of their traditions and their character peculiarly fitted to the attainment of American ideals." He found wide congruence between these ideals and those of Zionism. Indeed, they reinforced one another. "It became clear to me that to be good Americans we must be better Jews, and to be better Jews we must become Zionists."[3] He interpreted the Wilsonian New Freedom to include the concept of a new nationalism which proclaims it a duty for each race or people "to develop . . . for only through differentiated development will high civilization be attained."[4] For the Jewish people to fulfill its mandate of spiritual and cultural development it must have in "the fatherland a center from which the Jewish spirit may radiate and give the Jews . . . that inspiration which springs from memories of a great past and the hope of a great future."[5] Zionism, Brandeis argued, serves both the needs of the Jewish people and the interests of American democracy. One great contribution Brandeis made to American Zionism was to remove from it the specter of dual allegiance. Equally important was his organizational achievement. In 1914 he found a disorganized FAZ; by 1918, his leadership—"Men, money, discipline" was his demand—had forged a large, well-organized, smoothly running Zionist organization.

Brandeis came into leadership almost casually. He responded to a call to a meeting of Zionist leaders at the outbreak of the war, and found he was the only nationally known figure present. De Haas proposed him for the chairmanship and Brandeis agreed to head the Provisional Executive Committee for General Zionist Affairs. His first act was to establish an emergency fund, and he himself pledged the first thousand dollars. The plight of Jews overseas demanded funds, and American Jewry needed to respond. Political activity would also be necessary, and Brandeis took leadership in demand for a democratically constituted American Jewish Congress identified with the Zionist program. The successful congress campaign added thousands of new members to Zionist rolls. The Balfour Declaration of November 2, 1917, added thousands more.

In 1916 Brandeis was nominated by President Woodrow Wilson to the Supreme Court of the United States. After his confirmation, he resigned from the presidency of the Zionist organization, but continued an active interest in its affairs.

WASHINGTON VERSUS PINSK

The war over, the Zionist Organization of America (ZOA, formerly the FAZ), led by Brandeis's lieutenants under Justice Julian W. Mack, set out to undertake what they conceived as "the task before us," building up of the land of Israel. They felt that cultural enterprises and political activity had to be laid aside. All energies and funds should go for the physical and economic structure that a modern nation would need. Because sovereignty through settlement was the nineteenth-century American experience in nation building, the Americanized leaders of the ZOA thought it also the proper program for a Jewish Palestine.

The opposition developed immediately, both at home and abroad. Dr. Chaim Weizmann, moving into leadership of the World Zionist Organization, had been raised in Russian Zionism with its strong emphasis on cultural renaissance. He was allied with Labor Zionism, which was working to establish a Jewish Socialist state. European Zionists emphasized immigration and the political activity which would create a state. The ZOA's program of practical development was philanthropic Zionism, whose purpose was to build up the land and aid those who settled on it.

The conflict was dramatized as a confrontation between Brandeis and Weizmann, who declared, "There is no bridge between Washington and Pinsk." (Weizmann was born in the village of Motol, near Pinsk.) For Brandeis, Zionism demanded creation of an *organization* (or organizations), structured to fulfill the ultimate goal. Weizmann conceived Zionism to be a *movement* whose purpose was to alter radically the condition of the Jew. To an organization, one lends talents and gives money; a movement asks total commitment of oneself and one's resources. To put it starkly: The followers of Weizmann fully expected their leader to settle in Palestine as soon as practicable; no co-worker of Brandeis conceived such a possibility for him.

The membership of the ZOA was comprised in the great majority of East European immigrant Jews. They welcomed Brandeis's leadership and were grateful for his great contribution. They refused, however, to tolerate what they considered to be the high-handed and patronizing ways and the weak ideological commitment of those Brandeis brought into the leadership. So at the Cleveland Convention, they forced that leadership to resign. Political victory went to the group led by Louis Lipsky and Emanuel Neumann, but ideological victory ultimately went to the Brandeis group. Within a few years the Brandeis program was adopted in toto by those who had forced its adherents out. Philanthropic Zionism was the Zionism in America in the 1920s. Cultural programs and political action were discussed, but little more than that.

The Lodge-Fish resolution in 1922, a joint resolution of the United States Congress, gave formal American approval to "the establishment in Palestine of a national home for the Jewish people." The resolution bolstered flagging Zionist morale, but had no practical significance. American isolationism had already set in, and congressional resolutions were of little importance when America was in the process of cutting itself off from the family of nations.

The World Zionist Organization was pressing the Americans for funds and the pressure bore fruit. Half of the $20 million raised for Keren Hayesod, The Palestine Foundation Fund, came from America. Zionist fund raising competed with JDC activity, adding fuel to the Zionist-anti-Zionist conflict. The establishment in 1929 of the expanded Jewish Agency, which brought non-Zionists into decision-making power in heretofore Zionist matters, sapped whatever vitality was left in American Zionism at the end of the decade. In response to the bloody Arab riots in 1929, a segment of the American press, the Communist Yiddish press among them, spoke of the Arab attacks on Jews as a justifiable uprising against colonialist oppressors. The State Department remained unmoved and Congress silent. American Zionism could do little more than to hold rallies where the preachers spoke to the already converted. In 1930, Dr. Stephen S. Wise remarked: "There is a complete lull in things Zionist in America . . . the Zionist Organization is gone. The Arab riots . . . plus the killing of Zionism as a democratic mass movement . . . have robbed me of my faith."[6]

The masterful pulpit orator was given to hyperbole, but the situation was truly dire. America was beginning to experience the onset of the Great Depression, Nazism was on the rise in Germany and organized Zionism seemed in disarray.

"The pervasive influence of the Zionist ideal," however, an observer notes, continued in the thirties, drawing "consistent and impressive support from modern Orthodox and Conservative congregations." Even traditionally anti-Zionist Reform Judaism was changing its stance. In 1937, both its rabbinic and lay organizations "recognized the obligation of all Jews to cooperate in making Palestine a Jewish homeland—which they defined as a cultural and spiritual center."[7] The pressing need for a refuge for Jews in European countries wiped away fears of dual loyalty accusations.

Particularly impressive was the work of women's Zionist organizations. Hadassah expanded its medical services in Palestine, welcoming Jewish medical personnel fleeing Hitler's Germany, and accepted what became one of the century's greatest humanitarian endeavors, Youth Aliyah. By 1945, over 35,000 children had been rescued from Europe and settled in the *Yishuv* (Jewish community) in Palestine. Henrietta Szold, who left a career as scholar and editor to become founder and lifelong leader of Hadassah, made it the last great endeavor of her rich career of service to Jews and Judaism.

ZIONIST POLITICAL ACTIVITY

With Europe at war, Dr. Chaim Weizmann, on a visit to the United States in 1940, informed American Jewry that all the Zionist effort was now in their hands. Such a burden could only be borne by a united American Jewry. Non-Zionists had to be enlisted in the cause.

First at a conference convened in New York, in May 1942, the Basel platform was restated at the Hotel Biltmore, which gave its name to the new platform calling for "Palestine [to] be established as a Jewish Commonwealth integrated in the structure of the new democratic world." With the goal restated, the leaders of Zionism turned to forging a broad-based, organized support. During World War I, American Jewry had united in a congress to face its postwar world responsibilities. In 1943, promoted by the Zionist forces vigorously led by Dr. Abba Hillel Silver, and organized by Henry Monsky, the first son of the East European community to serve as president of B'nai B'rith, the American Jewish Conference was convened. Jewish communities throughout the land held elections for delegates. National Jewish organizations were represented. An address by Abba Hillel Silver, which no one present would ever forget, resulted in a 478 to 4 acceptance of the Biltmore Platform. Even the defection of the powerful American Jewish Committee could not diminish the joy of the occasion nor lessen the anticipation of a Zionist triumph.

The days and years ahead were difficult. Great Britain's White Paper kept Palestine's gates shut even to that pitiful remnant of a once great European Jewry which had survived the Holocaust. The task was clear: organized American Jewry had to exert whatever influence it had with the United States government to open the gates. In March 1944, President Roosevelt assured U.S. Jewry that the "American Government has never given its approval to the White Paper of 1939." He promised that, if reelected, he would help bring about the establishment "of Palestine as a free and democratic Jewish Commonwealth . . ." It was later revealed that he had given different private assurances to Arab leaders, but his pledge to the Jewish people was on the public record.

Between VE Day and the founding of the state, Zionism was the dominant force in American Jewry. From 1945 to 1948, enrolled Zionists increased in number from 387,000 to 711,000. Expectations ran high. An unofficial Zionist presence at the San Francisco Conference which established the United Nations in April 1945 laid the groundwork for the UN Resolution which two years later provided for the establishment of a Jewish state in Palestine. There was dancing in the streets of Jewish neighborhoods throughout the nation when the UN Resolution was adopted on November 29, 1947, and again on the night of

May 5, 1948, when the state was established. Many American Jews could take satisfaction in having helped bring about the day they were celebrating.

FOCUS
The American Jewish Religious Movements and Zionism, 1897–1948[8]

The half century between the First Zionist Congress in Basel, Switzerland, 1897, and the establishment of the State of Israel in 1948 witnessed a sweeping change in the American Jewish community's attitude toward Zionist ideology and programs. From general apathy and opposition by much of the religious establishment, American Jewry, masses and leaders alike, moved to full and active approval of the goals of Zionism and activities on behalf of creating a Jewish state. During those fifty years, Zionism was a major issue in the life of the American Jewish community and in the deliberations of its three religious groupings.

At the close of the nineteenth century, Reform Judaism dominated the American Jewish religious scene. Conservative Judaism was but a fledgling, Orthodoxy divided and disorganized. In the spring of 1897, word reached the United States that Theodor Herzl, who a year earlier had published a Zionist pamphlet, *Der Judenstaat*, was about to convene a Zionist conference in Munich. At a meeting in New York, on June 9, of rabbis and representatives of Jewish congregations and institutions, the following resolutions were adopted:

> that while every association of Palestine with the Jews arouses our interest and touches a responsive chord in Jewish hearts, we deprecate any movement tending towards the formation of a Jewish State in Palestine capable of being construed as casting doubt upon the citizenship, patriotism or loyalty of Jews in whatever country they reside.
>
> that we affirm our conviction that the true mission of Judaism is religious and not political.[9]

These resolutions expressed the mood and sentiments of the great majority of organized Jewry. *The American Hebrew* editorialized:

> We believe that the Munich Conference to be held in August will receive scant encouragement here from those who really represent Judaism. Zionism is favored here only as it stands for colonization in the Holy Land. The moment a political state is broached, all with one accord cry "hands off."[10]

The editorial reaction to the Zionist Congress itself, which was held in Basel, was more ambivalent:

. . . so far as its animating purpose was concerned, it [the Congress] was a failure . . . Yet we are not disposed to read absolute failure in a gathering of two hundred men and women, whose religious views run from the most orthodox to the most heterodox but who are bound together by the tie of kinship that runs back through the ages . . .[11]

The *American Hebrew* reflected the views of the elder statesmen of Conservative Judaism; the new generation, fired by the cause, supported it with zeal. A representative view was that of Rabbi Joseph H. Hertz, the infant Jewish Theological Seminary's first graduate. In its October 17, 1897, issue *The American Hebrew* gave a prominent place to his "After the Congress—A Resumé and a Retrospect." Hertz saw Zionism as a unifying force within world Jewry, as the only solution for Jews in a world ever more hostile to them. In addition, Zionism was characterized as a great spiritual force which calls forth "deep piety, moral enthusiasm and lofty idealism . . . It has promoted self-emancipation along with self-respect and self-knowledge."[12]

Most Orthodox rabbis were devoted to the return of the Jewish people to their homeland, and many were active in the Hovevei Zion movement. At the first convention of the Orthodox Jewish Congregational Union of America in 1898, a Zionist resolution was adopted:

The desirability and the necessity of offering to those of our brethren dwelling under the rigour of oppressive laws a refuge legally assured to them cannot be questioned. . . . The restoration of Zion as the legitimate aspiration of scattered Israel in no way conflicts with our loyalty to the land in which we dwell or may dwell at any time.[13]

At the close of the century anti-Zionists among the Orthodox in America were few, but there were some who felt that the restoration of the Jews to their own land was a matter for the Messiah, that human beings should not interfere in such eschatological matters.

Until 1897, Zionism might have been shrugged off by the leaders of Reform Judaism in America, but in 1898 the Central Conference of American Rabbis and the Union of American Hebrew Congregations issued a strongly negative resolution in response to the Zionist Congress at Basel and its program.

Resolved, that we totally disapprove of any attempt for the establishment of a Jewish state. Such attempts show a misunderstanding of Israel's mission . . . the promotion among the whole human race of the broad universalistic religion first proclaimed by the Jewish prophets. Such attempts . . . infinitely harm our Jewish brethren where they are still persecuted, by confirming the assertion of their enemies that the Jews are foreigners in the countries in which they are at home, and of which they are everywhere the most loyal and patriotic citizens.[14]

The "mission" of Judaism and the specter of dual loyalty were discussed in dozens of articles and hundreds of sermons by Reform spokesmen. One rabbi put it as follows:

The destruction of the Temple in Jerusalem by the Romans and the consequent dispersion of the Jews over the whole earth, was not a divine punishment, a catastrophe, but an act of divine Providence, a part of the plan of the Almighty . . . the establishment of a Jewish state in Palestine is opposed to the mission of the Jew. . . . Least of all will we Jews living here in America countenance any plan that even in the slightest degree reflects upon our love of this country and our attachment to this government. America is our Palestine, the flag of this country is our banner, the Statue of Liberty in our harbor is the symbol of our patriotism.[15]

These words of Reform spokesman Rabbi Rudolph Grossman expressed the sentiments shared by almost all Reform rabbis and their congregants. At the time of the First Zionist Congress, only Rabbis Bernhard Felsenthal and Gustav Gottheil, as we have noted, raised their voices for Zion. They were shortly joined by Rabbi Stephen S. Wise, who, upon his return from the Second Zionist Congress in 1898, said:

Thrilled and grateful, I caught then a first glimpse of the power and the pride and the nobleness of the Jewish people, which my American upbringing and even service to New York Jewry had not in any degree given me . . . The Jewish people became my own and I returned to my people.[16]

During the two decades between the First Zionist Congress and the Balfour Declaration, the physiognomy of organized Jewish religious life in America underwent a great transformation. Almost two million immigrants had come from Eastern Europe. Of those who sought religious affiliation, the great majority joined Orthodox and Conservative synagogues. Reform, though still the most prestigious and influential force in American Jewish religious life, was now but one of three organized religious movements on the American Jewish scene. During that brief span Zionism had become a potent force, the great majority of Orthodox and Conservative Jews in sympathy with its aims, if not members of the various Zionist organizations.

The Balfour Declaration afforded an opportunity to take the Zionist pulse of the Jewish religious community. The official Zionist publication, *The Maccabean* (January 1918), exulted:

Never has there been an occasion in American Jewry that can compare with the Great Zionist demonstration which was held in Carnegie Hall, New York, on Sunday evening, December 23, when 15,000 Jews gathered to give utterance to the gratitude they felt toward Great Britain for the momentous declaration which has given to the Jewish people a national status and a definite pledge that their 2,000 year old longing for the re-establishment of the Jewish State in Palestine will be realized.[17]

The various groups within the American Jewish religious community responded to the Balfour Declaration in conformity to their ideologies. In *The Political World of American Zionism,* Samuel Halperin states:

It was [Solomon] Schechter, perhaps more than any other individual, who won for the tiny Zionist following in America its first great accretion of strength—the Conservative movement in Judaism. Despite the threats and imprecations of the Seminary's Reform dominated Board of Directors, he warmly and decisively espoused the doctrine of Jewish national restoration in Palestine.[18]

Not surprisingly the United Synagogue of America, the organization of Conservative congregations founded by Schechter, hailed the declaration and its promise of a "national home for the Jewish people," affirming the movement's emphasis on Zionism as a means for the preservation of Judaism and the survival of the Jewish people.

The Reform Central Conference of American Rabbis notes "with grateful appreciation the declaration of the British Government by Mr. Balfour as an evidence of good will toward Jews." However,

. . . we do not subscribe to the phrase in the Declaration which says, "Palestine is to be a national home-land for the Jewish people" . . . We hold that Jewish people are and of right ought to be at home in all lands . . . Jews in America are part of the American nation. . . . We believe that our survival as a people is dependent upon the assertion and maintenance of our historic religious role and not upon the acceptance of Palestine as a homeland of the Jewish people. The mission of the Jew is to witness to God all over the world.[19]

The reaction of the Central Conference to the Balfour Declaration was far more temperate than its response to the Basel Platform. Nationalistic elements had made inroads into Reform thinking. "Our survival as a *people*" and "our *historic* religious role" pointed to acceptance of Jewish peoplehood and a stress on its historic experience, concepts rejected by classic Reform. Even the mission concept was

pressed into Zionist service. Reform proponents of Zionism now explained the Jewish mission to the nations in terms of a state which
would serve as a model commonwealth devoted to the service of God
through love of one's fellowman, of a nation motivated by prophetic
ideals and directed by the Jewish passion for social justice and human
brotherhood.

Reform anti-Zionists, however, were quick to point out that
Zionism in America was largely confined to immigrant Jews. In an
anti-Zionist "Statement to the Peace Conference," following World
War I, they declared: "We are voicing the opinion of the majority of
American Jews born in this country and of those foreign-born who
have lived here long enough to thoroughly assimilate American political
and social conditions. . . ."

It was the mass migration from Eastern Europe, overwhelmingly
Orthodox in affiliation, which provided the raw material for creation
of a religious Zionist movement in America. Orthodox Zionist strength
was organized in the Mizrachi movement, whose organ, *Ha-Ivri*, greeted
the Balfour Declaration in its lead editorial of November 16, 1917:

> The Declaration of the British Government ushers in a new era in
> the history of Zionism—indeed a new era in Jewish history. . . .
> Our great dream, the dream of return and redemption is becoming
> a reality. . . . [However] the Declaration has not as yet made the
> impression it deserves. The Jewish "street" has not responded, and
> the Jewish masses have not been moved to the extent we had
> expected. . . . Let us not forget that our brothers—our foes, have
> not ceased to undermine our national edifice . . . They still stealth-
> ily do their work, placing road-blocks and pitfalls on our path.[20]

The "brothers-foes" were those members of the Orthodox Jewish community who were anti-Zionists. Among these was the European spiritual head of Habad Hasidism, Shalom Dov Baer Schneersohn, whose
views were reprinted in New York in 1917.

> As for the question you ask about Zionism . . . We are not per-
> mitted to press for redemption, certainly not through physical
> endeavours and enterprises. It is not permitted for us to leave the
> Exile through force or might; not in this will be our redemption
> and salvation.[21]

A more direct anti-Zionist reaction to the Balfour Declaration
from the Orthodox camp was a pamphlet, *Shaalu Shlom Yerusholoyim,*
by Rabbi Baruch Meir Klein of New York, which said:

> So long as the Zionists were from the non-religious Jews, they
> were less harmful, and we kept our silence . . . Now that a group

of them have begun to put on a pious face, and have taken the name "Mizrachi" . . . the time has come to undertake the battle . . . I hope for the redemption, and it will come as soon as we shall repent. But this is not the redemption which Balfour promises us, and which deniers of the Torah, scoffers and rebels demand. No, no! Redemption will come from God, through the Messiah, the Righteous Redeemer. May he come soon, in our days, Amen! He will come. He must come! [22]

The leading article of the November 30, 1947, issue of *The New York Times* reported:

The United Nations General Assembly approved yesterday a proposal to partition Palestine into two states, one Arab and the other Jewish, that are to become fully independent by October 1. The vote was 33 to 13 with ten abstentions and one delegation, the Siamese, absent.

Another front-page article described the mood: "In the public lobby there were kisses and tears and excited laughter. In the delegates' lounge a rabbi cried, 'This is the day the Lord hath made; let us rejoice in it and be glad.' "

New York's Yiddish press reported the day's events with greater emotion and enthusiasm. A banner headline of that day's *Morgen Zhurnal* (Morning Journal) proclaimed: A JEWISH STATE—MAZAL TOV! A reporter described the jubilation of New York Jewry: "Wherever Jews met there was spontaneous joy. . . . All meetings, all gatherings which were held last night, all weddings, all family celebrations were turned into national demonstrations." [23]

All the leading Jewish religious organizations hailed the creation of the state and pledged their aid. The few voices raised in opposition were outside of the mainstream of organized religious life in America. The Rabbinical Assembly of America, in convention in Chicago on May 16, 1948, spoke the sentiments of the Conservative movement.

A new epoch in the immortal history of the Jewish people was opened hardly twenty-four hours ago—on the 14th of May, 1948, the 5th day of Iyar 5708, . . .

After almost 2,000 years of wandering and suffering—a Jewish State came into being—the State of Israel. Long live the State of Israel! . . .

To the New State, to its National Council and officers, to the Haganah, to all the workers and builders in Zion, we extend greetings. We express our profound faith that they will embody, in the new state, the ethical ideals enunciated by our prophets, and the Hebraic principles of social justice which will make it a blessing to all its inhabitants and radiate a beneficent influence of justice and peace throughout the world.[24]

The Central Conference of American Rabbis greeted the new state no less enthusiastically, at its annual convention in Kansas City, Missouri, June 22–26, 1948.

We salute the Republic of Israel and offer our Israeli brothers all possible encouragement and assistance in the maintenance of independence and in the achievement of security. We pray that Israel may go from strength to strength and that with God's help, it may soon attain peace and prosperity, that it may carry forward the spiritual revival, the Hebrew cultural contributions and the social and democratic advances already fostered in the Yishuv, for the enrichment of Judaism the world over, and the benefit of all humanity.[25]

The lay body of Reform Judaism, the Union of American Hebrew Congregations, at its 40th General Assembly, held in Boston, November 14–17, adopted a resolution that "enthusiastically hails the creation of the State of Israel. . . ." There had been division of opinion within the leadership on the wisdom of such a resolution, but at the General Assembly the vote was almost unanimous.

Perhaps the most unexpected reaction to the decision of the United Nations and the creation of the State of Israel was that of the anti-Zionist American Council for Judaism which, for the preceding five years, had worked against the creation of a Jewish state in Palestine. A temperate editorial in the December 1947 issue of the *Council News* stated:

The General Assembly of the United Nations has acted . . . We of the American Council for Judaism have opposed the partition of Palestine on many grounds, we have foreseen many dire consequences of a partition of Palestine. Now, however, that a decision has been reached we can only hope, with profound sincerity, that our expectations will prove mistaken. We hope that time will prove us false prophets. We wish the new countries well.[26]

A statement of policy by the Council's Executive Committee on May 21, 1948, reaffirmed its position that "the state of Israel is not the state or homeland of 'The Jewish People.' To Americans of Jewish faith it is a foreign state. Our single and exclusive national identity is to the United States."

Composed almost wholly of members of the Reform rabbinate and laity, the American Council for Judaism had been a source of contention in American Jewish life and of strife within the Reform movement. By 1948, however, its ranks of rabbinic leadership had dwindled to a half-dozen from the ninety-one who had called it into being in 1943.

Reform Judaism in 1947 and 1948 was almost unanimous in greeting the state and pledging support of its endeavors. Rabbi Abraham J. Feldman expressed it well in his presidential message to his colleagues of the Central Conference of American Rabbis:

> It seems to me that in the presence of the *fait accompli,* the half-century debate on the subject of Zionism should come to an end. After all the government of the State of Israel is not your government or mine . . . They will have our aid whilst they need aid, and our brotherly support as they require it. But the political controversy amongst us here should now be adjourned.[27]

The most varied reaction to the creation of the state was that of Orthodox Jewry. A lead editorial in the February 1948 issue of *Orthodox Jewish Life,* the publication of the Union of Orthodox Jewish Congregations, spoke for the vast majority of Orthodox Jews: "The decision of the United Nations to permit establishment of a Jewish state in partitioned Palestine is, in its essence, one of those acts of Divine Providence which seems to transcend the ordinary course of natural law."

"We must remember," another editorial notes, "that our people have yearned and striven not simply for a *state* but a *Jewish* state."

> Eretz Israel can fulfill its purpose only by creating a society which is predicated upon service to God and to mankind . . . Let those who go up to the Land divest themselves of the social concept derived from a non-Jewish environment, for they are called up to build a society, which, new though it is, has been in the making for ages, yes, even from the days of Father Abraham.[28]

The Agudas Harabonim, the organization of European-trained rabbis, declared:

> We see in the decision of the United Nations to establish an independent Jewish commonwealth in Palestine, the desire of Providence to recompense us in His mercy for the tragic losses we have suffered . . . We cannot for a moment imagine that the renewed Jewish commonwealth . . . can be based on any other foundation than that of our Torah and Faith. . . . Only through this shall we be worthy of a full ingathering of the exiles and a complete redemption, soon, in our days, Amen.[29]

Some of the leaders of Agudas Harabonim were also leaders of the ultra-Orthodox Agudas Yisroel group, which issued a similar state-

ment, interpreting the decision of the UN as the will of God. Though
formerly opposed to a state, Agudas Yisroel now accepted it because
God had willed it. But the state did not constitute redemption or obviate
the need to await the coming of the Messiah.

With the creation of the state, Rabbi Joseph Elijah Henkin, an
outspoken anti-Zionist before the establishment of the state, became
with the creation of Israel a friend and defender. Before the state was
in existence, he argued, one had the right to oppose it, but once it had
come into being one must help and defend it. "After the Jews have
thrown off the yoke of subjugation, though they have done so contrary
to the admonition of the Sages, it is now our duty to help them with
utter devotion." Anyone who would now deliver Jews into foreign
subjugation was "an informer and a persecutor of the Jewish people." [30]

Rabbi Henkin's remarks were addressed to those Orthodox Jews
whose opposition to Zionism now led them to oppose the founding of
the state and the state itself. These were the disciples of the Rebbe of
Muncacz, who issued a New York reprint of a violently anti-Zionist
volume which had first appeared in Hungary in 1936, and even more,
the followers of Rabbi Joel Teitelbaum, the Rebbe of Satmar, who
equated Zionism with heresy and atheism, and blamed the bitter tragedy
of the Holocaust upon the sin committed by the Zionists in seeking to
"hasten Redemption."

FROM AN ALLIED TO A UNITED COMMUNITY

The formal unity forced upon American Jewry by the crisis
facing European Jewry during World War I began to fall apart as the
situation "normalized" in the postwar world. The immediate needs of
almost a million displaced persons, sixty thousand orphans, pogrom-
shattered communities had kept the alliance intact, but discordant notes
began to be heard.

Zionists claimed that not enough of the funds were directed to
Palestine, thus preventing larger numbers of Jews from settling there
and fulfilling the promise held forth by the Balfour Declaration. The
chief fund raisers and fund providers were opposed to political Zionism.
Some, like Jacob H. Schiff, Louis Marshall and Felix Warburg, were
committed to help the Jews in Palestine as they would aid Jews anywhere; others, like the Joint Distribution Committee's most effective
fund raiser, David Brown, and Julius Rosenwald, the single most gen-
erous philanthropist, opposed any funds for the Yishuv. Brown felt
that the JDC's responsibility was to the Jews of Europe; let American
Zionists provide for their brethren in Palestine. Rosenwald's opposition
was even more pronounced, for he felt that the Holy Land was not
suitable for a modern agricultural or industrial society.

The Zionists, on the other hand, argued that the only secure future for European Jewry was in a commonwealth in Palestine. All aid to European Jewry which encouraged them to remain in Europe was a historic disservice to them. Minority rights granted them by peace treaties, they warned, were ephemeral, hopes for equal rights, security and well-being chimerical.

In 1924, the JDC established the American Jewish Joint Agricultural Corporation to handle its work in the Soviet Union, the Agro-Joint. Within four years, some $6 million had been contributed by the JDC to resettle about 35,000 Jewish families on farms in the Crimea. Zionists saw this as a direct affront and challenge. While colonization in Palestine was languishing for want of funds, large sums were being poured into the Soviet Union.

American Jewry was united in fund raising for overseas needs through the United Jewish Campaign. The circular letter announcing the 1926 campaign emphasized the work in Crimea, made no mention of money for projects in Palestine. Although they had been promised $1.5 million for work in Palestine, the Zionists withdrew in anger from the United Jewish Campaign and organized a separate United Palestine Appeal in 1925.

Of the $60 million raised by the JDC in the first decade of its existence (1916–26), only $7 million, some 12 percent, went to Palestine. In 1926, the leaders of JDC in a quiet drive to match a $10-million grant from the Russian government raised some $8 million, Julius Rosenwald contributing $5 million, Felix Warburg, $1 million, and John D. Rockefeller, Jr., $0.5 million.

Author Maurice Samuel cast a critical eye on what he called the "charity mania" in his *Jews on Approval:*

The drives for European Jewry and Palestine were only part of the picture in those years. Between 1914 and 1929 there was a great revival in American Jewish life. The money spent on social service, schools, hospitals, asylums and temples doubled and trebled. A building fever set in, for stone is by far the most durable memorial, as well as the most striking evidence, of public generosity. Million-dollar enterprises became common, and small communities ventured into synagogues, centers, Y.M.H.A.'s, which cost hundreds of thousands of dollars. Rabbis were eager to outshine one another in acreage and bricks, and gorgeous structures rose throughout the country. Once or twice mild warnings were issued: what was the good of these superb centers, these imposing places of worship, Saracen, Moorish, semi-Gothic and what not, when we had not developed the teachers? . . . Charity, too long a disproportionate force in Jewish life, will become the sole force, and Jews will aspire to enter the history of the future on a passport of philanthropy whose visas consist of cancelled checks. [31]

In 1929 the great champion of Jewish unity in America, Louis Marshall, died, but not before his most lasting accomplishment had been realized. Largely through his efforts, Zionists and non-Zionists joined in work for Palestine through the Jewish Agency for Palestine. That accomplished, the Joint Distribution Committee and American members of the Jewish Agency agreed to join in an Allied Jewish Campaign. Its goal was to be $6 million, of which $3.5 million would go to the JDC and $2.5 million to the Jewish Agency. What gave urgency to the need for a united effort was once again an overseas crisis. The anti-Jewish riots in Palestine evoked sympathy from all segments of American Jewry (the Jewish Communists excepted). Felix Warburg, who had been second only to Marshall in his commitment to a united American Jewry, hailed the joint campaign as the beginning of "a lasting and permanent unity in American Israel." The unity was short-lived, the partners agreeing to "separate their fund-raising activities." But the joint drive had succeeded in "laying the foundation in many communities, for enduring cooperation on behalf of Jewish causes."

When, three years later, a peril of unprecedented proportions confronted one of the world's leading Jewish communities, the Joint Distribution Committee and the American Palestine Campaign were ready to unite in joint fund raising. In 1933 Hitler came to power; in March 1934, the United Jewish Appeal was created. A campaign for $3.25 million was launched. By September 1935, only $1.5 million had been raised. A call by two hundred prominent non-Jews, bishops, deans of theological schools and university presidents and political and civil leaders, was issued, to little avail. By the end of October, the UJA's Executive Committee found it wisest to terminate the effort. It was recognized that "one of the advantages of separate campaigns was that both the Joint Distribution Committee and the American Palestine Campaign would be free to intensify their special appeals . . . for their respective programs in the field of European aid and reconstruction, and Palestine upbuilding." [32]

The statement of termination added that the decision "does not preclude the possibility of joint local drives. . . ." There seems to have been greater unity and desire for united efforts in the local communities than in the national bodies. American Jewish communal demand was for unity in *raising* funds, but not in their distribution. The manner in which the campaigns were organized and conducted affected local communal life, and the communities wanted the campaigns to be activities which would bring amity and unity. The issue was brought to a head in January 1937, when the National Council of Jewish Federations and Welfare Funds (CJFWF) initiated a series of consultations between representatives of the JDC and UPA "with a view of promoting the fullest cooperation between them and of securing from local Jewish Welfare Funds the maximum response to their appeals." [33] Both agencies would continue their separate existences, their fund-raising apparatus and activities, but they would give fullest cooperation to local campaigns. These arrangements presaged a united campaign and an increasingly important role for the CJFWF.

The Council, which by the late 1930s was beginning to exert considerable influence, resulted from a number of mergers of service bureaus designed to aid local community federations in communal coordination and fund raising. By the end of the nineteenth century, most Jewish communities had central charitable associations. (Some had two, one of and for the German Jewish community, another for the East European.) During the last quarter of the century, attempts had been made to establish a national organization which culminated in the National Conference of Jewish Charities, which subsequently evolved into the National Conference for Jewish Communal Service. Local communal organizations, called federations, grew in number as communities became stabilized, and by the end of World War I, reached forty-two. The Field Bureau of the National Conference and the research department of the American Jewish Committee merged to form the Bureau of Jewish Social Research. In 1932 the bureau urged the formation of the CJFWF, and three years later it merged into the council.

The mergers reflect a community assuming a sense of national communal identity. A pattern evolves which mirrors the American experience of nation building, acceptance of a federated form of national unity. The local bodies retained their independence but increasingly turned to the CJFWF to represent them in their relations with the national Jewish organizations. Recognizing that collectors of money retain a measure of control over the funds they raise, and that such control confers influence and the power of decision, the CJFWF worked at transferring major national Jewish fund raising to the local federations. At first the CJFWF made itself useful and, in time, indispensable to the federations as its service agency in campaigning, and as its coordinating body in its cooperation and confrontation with national Jewish agencies. In 1937, however, it could act the "honest broker," not yet the "power broker," so despite its attempts for fund-raising unity, the JDC and the UPA conducted their own independent campaigns.

Events intervened a year later to force unity upon American Jewry. On November 10, 1938, a nationwide pogrom swept Nazi Germany, which because of the broken glass windows and shattered showcases was given the name *Kristallnacht* (Crystal Night). Shops were looted, homes invaded, heads of families imprisoned. Most shocking was the desecration and burning of the German synagogues.

For American Jews, the gutted synagogues were an abomination and affront, their charred ruins an evil omen. For in the 1930s American Jews had experienced a new form of anti-Jewish agitation. Social bigotry and economic discrimination, which they had learned to cope with, was replaced by actions of uniformed Bundists and Silver Shirts, who had ties to and conjured up the strength of the virulent, powerful anti-Semitic movements of Europe.

The immediate response was a drawing together to aid those who had been victimized. In January 1939, the Joint Distribution Committee, the United Palestine Appeal and the National Coordinating Committee Fund (refugee aid) joined to form the United Jewish Appeal for Refugee and Overseas Needs. The joint campaign realized over $15 million, whereas separate campaigns a year earlier had raised about $7 million. As if to give symbolic answer to those who burned synagogues, the campaign of a united American Jewry named as its cochairmen, Abba Hillel Silver and Jonah B. Wise, two of America's most distinguished rabbis.

ANTI-SEMITISM

Burton J. Hendrick's *The Jews in America,* published in 1923, opens with a comment on anti-Semitism in America:

> The wave of anti-Semitism, which has been sweeping over the world since the ending of the Great War, has apparently reached the United States. An antagonism which Americans had believed was peculiarly European is gaining a disquieting foothold in this country. The one prejudice which would seem to have no decent cause for existence in the free air of America is one that is based on race and religion. Yet the most conservative American universities are openly setting up bars against the unlimited admittance of Jewish students; the most desirable clubs are becoming more rigid in their inhospitable attitude toward Jewish members; a weekly newspaper, financed by one of the richest men in America, has filled its pages for three years with a virulent campaign against this element in our population; secret organizations have been established for the purpose of "fighting" the so-called "Jewish predominance in American life"; Congress has passed and the president has signed an immigration law—it is just as well to be frank about the matter—to restrict the entrance of Jews from eastern Europe.[34]

America had long since been importing anti-Semitic prejudice and rhetoric from the Old World, as well as fashioning its own. The preface to *The Wonderful and Most Deplorable History of the Latter Times of the Jews* by Josephus Ben Gorion, published in Leominster, Massachusetts, in 1803, characterized the Jews "from that time to this day," as: ". . . runagates and land-loopers . . . they apply themselves to the most sordid and servile conditions, for commonly they are either *lombardiers* and brokers of the pettiest things . . . they are known to be the subtilest, and the most subdolous race of people on earth—as also the most fearful and pusillanimous . . ." The anonymous British author of the preface introduces to America the physical stereotype of the Jew: " . . . there is a kind of curse falled upon their bodies; witness those uncouth looks, and odd casts of the eye whereby they are distinguished from other people. As likewise that rankish kind of scent, no better indeed than a stink, which is observed to be inherent and inseparable from most of them." [35] This was the Jew many Americans "knew" long before they met one, if indeed they ever did.

Favorable portrayals there were, too, as for example Hannah Adams's picture of Charleston Jews in her *History of the Jews:*

> Open and charitable . . . for their enterprize and judgment, they have been entrusted with municipal office. . . . They have built an elegant synagogue. They have also societies for the relief of orphans . . . The dress and habits of the Jews of Charleston do not distinguish them from other citizens. [36]

Books published in America in the early years of the nineteenth century portrayed Jews both as renegades, pariahs, deicides, deformed by physical traits which set them apart from the rest of society and as useful, respected citizens who successfully integrated into the social fabric. Both portraits persisted throughout the nineteenth century, the former growing dimmer, the latter more distinct. The pluralistic character of American society made for tolerance of differences, but native tendencies to bigotry, reinforced by inherited traditions of prejudice, made for a vulnerability to anti-Semitic stereotypes in American literature. Patrician Henry Adams freely expressed his anti-Semitic sentiments, and populist demagogues made use of the stereotypical anti-Semitic rhetoric.

There were incidents of bias as well, such as the Seligman Affair. The Grand Hotel was proclaimed off limits, as was Coney Island toward the end of the century. But there were other hotels where Jews were welcome, and other desirable neighborhoods open to them. The riot at the funeral of Chief Rabbi Jacob Joseph was quite another matter, in which prejudice manifested itself in physical violence.

The New York Times of July 31, 1902, featured the incident on its front page:

RIOT MARS FUNERAL OF RABBI JOSEPH

Mourners and Hoe Factory Employees in Struggle

As the horde of mourners was beginning to pass the printing press factory of R. Hoe and Company . . . a bucket of water was thrown from one of the upper windows into the midst of the surging crowd of mourners. Bundles of paper saturated with oil, bits of iron, small blocks of wood . . . followed from the windows. . . . "Is this Russia?" shouted an old man, speaking with a foreign accent. The missiles . . . continued to pour down on the street, and the mourners . . . cast them back against the windows. . . . A riot call . . . brought 200 [police]men . . . It was evident from the action of the officers that they considered the mourners in the wrong. Slashing this way and that with their sticks . . . shoving roughly against men and women alike. . . . "It was a thing that even a Russian, with all his dislike for our people, would have been ashamed of," said [City Marshal Albert] Levine. "The men in the factory insulted us wantonly. Then the police, who should have protected us, clubbed us into insensibility."

But America was not Russia. Mayor Seth Low called it a discredit to the city and ordered a full investigation. The press denounced the police behavior. An editorial in *The New York Times* stated:

The incidents attending the funeral of Rabbi Joseph will be recalled with shame by every self-respecting citizen of New York. For their part in the affair the police are greatly to blame. . . .

The riot was an enactment on a grand scale of what was happening almost daily. Immigrant Jews were attacked by hoodlums and toughs, part of the "sport" of the unruly elements of immigrant neighborhoods. Yet there was public opinion to declare its outrage and public authorities from whom one could demand redress. Even the "riot" itself could not be compared to a pogrom; it was neither supported nor condoned, but widely condemned.

A more agitating, complex incident was the Leo Frank Case. The body of murdered Mary Phagan was found in the basement of the National Pencil Factory in Atlanta, Georgia, on the night of April 27, 1913. Leo Max Frank, Brooklyn-reared, Cornell-educated Jewish superintendent and part owner of the pencil factory, was arrested for the crime. Sentiment was whipped up by local demagogues playing on Southern prejudices against Northern exploiters. That the Northerner in this case was a Jew made prejudice against him easier to evoke. He was convicted (on evidence later discredited) and the prosecuting attorney was accorded a spontaneous hero's parade. The case was appealed to the Supreme Court, but the verdict held. The governor, uneasy about the questionable evidence on which Frank was convicted, commuted the death penalty to life imprisonment. Frank was incarcerated only two months before a gang broke into the prison and lynched him.

Disquiet among American Jews was pronounced. One did not need to be paranoiac to feel fear.

The notorious "Protocols of the Meetings of the Zionist Men of Wisdom" (a forgery by czarist secret service agents based on an anti-Napoleon III French tract) were published in 1920 under the title, *The Protocols and World Revolution,* by Small, Maynard & Co., and widely distributed. The introductory statement warned: "With the triumph of the Bolshevist revolution in Russia, a group of internationalists, most of whom were members of the Jewish race, seized the machinery of government . . . Was it a long planned, gigantic revolt of the Jewish race against Christendom and its institutions?" The question was meant to be rhetorical, but the introduction to the Russian edition of *The Protocols* was cited, and an alarm was sounded against a worldwide Jewish conspiracy:

> The "Protocols" are a program carefully worked out in all its details for the conquest of the universe by the Jews. The greater part of this program has already been realized, and if we will not come back to our senses, we are inevitably doomed.
>
> Shall America be as slow to realize the real danger of international Bolshevism as she was to recognize the menace of German imperialism? Shall America again be unprepared?[37]

America's leading industrialist, Henry Ford, used his newspaper, the *Dearborn Independent,* to publish articles, beginning in the spring of 1920, exposing "The International Jew and his satellites, as the conscious enemies of all that Anglo-Saxons mean by civilization." A booklet, published November, 1920, entitled *The International Jew—The World's Foremost Problem, Being a Reprint of a Series of Articles Appearing in the* Dearborn Independent, was distributed internationally. The articles dealt with such themes as "The Historic Basis of Jewish Imperialism," "An Introduction to the 'Jewish Protocols,' " and "Jewish Testimony in Favor of Bolshevism." A half year later, volume 2 of the *International Jew,* bearing the title *Jewish Activities in the United States,* appeared. The articles in this collection were even sharper in their attack: "The Scope of Jewish Dictatorship in the U.S.," "Rule of the Jewish Kehillah Grips New York," "Jewish Copper Kings Reap Rich War-Profits," and " 'Disraeli in America'—A Jew of Super Power" (the reference is to financier Bernard M. Baruch). A third volume, *Jewish Influences in*

American Life, is an all-out anti-Semitic attack on the Jews as a corrupting influence in American life: "Jewish Degradation of American Baseball," "Jewish Jazz Becomes Our National Music" and "How Jews Ruled and Ruined Tammany Hall." And there is a return to the *Protocols'* libel of a Jewish plot to dominate the world through Bolshevism and Zionism: "Jewish Hot-Beds of Bolshevism in the U.S." and "Will Jewish Zionism Bring Armageddon?"

The preface notes:

> The year has witnessed much notable discussion of the Jewish Question in magazines of quality. A few have descended to white-washing, a fewer still to sheer pro-Jewish propaganda; but such articles as those in the September *Century;* those in the *Atlantic* for February, May and July . . . these testify to the matter. The more serious religious press . . . the *Christian Standard,* the *Christian Century, The Moody Monthly* . . . have added materially . . . the religious press has shown itself to be freer of control than the secular.[38]

All efforts to persuade Ford to desist proved futile, but economic and legal force prevailed. The threat of a lawsuit and a boycott of Ford motorcars caused an apparent change of policy. In May 1927, seven years after the articles began, Louis Marshall made public a retraction by Henry Ford, in which the auto magnate promised to do all in his power to withdraw the scurrilous publication, and offered an apology to the Jewish people.

The Ford apology was exacted by Aaron L. Sapiro as part of an out-of-court settlement of a damage suit he had brought against Ford, for attacks on him by the *Dearborn Independent.* Sapiro wrote of the case:

> Ford maintained that there was a committee of Jews, headed by me, for the purpose of organizing and controlling the primary agricultural products of the world, so that the Jewish bankers could squeeze the nations of the earth of their primary foods. In this connection he named Bernard Baruch, Paul Warburg, Otto Kahn, Albert Lasker, Julius Rosenwald and Eugene Meyer. I spoke to each one to find out whether they would be available for attendance at Detroit at the trial. Otto Kahn refused saying, "I am not a Jew anymore." Eugene Meyer refused saying, "My wife, who is not Jewish, does not want me to be concerned with a Jewish case." Albert Lasker refused saying, "You can be a damn fool and fight a billion dollars, but don't ask me to do it." Julius Rosenwald declined saying, "I am too old to go through cross examination these days." Bernard Baruch said that he "would attend from wherever he might be, from anywhere in the world." Paul Warburg said he "would do anything" I wanted. . . .[39]

"He played with fire," Louis Marshall wrote in 1922, "and has given the sanction of his great office to what, after all, is a vulgar expression of Jew-baiting . . ." Marshall was not referring to Henry Ford, but to the president of America's oldest, most prestigious university, Harvard. "If President Lowell wishes to . . . ally himself with the vilest of European politicians, let him do it," Marshall wrote, and vowed, "We shall not make the way easy for him to accomplish his disgraceful purpose." [40] Marshall's anger was aroused by President Abbott Lawrence Lowell's announcement at the 1922 commencement that a faculty committee had been appointed to discuss a new admission policy. The administration had previously disclosed that "the proportion of Jews at the college," was a matter under consideration. The chairman of the committee voiced Lowell's position that to lessen discrimination against Jews at Harvard their numbers must be contained. "Today Jews are practically ostracized from social organizations. . . . If there were fewer Jews, this problem would not be so." [41]

Marshall and Jewish leaders, including a number of distinguished alumni of the college (Judge Julian Mack was a member of the Board of Overseers), viewed the issue as a matter of gravest importance. Harvard, after all, set the tone for the country. If America's citadel of learning practiced open discrimination, what could one expect of lesser institutions? How would one be able to argue with leaders of industry about discrimination in employment? Marshall warned the committee (of the thirteen professors serving on it, three were Jews), that establishment of a quota would stimulate "anti-Semitism in the United States and abroad, to an extent that can scarcely be estimated." It would constitute "a calamity to the United States and a menace to the Jews of the World."

The committee thereupon repudiated any "novel process of scrutiny," recommending a policy of "equal opportunity for all, regardless of race or religion." But the administration found ways to limit the number of Jews admitted, as did most of the country's major colleges and universities. The quotas were particularly harsh in the professional schools, none more so than the medical schools. Harsher still was the discrimination in university faculties. In the 1920s when some of America's leading lawyers and some of its most distinguished jurists were Jews—indeed, when a Jewish justice, Louis D. Brandeis, sat on the Supreme Court of the United States—the faculties of the nation's law schools had no more than a half-dozen Jews.

Marshall's involvement in both the Ford and Harvard matters was as president of the American Jewish Committee, for the struggle against anti-Semitism had risen high on the Committee's agenda. The Anti-Defamation League of B'nai B'rith was established in 1913 for the purpose the name describes, and the American Jewish Congress soon joined to constitute a growing cadre of "defense agencies," augmented later by the Jewish Labor Committee, the Jewish War Veterans and local communal agencies.

ANTI-SEMITISM: A NATIVE OR IMPORTED PRODUCT?

Defense of the security, status and rights of Jews was the ranking priority of the national Jewish communal enterprise in the interwar period. The prevailing opinion was that anti-Semitism was an import from the Old World, a product of medieval minds, blighted by prejudices formed in autocratic societies, deformed by parodies of true religion. The New World neither fashioned it nor would long tolerate it, if men were made aware of its menace and its danger.

In *The Nation* (March 21, 1923), Lewis S. Gannett argued a contrary view:

> Anti-Semitism, as it manifests itself in America, is essentially a part of a long Anglo-Saxon tradition of dislike of the newer arrival . . . [It] is, of course, a recent fact. It had to await the coming of the Jews . . . The children of that Jewish immigration are just coming of age as the present anti-Jewish feeling is reaching its maximum.

The cause, as Gannett saw it, was that "Anglo-Saxon Americans . . . do not want to be fused with other races, traditions, and cultures . . ." This would account for the fact that in America, anti-Semitism has expressed itself through exclusion of the Jew from social clubs, vacation places, neighborhoods, offices, certain jobs and professions, and by limiting their numbers where they could not be excluded. The rhetoric had been imported from Europe, not the physical manifestations— pogroms, expulsions and the like.

Gannett's thesis was called into question by the anti-Semitism of the 1930s, where the ties of American anti-Semitic groups with those in Europe were clear. The brown shirts and swastika armbands of the Nazi-inspired German-American Bund could be seen on city streets. Catholic priest Father Charles E. Coughlin revived in the 1930s, in a long series of radio broadcasts, the Bolshevik specter, accusing Jews (leading bankers, no less) of fomenting and launching the Russian Revolution. The discredited *Protocols* was reprinted in his newspaper, *Social Justice*. Coughlin justified the spread of anti-Semitism in America, "because the people sense a closely interwoven relationship between Communism and Jewry." His superiors in the Church would not silence him. George Cardinal Mundelein of Chicago explained: "As an American citizen, Father Coughlin has the right to express his personal views on current events, but he is not authorized to speak for the Catholic

Church. . . ." [42] Rabble-rouser Joe McWilliams forged his *Christian Front*
constituency from urban ethnics.

Opponents of anti-Semitism chose to view it as an "import,"
alien to the American experience, in conflict with the American promise
of freedom and equality. Americanism could therefore be invoked to
contain it and defeat it. Americans were enlisted in its denunciation and
their words were widely disseminated. In 1921, *The Peril of Racial
Prejudice,* a statement protesting the *Protocols,* was published in America
and abroad:

> The undersigned, citizens of Gentile birth and Christian faith, view
> with profound regret and disapproval the appearance in this coun-
> try of what is apparently an organized campaign of anti-Semitism
> . . . These publications . . . are introducing . . . a new and dan-
> gerous spirit . . . that is wholly at variance with our traditions and
> ideals and subversive of our system of government . . .

One hundred leading Americans, including President Wood-
row Wilson, former president William H. Taft and William Cardinal
O'Connell, were its signatories. It was reprinted when "the rise of
Hitlerism and the spread of Nazi falsehoods" revived the *Protocols.*

Identifying anti-Semitism as an antidemocratic sentiment, "at
variance with our traditions . . . subversive of our system of government," the American Jewish Committee published *The Authoritarian
Personality* which argued that prejudice against Jews emanates from a
personality type that is a threat to the "very survival of democratic
society." The Committee underwrote studies, and convened conferences "not merely to describe prejudice but to explain it in order to
help in its eradication." [43] Jews had a primary interest, but as the Protest
of the One Hundred stressed, anti-Semitism was an American problem:
"We believe it should not be left to men and women of Jewish faith to
fight this evil, but that it is in a very special sense the duty of citizens
who are not Jews."

Nonetheless, it was organized Jewry not the "citizens who are
not Jews" who carried on the campaign. The Anti-Defamation League
identified bigots and bigotry. It undertook to educate the public about
the Jew and Judaism, about the contributions both made to the course
of Western civilization and the well-being of mankind. Its longtime
chairman, Sigmund Livingston, concludes his volume *Must Men Hate?*
with two appendices. One: "Seven Hundred Jews Who Have Made
Notable Contributions to Modern Civilization." Two: "Jews in the
American Armed Forces in the Present War Who Received Official
Awards." The introduction to the volume is a statement of faith: "Any
person who will try honestly will find real satisfaction, and even ex-
hilaration, in the conquest of . . . prejudices . . . *Teach the truth and*

unmask every falsehood . . . An intellectually honest man, knowing the truth about the Jew, cannot be an anti-Semite." *Must Men Hate?* was published in 1944, eleven years after the rise of Hitler, when reports on ghettos, extermination camps and crematories had already reached these shores.

Other Jewish "defense agencies" took on tasks peculiar to their interests. The Jewish Labor Committee established bridges to the labor movement; the Jewish War Veterans stressed the patriotism of the Jew; the American Jewish Congress undertook vigorous public protest against anti-Semitic manifestations, and organized mass demonstrations against Nazism and a boycott of German goods. Immediately after the war, it turned its energies to social legislation "in activities designed to strengthen American democracy, eliminate racial and religious bigotry, and advance civil liberties."

Throughout the interwar period, advertisements for jobs in the daily press openly stated, "No Jews need apply." In a survey conducted in 1926, discrimination was justified on such grounds as, "We find Protestants . . . more trustworthy than Catholics or Jews"; "Everyone in the office is a Christian . . . it would be more convenient to continue on that basis"; and "Sometime ago we had the Bolshevik class of Jews in our place who caused a strike." The Jewish-owned *New York Times* accepted ads which called for excluding Jews from jobs and places of residence.[44]

There were even uglier incidents. In June and July 1927, *The New York Times* carried reports that in Kings County Hospital, Brooklyn, three Jewish interns were assaulted by some twenty others who gagged and bound them and ducked them into ice-cold water.[45] The incident was a mark of the prevailing pattern of prejudice against Jewish doctors in a city hospital in a borough with a large Jewish population. The mayor ordered an investigation. The superintendent of the hospital was suspended but later reinstated.

Overt anti-Semitism in America did not go much further. Not a single pogrom is recorded. No political party of any consequence espoused it. Anti-Semitism was condemned by the Catholic Church and main-line Protestantism. American traditions and ideals were invoked to condemn it; and the pluralistic society produced and sustained a tolerance which would not permit excesses. Its chief expression remained in Jewish exclusion from significant aspects of American life.

Neither the exertion of Jewish agencies nor the efforts of men of goodwill brought an end to open discrimination. Practical necessities accomplished what lofty ideals could not. In the early 1940s the needs of a nation at war opened opportunities of employment more genuinely on the basis of ability; the need for social stability in the postwar era led to legal abrogation of many institutionalized discriminations.

11.

From Dusk to Darkness

AMERICAN JEWRY ENTERED THE 1930s DISTURBED BY THE COLLAPSE OF THE stock market, which seemed the beginning of worse to come; worried about rising anti-Semitism in Europe; and shocked by news of Arab pogroms in Palestine that called the viability of the Zionist enterprise into question. The bright promise of the Balfour Declaration seemed nullified by the attacks on Jewish worshipers at the Western Wall in Jerusalem, the murder of yeshiva students in Hebron, and the Mandatory Power's unwillingness or inability to restore order or offer protection.

The reaction of American Jewry was immediate. Protest meetings were called, climaxed by a rally in Madison Square Garden in New York, attended by 25,000. The massacre was angrily denounced from synagogue pulpit and in the Anglo-Jewish and Yiddish press, as was the British government for its do-nothing policy. Resolutions were adopted; friends in high places were called upon. Members of Congress expressed sympathy and announced support for the Zionist cause. Congressman Hamilton Fish, Jr., of New York, stated, "For a long time I have been a convinced Zionist, but never more convinced than since the cold-blooded murder of over one hundred defenseless Jews in Palestine." Senator Arthur Capper of Kansas announced that the American people were behind the movement "to make Palestine a real home for the Jewish race."[1] Congressman W. E. Evans of California acknowledged that "the tragedies that are daily occurring in Palestine are of great and vital concern to the American people."[2] This was a matter, he said, for the State Department to handle. But the State Department—

despite rallies and pleas, despite the fact that about a dozen Americans had been murdered—did nothing. The British government would not alter policy, and the United States would do nothing to discomfit a friendly power.

The American daily press joined in an outpouring of sympathy for the victims. New York newspapers, *The Times,* the *Telegram,* the *Journal* and the *Sun* blamed the British for not standing up to the promise made to the Jewish people. Some liberal periodicals took the occasion to denounce Western imperialism; *The Nation,* for example, stating:

> The British have failed to give the Jews the protection they promised, but the Arabs have also their prior grievances. . . . The pledges to the Arabs were shamelessly flouted. Sometime, somewhere, this Western domination of Arab lands will cease. There will be no end to Arab agitation until it does.[3]

The *Jewish Daily Forward,* the leading Yiddish daily, which, under the editorship of Abraham Cahan, had turned from a doctrinaire Socialist anti-Zionist stance to one of benevolent neutrality, condemned the riots, expressed sympathy for beleaguered fellow Jews and called for a reversal of the Zionist program.

The first reaction of the Communist Yiddish daily, the *Freiheit,* was to call on the world proletariat to oppose "the Arab nationalist movement" which is under "the leadership of Arab effendis and the bourgeois intelligentsia." It labeled the attackers "hooligans" supported by the British, and spoke favorably of the "Zionist youth who fought bravely against the Arab pogrom makers." When the Communist commissars moved quickly to suppress such "cosmopolitan" Jewish sentiments, the *Freiheit* did a complete about-face. Now its headline declared that THE ZIONIST-FASCISTS HAVE PROVOKED THE ARAB UPRISING. To atone for his deviation from the party line, editor M. Olgin pointed an accusing finger: "You [the Zionists] are playing with the blood of misled people . . . The blood will fall on you . . . You are murderers . . ."[4] A protest march against the pogroms was held on August 27; the Jewish Communists countered with a banner headline in the *Freiheit:* ENGLISH TROOPS AND JEWISH LEGIONAIRES IN BLOODY MASSACRE ON ARABS: THOUSANDS DEAD AND WOUNDED; HAIFA IN FLAMES. At a meeting in Irving Plaza Hall in New York City the next day, the faithful adopted a resolution which began: "The assembled Jewish workers send their brotherly greetings to the rebellious masses in Palestine," and concluded: "Long live the Revolutionary Uprising of the Arab masses in Palestine!" A later *Freiheit* headline declared: THE BLOOD IS ON YOUR HANDS, ZIONISTS AND ZIONIST FELLOW TRAVELERS.

The *Freiheit* had been established seven years earlier, when the *Forward* chose to remain Socialist. A number of leading *Forward* writers and poets left for the new paper, which offered them greater opportunity for literary creativity and was more oriented toward Russian Yiddish culture.

Now, in 1929, four of the most distinguished of the group left the *Freiheit* in protest against its stand on the riots. Abraham Raisin proclaimed: "I want no revolutions through pogroms on the Jews. When the Jewish people are in trouble I suffer with them . . . I am no Zionist, but I have the greatest respect for the Jewish colonists who, having built up their colonies through sweat and blood, are now being destroyed by the Arab pogromists . . ." Three others who left, poets H. Leivick, Menachem Boraisha and novelist Isaac Raboy, protested: "The greetings to the so-called 'Arab Revolutionists' are greetings for frightful outrages committed on innocent men, women and children."[5] Poets David Ignatow and Lamed Shapiro left as well. Moishe Nadir, who remained to accuse the departing writers of self-serving motives— "attracted by the fat roast," he accused—did the same ten years later, when he joined Melech Epstein, Louis Hyman, novelist Joseph Opatoshu and playwright Peretz Hirschbein in leaving the *Freiheit* for its defense of the Hitler-Stalin Pact.

The "Jewish masses" responded to the *Freiheit*'s stance with a boycott. News dealers refused to sell the paper. Subscribers canceled and readers departed. Melech Epstein recalled an incident in Chicago on Wednesday, September 9, a day the Orthodox rabbinate designated as a Fast Day to mourn the victims. He asked a middle-aged woman at a newsstand for a *Freiheit*. She replied, "I am too weak to fast, so the least I can do is not to sell the *Freiheit* today."[6]

Communism was a force to contend with in the Jewish community from the twenties through the forties. In the postwar decade it concentrated on capturing the clothing unions and almost succeeded with the ILGWU. In the thirties, it was strengthened by the Great Depression and in the forties by the war alliance of the United States and the Soviet Union and by their joining together to help establish the State of Israel. The disclosure in the sixties of Stalin's anti-Semitic excesses was a hard blow, and defection among leaders and rank and file followed.

THE GREAT DEPRESSION

The Depression affected American Jews as it affected other urban Americans. Unemployment and underemployment knew no ethnic bounds, but its debilitating effect was more profound on Jews. The discrimination in employment that developed in the twenties intensified in the Depression years of the thirties. The psychic disorientation which the economic crisis caused to many was even more pronounced for

Jews. It shook their confidence in America. To see the American dream turn into a nightmare destroyed their morale; for more than others, they had made America the source of their security, the object of their devotion.

The Depression also threatened the viability of the vast network of social, cultural and religious institutions American Jews had created to serve their needs and assure Jewish survival. Maintaining voluntary institutions in an economic crisis is low in priority for a family that needs food, rent or mortgage payments. The personnel needed adequately to staff pulpits, classrooms and offices was depleted, and those who remained were often embittered by continuing conflict with the leaders of institutions which employed them but could not adequately compensate them.

Small wonder, then, that Jews were among the most enthusiastic supporters of the New Deal. Judge Jonah B. Goldstein's quip that the American Jew had three worlds: "*Die velt* [this world]; *yene velt* [the world to come]; and *Roosevelt*," was an apt revelation of the adulation Jews felt for the president. Roosevelt represented the promise of Depression defeated, prosperity reestablished and faith in America restored.

In the meanwhile, the option of *aliyah* to Palestine became a prospect to be seriously considered. There had been a sporadic *aliyah* from America from the beginning of the century, but the number of emigrants was very small. Of Zionist leaders only Judah Magnes, Henrietta Szold and Irma Lindheim had settled in Palestine, for the future looked far brighter in the Land of Promise than in the Promised Land. But in the early thirties, as a longtime Zionist phrased it, "It will be more pleasant to starve in Palestine than in America. At least *there* we will be doing it for a cause." So young American Zionists began to sing a song of parting:

Goodbye, America,
Goodbye, Yankee fashion.
I'm going to Palestine,
To hell with the Depression!

and the young Labor Zionist Habonim group began to prepare for *kibbutz* life in training camps in New Jersey. Some did reach the Promised Land and were among the founders of *kibbutzim,* notably Gesher Haziv and K'far Blum.

LITERATURE AND POPULAR CULTURE

"It is from the Russian Jews, who are the mass of poor Jews in America, that the real contribution to American life is likely to come, because their aspirations are spiritual, their imagination alive," wrote the editor of *Harper's Weekly* in 1916. In 1917 appeared the first and best of the novels about immigration, *The Rise of David Levinsky,* by Abraham Cahan. This classic describes the coming of a penniless *yeshiva bachur* from Russia to New York in the 1880s, as Cahan himself had come. The hero rises to become a millionaire clothing manufacturer, sacrificing along the way the piety, the love of learning, the ideals of social justice and even the hope for simple family joys that might have been his heritage. It is both a statement of what might have become of a gifted, ambitious young immigrant like Cahan had not Socialism become his new religion, and a sad, poignant farewell to the values of the world he had left.

"The Promised Land" was the name given by Mary Antin to the new country, and the title she chose in 1912 for her paean of praise to the freedom of America as contrasted to the repressions of the Old World. To become one with the beckoning new society, she saw it necessary to discard Jewish ties.

Among other writers on the immigrant experience, Anzia Yezierska found poverty and near-desperation, as told in *Hungry Hearts* in 1920; yet she was sustained, as she reiterated thirty years later in her autobiographical *Red Ribbon on a White Horse,* by a fanatic love of education and by the hope that America might yet become the Golden Land of justice the immigrants had envisioned.

The newcomers' problems and disillusionments, and the second generation's defection to the lures of American society, were treated by Sholem Asch in *East River,* by David Pinski in *The House of Noah Eden* and by Charles Reznikoff in *By the Waters of Manhattan.* Leftist or "proletarian" writers of the twenties and thirties also wrote harshly of the ghetto and its offspring. The bewilderment of a Jewish immigrant child whose parents are undergoing their own struggle in the new world is evoked by Henry Roth in *Call It Sleep.* Terrified by his sordid surroundings and hated by his father, the boy clings to his mother. He almost meets death while seeking a glory he has glimpsed in a passage from the Prophets he has overheard at *heder.*

A masterly novel of second-generation Jews growing to young adulthood in the Chicago of the thirties is *The Old Bunch,* written in 1937 by Meyer Levin. The conflicts between the old and young generations, the encroachment of social evils and urban turmoil on the individual, the love of learning and desire to serve humanity that mark some of the characters all ring true in this panorama of American life.

Socially conscious Jewish playwrights of the thirties and forties, like Clifford Odets in *Awake and Sing,* and Elmer Rice in *Street Scene,* showed the shortcomings of American life through the medium of Jewish characters. Lillian Hellman in serious vein and such lighter playwrights as S. N. Behrman and George S. Kaufman were mainstays of Broadway.

Poets such as Louis Untermeyer and Babette Deutsch contributed much to American poetry in the first half of the century. Charles Reznikoff, closer to Jewish roots, sang of his heritage as Jew in the Diaspora, while the Canadian A. M. Klein summed up in his masterpiece of prose-poetry, *The Second Scroll,* the entire range of Jewish experience. Others whose Jewishness furnished subject matter for their poetry include Howard Nemerov, Hyam Plutzik, Delmore Schwartz and Muriel Rukeyser, who wrote that refusing the gift of being a Jew would be choosing "death of the spirit."

Most perceptive of the analysts of the Jew and his world was Maurice Samuel, who became best known for his analysis and translation of Yiddish literature, in *Prince of the Ghetto* (about Y. L. Peretz) and in *The World of Sholom Aleichem.* In *The Great Hatred,* Samuel argues that the basis for anti-Semitism is amoral man's rage against the group which imposed moral restraints on his pagan passions. *The Gentleman and the Jew* argues that the world suffers because it idealizes the gentleman, who fights gallantly in the pursuit of power and honor, while the Jewish prophetic ideal, the moral, compassionate human being, is rejected.

FOCUS
Anger, Alienation . . . Escape

Words are the weapons of the weak. The sons of the immigrant generation took up these weapons in their battle against an America which would not let them in and then justified the exclusion by claiming that the Jews preferred to remain apart. Morris Raphael Cohen, one of the keenest minds and most memorable teachers on the American academic scene, recalls in his autobiography his frustrating struggle for a faculty appointment. Ludwig Lewisohn, among the most gifted students and teachers of literature, writes with bitterness of the bigotry which he met when he attempted to enter the intellectual and academic world.

Novelists Samuel Ornitz, Jerome Weidman and Budd Schulberg threw their battling, clawing, conniving Meyer Hirsh (in *Haunch, Paunch and Jowl*), Harry Bogen (in *I Can Get It for You Wholesale*) and Sammy Glick (in *What Makes Sammy Run?*) at America as if to say, "Add these to your pantheon of robber barons; they are no less adept in the acquisitive virtues you value than Vanderbilt, Fisk or Gould." Clifford Odets' rage was of a milder sort, but no less visceral in his *Awake and Sing.* Grandfather Jacob sums up what America has done to the youthful dreamers: "He dreams all night of toilets like a monument."

The American reading public was fascinated by these bitter outpourings. Such alien voices—how unlike the tempered anger of Upton Sinclair or the gentlemanly criticism of Sinclair Lewis! Michael Gold's manifesto, *Jews Without Money,* published in 1930, went through seventeen printings in a decade. Within the first five years of publication, it was translated into French, Swedish, Romanian, Spanish, Yugoslavian, Italian, Japanese, Chinese, Ukrainian, Russian, Yiddish, Bohemian, Bulgarian, Dutch and Tartar. He wrote of poor Jews, of Jews who "had fled from European pogroms";

> with prayer, thanksgiving and solemn faith from a new Egypt into a new Promised Land.
>
> They found awaiting them the sweatshops, the bawdy houses and Tammany hall. . . .
>
> Earth's trees, grass, flowers could not grow on my street; but the rose of syphilis bloomed by night and by day.

Gold's novel ends as pious works are meant to end, with a doxology, a proclamation of fealty to his new "Red God":

> O workers' Revolution, you brought hope to me . . . You are the true Messiah. You will destroy the East Side when you come, and build them a garden for the human spirit.
>
> O Revolution, that forced me to think, to struggle and to live.
>
> O great Beginning!

There were other gifted sons of immigrant fathers who took up verbal weapons and used them not to lacerate the hostile world about them but to dissect the perplexing world within themselves.

Isaac Rosenfeld's *Passage from Home* is the story of the son who runs away from his father to an aunt, through whom he wants to enter the world outside, by arranging an ill-omened affair between her and a Gentile. His attempt to return to home and love is also a failure. Rosenfeld's parable is of the prodigal son, who cannot enter the world outside, nor return to the world he had to leave. It echoes a theme found in Yiddish and Hebrew literature of the late nineteenth and early twentieth centuries: the modern Jew lives in stark alienation. Rosenfeld and the novelists of the next decades declared alienation to be the condition of modern man, of the thinking, sensitive American. In adopting the posture of alienation Jewish intellectuals justified their defection from the world of their fathers, and thought they placed themselves in the world of the American intellectual elite. "The alienated Jewish intellectual . . . ," said sociologist Daniel Bell in "A Parable of Alienation" published in the *Jewish Frontier* in 1946, "can only live in permanent tension and as a permanent critic." And as if to anticipate the rebuke that to do so is to escape obligation to community—people and heritage—Bell declares alienation a moral imperative. "As long as moral corruption exists, alienation is the only possible response."

The Jewish intellectuals, raging, alienated or otherwise, at first finding the pages of "American" quality journals closed to them, took advantage of the hospitality which Jewish journals extended, notably *The Menorah Journal*. Begun as the publication of the Menorah Society, an intercollegiate Jewish fellowship with chapters on the leading campuses, it was for almost four decades from 1915 the finest journal American Jewry produced. Mordecai M. Kaplan, Horace Kallen, Israel Friedlaender, Harry A. Wolfson, Salo Baron, Marvin Lowenthal, Maurice Samuel and a Who's Who of Jewish scholars and thinkers were introduced to the intelligent Jewish reader in its pages. Editor Henry Hurwitz and his gifted co-worker Elliot E. Cohen also made it a journal which introduced Jewish art and literature and sought out the contributions of young Jewish writers of promise. Clifton Fadiman, Irwin Edman, Lionel Trilling were published there before fame opened other avenues to them. Nor was *The Menorah Journal* alone. The tradition of Anglo-Jewish journals of quality begun by *The Occident* in 1843 continued to offer the Jewish reader a wide choice of intellectual fare. A number of the local Anglo-Jewish weekly newspapers, as for example *The Boston Jewish Advocate,* were papers of quality, sometimes surpassing the local press.

The world at large knew far less of Jewish literary figures than of Jewish purveyors of popular culture: songwriters, popular playwrights, columnists; but, most of all, those they saw on the vaudeville stage. In the 1940s, Ben Hecht remembered them as he found them in New York in the 1920s.

> Twenty-five years later most of these antic performers are still the singing, talking and dancing stars of the nation . . . what a troupe they were in their heyday! What a wild yap of wit and sweet burst of song came surging out of the Jewish slums of the twenties! The Marx Brothers, Al Jolson, George Jessel, Fanny Brice, Eddie Cantor, Jack Benny, Jack Pearl, Bennie Fields, Lou Holtz, Ed Wynn, Joe Laurie, the Howard Brothers, Julius Tannen, Phil Baker, Phil Silvers, Milton Berle, Belle Baker, Harry Richman, Ben Bernie, the Ritz Brothers, Smith and Dale, Ben Welch, Harry Green, Ray Samuels, Jackie Osterman, George Burns—these are some of them.
>
> There were others . . .
>
> In their presence Jewishness was not Jewishness. It was a fascinating Americanism.[7]

THE SILVER SCREEN

The early twentieth century witnessed the birth of the moving-picture industry. As a new industry, it was free of vested interest, a high risk venture with an uncertain future. Unattractive to well-established prudent entrepreneurs, it was enticing to venturesome and imaginative members of the immigrant community, who without money or connection had nothing to lose and fortunes to gain. A Jesse Lasky, a Marcus Loewe, and later a Louis B. Mayer and a Samuel Goldwyn had the vision, daring and organizational ability that might have carried them to the highest reaches of any industry.

Initially, Jewish participation in this newest medium of America's popular culture was in production and distribution. Later, creative sons and daughters of immigrant Jews made their mark, as the movies also became a major art form. The producer Irving Thalberg, actors Paul Muni and Edward G. Robinson, and a host of writers and directors found success in Hollywood. The foundation they laid enabled an even greater number of third-generation American Jews to become a highly visible and powerful element in many aspects of the television industry.

During the years of Jewish leadership of the movie industry two films were produced which dealt with Jewish themes. Samson Raphaelson's *The Jazz Singer* in 1927, and Fannie Hurst's *Symphony of Six Million* (the number refers to the population of New York) in 1932. Adapted from a successful Broadway production, *The Jazz Singer* epitomizes the generational conflict between immigrant parents and their American children in the story of Jakie, the son of Cantor Rabinowitz, who takes the name Jack Robins and rises to fame on the vaudeville stage. The father's hope that his son would continue the family tradition of service to God as a cantor is thwarted by the son's ambition to gain fame by pleasing the public. The pain of the father, the pangs of guilt of the son, the proverbial prodigal's return to chant Kol Nidre to a father on his deathbed and a congregation met on the eve of the Day of Atonement, the loving acceptance by the mother of the non-Jewish prospective daughter-in-law, are on the screen blended into a "happy ending." The forgiving mother is rewarded by her now famous son singing "Mammy" to her on bended knee and in black face. Those seated in the movie house experienced a moment of solace that perhaps the conflict between generations with which so many could identify might have a happy ending. But, once out of the theater, they returned to a world in which the pains of the parents persisted, the guilt of the children lingered, and life denied Hollywood happy endings.

The review of *Symphony of Six Million* in *The New York Times* was headlined, A CLEVER JEWISH SURGEON. The Klauber family is caught up in the ambition to succeed in America. The chosen vehicle for upward mobility is son Felix who is spurred on to become a doctor. The immigrant father buys his young son a pair of "surgeon's gloves" and a surgeon he does become. The family glories in their son's rise from practicing medicine in an East Side clinic with patients who need him to a lucrative Park Avenue practice and a clientele whom he pampers. An unsuccessful operation on his father and the realization that his profligate life has eroded his skills cause Felix to return to the old neighborhood and his old sweetheart, to announce: "I dedicate these two hands in the service—that the lame may walk, the halt may be strong—lifting the needy and comforting the dying. This is my oath in the Temple of healing."

Hollywood caught some of the tensions in the immigrant community: generations in conflict, ambitions realized and the prices paid, a happy ending which could not quite erase the misery that preceded it. Hollywood sometimes presented the world as it was, but far more often, it afforded its audience the experience of being part of the world it invented—a world free of ambiguities and uncertainties. Virtue was rewarded, sin never went unpunished. Hero and villain were clearly identified, and at the end of trials and tribulations, pain and suffering, striving and sacrifice, there was almost always the happy ending. A vulgarized version of the Judeo-Christian tradition of an ordered, morally unambiguous universe, presided over by a stern but benevolent Deity, was the world Hollywood placed before the vast audiences who weekly worshiped the secular saints of the silver screen in the cathedral theaters which dotted America. The descendants of priests and Prophets created for the secular city a canon and liturgy on celluloid—a faith as fragile as the product on which it was printed.

MUSIC AND ART

East European liturgical music was introduced to America by cantors such as Baruch Shorr of Lemberg, Pincus Minkowski of Odessa and Zeidel Rovner of Kishinev and London. The most popular and most beloved of all cantors was Yossele Rosenblatt, but David Roitman, Mordecai Herschman, Shmuel Vigoda and Berele Chagy had their worshipful followers in synagogue and concert hall.

The names of A. W. Binder, Jacob Weinberg and Herbert Fromm became well-known as composers of music for the American synagogue. The most significant new work to be created for Jewish prayer was *Avodat Kodesh* by Ernest Bloch, well-known as composer of the *Baal Shem Suite* and *Schelomo*. Other composers of liturgical music included Lazar Saminsky, Frederick Jacobi and Max Helfmann. From the Yiddish theater, composers like Sholom Secunda and Abraham Ellstein began immediately after the Second World War to devote their creativity almost exclusively to the synagogue.

In the performance of music, Jews have been particularly active. The roster of the leading American instrumentalists of the twentieth century is filled with names like Jascha Heifetz, Yehudi Menuhin, Mischa Elman, Nathan Milstein, Arthur Rubinstein, Vladimir Horowitz,

Emanuel Feuermann and Isaac Stern, and among Jewish singers who have achieved world prominence, Jan Peerce, Richard Tucker, Robert Merrill, Beverly Sills and Roberta Peters.

Outstanding in American musical accomplishment are the names Aaron Copland, whose music for the ballet, opera and symphony hall is among the most acclaimed and most popular; Marc Blitzstein, composer of music dramas; Arnold Schoenberg, who revitalized the field of musical composition with his twelve-tone scale; and Kurt Weill, who escaped Nazi Germany to continue his distinguished career for the musical stage. George Gershwin began as an apprentice composer in the Yiddish theater and turned to Tin Pan Alley. His *Rhapsody in Blue* was the first jazz composition to receive a performance in Carnegie Hall.

While Jewish influence in much of the music produced by Jewish composers and artists can only be guessed at, many works are avowedly on Jewish themes. The multitalented director-composer Leonard Bernstein created the *Jeremiah Symphony,* with liturgical passages, and a new setting to Hebrew psalms in the *Chichester Psalms.* Stefan Wolpe wrote in the modern mode a variety of classical Jewish art songs. In musical theater, well exemplified by Jerome Kern, composer of the classic American light opera *Show Boat,* and in popular song, Jewish composers have been numerous. For over a half century America has heard and has sung the songs of Irving Berlin. His "God Bless America" has become more widely sung than the national anthem.

Jewish artists born in Eastern Europe and coming to America around the turn of the century, many of them studying for some time in Paris, brought modern European influences with them. Max Weber, whose work included evocations of East European life, went from Cubism to New York Expressionism. William Meyerowitz, disciple of Cezanne, often used themes from Jewish folklore. In a more realistic style, tending toward the romantic, the brothers Moses and Raphael Soyer, sons of the Hebrew writer Abraham Soyer, portrayed sympathetic scenes and human figures, often taken from Jewish or immigrant life. During the Depression years, Jewish among other artists expressed strong social criticism through their work. William Gropper, Marxist from the Lower East Side, used the medium of caricature. Others whose work tended toward moral comment were Joseph Hirsch and Jack Levine.

The work of many of the artists expressed elements of Jewish background, such as the Biblical themes of Ben Zion, and the Near Eastern effects of the primitive, Morris Hirschfeld. Todros Geller's feeling for Jewish culture served well in his creation of synagogue windows and other functional Jewish art. Ben Shahn, a lover of the letters of the alphabet, used his dramatic artistic gifts to further social causes in which he believed, and to add to Jewish ritual art as well. William Zorach, master worker in structural forms in stone and wood, taught and influenced a large school, including the outstanding Chaim Gross. Sculptor Jacques Lipchitz, whose themes of struggle are often illustrated through Jewish subjects such as the birth of Israel, was said to be the first to translate concepts of abstract painting into sculpture.

As revealed in Avram Kampf's *Contemporary Synagogue Art,* congregations in the United States have been attempting to utilize contemporary art forms to add to the beauty of their synagogue buildings and to "awaken an intrinsically religious feeling." Outstanding among synagogue architects is Percival Goodman, who brought to the buildings he created a modern aesthetic while retaining in them the functional and traditional requirements of the synagogue. Boris Aronson, Ilya Schor, A. Raymond Katz and Ben Shahn are among the artists who have, in stained glass and sculpture, arks and doors and pulpits, aided Jews to "worship the Lord in the beauty of holiness."

EXILES AND EMIGRÉS

Restrictive immigration laws permitted only a trickle of Jewish immigrants to enter the United States in the years between the wars, even when victims of Nazism were seeking a haven. But a number did enter in the 1930s, and they made their impress on American and Jewish life.

World-renowned scientists, of whom Albert Einstein was the most noted, played a key role in leading America into the nuclear age. University faculties were strengthened by the arrival of scholars in all disciplines. Social scientists Hannah Arendt and Hans J. Morgenthau, for example, helped America understand the nature of totalitarianism and the power relationships between nations. Artists, writers, composers infused into American culture the rich heritage of the West European.

The Jewish community was enriched by the scholars who came and by the newly arrived community, which was marked by a high level of general and Jewish culture. Three rabbinic seminaries joined to bring Ismar Elbogen, historian. Nahum Glatzer introduced the thought of Franz Rosenzweig to America and played the central role in the establishment of Jewish studies at Brandeis University. The most influential and widely read American Jewish theologian in the postwar era was Warsaw-born, German-trained Abraham Joshua Heschel. A small but important group brought the way of life of the neo-Orthodoxy of Samson Raphael Hirsch, full involvement in general life and culture and strict religious observance. They set the pattern for the modern Orthodoxy which developed in the postwar years.

After World War II, some relaxation of immigration quotas permitted survivors of the Holocaust to enter. An appreciable number were soon involved in communal activities, and some rose to positions of leadership, lay and professional.

Among the new arrivals were Hasidic communities which re-established their old way of life in the Williamsburg, East New York and Boro Park sections of Brooklyn, and in self-contained communities in rural New York State. Most notable of these have been the Habad Hasidim, followers of the Lubavitch Rebbe, whose emphasis has been on bringing back to Jewish observance those who had strayed from it or had never experienced it; and the followers of the Satmar Rebbe, militant anti-Zionists, bent on retaining a way of life free of influences of the modern world.

THE UNITED JEWISH APPEAL

During the quarter century 1914–39 American Jewry had come of age; over a million were added to the population, bringing it close to five million, one-third of world Jewry. The community established one thousand new congregations, built synagogues and community centers and trained the personnel to staff them. It devised strategies with which to confront bigotry and discrimination and fashioned agencies to employ them. America as a land of cultural pluralism which replaced the melting pot concept made American Jews more comfortable in their cultural and religious otherness, provided justification for Jewish cultural endeavor and gave "legitimacy" to Zionist activities. Acceptance of fraternal responsibility for the well-being of overseas brethren conferred maturity and made for unity. At the period's beginning, the Jewish community was so divided that even in the war years it could not unite into one fund-raising organization; at its end one united campaign was willed by the community—the United Jewish Appeal. It took a traumatizing crisis abroad to force this unity, but the elements were ready and awaiting a catalyst.

A Review of the Year 5700 (July 1939–June 30, 1940) in the *American Jewish Yearbook* states:

> The outbreak of the European war in September and the rapid extension of Nazi domination over the greater part of Europe, with its profound effect on Jewish life overseas, and its serious threats to democracy throughout the world, held the focus of attention of American Jewry during the period under review. In the United States there remained the only important Jewish commu-

nity in the world, operating within the framework of the democratic way of life, in a country still at peace. The rapid march of events abroad imposed upon American Jews the twofold responsibility of extending material aid and moral support on an unprecedented scale to the victims of Nazi war and persecution, and of strengthening the communal and cultural bases of Jewish life in America . . . the effects of the war on Palestine held the attention of the American Jewish community which became practically the sole remaining source of moral and material support for the Jewish settlement there. . . . Above all, the necessity of caring for refugees and other victims of the war resulted in an unprecedented expansion of relief efforts. The United States became the center of Zionist efforts and assumed the leadership in Jewish life throughout the world.[8]

In this atmosphere of crisis and peril abroad and heightened responsibility at home, the United Jewish Appeal was born. At the end of the 1940 campaign, the cochairmen, Rabbis Abba Hillel Silver and Jonah B. Wise, announced that "as of December 31, 1940, the United Jewish Appeal will cease to function as the agency for the collection and distribution of new funds for the 1941 programs of the Joint Distribution Committee, the United Palestine Appeal and the National Refugee Service."[9] The three constituents announced individual campaigns, but they had not properly assessed the mood of the Jewish community. The announcement aroused such vigorous protest from all parts of the country that the constituent agencies thought it wise to reconsider. Within a month, an agreement to reconstitute the UJA was reached. What became increasingly obvious was that the power of decision was flowing from the national agencies to the local communities; that those who raised the funds were determined to have an increasing voice in how this would be done. The United Jewish Appeal was being willed a life of its own not by the agencies who begat it, but by the communities who used it and in the process were united by it.

November 1942 marked a turning point in the fortunes of war for the Allied armies. They were soon able to liberate North Africa and parts of Italy. The push eastward to liberate Nazi-enslaved countries was on the way. The prospects of peace seemed to permit ideological and practical conflicts to come to the fore, most pronounced of which was the Zionist–anti-Zionist confrontation.

In preparation for a postwar world, and the place of Jews within it, the American Jewish Committee issued a position paper which called for an international trusteeship of Palestine under the United Nations which would safeguard Jewish settlement and permit Jewish immigration "to the full extent of the economic absorptive capacity of a self-governing commonwealth." The Zionists termed this an anti-Zionist position and argued that it made negotiations for joint action impossible. Others stated that it left sufficient room for cooperation if not agreement between Zionists and non-Zionists. Among these was Henry Monsky, president of B'nai B'rith, who called for convening an American Jewish Assembly "to establish a common program of action in connection with post-war problems." One of three items on the agenda, "the implementation of the rights of the Jewish people with respect to Palestine," had a definite Zionist ring to it, so both the American Jewish Committee and the Jewish Labor Committee absented themselves from the convening meeting. Only after long negotiations did both agree to participate in the American Jewish Conference—from which the American Jewish Committee soon departed. In such an atmosphere of communal tensions the United Jewish Appeal brought a needed unity to American Jewry, now the largest in the world, and the only one to whom the Jews of a war-torn world could look for "material aid and moral support." Reviewing the 1939–44 period, Joseph J. Schwartz, head of European operation for the JDC in those years, wrote (in 1955):

> During these five years of war and Nazi persecution, 5,814,000 European Jews perished in gas chambers, in slave-labor camps, in ghettos and during deportation. But the survival of 1,430,000 Jews in Western, Central and Eastern Europe (excluding the Soviet Union) was, to more than a modest degree, the result of the lifesaving mission of the Joint Distribution Committee. Operating in Portugal, Switzerland and Turkey, J.D.C. untiringly provided aid through various channels, including diplomatic missions of neutral countries and the underground . . . In spite of numerous obstacles and perilous conditions prevailing in German-occupied Europe, the J.D.C. and the Jewish Agency were able to rescue 162,000 Jews from *Festung Europa* during 1939–1944 of whom 50,000 were brought to Palestine.
>
> At the end of 1944, U.J.A. funds provided relief to distressed Jews in forty-eight countries: seventeen in Europe; eleven in Arab and Middle Eastern lands; seventeen in Central and South America and three elsewhere.[10]

1946: A YEAR OF TESTING

The first postwar National Conference of the United Jewish Appeal for Refugees, Overseas Needs and Palestine was held in Atlantic City on December 15–17, 1945, the most representative assembly of American Jewry ever gathered. The participants were burdened with the knowledge that less than 1.5 million Jews were now left of the once

great European Jewish community. Survivors of the death camps confronted the conference, and in response, the assembled leaders of America's Jews, under the insistent prodding of campaign director, Henry
Montor, unanimously voted to undertake a campaign for $100 million.
It was a long arduous task to get the allocated quota. A veteran UJA
professional recalls: "I remember going to some communities and having battles and coming back. They wouldn't accept the whole quota,
so I had to go back [and] reopen the whole thing . . . Of course, the
$100 million was exceeded." The success of the campaign established
UJA hegemony in the postwar American Jewish community. Seven
years earlier, the local communities had forced a united campaign upon
leadership and the founding agencies; now the UJA began to impose
its demands upon the communities. The 1947 campaign raised some
$125 million; and the campaign of the year of Israeli statehood, 1948,
close to $160 million. Such unprecedented giving, both in size of con-
tributions and numbers of gifts, ushered in a new era in American Jewish
philanthropic endeavor. It demonstrated the capacity of American Jews
to give, and their readiness to do so. Other charitable enterprises found
that a donor, having given to one cause, was easier to solicit for another.

The dramatically successful campaign of 1946 was the last campaign headed by three cochairmen representing the constituent agencies.
Beginning with 1947, one national chairman symbolized not only the
unity which the UJA had effected, but its independence as well. The
first to serve was Henry Morgenthau, Jr., who brought to this position
a long and distinguished career of public service, including more than
a decade as secretary of the treasury in the cabinet of President Franklin
Delano Roosevelt. Morgenthau came to Jewish service late in life, but
the prestige he brought was vital to the cause. Some of America's most
influential Jews questioned whether the constituent agencies of the UJA
had not stepped beyond the boundaries of philanthropy to become
engaged in activities which might not be consonant with the national
interests of the United States and its Allies. Morgenthau's commitment
provided quasi-governmental approval for what the UJA and its component agencies were doing.

During the Montor-Morgenthau era, the center of American
Jewish philanthropic concern was shifted from Europe to Israel, which
made the involvement of non-Zionists like Morgenthau all the more
important. Even more vital was Montor's contribution. To him, the
overriding concern was the rescue and rehabilitation in Palestine of
Sheerit Hapleta, the "Surviving Remnant" of European Jewry. To the
dramatic appeals which he orchestrated, Montor also brought the organizational techniques first fashioned by Joseph Willen of New York's
Federation of Jewish Philanthropies: organization by localities, professions and *landsmanshaften;* precampaign pledging, parlor meetings, card

calling. Above all, he brought to the campaign a vision of the philanthropic potential of the American Jewish community.

IN AND WITH THE COMMUNITIES

Montor was succeeded by Dr. Joseph J. Schwartz, the JDC director in Europe. The American Jewish community had built its institutions—synagogues, schools, community centers—in the 1920s. The thirties were the years of the Great Depression, the forties years of war, rescue and rehabilitation. The postwar years had also seen the relocation of the Jewish population from the city to the suburbs. New facilities for the established and newly created institutions were high communal priorities. Competition for the philanthropic dollar ensued. Schwartz was selfless in his labors for the UJA, but he also recognized that there were legitimate communal needs which had a justifiable claim on the communal till. In the long run, the welfare of the UJA and the causes it aided would best be served by a strong and committed community. Synagogues, schools, centers, might be competitors to today's campaign, but they would also be the surest guarantor of tomorrow's success.

The general chairman during these years was Edward M. M. Warburg, son and grandson of the leading communal leaders of the previous generations, Felix M. Warburg and Jacob H. Schiff. He and Schwartz were able to report that in its first fifteen years the UJA had received over $1 billion. With those funds it sustained the 1.5 million survivors of the war; it assisted in the emigration of 885,000 Jews, 90 percent of these mainly from Arab states to Israel, where it helped in their settlement and economic integration. In all, some 2.5 million persons had been aided.

In his valedictory report in 1955, Schwartz pointed out that about 2 million American Jews were in an economic position to contribute. From these "the U.J.A. year in and year out receives the third largest sum made available to any American fund-raising body. . . . Only the U.S. Community Chest movement . . . and the American Red Cross raise greater funds than the U.J.A., and even then not always. . . ."[11]

FOCUS
The Holocaust Years in an American Jewish Community

"Never before in history," Hayim Greenberg, intellectual mentor of American Labor Zionists, wrote in the *Yiddisher Kemfer* February 12, 1943, "have we displayed such shamefully strong nerves as we do now in the days of our greatest catastrophe. We have become so dulled that we have even lost our capacity for madness." At the end of August

1942, he and other Jewish journalists and writers had heard from a representative of the American Jewish Congress that Hitler intended to annihilate all European Jewry. This information had come in an August 8, 1942, cable from the Geneva office of the World Jewish Congress to Dr. Stephen S. Wise. It had been relayed by the State Department, which, after holding it up for twenty days, then asked Dr. Wise not to disclose publicly its contents until they had been confirmed at the end of November. In his article Greenberg confessed: "If it is still possible to do anything then I do not know who should do it and how it should be done. I only know that we are all—all five million of us, with all our organizations and committees and leaders—politically and morally bankrupt."[12]

Pain, frustration and shame marked the more sensitive American Jewish leaders: pain, as news of the scope and intensity of Hitler's war against the Jews kept arriving; frustration, at attempts at rescue through emigration of German Jewry; and shame, at the rebuffs to American Jewry by an ostensibly friendly American administration. The Evian Conference on refugee problems in July 1938, convened by President Franklin D. Roosevelt failed to find haven for the victims of Nazi persecution. The *S.S. St. Louis,* with its 936 men, women and children (930 of whom were Jews) was refused entry in 1939 to any port of the "Mother of Exiles," and had to return its cargo of refugees back to Europe. The British White Paper of 1939 limited Jewish immigration to Palestine for the next five years to 75,000 and none thereafter. The shame was the shame of the powerless, fearing to admit powerlessness lest such confession lead to utter despair and the suicide of will. In addition there was the feeling of bewilderment: "Who should do it and how it should be done."

The America they lived in was not tolerant of civil disobedience or public protest against the government. Ten years earlier, when war veterans seeking aid for themselves and their families in the Great Depression, had assembled in Washington to urge a Bonus Bill, the army—infantry, cavalry and tanks—was called out to disperse them. And these were war veterans, and America was at peace. What militant public protest could be mounted in the midst of the war by a Jewish minority, accused by many of having hastened America's entry into the war?

America's isolationist sentiments had been enacted into law by Congress, declaring America's neutrality in 1939. America's opposition to aid was borne out by the sad fate of the proposed Wagner-Rogers Bill introduced in February 1939 to admit 20,000 German [sic!] children above the quota during the next two years. Patriotic organizations including the American Legion and the Daughters of the American Revolution mounted a campaign against it, a sentiment shared by two of every three Americans polled on the issue by the Gallup organization. Pro-Nazi sentiments were publicly demonstrated in the streets of New York.

Stephen S. Wise was being reassured by President Roosevelt of his sympathy, and Wise urged American Jewry to accept such reassurance in good faith. What alternative was there? Roosevelt had led a reluctant nation to rally behind the Allies, defied Congress in extending aid to the beleaguered British. He alone could muster the economic, political and military resources to defeat the Nazi menace. Turn from Roosevelt? To whom?

With the rise of Hitler, American Jews had undertaken what measures they could for rescue. The American Jewish Congress urged a boycott against German goods, widely practiced by American Jews, though the American Jewish Committee feared the effect of such policy on the Jews of Germany, then threatened politically and economically, but not yet in danger of their lives. Joined by religious and political leaders Wise led an anti-Nazi protest march in New York City. Attempts at easing immigration restrictions caused State Department officials to complain of Jewish pressure. American Jews signed affidavits in the thousands enabling German Jews to enter the country. The JDC continued its work throughout the war.

After the contents of the Geneva cable were made public, President Roosevelt was presented a Blue Print for Extermination report. A day of mourning was declared. Protest meetings were called, a mass rally at Madison Square Garden asked the Allied nations to negotiate with Germany for rescue of Jews. Among the three commissions established by the American Jewish Conference convened in 1943 was the Commission on Rescue. Protests by Secretary of the Treasury Henry Morgenthau to President Roosevelt against State Department obstructionism, especially by Assistant Secretary Breckenridge Long, resulted in the establishment on January 21, 1944, of the War Refugee Board to help rescue Jews and offer them relief "consistent with the successful prosecution of the war."

Successful prosecution of the war was the first priority of America and the Allies. Efforts to rescue Jews in Nazi-occupied Europe were weighed against this objective. Arthur Morse in his *While Six Million Died* (1968) and Henry Feingold in his *The Politics of Rescue* (1970) document America's sad record of silence and inaction during the Holocaust years.

The record of American Jewry during these years has been subjected to criticism: it was too credulous, too apathetic, too timid. The enormity of the annihilation was certainly not fully grasped at the time. As Hayim Greenberg attests, American Jewry did not know what if anything would help. That efforts for fellow Jews caught up in what was later called the Holocaust were too timid was perceived by but few. That these were shamefully meager was adjudged only later. That more was not done was due more to impotence than indifference.

What of American Jewry in the Holocaust years? What did it know and how did it react?

In "What Did They Know? The American Jewish Press and the Holocaust,"[13] Alex Grobman concludes that "the average Jew in America had access to more information than is generally believed." In the summer 1943 issue of *The Menorah Journal*, Elma Dangerfield told "The Tale of Warsaw and Treblinka."[14] From *Hitler's Ten Year War on the Jews* (1943) readers learned that "By Sept. 1943 not less than 1,600,000 Polish Jews had perished."[15] In the same year, *The Black Book of Polish Jewry* devoted full chapters to extermination[16] (noting, e.g., the Chelmno gas chamber), Treblinka, battle of the Warsaw Ghetto, etc. Among the sponsors of this volume depicting the systematic annihilation of Jews in all its gruesome details were Mrs. Eleanor Roosevelt, Professor Salo Baron, Congressmen Sol Bloom and Emanuel Celler, Professor Albert Einstein, New York's Mayor Fiorello La Guardia, Secretary of the Interior Harold Ickes, Senator Robert Wagner, et al.

Consider one Jewish community, that of Rochester, New York, in the years 1941–44. It had a strong tradition of participation in organized activity for Jewish concerns at home and abroad. National conventions of the Central Conference of American Rabbis, the Federation of American Zionists and Hadassah had been held there. Its charitable activities were centralized in the United Jewish Welfare Fund, and the Jewish Community Council dealt with matters affecting the total community. Reform and Conservative temples, sixteen Orthodox synagogues and a Jewish community center, the Jewish Young Men's Association, served its spiritual and cultural needs. It was kept informed on world and national Jewish events by its weekly *The Jewish Ledger*, a newspaper of quality.

In the Holocaust years, the *Ledger* published article after article, columns and editorials about the ongoing destruction of European Jewry. Caught up in the war-time atmosphere in which the press was expected to buoy up spirits, the emphasis was more on resistance and heroism than on annihilation. But the tale of massacres, growing in scope and intensity, were before the reader.

In "A Review of 1943," which appeared in most Anglo-Jewish newspapers in America, William Zuckerman wrote: "1943 will go down as the blackest year in Jewish history . . . For in that year the Nazi terror against the Jews reached its culmination point and the Nazi extermination of European Jews was almost complete."

Although the scope of "this greatest mass-massacre of a people" was not yet fully known, its dimensions were beginning to be apparent.

The American Jewish Congress reported that of Holland's 180,000 Jews only 25,000 remained in internment labor camps, and less than 10 percent of Poland's 3 million were still alive. Mass deportations and massacres had taken place in France, Belgium, Greece, Slovakia and other Nazi-occupied countries. "Nearly three million Jews were deliberately murdered by the Nazis . . . in 1942 and 1943," Zuckerman reported. "This is certainly the greatest massacre of unarmed and innocent people known in European history . . . European Jewry as an organized body has been mercilessly obliterated."[17]

The Jews of Rochester, New York, read this report in *The Jewish Ledger* on January 7, 1944. A week later they were informed by Mr. Zuckerman of the revolt in the Warsaw Ghetto, and of some organized Jewish resistance to the Nazis in ghettos and by guerrilla bands. An editorial spoke of "too much spurious pessimism in our midst" and announced: "Light is breaking even in these dark and dismal days . . . Our pleas are being heard in places formerly closed to our tears . . . There are favorable winds blowing for us in London and Washington."

The establishment of the War Refugee Board was hailed as one such favorable development. [That it was far too little and far, far too late became obvious only later.] What the board was gearing up to do was already being accomplished, said the editorial, by "the Jewish guerrilla fighters . . . who are concerned chiefly with saving Jewish victims from Nazi concentration camps and Nazi executions." Readers' spirits were buoyed up by the report:

> The Jews who have remained in Poland are no longer being slaughtered and exterminated. They hit back and hit hard, as guerrillas, as partisans and underground workers. The cumulative effect of their resistance is beginning to tell on the Germans.[18]

In his syndicated column, published March 3, 1944, Zuckerman informed American Jews that "Millions of Germans are now in the same position as the Jews, hunted, deported, uprooted, driven from place to place."

The invasion of Hungary brought reporter, editor and reader back to harsh reality. On March 31, they learned that "the 900,000 Jews of Hungary are in a trap from which there appears to be little hope of escape." An editorial is both accusation and plea:

They Might Have Been Saved

> The invasion of Hungary has provided Hitler's slaughterhouses with 800,000 fresh Jewish victims . . .
>
> And yet the tragedy might have been spared then, if the Allies acted with sincerity, wisdom and determination. Thousands might have been saved . . . if, by the good offices of the Allied

Powers, temporary domicile were secured for them in neutral countries. It might not be too late yet if both Germany and Hungary are sternly warned that the guilt of extermination of the 800,000 Jews will pitilessly be visited upon them, that there is a seeing eye and an avenging hand to mete out just retribution for what harm might befall them at the hands of their tormentors.[19]

From the pages of *The Jewish Ledger,* Rochester, New York:
On July 17, 1942, page 1, a boldface, double-column story, quotes Arthur Cardinal Hinsley, Catholic primate of England:

"In Poland alone the Nazis have massacred 700,000 Jews without the semblance of a trial. Innocent blood cries out to Heaven for vengeance."

On November 13, 1942, page 1:

NAZIS MURDER THOUSANDS IN THE UKRAINE

All Jews who have remained in Berditchev have been exterminated.

On December 25, 1942, page 1:

Text of Declaration of Allied Nations
The Ghettoes established by the German invaders are being systematically emptied of Jews . . . none of those taken away are ever heard from again . . . The able-bodied are slowly worked to death in labor camps . . . The infirm are left to die of exposure and starvation or are deliberately massacred in mass executions . . .

On April 9, 1943, page 1:

GESTAPO ARRESTS ALL FRENCH JEWS FOR DEPORTATION

In Paris aged Jewish men and women are being dragged off the streets and sent to internment camps at Drancy, from where they are deported eastward . . .

On May 28, 1943, page 1:

MASS EXECUTIONS CONTINUE IN POLISH GHETTO AREAS

During the Holocaust years, Rochester's Jews were reading about ghettos, concentration camps, death camps, gas chambers, about deportation, starvation and extermination. But those were also America's war years, when it was felt that national needs demanded all exertion for the war effort and that national interest dictated that to sustain morale life had to go on as normally as possible.

What was the organized Jewish community engaged in during those fateful years 1941–44?

In the minutes of the Executive Committee of the Jewish Community Council of Rochester [20] for that period there is hardly a mention of that which was appearing on the front page of the local Anglo-Jewish newspaper. One lengthy discussion is most instructive.

On February 1, 1943, a representative of the Jewish Labor Committee requested that the council sponsor a mass meeting to protest the Nazi treatment of Jews in Europe. The subcommittee appointed to consider a mass meeting concluded that such a meeting should have been held, but because of the Welfare Fund campaign and other reasons, the meeting had been postponed. In December such a meeting no longer seemed timely, but the subcommittee chairman suggested that since persecutions of Jews continued, it might be advisable to consider a mass protest meeting once again.

The perception in 1943 by leaders of the Jewish community was that the atrocities, "persecutions" as they called them, were tragic sporadic events. There was apparently no awareness of a sustained program of extermination with a goal of total annihilation.

The minutes of the Executive Committee of the United Jewish Welfare Federation of Rochester[21] reports concerns and activities which continued from prewar years: the fight against anti-Semitism locally and nationally, the annual federation campaign. Growing concern for overseas needs during the war years resulted in increased contributions, but the deliberations of the Committee show a remarkable absence of discussion of atrocities and annihilation in Nazi Europe.

What was happening in the congregations? The most Zionist committed was Conservative Beth El, and its rabbi's sermons dealt with Zionistic concerns, "Palestine and the Future of the Jews," "Britain's Policy in Palestine," an attack on *The New York Times* for its opposition to a Jewish army, "Times Change But Not *The Times*," a plea for membership in Zionist organizations, "Palestine—Haven or Home," and the like. Other concerns were the war effort and the threat of anti-Semitism. Some sermons touched on what was happening to European Jewry under the Nazis, but only tangentially, e.g., "Racial Theories of Nazism and Anti-Semitism" and a review of the play *Tomorrow the World,* which dealt with the question of what to do with the generation of Germans raised under Nazism.[22] The scope of the European Jewish tragedy did not as yet register.

What was organized Rochester Jewry doing during the war years? The pages of *The Jewish Ledger,* the minute books of the Community Council and of the Welfare Federation, and the *Beth El Bulletin* define six areas of activities.

1. Care for the German Jewish refugees settled in Rochester. Their number was not insignificant, and for some their need for help persisted for a considerable time after their arrival. From 1939 to 1942,

almost half the immigrants to the United States were Jews, some 120,000 of 225,000. Of those who remained as permanent residents, two-thirds were Jewish.

2. The Jewish community was waging a war against anti-Semitism, locally and nationally. In 1941, the Federation was deeply concerned about the growth of anti-Semitism in Rochester's largest ethnic group, the Italians, who held the Jews responsible for the passage of the Lend-Lease Act. Loyalty to the mother country was strong among Italians, and the Jews felt threatened.

3. The Federation was involved in fund raising. Each year the number of contributors and the sums realized increased, from $70,000 in 1938 to $1.4 million in 1948, a twentyfold increase in one decade.

4. The community was playing its role in American Jewry's quiet activity to persuade the United States and its Allies to use their good offices with neutral nations to intercede on behalf of the Jews in Nazi-occupied Europe. It was felt that it had to be done quietly through well-placed friends to prevent enemies of the war effort from labeling the war against Hitler as a "Jewish war."

5. The organized Jewish community was deeply involved in political activity for the revocation of the British White Paper of 1939 which curtailed immigration into Palestine, and in laying the political and financial foundation for a future Jewish commonwealth there. The chosen instrument for this enterprise was the American Jewish Conference. The Rochester Jewish community joined with sister communities in electing and sending its delegates.

6. Above all, every one of the community's institutions and organizations were involved in aiding the war effort. It was widely recognized that the outcome of the war would affect the course of human civilization, most profoundly the fate of the Jewish people. Winning the war was a matter of life and death; all other causes and interests took a secondary place, so top priority went to the War Bonds sale, and the drives to marshal America's resources and bolster the morale of a nation at war. Families opened their homes to the men stationed at the nearby Sampson Naval Base. The rabbi of Beth El, then a congregation of four hundred families, had to sustain the spirits of the families of more than one hundred of his congregants who were serving in the armed forces, and assuage the grief of five who lost sons in battle. His colleagues had similar tasks.

The story of Rochester Jewry in the war years is the story of American Jewry in that era. But what of the Holocaust? Rochester's Jews, American Jewry, knew so much; why didn't they do more?

They read about the terror and the atrocities visited upon their brethren in Europe. They knew about torture and mass murder, but they did not know about *the Holocaust*. That was a perception and a concept which came years later. They read of atrocity after atrocity, each new one dissipating to some degree the impact and immediacy of the earlier; and they apparently did not recognize them as component parts of a total, integrated whole. It was only with the wisdom granted by hindsight that American Jewry began to perceive that what they had been reading about was a program aimed at total annihilation of the Jewish people, what we know today as *the Holocaust*.

The postwar community also learned that the first, most persistent war Hitler waged was against the Jews. Having survived him, Jews were determined not to permit him a posthumous victory. Hence, the frenetic political activity for the establishment of the State of Israel; the campaigns to finance rescue and rehabilitation of survivors, and later efforts to relocate Jews from Arab countries and the Soviet Union. A generation living with the memories and the unfolding knowledge about the Holocaust felt justified, even compelled, to turn its energies and resources to Jewish interests. The redemption of the world was a messianic enterprise; the survival of the Jewish people was the immediate task. For most American Jews this meant philanthropic and political activities in behalf of Jews everywhere.

Part Three

At Home in America

For Judaism to become creative once again, it must assimilate the best in contemporary civilizations. . . . To survive, Judaism must . . . absorb some of the very forces and tendencies that threaten it.
—Mordecai M. Kaplan

12.

At the Tercentenary

IN 1954 AMERICAN JEWRY PAUSED TO TAKE STOCK. THE OCCASION WAS the year-long celebration of its tercentenary, the three hundredth anniversary of the landing of "the twenty-three" in New Amsterdam in 1654. On such occasions self-congratulations are in vogue, and they were not wanting at this one. In a special tercentenary issue of the *Jewish Quarterly Review*, editor Abraham A. Neuman wrote:

> Looking back upon past horizons in many lands where Jewish communities lived we become conscious of our relatively high accomplishment under American skies. We also come to realize that the evolution of Jewish culture in America is still in its early stages.[1]

In his introductory article to the tercentenary issue of the journal *Judaism,* Robert Gordis noted:

> The thinkers and leaders represented in the following pages share in common a faith in tomorrow, a conviction that American Jewry has its future before it and not behind it and that its children can attain a creative and meaningful Jewish life here in America.[2]

The mood, then, was that which Browning had his Rabbi Ben Ezra proclaim, "The best is yet to be."

President Dwight D. Eisenhower was the guest of honor and main speaker at the tercentenary's central event, a dinner at the Sheraton-Astor in New York City. The former commander in chief of the Allied armies commended his hosts for coming of that people which gave "new dimensions of meaning to the concepts of freedom and justice, of mercy and righteousness, kindness and understanding—ideas and ideals which were to flower on this continent . . . ," whose "chief enemies a decade and more ago were Nazi and Fascist forces which destroyed so many of our fellowmen." It was not lost on the audience of eighteen hundred that among those destroyed were one-third of the Jewish people. "Thank you for the honor of being with you," the president concluded.

A half-century earlier, on Thanksgiving Day, 1905, American Jewry had celebrated "The Two Hundred and Fiftieth Anniversary of the Settlement of Jews in the United States" in Carnegie Hall. The chairman of the celebration then was Jacob H. Schiff, who read a letter from President Theodore Roosevelt: "My Dear Sir: I am forced to make a rule not to write letters on the occasion of any celebration . . . I make an exception in this case because [of] the lamentable and terrible suffering to which so many of the Jewish people in other lands have been subjected . . ." He went on to say, "The Jews of the United States . . . have become indissolubly incorporated in the great army of American citizenship . . . They are honorably distinguished by their industry, their obedience to law, and their devotion to the national welfare."[3]

Good and appropriate words! A half-century later, they would have sounded patronizing. In assessing the character, status and strength of American Jewry at its tercentenary, it should be noted that in 1905, President Theodore Roosevelt sent a letter, motivated by sympathy. The status of the Jewish community at the beginning of the century was such that Roosevelt perceived that it needed public reassurance of its integration into the American fabric as good and loyal citizens. A half-century later, President Eisenhower came in person and spoke to this group of Jewish citizens as he would to any other. His presence was a gracious act, to be sure, but motivated mainly by his recognition of the position of influence which American Jewry, grown sixfold in half a century, had attained in America.

At first apologetic about its influence, the American Jewish community learned quickly that the perception of power bestows power. In the quarter of a century which followed the tercentenary, American Jewry increasingly availed itself of all its resources to protect and promote its interests. The free exercise of decision made the American Jew feel at home in America.

At home—yet not quite at home!

American Jews perceived that the economic integration which afforded them affluence was marginal, the social acceptance which conferred status was limited, and the cultural and religious camaraderie that provided status was fickle. Added to these tensions in the neighborhood were problems within the house itself. A declining birthrate made survival of a viable community problematical, as did an exploding rate of intermarriage, and an ambivalent sense of identity. Political scientist Charles S. Liebman described this sense of unease: "The American Jew is torn between two sets of values—those of integration and acceptance into American society and those of Jewish group survival. . . . The behavior of the American Jew is best understood as his unconscious effort to restructure his environment and reorient his own self-definition and perception of reality so as to reduce the tension of these values."[4]

No matter how integrated into the warp and woof of American society American Jews felt themselves to be, they knew that theirs was a dual identity, American and Jewish. The pluralistic character of America permitted them, if they so chose, to "bear the burden of both commitments," as church historian Winthrop S. Hudson felicitously expressed it. As individuals and as members of the American Jewish community, their life was affected simultaneously by what was happening in America, and by what world Jewry was experiencing.

In the quarter century which followed the tercentenary, America was shaken by the McCarthy era, the civil rights revolution, the Vietnam War and the apparent lessening of its global political power and economic dominance. These events touched the American Jews deeply. Most had taken a stance in the liberal segment of American society. The majority of the old Socialists had become Social Democrats and hailed Franklin Delano Roosevelt as the practical exponent of the social democratic doctrine. They were joined by the great majority of American Jewry who saw in FDR the embodiment of what they conceived to be the promise of America, a gifted son of aristocratic America, placing his talents in service of the common people. His social and economic programs permitted the socially conscious American Jews to channel their messianic energies into acceptable American endeavors.

Senator Joseph McCarthy and the forces he unleashed caused most American Jews grave unease (coupled with embarrassment that two of the senator's aides were Jewish). They were discomforted more than others because, as a group, they had staked most on the liberal tendencies in the American ethos. In an America that seemed to be cutting itself off from its traditional moorings, could the Jew feel safe? That a disproportionate number of McCarthy targets bore Jewish names added to the apprehension. For a generation whose memories of the rise of Hitler were fresh wounds, the fear engendered by the rise of McCarthyism was not unfounded.

The civil rights revolution enabled the Jew to join in a revolution to which the government itself had consented, and to which dominant forces in American society gave allegiance and aid. It brought Jewish community federations into joint enterprise with councils of churches. Rabbis joined ministers and priests in conferences and on protest marches. Jewish leaders sat down with the power elite of their communities. Camaraderie bestowed an egalitarianism—and this time not an equality with the persecuted but with the benefactors. It was a heady wine which the American Jew drank in the fifties and early sixties when the civil rights revolution marched to its early victories. Later, Jews found that the newly uplifted Blacks were vying with them for the rung on the economic ladder to which they had risen. Black leaders in the process of emancipation turned away from the programs of the white and often Jewish do-gooders to autoemancipation. In response, activist American Jews and organizations sought out new interests and turned to a more conservative stance in ideological statement and practical programs.

For Jews the sources of unease about the Vietnam War were legion. Invincible America was being proved vulnerable. Isolationist sentiments were in the air. Did this vulnerability and isolationism of America bode ill also for the State of Israel? The American Jews knew that few of their sons were serving in that war, while many of their children actively opposed it. Was such nonparticipation and opposition threatening to their status as the most loyal of Americans?

The waning of American dominance in world political influence and economic power particularly disturbed American Jews. Apprehensive of the social unrest which can erupt in a nation experiencing change in status, they feared that a weaker America could not be called upon, as it had been again and again since 1840, to come to the aid of beleaguered Jewish communities abroad. The memory of the influence a powerful America exerted in the United Nations for creation of the State of Israel was still fresh. In the late forties and in the fifties, America's power seemed irresistible. In the 1960s and increasingly in the 1970s, nations large and small delighted in ruffling the feathers of the once dominant American eagle.

There were those individuals and groups who pointed to America's inherent strength, arguing that America's apparent impotence lay in its lack of will in pursuit of its interests; its chief weakness was a weakness of resolve. An increasing number of Jews found comfort and congruity of interests with such sentiments. The "New Conservatism" found a number of its leading ideologists among Jewish intellectuals, some of whom had come in out of the Left. Jewish organizations and journals of opinion became important proponents of a more politically and economically resolute America. And this too became a source of unease. The old alliances severed and the new ones forged demanded an expenditure of emotional energies. A new vocabulary of relationship had to be established, for one does not speak the same language with the conservative Moral Majority as one did with progressive main-line Protestantism.

The economic rise of the Jew in post–World War II America is an authentic success story. The sons of shop laborers and small storekeepers, Jews increasingly entered the free (self-employed) and salaried professions at a time when America was moving toward giving greater economic rewards to the service professional. Many became successful entrepreneurs and made their mark in soft-goods manufacturing, in merchandising and in the communications complex. They are well represented in ownership, management and technology in the electronics industry, but the executive suites of the basic industries which are the sinews of America—oil, steel, transportation and finance—remain largely without Jews.

American Jews enjoy a twofold freedom: They are free citizens of the republic and free in their relation to the Jewish community. Theirs are full civic rights and political equality. They can choose whether to affiliate with the Jewish community and to what degree. This freedom, however, is tempered by social practice and communal pressure. Barriers to educational institutions and employment opportunities have greatly diminished in present-day America. There remains, however, the "five-o'clock shadow" which separates associates and neighbors when the working day ends. Exclusion from restricted clubs does not seem to trouble Jews as it once did. The opening up of neighborhoods which once excluded them and the availability of job opportunities but recently closed to them make social exclusion a minor irritant. Associates in the salaried professions, which the Jews entered in increasing numbers, seem far more open to social integration than were those in the business community or the free professions.

Nor is American Jews' choice of identity and affiliation free in the absolute. Those born to Jewish parents are invited to associate with and pressured to contribute to Jewish causes. Often their children will demand of them an identity more distinctive than merely "American." Their non-Jewish neighbors still identify them as Jews, with less rancor, perhaps, but with persistence. On occasion, this extends even to those who have converted to Christianity and become active members of a church. Rabbis have quoted ministers informing them matter-of-factly, "We have some of your people in our church."

The great majority of American Jews have chosen to retain a Jewish identity and to express it through Jewish association, generally through synagogue membership. Jewish historian Salo Baron noted in 1942: "In Western Europe and in America . . . The religious congregation has continued to attract the relatively most constant and active participation of a large membership . . . Total congregational mem-

bership vastly exceeds, numerically, Jewish membership in purely philanthropic undertakings."[5] In the 1950s, American Jews viewed America
as the land of the three great faiths, and saw themselves as American
Jews, members of the American-Jewish religious community, just as
their neighbor was an American Protestant or an American Catholic.
In the late sixties a shift from religious to ethnic self-designation took
place throughout America. The seventies have been called "the decade
of the ethnics."[6] The Six-Day War of 1967 evoked a strong sense of
"peoplehood" in the hearts of many American Jews. The larger presence
of the State of Israel in their lives, the upsurge of ethnic pride in other
groups and the tensions, crises and ferment in American life in general
left American Jews with an identity crisis.

In the seventies the survival of the American Jewish community,
once thought certain, began to be questioned. Freedom, affluence and
influence may make life more viable, those concerned argued, but they
do not assure Jewish survival. The low birthrate, increasing intermarriage, a society ready to assimilate all who choose to enter, a persistence
of anti-Semitic sentiments—dormant in prosperity, ready to flare up in
times of social or economic turmoil—remained real and present dangers.
Moreover, as religious loyalties and observances grew weaker, so too
did attachment to Jewish identity.

DEMOGRAPHY[7]

The Jewish population of the United States rose from some 5
million in 1954 to an estimated 5,920,900 in 1980. This evident increase
should hearten those concerned with Jewish survival in America, but
analysis leads to a pessimistic prognosis. During the quarter of a century
in question, the percentage increase in the population of the United
States was 37 percent, but only 17 percent in the Jewish population.
During the 1970s there was virtually no increase in the Jewish population, while the population of the United States increased at the rate
of 1.5 percent annually. Two more factors make the picture even more
somber. The demographic statistics are of "persons in Jewish households," not number of Jews. Since the 1970 National Jewish Population
Study estimated that the percent of non-Jews resident in Jewish households is 7.4 percent, the total cited must be decreased to 5,482,753.
During the period in question, there may have been as many as 350,000
to 400,000 Jewish immigrants into the United States and very few
emigrants from it, which would further reduce the statistics of increase
through natural growth of the Jewish population.

In 1957, the comparatively lower Jewish birthrate was reported
by the U.S. Bureau of the Census:

Catholics	3.1
Protestants	2.8
Jews	2.1

Charles F. Westoff and Norman B. Ryder reported the following birth-rates for 1970 in *The Contraceptive Revolution* (Princeton 1977):

Catholics	3.6
Protestants	2.9
Jews	2.1

During the next decade, American Jewish fertility dropped below zero population growth. Demographer Sidney Goldstein reports a continuing decline in Jewish fertility ratios (i.e., the number of children under 5 years of age per 1000 women aged 20–44), recorded in studies of Jewish communities. In two decades it had decreased from, for example: 528 in Lynn, Massachusetts; and 596 in Des Moines, Iowa, in 1955–56; to 342 in Houston, Texas, and 231 in Kansas City, Missouri, in 1975–76. These numbers may be compared with a U.S. white urban population fertility ratio in 1960 of 635. In 1970 the national figure had fallen to 485, but the comparable Jewish figure was 352. In 1980 the Jewish birthrate had fallen to 1.6, about one-third below that of America's 2.2, and far below the replacement level.

During the half century 1930–79, a proportion of Jews followed their neighbors out of the Northeast and the North Central states to the South and the West. This internal migration has made the Los Angeles Metropolitan Area and the Greater Miami Area (including Fort Lauderdale and Hollywood) the second and third largest areas of Jewish population, with 503,000, and 355,000, respectively. Notable increases have been made in the Jewish population of San Diego, Phoenix, Denver, Atlanta, Houston, Dallas and other Sunbelt cities. In the main, however, American Jewry continues to inhabit America's largest cities. Over 75 percent of America's Jews live in ten metropolitan areas—New York, Los Angeles, Philadelphia, Chicago, Miami, Washington, Boston, Baltimore, Detroit and Cleveland, areas in which 20 percent of Americans live. Twenty percent of world Jewry lives in the Greater New York area.

A case study of one community provides a picture of what has happened in two decades in an established Northeastern Jewish community. Demographic studies of the Jews of Rochester conducted in 1960 and again in 1980[8] disclosed that the Jewish population had declined from an estimate of 21,500–22,500 to 18,400–20,800. The number of households had increased, but the number per household had gone down, indicating the decline of the extended family and the increase of nuclear families and persons living alone. The age distribution also underwent a significant change, the median age rising from 38 to 43. In 1960 the percentage of those above 65 was 13; by 1980 it had increased to 19.1. On the other end of the scale, those under 20 had decreased from 32.4 to 22.4 percent, the most drastic change occurring in the youngest group. The percentage of those aged 5 through 9 declined from 8 percent to 3.7 percent, and those below the age of 5 fell from 6.9 percent in 1960 to 3.1 percent in 1980. Rochester Jewry had aged. The number of children had decreased and this pattern continued. Its effect on communal institutions is indicated by a more than 40 percent decline in religious school population, and in planning a new, larger home for the aged.

Over 45 percent of Jewish wage earners in 1980 were professionals or semiprofessionals. The same number were managers, agents or in sales. Only 10 percent were laborers. The high educational level, double that of the general population, continued, accounting for the considerably higher mean income. The move from city to suburbs, which began at the end of World War II, accelerated. In 1960, 63.6 percent of Greater Rochester's Jews lived in the city; in 1980, the percentage was only 24. Most of these live in areas contiguous to the suburb with the largest percentage of Jews, Brighton. Fully 85 percent were born in the United States, up from 79 percent in 1960.

During the latter decades of the nineteenth century and in the early decades of the twentieth, the manufacture of men's clothing was one of Rochester's major industries. Both employers and employees were largely Jewish, as was true throughout the country at that time. In 1980 only one clothing factory remained. The sons and daughters of the clothing factory workers who have continued to live in the area are doctors, lawyers, accountants and pharmacists, or are employed as managers, physicists, chemists and engineers at Eastman Kodak, Xerox or the other technological industries which sustain the area's economy. There are few Jewish-owned factories or businesses in Rochester today. Very few family businesses remain to return to after one's higher education, which almost always is pursued away from Rochester (though the city boasts a major university and a number of colleges). An increasing number of Jewish Rochester's sons and daughters make their homes elsewhere, most in the larger metropolitan areas, and in the growing cities of the Sunbelt. This pattern of relocation has had a profound effect on family and community stability.

A significant change in Jewish religious observance is reported in the 1980 Rochester Jewish community population study.

> Religious practices such as lighting candles on Friday night, fasting on Yom Kippur, having or going to a seder, and keeping a kosher home have . . . declined. . . . For example, 29 percent report that

they "always" light candles on Friday night compared to 45 percent who say they "always" lit candles ten years ago and the 68 percent who say that candles were always lit in their parents' home. As for keeping a kosher home, 28 percent claim they now always do, 39 percent say they used to ten years ago, and 62 percent remember that their parents kept a kosher home.

The number of kosher butchers has declined from ten to two, though one is now of supermarket size. Frozen kosher meat and poultry are available in a number of supermarkets, and there is one kosher delicatessen.

In 1960, only 11 percent said that they had not attended synagogue services during the past twelve months. That percentage has grown to 29. Though the membership in congregations has remained relatively stable, there has been a change in religious identification. Those who term themselves Reform have increased from 32 to 42 percent. Conservative Jews have retained a 36 percent figure, but the percentage of Orthodox has fallen from 25 to 12. Yet during this time, a day school, Orthodox in orientation, has more than doubled its size, and a Yeshivah has established itself in the community. It is also worth noting that whereas twenty years ago there was considerable ideological objection to the day school, such opposition has completely disappeared, and the ready acceptance of the Yeshiva by all elements of the community has come as a surprise to those who remember heated communal debates of two decades earlier. Almost 70 percent of the families (a slight drop from 1960) are members of the dozen congregations in town, though two, the Conservative Beth El and the Reform B'rith Kodesh, divide equally more than 60 percent of the affiliated. Almost every home (over 85 percent) has a Bible, a prayer book and a Passover Hagaddah. Twenty-eight percent have visited Israel.

Participation in philanthropy, general and Jewish, has decreased. The number contributing to the Community Chest has gone from 93.2 percent to 75.4 percent, and to the United Jewish Welfare Fund from 92.9 percent to 78.6 percent. In households with an annual income of over $50,000, however, the percentage contributing to the Welfare Fund is over 90.

The profile is of an American-born, suburban, numerically declining community of aging free and salaried professionals and administrators, whose religious affiliation has remained steady but whose lives are less and less directed by religious disciplines. It is a highly educated, relatively affluent community, its members comfortable in their dual identity as Americans and as Jews. In a word, it is the kind of American Jewish community which most are on their way to becoming. Rochester "got there early" because of the nature of its industry. The technologically sophisticated industries needed the scientific, technological and managerial skills which many American Jews had acquired through education. The route from sewing machine and store counter to operating table, courtroom and laboratory was traveled by Rochester Jewry earlier than by most. Increasingly it is becoming the occupational road for more and more of America's Jews. The demographic, social and religious profiles of other communities in the future will more and more reflect that of Rochester's today.

THE ORGANIZED COMMUNITY

The American Jewish community of the postwar era was at one and the same time quantitatively highly organized but functionally disorganized. The *American Jewish Year Book* for 1980 lists as "National Jewish Organizations" 29 in the field of community relations; 34 cultural; 22 dealing with overseas aid; 148 religious and educational organizations and institutions; 18 in social, mutual benefit; 33 in social welfare; and 70 Zionist and pro-Israel.

Over three hundred national organizations serve the various and varied needs and interests of American Jewry, yet there is no one overall representative body mandated to speak for and act for a united organized Jewish community. Within the subgroupings there are coordinating bodies, but these are largely without power, smaller in budget, staff, program and influence than the independent organizations which they "coordinate." Thus, in the field of community relations, the American Jewish Committee, the Anti-Defamation League of B'nai B'rith and the American Jewish Congress outstrip in power and program the National Jewish Community Relations Advisory Council. The American Zionist Council is the "coordinating and public relations arm of the twelve national organizations which comprise the American Zionist movement," but the twelve remain autonomous and the council exists at their sufferance. Similarly, the Synagogue Council of America "acts as the over-all Jewish religious representative body of Orthodox, Conservative and Reform Judaism . . . ," but the national organizations of these religious movements have delegated virtually no power to the Synagogue Council. Each of the constituent bodies retains a veto on policy and pronouncement by the council, thus rendering it ineffectual as a spokesperson for American religious Jewry.

It may be said that American Jewry is a community of organizations lacking organization. This reality is the product of the unique factors in American political, social and religious life reflected in the American Jewish historic experience.

The American Jewish community is a voluntary community. In Europe of an earlier era a Jew was born in the community—*kehillah* or *gemeinde.* To dissociate oneself from one's community of birth, one had to undertake an active act of dissociation, generally religious conversion. In America, the person is born a citizen of the nation. To become a member of an ethnic or religious community demands an act of affiliation through formal membership or association through will and activity. The American Jew, then, has the choice of affiliating or not, and through which institution, organization or movement to express that association. This makes for a multiplicity of organizations and institutions expressing the wide variety of interests and commitments. It works against one overall body, any part of whose policy or program might be counter to the views or interests of the individual.

Many Jews felt that an organization which did not have a parallel in the general community would stand in the way of their full acceptance into America. The parallel institution which the Jew established was the synagogue. The development of America and its secularization brought the government and the civic community into the everyday life of the people. Education was provided by the government; social care and welfare became a community responsibility. This development was reflected in the Jewish community in the transfer of charitable and social-welfare activities from the synagogue to organizations and institutions established for a specific purpose—orphanages, hospitals, charity societies and relief organizations for local and overseas needs.

Attempts to organize a representative body of American Jewry all came in response to world Jewish crises which reminded the American Jews of their common Jewish destiny. The Mortara Affair in 1858 resulted in establishment of the Board of Delegates of American Israelites; the American Jewish Committee was organized in the wake of the Kishinev massacre of 1903 and the pogroms of 1905 in Russia. Planning for the postwar needs of World War I resulted in the American Jewish Congress; and World War II, the American Jewish Conference. In all cases, unity was short-lived. In recent decades, there has been little talk and no attempt to establish an overall representative body. The institutions and organizations of American Jewry guard their independence and prerogatives, unwilling to surrender either a measure of power or a modicum of independence. In time of special need, the Conference of Presidents of Major American Jewish Organizations acts as spokesman for American Jewry.

The past decades have seen the proliferation in number and growth in power of the local Jewish community councils and welfare funds. The great fund-raising efforts which have been the leading activity of American Jewry necessitated such organized Jewish communal efforts. Within the individual Jewish communities, local councils or welfare funds wield vast power. They have expanded their activities beyond fund raising to community planning and community-relations activities and, of late, into the fields of Jewish education and culture. There are today some 230 local federations, and their power continues to grow.

This growth of power and broadening of interests are true also of the national organization, the Council of Jewish Federations and Welfare Funds. Its stated purpose is to aid local agencies in "fund-raising, community organization, health and welfare planning, person-nel recruitment and public relations," but because it brings together the effective leaders of the American Jewish community, and since it ex-ercises considerable influence on allocation of funds, it has become the recognized locus of decision making in American Jewish life. Thus, when a group of Jewish students wanted to effect a reordering in prior-ities of allocations, it came in protest to the General Assembly of the CJF in 1968 and found a platform to put forward its pleas for Jewish education. In expanding its field of concern, the Council was instru-mental in the founding in 1960 of the National Foundation for Jewish Culture. A decade later, the foundation began a program of "lump sum" budgeting, receiving from local welfare funds a "lump sum" allocation, which, in turn, it distributes to its members' agencies in the field of Jewish culture.

There are those who see the imminent expansion of the Council's activities into more areas affecting Jewish life. All indications point to the Council's becoming more and more the effective, if not the official, overall representative body of American Jewry. It claims to be a service agency, without ideology or program, but allocation of funds and choice of fields of interest and activities are in themselves the results of ide-ology, since they express a point of view, necessitate priorities and constitute commitment to a system of values. It seems likely that, with the continued growth in power and program of the Council, with the new interest in ethnic identity and increased commitment to the concept of community in America, the issue of an American Jewish democratic representative body will again come to the fore. Those who argue for it will point to the strength which unity would bring in relationships with other bodies in America and abroad; to the efficiency which unity brings; to the ability of the total community to undertake self-study and carry on orderly planning; to the desirability of priorities in Jewish life being established by democratically elected representatives rather than by those who exercise the weight of wealth. Such a body, through local counterparts, might serve as a means of affiliation or identification for individual Jews whether their Jewish allegiance be religious, cultural, national or social. Those arguing against such a body declare that Jews are both citizens of a state and members of civic entity. How can they be part of a political entity for which there is no parallel in the general community? Must Jews be and continue to be "different"? They believe it would not be tactically wise for Jews to speak in one voice. They would further state that, in practice, it would be impossible for all Jews to adhere to such a body.

As the concerns of American Jewry turn inward, a confrontation continues between those who value the order, strength and efficiency of unity, and those who esteem the freedom, variety and creativity that a loose federation of independent bodies makes possible.

RELIGIOUS LIFE

In the period between the two world wars, American Jewry followed the general nationwide trend of increasing affiliation with religious institutions. In 1951, it was estimated that 3.4 million Jews, some 68 percent of America's 5 million, were associated with a synagogue. Some analysts claimed that beyond the physical growth of Jewish religious institutions, there was a discernible interest in and concern with religion in the postwar decades. Less sanguine observers suggested that the increase in the number of synagogues should be ascribed primarily to geographic and social factors. Whether the increase in the number of congregations was due to sociological forces or religious revival was debated throughout the 1950s. Certainly, the physical growth in institutions and activities took place in the new suburbs which became the areas of Jewish residence in postwar America. A 1959 survey article in *The New York Times* about the proliferation of congregations in the New York area disclosed that since 1947, 99 new congregations had sprung up in the suburbs, 31 Reform, 33 Conservative and 35 Orthodox. The "cathedral" synagogues of the inner city, built in the twenties, were abandoned, and new multipurpose synagogues blending into the suburban landscape were constructed, staffed and programmed to "meet the spiritual, cultural and social needs of every member of every family."

Jewish life increasingly centered on the synagogue, expressing itself through its activities. As the Jewish home became more assimilated and as the life-style of Jews became more like that of their middle-class neighbor, for many, synagogue activities and projects became the chief, if not the sole, expressions of Jewish life. Concern was voiced, warning that the synagogue could not take the place of the home as the locus of Jewish living, that institutional activities could not compensate for the loss of the Jewish way of life. Religious leaders warned against treating religion as "leisure activity," and sought to emphasize the "relevance" of Judaism for the contemporary Jew.

In the 1950s, a new breed of students began to apply for admission to Jewish theological seminaries. Heretofore, most of the students had entered rabbinical studies with a personal experience of Jewish life in observant Jewish homes and with a background of Jewish learning. Now, a significant number of students raised in homes only peripherally Jewish discovered Judaism in summer camps, or in university courses in religion, and turned to seminary studies to prepare for a life of Jewish religious service and/or scholarship. Because of the changed nature of its student bodies (in 1957–58 more of its students were graduates of Harvard than of Yeshiva University), the Jewish Theological Seminary reorganized its curriculum in 1957, placing greater emphasis on traditional text studies and calling for more stringent demands for religious observance. The Rabbi Isaac Elchanan Theological Seminary of Yeshiva University broadened and liberalized its ordination (*semihah*) program, and the Hebrew Union College–Jewish Institute of Religion strengthened its study of sacred texts and the Hebrew language. All also require a period of study in Israel.

The 1960s saw a rise in Jewish theological interest and writing. Jewish thought became a central concern of a small but influential group of Jewish scholars. The "existentialist" mood was evidenced in the popularity of the writings of Martin Buber, Franz Rosenzweig and Abraham Joshua Heschel, and in renewed interest in Hasidism. On the campus, "radical" Jewish students were seeking a new view of God, world and self, and a personal new experience of the Jewish tradition. Significantly, much creative Jewish theological thinking and writing, as well as innovative institutional experimentation, took place outside of the religious establishment and without organizational sponsorship. The *havurah,* a commune for Jewish religious living, was a notable creation of that period.

In the late sixties and in the early seventies, there was a perceptible weakening in organized Jewish religious life, reflecting, in part, the general crisis in organized religious life in America. Church membership and attendance declined, many aspects of Roman Catholic life were in disarray, and main-line Protestant bodies were experiencing serious declines in adherents, support and influence. Only the fundamentalist and Adventist churches were healthy and growing. In the Jewish community, the number of synagogues was declining. Some closed down because of neighborhood changes, with remaining ones merging. Synagogue membership dropped, and the median age of members rose. Only "fundamentalist" Orthodoxy seemed to be on the increase. Traditionalism was reemphasized even among the Orthodox groups that sought to grapple with the implications and demands of modern American society. Right-wing Orthodox groups in the large urban centers increased in numbers, through accretion from other groups and a high birthrate. The Hasidic Habad or Lubavitch movement brought imaginative educational campaigns into communities and onto campuses, gaining "converts" among noncommitted Jewish youth.

On campuses, courses in Jewish studies proliferated. Students organized "free Jewish Universities" for expanded Jewish studies, and kosher eating clubs grew in number. In the 1970s, despite challenges and losses the synagogue remained the central institution of American Jewry.

EDUCATION AND SCHOLARSHIP

Student enrollment in Jewish schools rose from 240,000 to 400,000 between 1948 and 1954. Fifty-two percent attended Sunday schools, the remainder weekday and all-day schools. The next two years witnessed a 22 percent increase in students (paralleling the growth of Protestant and Catholic schools). The increase continued up to 1962, when the total enrollment was reported as 588,955. Then, partly as a result of the decreasing Jewish birthrate, a decline set in.

A significant development in the post–World War II years was the rise in enrollment in Jewish all-day schools. Previously, such schools drew their students almost entirely from Orthodox families. In the 1970s, almost one of every seven students enrolled in any sort of Jewish school was in a day school, a considerable number from non-Orthodox homes. The percentage was even higher in the large metropolitan areas where parents enrolled children in Jewish day schools not only for religious or cultural reasons, but also because of the difficulties besetting the urban public school system. The curricula of the afternoon weekday schools, be they Orthodox, Conservative or Reform are remarkably similar. The differences are more structural than ideological, the Conservative and Orthodox requiring more hours per week and more years of attendance than the Reform. In all schools, there is considerable emphasis on Hebrew language, though achievement rarely matches aspirations. The achievement levels of the day school in Hebrew language, literature, history and Bible studies are notable, both because more time is devoted to Jewish studies each week and because pupils react with more seriousness toward a school which is their total arena for formal education. In 1976, the American Association of Jewish Education reported that while attendance in the one-day-a-week schools had dropped from 42.2 percent to 30.2 percent, attendance in day schools rose to 25.4 percent, an increase of 28 percent over a ten-year period.

The Holocaust brought to an end the dependency of American Jewry on European Jewish scholarship, cultural leadership and religious guidance. The great centers of Jewish culture, their institutions of learning, the books they published, the journals they issued, were destroyed. Some European Jewish scholars and writers were brought to America before the war; some came after; but compared to those who perished, they were few in number.

Of necessity, American Jewry had to intensify its efforts to produce its own scholars, and in this it was largely successful. The heads of its major theological seminaries, Drs. Gerson D. Cohen of the Jewish Theological Seminary, Alfred Gottschalk of the Hebrew Union College and Norman Lamm of Yeshiva University, were all trained in America. This is also true of highly respected professors of one or another aspect of Jewish studies at Harvard, Columbia, Pennsylvania, Brown, Berkeley, UCLA, Brandeis, Dartmouth. The output of scholarly works published by leading publishers and university presses continues to increase year by year. In such areas as Biblical studies, Jewish history and Jewish thought, America vies with Israel as the world center of Jewish scholarship. The *Jewish Quarterly Review,* the *Hebrew Union College Annual,* the *Proceedings of the American Academy for Jewish Research, Jewish Social Studies* and *American Jewish History* are respected scholarly journals. Periodicals such as *Judaism, Midstream, The Jewish Spectator, The Reconstructionist* and *Sh' ma* serve as forums for serious discussion of Jewish issues. The American Jewish Committee-sponsored *Commentary* has a wide general intellectual readership.

As late as the fifties, there were only two chairs of Jewish studies at major American universities. Harry A. Wolfson taught Jewish philosophy at Harvard and Salo W. Baron, Jewish history at Columbia. Baron is this century's preeminent Jewish historian. A master of the whole spectrum of Jewish experience, he sees Jewish history in the setting of world history. In his three-volume *The Jewish Community,* he attributes the community's viability to its ability to accommodate to new political conditions and social challenges. His monumental, multivolumed *A Social and Religious History of the Jews* is a complete reassessment of Jewish historical experience, stressing its uniqueness in its emphasis on social patterns and spiritual goals. Wolfson undertook a rewriting of Western philosophy as it came into contact with the several religious traditions, beginning with Philo of Alexandria and concluding with Spinoza of Amsterdam.

Baron and Wolfson were joined in scholarly eminence by Saul Lieberman, whose works on the Palestinian Talmud and the Tosefta, and the influence of Hellenistic civilization on Jewish life and thought in Talmudic times, established him as the preeminent scholar of rabbinics. H. L. Ginsberg reigned in Biblical studies. Abraham Joshua Heschel, scion of Hasidic aristocracy, became the most widely read and most highly regarded Jewish theologian in America. Joseph D. Soloveitchik and Louis Finkelstein were acclaimed as the rabbinic scholars and theologians of modern Orthodoxy and Conservative Judaism, respectively. American-born and American-trained Jacob R. Marcus in American Jewish history, and Robert Gordis and Harry Orlinsky in Bible studies have produced a second generation of American scholars. An altogether too brief listing of American-trained scholars who came to the fore in the 1960s would include Judah Goldin and David Weiss in rabbinics; Moshe Greenberg, Nahum Sarna and Yohanan Muffs in Bible studies; Ellis Rivkin, Gerson D. Cohen, Jacob Neusner, Isadore Twersky, Yosef Haim Yerushalmi and Howard M. Sachar in various branches of historical studies; Marshall Sklare and Charles S. Liebman in the sociology of the Jew; and Eugene Borowitz, Seymour Siegel, Jakob Petuchowski and Arthur A. Cohen in Jewish thought.

Even in the times of academic retrenchment, the number of American universities offering courses of Jewish studies kept growing, though there has been a leveling off in the seventies and eighties. What is perhaps most noteworthy is that American Jewish institutions of higher learning have by now produced their own faculties.

JEWS AND THEIR NEIGHBORS

Post–World War II America saw a virtual elimination of anti-Jewish quotas in industry, education and housing. Jews found full-employment opportunities in heretofore restricted occupations such as engineering. Not only did quotas limiting the percentage of Jewish students in colleges fade, but college faculties were opened to Jews, who entered the teaching ranks in significant numbers. Nonetheless, pockets of anti-Semitism persisted. As late as the 1950s, anti-Semitic slander accused Jews of Communism and depicted the Soviet Union as an instrument of an international "Zionist" conspiracy. In the late fifties racial desegregation in the South and the situation in the Near East were exploited for anti-Semitic purposes. The press gave wide coverage to anti-Jewish activities, and generally condemned them; even veiled anti-Semitic sentiments expressed by a public or elected official evoked universal censure.

Official and formal relationships among Jewish, Catholic and Protestant groups remained firm, warm and active. They not only labored to establish stronger ties and to foster understanding between their constituents, but also joined in an effort to erase racial discrimination. Leaders of the "three faiths" marched together in Selma and Birmingham in the early days of the civil rights movement, joined in protest against bigotry and worked for racial integration in American life.

In 1962, American church historian Franklin H. Littell commented on what he called "a dramatic ceremony during National Brotherhood Week, February 1961."

The non-fiction award of the year was granted to a book entitled, *An American Dialogue*. This book, written in collaboration between a brilliant Protestant theologian (Robert McAfee Brown) and a distinguished Catholic theologian (Gustave Weigl), with an introduction by one of the greatest contemporary Jewish scholars (Will Herberg) marked the high point to date of an expanding network of discussions between representatives of the three major faiths in the Republic. These discussions, sometimes spontaneously emerging on a local basis and sometimes fostered by national movements like the National Conference of Christians and Jews and the Association for the Co-ordination of University Religious Affairs, call for a maturity and self-understanding which all three faith groups have yet to gain in a setting of voluntarism and pluralism.[9]

Less than a decade later, it all sounded dated. "Brotherhood Week," and " 'Dialogue' Discussions" had all but departed. Ethnicity tended to replace the "three major faiths" concept as a force in American life. The 1960s saw a gradual breakdown in interfaith relations and activities. This was dramatically revealed in the spring of 1967. When the future of the State of Israel seemed in jeopardy, most American Jews believed their own status and security were tied to the fate of Israel, but they found almost no understanding on the part of the organized Christian community with whom they had ties forged by shared enterprises. In the wake of the Six-Day War, an assessment of the situation disclosed that most American Christian leaders and organizations had remained silent before the war and many had turned cool thereafter. There was great soul-searching among those who had built bridges to the Christian community and found that when they were needed, the bridges collapsed.

What happened in 1967 was only the visible expression of a process under way for years. Interfaith came to an end because the needs which established it seemed no longer to exist, and the energies which propelled it were turned to other interests. Jews had entered interfaith activities with enthusiasm, for they saw in it a dignified vehicle for strengthening their acceptance, status and security in America. Christians of goodwill participated in activities which expressed Christian love, particularly for a people to whom they had long denied it. But as Jews found ever wider acceptance in America, their need for "interfaith" decreased. The Christian community redirected its love to groups more in need of it. First interfaith activity turned to common endeavors in the service of the civil rights struggle, and interfaith commissions on religion and race did effective work. But soon the Black community rejected these as paternalistic and patronizing. Christian sentiments of ecumenism, once expressed in interfaith activities, found more meaningful operations in intrafaith projects, a development made possible by a new openness in Catholicism engendered by the spirit of Vatican II.

The new realities of American life, characterized by the Black "Revolution," spurred the Jewish community to consider anew its position within an ethnically pluralistic society. In an essay which appeared as an introduction to a catalog of an exhibition, "Harlem on My Mind," at the Metropolitan Museum of Art in the winter of 1969, a seventeen-year-old Black girl wrote (later found to be cribbed from a respected work of sociology): "psychologically Blacks may find that anti-Jewish sentiments place them, for once, within a majority. Thus, our contempt for the Jew makes us feel more completely American in sharing a national prejudice."

After a generation in which being Jewish seemed no handicap in America, during which the Jews seemed firmly incorporated into the American landscape, to hear such an observation sent a shudder through the Jewish community. A disclaimer was placed in the catalog; then the catalog was quietly withdrawn, but the uneasiness remained. It was not comforting to be reminded that a "national prejudice" had persisted throughout the era of goodwill; it was galling to hear that America's most persecuted minority felt that it could lift itself into American society—psychologically, at least—by sharing in its anti-Semitic prejudice.

Areas of residence in the Northern cities to which Blacks were arriving in the fifties and sixties had just been left by Jews, but Jewish landlords and storekeepers remained. The 1968 teachers' strike in New York City, which, in the eyes of many, was a manifestation of the conflict which pitted Black aspirations and Jewish interests against one another, heightened the tension between the groups. A serious confrontation, characterized by the title of one of a number of such books, *Black Anti-Semitism and Jewish Racism,*[10] was expected to develop. The situation was exacerbated by a number of Black activist spokesmen aligning themselves with Third World anti-Israel forces and hailing the Palestine Liberation Organization as a movement of national liberation, its terrorist activities notwithstanding.

To everyone's relief, the expected confrontation was limited to words. But it also had become evident to many Jews that beneath a placid surface, caldrons may be seething.

A sober assessment of the community's status seemed in order. In a widely discussed article in *Commentary,* "The Black Revolution and the Jewish Question," Earl Raab urged that there be a renewed understanding of pluralistic politics, one which was already being expressed "in a new tendency to ask seriously a question which has been asked jokingly for a number of decades: 'Is it good for the Jews?' "[11] There was an "inward turning" in the American Jewish community. Among its expressions was increasing concern for the welfare of the

Jews in the Soviet Union, and an unprecedented and unapologetic militancy in defense of Jewish interests at home and abroad.

As early as 1954, Abraham Joshua Heschel warned of a Soviet-government-inspired "cultural genocide" which threatened Russian Jewish life with extinction. Elie Wiesel's *Jews of Silence* dramatized their plight. The post-1967 Jewish national awakening in the Soviet Union, and increasing demands by Soviet Jews for migration to Israel, served as a stimulus to greater involvement by American Jews. Their response was immediate and vigorous. An extreme manifestation of this activist spirit was the emergence of the Jewish Defense League, whose methods of direct militant action were unprecedented in American Jewish life. Denounced by the organizations of the Jewish establishment, and disapproved of by most Jews, it nevertheless gained some grass-roots support, particularly among the young.

A segment of the Jewish intellectual elite, some with well-earned liberal credentials, began the "serious questioning" which Raab called for, and *Commentary* magazine became one of its foci. The old alliance of Jewish intellectuals with liberal forces was shattered for many by what they conceived to be excesses which threatened Jewish interests. The anti-Israel stance of the New Left, a threat in itself, also reminded many of the anti-Zionism of the Old Left prior to World War II. A Columbia professor, shocked to see a red flag flying from a building occupied by students in their 1968 takeover of the campus, became an early neo-Conservative. Some pointed to a congruency of interest between Conservative doctrine and Jewish well-being. Critics accused these neo-Conservatives of opportunism, of accepting as their credo the American ambition of "making it." Be that as it may, they seem early to have recognized America's turning to the Right, and became part of its intellectual vanguard. Moreover, their position within the Jewish community was enhanced by the right-wing Likud victory in Israel.

Liberals urged caution, saying that decades of Jewish and liberal alliance should not be lightly dismissed. They pointed to a basic liberality in the Jewish tradition, and reminded Jews that historically they have fared better in liberal eras and under liberal regimes. As for Israel, they urged that a distinction be made between the incumbent government's policies and the national good. In all quarters Raab's observation was well taken:

> The past quarter of a century turns out not to have been, as some envisioned, the passageway to some terminal American dream. It has been a staying ground for some as yet indistinct future American design. The Jews, somehow in trouble again, need to make their own particular sighting on that future.[12]

CULTURE IN THE POSTWAR ERA

After World War II, American Jews gained access to new opportunities in study, employment and residence. War veterans returned, married and moved their families to the suburbs. The GI Bill of Rights made it possible for former servicemen and women to study at universities of their choice, and Jews did so in numbers twice the national average. New laws barring discrimination opened the salaried professions that attracted young Jews in ever-increasing numbers.

Organized Jewry responded by reordering its agenda to reflect a more universal interest. The defense agencies placed their struggle against anti-Semitism in the wider context of strengthening democratic forces in American life. Typical was the change of focus of the American Jewish Congress, described by sociologist C. Bezalel Sherman.

> In 1945 the Congress embarked on a program based on proposals submitted by Alexander H. Pekelis, which fundamentally altered its character. Proceeding from the premise that the well-being of Jews depended on a liberal political and social climate, the Congress became increasingly involved in the promotion of social legislation and in activities designed to strengthen American democracy, eliminate racial and religious bigotry, and advance civil liberties.[13]

Under the imaginative leadership of Louis Finkelstein, the Conservative Jewish Theological Seminary's thrust into the wider world was through its Conference on Science, Philosophy and Religion, which involved Jewish and non-Jewish academicians and clergymen in convocations, lectures and courses on subjects related to the moral and spiritual life of the nation. The Reform Hebrew Union College encouraged non-Jewish students of Judaica to pursue graduate work under its auspices. The Orthodox Yeshiva College, a small liberal arts college attached to the Rabbi Isaac Elchanan Theological Seminary, when Samuel Belkin assumed its presidency, expanded into Yeshiva University, a complex of facilities which came to include a school for graduate studies, a school of social work, the Albert Einstein College of Medicine and the Benjamin N. Cardozo Law School.

American Jewry's most visible incursion into academia was Brandeis University, the only Jewish-sponsored, nonsectarian university in the United States. "When we started in 1948," first president Abram L. Sachar reminisced, "I thought it might take a century to put such a university together, but over eighty buildings were put up by one president in his twenty years of service." Within a decade of its founding, it attained a respected place among American universities. The American Jewish Committee turned from sponsoring the more parochial *The Contemporary Jewish Record* to publishing *Commentary,* and, as critic Alfred Kazin described it, "as the first issues began to appear at the end of that pivotal year of 1945, I was vaguely surprised that it dealt with so many general issues in so subtly critical and detached a fashion, regularly gave a forum to non-Jewish writers as well as to Jewish ones."[14] *Commentary,* its editor Elliot E. Cohen and the committee were criticized for the magazine's "non-Jewish" character. It was so by design, seeing its role as a Jewish presence in the larger cultural scene. In time articles of Jewish interest increased in number. On occasion there was an attempt at wedding the traditionally Jewish with the contemporary American. Thus, Norman Mailer was invited to comment on Hasidic tales, but the attempt at making of Mailer a pop Buber did not quite succeed. Editor Norman Podhoretz's ability to discern portending social and political trends caused *Commentary* to publish articles on Jewish themes, and made it the forum for the forces moving America from Liberalism to neo-Conservatism.

World War II left its mark on American literature. Anti-Semitism, previously almost a taboo subject, was dealt with in a series of best-selling novels. Arthur Miller's *Focus* and Laura Z. Hobson's *Gentleman's Agreement* each has a non-Jewish hero who, mistakenly regarded as a Jew, has his eyes opened to the plight of the victim. Noah Ackerman in Irwin Shaw's *The Young Lions* is a victim of barracks-room anti-Semitism while the war against the Nazis goes on. The two Jewish soldiers in Norman Mailer's dazzling first novel, *The Naked and the Dead,* are differentiated by the way in which each accepts the predicament of being a Jew.

The flood of writings about Jews having begun, young college-educated Jewish writers found publishers for novels reflecting other aspects of American Jewish life. Herman Wouk's *Marjorie Morningstar* portrayed the shallowness of the middle-class, Americanized Jew bereft of his own heritage, a subject Philip Roth and others turned to. Saul Bellow's major novel of a Jewish rogue, *The Adventures of Augie March,* portrays an urban Jewish countertype to *The Adventures of Huckleberry Finn.* Bernard Malamud depicts a struggling Jewish grocer as a saintly inspiration to an orphaned Gentile in *The Assistant.* The Jew as peculiarly affected by experiences such as immigration, exile and the Holocaust was presented in such different works as Herbert Gold's *Fathers,* which spoke for many an estranged son of immigrant parents; and Edward Lewis Wallant's *The Pawnbroker,* which depicted the blunting of human sensitivity and the possibility of its awakening after the Nazi experience.

In the fifties and sixties, writers, publishers and the reading public, learning more about the Holocaust and captivated by the establishment of Israel, found continued interest in the Jew as a literary subject. Leon Uris's *Exodus* became a source of popular knowledge about some of the events surrounding the birth of Israel. Non-Jewish writers produced books of Jewish interest: John Hersey wrote about the Warsaw Ghetto uprising in *The Wall,* and James Michener produced *The Source,* on the history of the land of Israel through the ages.

Writing about the American scene as they saw it, Saul Bellow, Bernard Malamud and Philip Roth attained the leading roles as Jewish novelists and short-story writers. In a group of incisive stories, collected in *Goodbye, Columbus,* and in a novel of intermarriage, *Letting Go,* Philip Roth astutely commented on the bourgeois failings, spiritual insufficiency and loss of identity of the assimilated American Jew. Charles Angoff, who himself wrote a saga of the American Jew in the person of the literate, sensitive David Polonsky, spoke of a type of Jewish novel "racked with self-degradation and obsessed with various aberrations, sexual and otherwise." Fulfilling this description, Roth's *Portnoy's Complaint* was the novel-sensation of 1969, described by *The New York Times* as "one of the dirtiest books ever published . . . also one of the funniest." In its self-abasing ridicule of a monstrous Jewish mother and sex-obsessed son, it has been said to "cap—or put a yarmulke on— the American Jewish genre." Roth himself, in *The Ghost Writer,* later exposed the self-searching he had undergone when he was accused of betraying his people through his art.

Sensitive and often mystical in approach, Bernard Malamud created Jewish characters who are ordinary, often almost mute, but who attain nobility in their endurance and in their striving for integrity. Morris Bober, in *The Assistant,* and Yakov Bok, in *The Fixer* (representing the historical Mendel Beiliss who was falsely accused of killing a Christian child in czarist Russia), suffer their way to a kind of saintliness. In *A New Life,* and in many short stories about the poor and outcast, Malamud often portrayed the *schlemiel* as hero.

Two unique figures on the American Jewish literary scene are Elie Wiesel and Isaac Bashevis Singer. Wiesel, a survivor of Auschwitz, first reached the American reader in *Night,* his most moving statement. Later books dealing with the Holocaust, Israel and the "silent" Jews of Russia have spoken to the conscience of the world. Singer, a Yiddish writer born in Poland, writing in New York, became a favorite of the general American reading public. He dealt only rarely with American subjects, but his narratives of East European Jewish life, passion-laden, invaded by the supernatural, have appealed to a wide variety of readers, and won him the Nobel Prize for Literature in 1978.

Among the many who contributed to the "Jewish school," Chaim Potok stood out as one who wrote from within the Jewish tradition, free of self-flagellation. *The Chosen,* a tale of two boys growing up in Orthodox Jewish communities in Brooklyn, provided an intimate look into a little-known ethnic group, a society where adolescents as well as adults pursue learning, and where teenagers are concerned about the best way they may serve humanity. Abraham Rothberg's historical novel *Sword of the Golem* and Cynthia Ozick's collection of short stories, *The Pagan Rabbi,* are works displaying similar Jewish sensibilities.

Allen Ginsberg was the leader of beat poets of the fifties and sixties. His howls against society include *Kaddish,* a lament for the warping of his youth by his psychotic mother. One hears an echo of Yehudah Halevi in Karl Shapiro's poem "Israel" which celebrates the birth of the state while the author remains in exile "chained in a western chair" *(Poems of A Jew,* 1958).

Arthur Miller and Paddy Chayevsky were but two of numerous playwrights who wrote for the theater, for films and for television. A revival of nostalgic interest in European and Yiddish backgrounds led to plays reminiscent of the old Yiddish theater; and *Fiddler on the Roof,* based on Sholem Aleichem's Yiddish stories about Tevye the Milkman, became one of the popular classics of musical comedy. Jewish literary critics Lionel Trilling, Philip Rahv, Paul Goodman, Leslie Fiedler, Irving Howe and Alfred Kazin were among the leading arbiters of literary taste for all America.

The major American novelist of the period was Saul Bellow, 1976 Nobel Prize laureate in literature. A man of broad general and Jewish culture, he presented alienated heroes like himself—urban, intellectual, tormented by lack of fulfillment and by petty harassments, seeking salvation— in *Herzog, Mr. Sammler's Planet, Humboldt's Gift* and *The Dean's December.* Like most American Jewish writers a son of immigrants, Bellow's career mirrors the great strides made by American Jews as they moved from immigrant to significant contributor to American cultural life. Writer and critic John Leonard wrote in *The New York Times* when Bellow was awarded the Nobel Prize:

> If Saul Bellow didn't exist, someone exactly like him would have had to have been invented . . . a very special sort of novelist, a highbrow with muscles, to tell the story of the Jewish romance with America. . . . One form of the Jewish romance with America was being worked out in popular culture—in Hollywood and in the theater of musical comedy. It was assimilationist: Look at us, we're just as American as you are; we're more American because we are feeding you your dreams.
>
> This was not what the New York intellectuals had in mind. Critics and explicators of the great texts of modernist literature, haunted by Europe, having been through the revolving door of Hitler and Stalin, at home with the problematic as a mode of knowledge, didn't want to disappear into American culture; they wanted to enrich it, to make it grow up.[15]

13.

Zionism, Philanthropy and Politics

NO SOONER HAD THE CELEBRATIONS MARKING THE FOUNDING OF THE STATE of Israel come to an end when American Jewry was called upon to aid the new state in fighting for its existence. The energies and resources of American Jews were placed in service of helping European, Near Eastern and North African Jews move to Israel, and of rehabilitating and settling them on the land. The effort required skilled organization, unprecedented philanthropic campaigns and political activity as well.

In the 1920s and 1930s, American Zionists were joined in a debate on emphasis and priority: political activity or the practical labor of rebuilding, ideology or philanthropy. Movements rooted in ideology demand political commitment of their adherents. Organizations deal with more mundane concerns. In America, Zionism expressed itself more through organizations due, in part, to the American temper, which is more given to practicality than ideology, and in part to the role the American Jew was assigned in the Zionist program, that of influence and philanthropy.

Zionist organizations in America maintain an ideological stance, but their life is in their practical function. They are joined together in a loose confederation, the American Zionist Council. To the left are the Labor Zionist Organization of America and the Pioneer Women, and the lesser in number Progressive Zionist League and the United Labor Zionist Party. The centrist organizations are the Zionist Organization of America and Hadassah, the women's Zionist organization.

The latter, by far the largest of the Zionist organizations, has an enviable record of continuing service to medical, public-health, child-welfare and vocational education institutions in Israel. In America, it carries on a program of education and publishes *The Hadassah Magazine*. To the right is the United Zionist-Revisionists, which has gained considerable strength with the coming to power in 1977 of its ideological counterpart in Israel, the Revisionist dominated *Likud*. The religious Zionists of America consist of Mizrachi-Hapoel Mizrachi and Mizrachi Women, now called AMIT. All groups sponsor educational activities in the United States and social welfare institutions in Israel.

Opposition to Zionism in post–World War II America has come from the extreme left and right of Jewish life. The American Council for Judaism opposed Zionism for its nationalism, seeing it as a hindrance to national, civic, cultural and social integration of the American Jew into American life. The followers of the Rebbe of Satmar oppose Zionism as an antireligious force, which usurps the role to be played by the Messiah.

After the Six-Day War, strong anti-Zionist and anti-Israel sentiments were expressed by the New Left. Israel was accused of imperialism, of being an instrument of international capitalism in subjugating and exploiting the peoples of the Near East and the Afro-Asian populations of the Third World for American interests. That Jews were among the leadership of the New Left pained the great majority of American Jews and amazed and perplexed Israelis.

Over the years, United States policy in the Near East has remained constant in principle and purpose, but has changed in its practical relations with the State of Israel. The Middle East is to serve as a bulwark against Communist expansion, and the United States seeks to reduce tension between Israel and the Arab states to protect its economic and strategic interests. In 1954 the State Department declared "a policy of impartial friendship" to all countries in the area. When, in October 1956, Israeli forces occupied the Sinai Peninsula, the Eisenhower administration pressed for Israeli withdrawal. American Jewry urged Washington to propose to the General Assembly of the United Nations that Israel and the Arab states be required first to enter into peace negotiations. Finally, however, Israel yielded to American insistence of withdrawal, and President Eisenhower wrote to Premier David Ben-Gurion that "Israel will have no cause to regret" its action.

Throughout this period of Israeli-American tension, American Jewry remained constant in its support of the Israeli position, which it claimed was in the best American interests. The moral argument it mounted was that as the leader of the free democratic world the United States owes special obligations to the one free, stable and democratic state in the Near East. Practical reasoning maintained that a free, strong

Israel is the best deterrent to Russian domination of the Middle East. American Jewry's political activity in friendship for Israel has been resolute, skillful and of consequence.

Of the impact of the Six-Day War, political scientist Daniel J. Elazar wrote:

> June 1967 marked a watershed in contemporary Jewish affairs. The six day war united the members of the generation that witnessed the founding of the state with those of a new generation, one that grew up accepting the existence of Israel as a matter of fact, only to encounter suddenly the harsh possibility of its destruction, making both generations deeply aware of the shared fate of all Jews, and the way that fate is now bound up with the political entity that is the State of Israel . . . Even Jews farthest removed from Jewish associations "instinctively" realized how crucial the survival of Israel was to their own welfare as individuals.[1]

Changes in the psyche of the American Jew wrought by the war were put to the test a half-dozen years later on Yom Kippur, 1973. American Jews were in their synagogues when news of the Egyptian and Syrian attack on Israel reached them. The result was a coalescing of political, economic and emotional support that underscored the strong sense of Jewish unity which the Six-Day War had brought to the fore. Elazar also assessed the impact of the Yom Kippur War:

> As a result of the Yom Kippur War . . . American Jews (who do not wish to assimilate) have to confront the fact that they have different interests from other subgroups within American society, interests which transcend their American background . . .
>
> After the Six Day War, it was widely suggested that Jewry had entered into a post-emancipation age. The willingness of young Jews to express their Jewishness openly, precisely because they had grown up in an emancipated modern society, was the surest sign that this was a fact. The Yom Kippur War may have brought us to a post-Zionist age, in the sense of the Jewishness of the Jewish people—not in the ways of nineteenth century nationalism, or eighteenth century emancipation, but in a new version of Jewish living . . .[2]

Elazar's perception of the special interests of America's Jews, which may be different from or in conflict with the interests of other groups in American society, may be illustrated by the reaction of the American intellectual elite to the Yom Kippur War. A letter to *The New York Times* expressing sympathy for Israel and opposing Arab aggression was signed by Saul Bellow, Irving Howe, Alfred Kazin, Meyer Shapiro, Lionel Trilling and Michael Harrington.[3] Only one, the last named, was not a Jew. Israeli novelist Aharon Megged, visiting in the United States two months after the cease-fire, in a letter to *The Times* challenged: "I have been appalled to witness the silence of American intellectuals in the face of the latest events . . . will not a few voices of courageous and conscientious intellectuals be heard at this troublesome time?"[4] Some of America's non-Jewish writers and intellectuals did lend their names to pro-Israel advertisements, but as Irving Howe accused:

> Various intellectual prominences are silent . . . Where is the great poet, conscience of America? Where is the sensitive psychiatrist, who studies collective brainwashing? Where is the brilliant novelist, champion of the new, darling of the young?[5]

In the days preceding and during the Six-Day War and during the Yom Kippur War, American rabbis found that ministers and priests solicited for public expressions of concern, all too often responded with an "even-handed neutrality." This indifference to the fate of Israel led, as we have noted, to an estrangement between the Jewish and Christian religious establishments. Jewish intellectuals felt a similar sense of abandonment. Their involvement in Jewish causes became more pronounced and less apologetic, their writing on Jewish matters less self-conscious.

Both the Six-Day and Yom Kippur wars were traumatic for the Jews in America, but a renewed sense of Jewish peoplehood emerged. The victory in 1967 was celebrated by American Jews as their victory; in 1973, American Jews felt the Egyptian and Syrian armies threatening them, though they were six thousand miles away.

The tie of American Jews to Zion was expressed organizationally by the reconstitution in 1971 of the Jewish Agency. At the Agency's First Assembly, Max M. Fisher proclaimed the sentiments of American Jewry in its relationship to Israel:

> Out of this land once came a great message to the world: justice, freedom and human dignity. And we Jews, we choose to believe that out of this land will yet come another such message. To be given a chance to make our contribution to that goal, to be able to do our part by re-establishing our people, to build for the peace that will surely come, to have a small share in creating that Israel . . . . All this is a privilege beyond price.[6]

While American Jewry awaited the fulfillment of the Zionist dream, it built bridges to Israel. The American tourist became a commonplace in Israel. Of greater significance was the number of young American Jews studying in Israel, often a year or longer at the Hebrew University in Jerusalem or at Tel Aviv, Haifa, Bar Ilan or Ben-Gurion universities, or at one of Israel's *yeshivot* or other religious institutes.

The *kibbutz,* as a successful form of cooperative living, attracted many to a summer's, half-year's or year's residency.

Prior to 1967, *aliyah* in any appreciable numbers was demanded by Israeli leaders, with lip homage being paid at Zionist conventions. After 1967, the call for *aliyah* met with a response that gave its proponents hopes for an American immigration of some consequence. The movement, however, was short-lived. The Yom Kippur War and the economic and social problems of Israel have kept the numbers low, and have caused some who attempted settlement to return to the United States. An increasing migration of Israelis to America has become a matter of grave concern to the State of Israel. The ties of American Jewry to Israel remain strong, however, none stronger than the continuing philanthropic enterprise of the United Jewish Appeal.

PHILANTHROPY

In the decade which ended in 1954, Jewish community federations raised over $1.3 billion dollars. The early campaigns were launched to meet the needs of the Jews left homeless in war-blasted Europe. By 1951, almost all the displaced persons had been resettled from Europe, with some 90 percent in Israel; but 1954 saw the intensification of large-scale immigration from North Africa.

After the UJA's campaign of 1948, there had been sharp annual declines. In the year of tercentenary, American Jewry was turning more to its domestic needs, and allocations reflected this change, with the UJA share declining by almost 10 percent.

It became clear to the UJA that in the years ahead it would not only have to dramatize the appeal, but also be able to stand up to local welfare funds (who did the actual collecting of the monies) in negotiations for a "fair share" of the campaign income. To undertake this task William Rosenwald, philanthropist son of philanthropist father, was designated national chairman and Rabbi Herbert A. Friedman the professional head. Coming from local communal campaign involvement in two typical American Jewish communities, Denver and Milwaukee, Friedman knew what national UJA leaders had been claiming, that the potential in the American Jewish community had not yet been adequately addressed, and that only the UJA's appeal could tap that reservoir. In 1956 and 1957 a means to exploit the latent support for overseas needs was created: special funds to which one could contribute beyond one's usual pledge. In 1956, it was called the UJA Special Survival Fund, and in the next year, the UJA Emergency Rescue Fund. The $140 million raised in 1957 was a one-third increase in only two years. "Almost all the increased campaign results for 1956 were channelled to the UJA," the *American Jewish Yearbook* reported. Leaders of many local welfare funds, while pleased by the sums realized, felt that too little was remaining in their city and in this country. Conflicts between local communities and the UJA ensued, and the individual communities turned for guidance and support to their national body, the Council of Jewish Federations and Welfare Funds. They delegated power to the CJFWF so that it could face the UJA from a position of strength. In the late fifties the CJFWF began effectively to represent the organized American Jewish communities, and the 1960s witnessed transfer of the central power position in American Jewry from the national organizations to the CJFWF. In the year following establishment of the State of Israel, Prime Minister Ben-Gurion dealt with Jacob Blaustein, head of the American Jewish Committee, as the representative of effective power in the American Jewish community, protest by the Zionists notwithstanding. (Ben-Gurion knew that in a voluntary community true power lies in the purse and in the ability to persuade.) Two decades later, when the need to reconstitute the Jewish Agency became compelling, Louis Pincus, chairman of the Executive Board of the agency, turned to Max M. Fisher, president of the Council of Jewish Federations, to join him in organizing the new body.

Henry Morgenthau, Jr., came to UJA leadership from the highest executive office held by a Jew in America, until then, secretary of the treasury. His successor as UJA general chairman, Edward M. M. Warburg, donned the mantle of leadership worn before him by father and grandfather. William Rosenwald continued the services initiated by his father, whose philanthropy had set new standards for the Jewish community. For over one hundred years, leadership in the Jewish community had been the prerogative of Jews who came from the German states, or their children and grandchildren. Morgenthau, Warburg and Rosenwald were the last national leaders to be thought of as members of that elite. The postwar years witnessed the ascendancy of the sons and daughters of the East European Jewish immigrant community into positions of leadership. The "old guard" leadership was provided by history; the new leadership was "geographic," coming to the national scene from leadership in their local communities, and was thus part of the process of "natural democracy."

Joseph Meyerhoff, a communal leader in Baltimore, who became general chairman in 1961, immigrated with his family from Russia in 1906. The father of Morgenthau, Henry, Sr., had been a doctrinaire anti-Zionist; Julius Rosenwald, father of William, was a practical anti-Zionist; Felix Warburg and Jacob H. Schiff, father and grandfather of Edward, had been non-Zionists; but the father of Meyerhoff was a Zionist. His son recalls:

> As a matter of fact, in the early nineteen hundreds he went to Palestine from Russia to see if he should move his family there. . . .

He lived there for several months, and came away convinced that it was too rough a place to raise a family. So he went back to Russia. My father was head of the local defense group [against pogroms] in the small town near Poltava where he lived. They came searching for arms in the middle of the night . . . put my father in political prison for two months. . . . In 1906, when my father was able to get a passport, we all came to the United States to Baltimore.[7]

Many communities had had separate local and overseas campaigns. Most often, the older German Jewish community was identified with the local, and the more recent East European group with the overseas. The two campaigns not only reflected the divided community but also prolonged division. The joint campaign which overseas needs required did much to unite the community not only for fund raising, but also for all manner of communal endeavor. The last such division, in New York City, was erased by the Yom Kippur War.

Meyerhoff's successor, Max M. Fisher, came to national leadership through activity in the Detroit Jewish community as president of its Jewish Welfare Federation, one of the most powerful in the nation. He went on to become president of the Council of Jewish Federations and Welfare Funds, while at the same time serving as chairman of the United Israel Appeal. Later he became chairman of the board of governors of the reconstituted Jewish Agency, as well as chairman of the executive committee of the American Jewish Committee. He thus held leadership positions in all the power bases of the American Jewish community. In a sense, he represented the final consolidation of the Jewish community into a unified entity.

THE SUMMER OF '67 AND THE FALL OF '73

Accounts of spontaneous and enthusiastic giving in the summer of 1967 have become part of American Jewish folklore. At a luncheon in New York, one man pledged $1.55 million, and four others $1 million each. It was reported that $15 million were pledged in fifteen minutes. Fifty families in Boston contributed $2.5 million dollars to launch the drive. In Cleveland $3 million was raised in a day and over a million in St. Louis overnight. Throughout the country, children went into the streets with pails, milk bottles and cans to collect for the emergency. On campus, students went from door to door in their dormitory buildings. Yeshiva students spread through the Times Square and garment districts of New York, taking contributions in bed sheets.

The years 1971–72 saw the beginning of increased immigration to Israel from the Soviet Union. This new wave, as dramatic as it was unexpected, brought 13,000 in 1971 and 35,000 in 1972. For more than half a century, the second largest Jewish community in the world had been cut off from world Jewry. The Soviet gates had first opened in 1966–70, permitting a slow trickle of refugees to Israel, a little more than 5000. The possibility that the trickle might become a wave moved world Jewry to action. American Jewry took the lead in pressing the U.S. government to use its influence on the USSR. It also assumed economic responsibility for resettling those permitted to leave.

When at 2:00 P.M. on October 6, 1973, Arab armies from the west and from the north attacked Israel, the Jews of the East Coast of America were on their way to their synagogues for Yom Kippur services. In the Midwest it was 7:00 A.M., on the West Coast, 5:00 A.M. It was from the pulpits that America's Jews first heard the news. Prayer took on a new significance and urgency. There was urgency, too, for the Holy Day to come to an end, so that the practical work which this new and apparently greatest emergency demanded might begin. A contemporary observer reported:

> The response was everything anyone expected and more . . . stories of men borrowing money at high interest rates to provide cash, people mortgaging their houses, women giving jewels . . . Congregations called special meetings to pray for Israel's victory and to raise funds to make that victory possible . . . On Tuesday night, October 9, communities across the country held open rallies to raise funds . . . sound trucks were driven through the streets of Jewish neighborhoods and suburbs asking for contributions. Hats and coin boxes were passed at rallies . . . Student gifts for the UJA far exceeded any previous campus effort, with $700,000 reported the first month alone . . . There were three gifts of $5 million, of $2 million or more and some forty gifts of $1 million or more . . .

But he adds:

> The major funds came from the relatively small number of very big donors and generally from those who had already been identified as big contributors . . . Relatively few new people came forward . . . .[8]

THE UJA AT FORTY

In 1979 the years of the United Jewish Appeal numbered the Biblical forty. It was a time which witnessed the destruction of European Jewry and the rescue and rehabilitation of the saved remnant; the fulfillment of a two-millennial dream in the founding of the State of Israel; the military, political and economic battles waged by the fledgling state; its almost fivefold growth in its three decades; the *aliyah* to Israel of the Jewish communities of the Muslim countries of North Africa and the Near East; the unanticipated Jewish emigration from the Soviet Union; and the emergence of American Jewry into a united, affluent, influential community accepting the responsibilities of leadership in world Jewry. In all of these, the UJA and its beneficiary agencies, the JDC and the United Israel Appeal/Jewish Agency, played a central role.

To sum up the contribution of the UJA to the fashioning of the American Jewish community: it provided both motivation and means for uniting a community ready for unification and it forced campaigns unprecedented in scope upon the individual communities, unearthing an unanticipated potential for philanthropy in American Jews. The benefits of these campaigns was major and direct. Central communal campaigns raised $57.3 million in 1945; refugee plight raised the sum to $131.7 million in 1946; and the founding of the State of Israel, to $205 million in 1948. Giving then leveled off, but never to a sum below more than twice that of the pre-1946 figure. Similarly, the Six-Day War raised the campaign results from $136 to $317 million; in the years following, the average remained well above twice the 1966 figure. The increase in the post–Yom Kippur War campaign was a $280-million jump to $660 million.

In the late 1960s and 1970s a substantial and increasing percentage of the total campaign, rising from 20 percent to 50 percent, remained in the community coffers, to be allocated by it to local and national needs. The local communities also benefited from a cadre of young leaders, educated, trained and motivated by the UJA, who took positions of leadership in all manner of communal enterprise.

In its first forty years of existence, the UJA was allocated $4.9 billion of a total $7.8 billion raised by central community campaigns. In addition, it obtained over $60 million for the Israel Education Fund, and helped create the atmosphere which made possible the sale of some $3.5 billion of State of Israel bonds.

Despite the achievements of the UJA, critical voices have been raised regarding its impact on the economy of Israel and communal life in the United States. Two such criticisms came from Israelis. The *Jerusalem Post* of March 25–31, 1979, reported:

> Abraham Shavit [chairman of the Israeli Manufacturers Association] called for a stop to the present system of UJA fund-raising which tended to represent Israel as a poor and deprived society, which needed charity. "The UJA raised $270 million for us last year, while exports brought $7 billion. The campaign does untold damage to the *Aliya* efforts and to our efforts to sell sophisticated products abroad."

Shavit recognizes the good done by the monies raised, but is critical of the manner in which they are raised.

The observation of Israeli political scientist and journalist Yosef Goell is even more challenging. In an article in the April 22–28, 1979, issue of the *Jerusalem Post,* Goell points to the problem which fund raising creates in the American Jewish community. "For American Jewry, the long-term and continuing Israeli emphasis on money donations has served to distort the terms of affiliation of many Jews with organized Jewish communities. The criterion of "How much have you given?" has become so central, that many people have kept away from affiliation." Goell may have overstated his case, but the issue touches two central problems confronting American Jewish life: the relationship between American Jewry and Israel, and the relationship between the individual American Jew and the organized Jewish community. Has the incessant emphasis on fund raising indeed relegated the relationship between the communities of America and Israel to that of donor-recipient? Is the place and worth of an American Jew within his or her community determined solely or largely by the size of the monetary contribution? Will American Jewry keep from active leadership some of its most thoughtful, creative, and committed men and women?

SOURCE
The American Jew—As Others Saw Him

In the January 1872 issue of *The Galaxy,* W. M. Rosenblatt concluded his informative and perceptive essay, "The Jews: What They are Coming To," with the prediction:

> Within fifty years . . . the grandchildren, at the latest, will be indistinguishable from the mass of humanity which surrounds them. . . . Of that ancient people only the history of their perils and their sufferings will remain, and the change that came over them in an enlightened age.[9]

A century later, the cover page article of the March 1, 1971 *Newsweek* was *The American Jew Today.* Excerpts follow:

> He is one American in 30, born to a people, a faith, a history which he can embrace, reject or ignore, but cannot easily forget. He thrives in cities, is overwhelmingly middle-class and consistently votes liberal. Sociologists assure him that he is, on average, wealthier than his neighbors and far better educated. Historians remind him that he is more secure today than his forefathers ever were over the last 2,000 years. He is the American Jew. . . .
> Most American Jews today share a new sense of pride in

themselves and their community. The key to that pride lies in Israel. The whole world has marveled at the determined strength of the tiny nation carved from the desert, but Jews have marveled most of all. "The Israeli victory in the six-day war in 1967," says Sol Linowitz, former board chairman of Xerox Corp. and the U.S. ambassador to the OAS, "was the end of the image of the Jew as a loser." . . .

"The twenty-year period from the end of World War II until 1967 was the Golden Age for Jews in America," says Bertram Gold, executive director of the American Jewish Committee. By 1965, nearly half of the Jewish families in America enjoyed solidly middle-class status. . . .

The proportion of Jews in college is twice that of the general U.S. population. And the proportion of Jews enrolled in graduate and professional schools is triple that for students in the general population. Although Jews account for only 3 percent of the U.S. population, they provide more than 10 percent of all American college teachers; at prestigious universities such as Harvard, Jews represent as much as one-third of the faculty. The most blatant forms of prejudice against U.S. Jews have been largely chipped away in the last quarter century. In part, it appears that once Americans became aware of the full horror of the Nazi ovens, they found it far more difficult to tolerate many of the petty forms of anti-Semitism that had so long been a commonly accepted facet of U.S. society. Whatever the reason, by the mid-'60s, more and more Jews were testing the election process and discovering that they could be chosen for the Statehouse or for Congress.

They also achieved an extraordinary degree of importance in American intellectual life. . . . Says Alfred Kazin, the noted critic, "I don't think that there has been anywhere in the history of the Jewish people anything quite like the influence that Jewish intellectuals have exerted on American culture."

Some observers . . . predict that the position of the Jew in America is more likely to deteriorate in the immediate future than to improve. But it seems equally possible that in a time when more and more Americans are learning once again to appreciate the nation's historic ethnic diversity, Jews will be freer than ever before to be themselves.

The cover story of the April 10, 1972, issue of *Time* was titled *What It Means to be Jewish*. Excerpts follow:

"I know what one must do to be Jewish," writes author Elie Wiesel. "He must assume his Jewishness. He must assume his collective conscience. He must assume his past with its sorrows and its joys." . . .

Where their parents had found new faiths in Marxism, Freudianism and a succession of liberal causes, many younger Jews followed their contemporaries into the New Left or exotic religious movements such as Krishna Consciousness, Scientology or even the Jesus Revolution. For others, young and old, Judaism has been reduced to what one young Jew contemptuously calls a "gastronomical experience": blintzes, bagels and lox, gefilte fish.

Paradoxically, during roughly the same period, assimilation ran into a countertrend. Orthodox and Conservative Jewry experienced a pronounced new growth in the U.S. Orthodox Rabbi Joseph B. Soloveitchik describes the change: "When I came here in the 1930s [from Germany], there was a certain naïveté, a great pride, a confidence in the American way of life. I'm not sure what the American way of life was, but everyone—including a great many Jews—thought it was best. Jews wanted to disappear." Now, says Soloveitchik, "America is reaching for values above historical change"—values that he believes Orthodoxy provides.

Theologian Abraham Joshua Heschel, professor of ethics and mysticism at the Conservatives' Jewish Theological Seminary in Manhattan, is the godfather and poet of [the] school of thought . . . that faith must underpin any lasting sense of Jewish identity. . . . For Heschel, the task is "being what we are, namely Jews; by attuning our own yearning to the lonely holiness in this world, we will aid humanity more than by any particular service we may render." . . . A cross-denominational group of theologians . . . [including] Reform Eugene Borowitz, Conservative Seymour Siegel and Orthodox Norman Lamm [tries] to promote, explains theologian Siegel, the idea that Jews "are *not* a people like all other people, nor a religious society promoting certain metaphysical principles and ideas, but a group joined together in relation to God."

The Covenant theologians—and many other religious Jews newly interested in *halakhic* (Jewish legal) observance—generally agree that the Jews' special relationship with God demands some kind of loyalty to traditional Jewish law. "Without law the Covenant is empty and even meaningless," says Siegel. "There can be no Covenant without observance." While more liberal Jews are willing to search for the common denominator of faith within a broader idea of Jewish peoplehood, the Orthodox are more demanding: faith must come first, peoplehood second.

In his short story "Monte Sant' Angelo" Arthur Miller writes of the Jewish experience: "The whole history is packing bundles and getting away." That may have been. Now the business, Jews hope, is unpacking bundles and settling where they are.

SOURCE
American Jews—As They Saw Themselves

A symposium on the 1980s in the Spring 1981 issue of *Judaism* finds the mood of American Jews ranging from an uneasy concern to a guarded optimism.

1. Lothar Kahn, professor of modern languages at Central Connecticut State College, presents a disquieting "description of current trends affecting the physical security and spiritual vitality of the Jewish community."

It appears that the American Jewish community is not in the same good shape it was in at the onset of the Sixties and Seventies. American Jews are still free and vigorous, more uninhibited about their Jewishness than any Jews in the Diaspora present or past, but they seem vaguely more apprehensive. . . .

There is the malaise that derives from the discovery that old socio-political positions are no longer viable and that new ground is not easily broken. Foreign and internal developments alike have pushed Jews, much against their traditions and inclinations, into a more conservative stance. Many Jews, always left of center, allied first in the past century to Liberal movements, then later to Socialist parties, suddenly find themselves in the enemy camp. . . . The Eighties appear a decade when American Jewry, by and large, will try to stake out new political ground. . . . Whether, in the light of new threats, their old commitment to social justice (their secularized God), can retain its erstwhile strength remains to be seen.

[Another] malaise, an import from the general society, pertains to the laxity of standards and the relativization of all values. . . .

The Jewish family is crumbling; the use of drugs and alcohol is increasing. . . .

Young American Jews seem attracted to a variety of secular gods: socialism with a human face, different forms of humanism, occasionally radical and revolutionary movements. If they are attracted to more specifically religious movements, they are likely to be of the lunatic fringe kind, with just a tinge of the kinky in them. . . .

Internally the house of Judaism looks older somehow in 1980, mustier, less sturdy.

2. Sidney H. Schwarz, rabbi of Reconstructionist Congregation Beth Israel, Media, Pennsylvania, notes a "widening gap" between Israel and American Jews.

The discussion of Israel-Diaspora relations, in recent years, has moved from one of theoretical musings to one of heightened urgency and even despair. While the Israeli government has sought to maintain the facade of the ever-right, ever-injured party, American Jews have cut back on their one-time unqualified support of Israeli policy. Despite concerted attempts in some quarters of the American Jewish community to keep dissenters in line, there is an unfortunately widening rift between American Jews and Israel. . . .

To continue to minimize the differences, or cover them up by repressing dissent, can lead only to disaster.

3. Richard Maas, first chairman of the National Conference on Soviet Jewry and past president of the American Jewish Committee, hails the democratization which has taken place in American Jewish communal life.

Since World War II we have witnessed sharp changes in the concept of leadership and in the manner in which leaders function. There is no longer a small cadre of people who speak for the "Jewish Community" or to whom American Jews are willing to entrust the authority for spokesmanship. . . . Attempts will undoubtedly be made during the next decade to establish "one voice" for American Jewry, but the effort will, and should, fail. The American Jewish community is as diverse and as independent as the pluralistic society in which we live and a return to the European-style kehillah would sacrifice the vitality and intellectual ferment which has characterized our growth and our strength.

By democratizing Jewish life we have diverted the beam of public attention from individuals and focused it on organizations. It is my belief that in this process we have lost nothing—rather, we have gained strength and maturity. This trend will continue for the benefit of all Jewry and will make possible new generations of leaders, coming from within the ranks of our complex organizational structure. So be it!

4. Theodore R. Mann, a past chairman of the Conference of Presidents of Major American Jewish Organizations, argues that optimism is realism.

Alarmist reports notwithstanding, the perception of a worsening shift in the American public's attitude toward American Jews simply has no basis in reality. . . .

Ours is a nation increasingly dedicated to the concept of pluralism. A nation which, in addition to its tradition of individual freedom, also welcomes and encourages a variety of separate cultural streams, is, indeed, different from any nation which preceded it. Where many groups cherish their ethnic identity, Jews will be more secure in openly cherishing theirs. . . .

We will not be overwhelmed by the magnetism of mainstream American culture. . . .

My own experience in scores of Jewish communities all over America tells me that our people's self-image is healthy and improving and, in the main, American Jews have gone about as far as they care, or will care, to go on the road to assimilation. Wherever I travel, I see and am aware of developing feelings of identity, community and pride.

FOCUS
In Political Life—A Retrospective View

In the administration of Ronald Reagan, Jews were conspicuous by their absence. Not one Jew could be found in the cabinet or in the upper echelons of the White House staff. Gone from the Senate were its most influential Jewish members, and in considerations for a Supreme Court appointment, no one spoke any longer of the "Jewish seat." What made this absence of Jews all the more noticeable was that the Jewish presence had grown perceptibly during the postwar years, most noticeably since the Kennedy administration. Abraham Ribicoff, Henry Kissinger, Harold Brown and Philip Klutznick in cabinet positions, Arthur Goldberg and Abe Fortas on the Supreme Court bench, Sol M. Linowitz, U.S. representative to the Organization of American States and Walter Annenberg, ambassador to the Court of St. James's were among the most prominent, and their number was supplemented in appointive and elective offices in the first and second echelons of government service.

The Jewish political traditions in America are as old as the Republic. In 1806, when the Jewish population numbered no more than 2500, twenty-seven-year-old Myer Moses, in an address at the fifth anniversary celebration of the Hebrew Orphan Society in Charleston, South Carolina, mused: "May we not fondly cherish the pleasing hope, that from among the Hebrew Society, there may spring a WASHINGTON for the field; a JEFFERSON for the cabinet."[10] The hope was indeed fulfilled. A well-founded tradition has it that a student at the Hebrew Orphan School was Judah P. Benjamin, son of "indigent parents," who rose to serve in the cabinet of the Confederate States as attorney general, secretary of war and secretary of state from 1862 to

1865. He had also served as senator from Louisiana, but had long since dissociated himself from the Jewish community. This was also true of a senator from Florida who announced his dissociation by a name change from Levy to Yulee. Louis C. Levin of Philadelphia kept his name, but little else that was Jewish, when he served in the House of Representatives in the mid-nineteenth century as a member of the Know-Nothing party.

At the beginning of the nineteenth century, Mordecai M. Noah received a political appointment as U.S. consul to the Barbary States. There was reluctance at appointing a Jew to serve in a Christian country, but it was thought that a Moslem state might be more tolerant. When his religion proved an impediment, Noah's appointment was withdrawn by the U.S. government, much to his ire and that of his fellow Jews, notably Isaac Harby, who wrote a strong complaint to James Monroe. A century later, Oscar S. Straus was appointed ambassador to Moslem Turkey, a post later awarded to fellow Jew, Henry Morgenthau, Sr. Straus was the first Jewish member of the cabinet, serving as secretary of commerce and labor in President Theodore Roosevelt's administration. Morgenthau's son, Henry Jr., served as secretary of the treasury in Franklin Delano Roosevelt's cabinet. These were positions of honor but little power, awarded to able men loyally doing their best for their political patrons. The positions of genuine power were filled from the Establishment, membership in which was circumscribed by family and social standing.

There were Jewish members of Congress elected by their districts without regard to their religion, and there were those whose Jewishness was an important factor in their election. An example of the former was Lucius N. Littauer of Gloversville, New York, of the latter, Henry M. Goldfogle, Tammany's congressional gift to the Jews of New York in the first decades of the twentieth century. A loyal party man, and a Jewish communal figure (he was later president of Reform Congregation Rodeph Shalom), Goldfogle served both his political bosses and his constituency, and could be counted on to be the "Jewish voice" in the halls of Congress, though not always to the satisfaction of all elements. In 1914, and again in 1916 and 1920, the Jews of the Lower East Side elected Socialist labor lawyer Meyer London to the House. Sol Bloom, Adolph Sabath and Emanuel Celler had long careers in the House, their legislative longevity elevating them to positions of some influence.

The most visible Jewish political figure of the 1930s and 1940s was Herbert H. Lehman. Scion of a distinguished Jewish family, he became a political associate of Franklin D. Roosevelt, and rose to the governor's mansion in Albany and then to the United States Senate, ending his career of service as head of the War Refugee Board.

Particularly distinguished was the Jewish representation on the United States Supreme Court. Louis D. Brandeis, in association with Oliver Wendell Holmes, gave the Court a liberal legal climate receptive to post–World War II advances in civil rights and economic democracy. Benjamin N. Cardozo's briefs have become the model of lucidity. Felix Frankfurter brought to the bench the vast legal knowledge and keenness of mind which had made him a leading professor at the Harvard Law School. More recently, Arthur Goldberg's brief tenure came to an end when President Lyndon Johnson persuaded him to head the U.S. delegation to the United Nations; and the short tenure of Abe Fortas on the Supreme Court ended with his resignation.

The role of Jewish presidential advisers has generally been overestimated. Bernard Baruch did not discourage the media's descriptions of his influence as "adviser to presidents." Judge Samuel Rosenman was a respected counselor to President Franklin D. Roosevelt, but the influence of labor leader Sidney Hillman was vastly exaggerated, based on Roosevelt's widely quoted instruction to his lieutenants to "Clear it with Sidney" on the choice of an acceptable vice-presidential candidate.

Jacob Javits possessed the political acuity and intellectual vigor which should have taken him to a position of power, but he was a liberal in Republican garb, and a Jew in that most Protestant of clubs, the United States Senate. Only toward the end of his career did he begin to exert real influence.

German-born Henry Kissinger rose to the highest position held by a Jew in the American government, secretary of state. An early protégé of Nelson A. Rockefeller, Kissinger later joined President Richard M. Nixon, whose foreign affairs adviser he became. Kissinger was the architect of a reoriented American foreign policy: détente with Russia, reestablishment of relationships with China, launching a peace effort in the Near East.

The Jew has appeared in American politics; the Jews as a group, unlike the Irish and later the Italians, have not. Jews have never attempted to build political machines. The organized Jewish community has opted to retain a political fluidity to enable it to deal with the variety of power bases on the political scene. Jewish political power brokers have been as much used as rewarded by the political figures they serve. But Jewish voters have become more sophisticated and they have become more demanding of those asking for their votes. They are not loath to admit that there have been and are certain issues which have outweighed all others, among them unrestricted immigration, militant opposition to anti-Semitism, the outlawing of discrimination, the extension of civil rights, separation of Church and State, the welfare of fellow Jews everywhere and the security of the State of Israel.

Earl Raab's assessment of Jewish political power is most astute:

Although Jews accumulated a great deal of political power in those
few big cities in which they were concentrated, it was transmissible
to the centers of national power only under special circumstances.
The acid test was the extent to which the Jews could exert influence
on the decisions . . . concerning foreign policy. For the most part
they have had and continue to have very little influence beyond
what might be called the Rule of Marginal Effect. The sentiment
of the American Jewish community, no matter how strongly pressed,
will influence American foreign policy only to the extent that it
doesn't make any substantial difference to what are *otherwise* considered the best foreign-policy interests of the United States.[11]

14.

Changes and Challenges

THE YEAR 1981 WAS THE CENTENNIAL OF THE BEGINNING OF THE MASS MI-
gration from eastern Europe which brought more than two and one
half million Jews to America. The migration itself lasted some forty
years, an average adult life span. The effective, vital life of the institutions which the immigrant community created—the Yiddish press
and theater, the Talmud Torah schools and the Yiddish *folkshuls,* the
Orthodox Yiddish-oriented neighborhood synagogues, the all-purpose
religious functionaries, the Jewish leadership and membership of the
garment-worker unions, and the Yiddish speaking fraternal orders—
was of similar duration.

The once mighty *Jewish Daily Forward* is now a slim weekly
tabloid, as is the *Freiheit;* and the weekly *Algemeiner Journal* is sustained
by an Orthodox Yiddish-speaking community which arrived after World
War II. The Yiddish theater, with English commentary, is revived
annually. The Socialist Workmen's Circle (*Arbeiter Ring*), once boasting
a membership of over 80,000 supporting a whole network of schools
and camps, lecture forums and publications, the Labor-Zionist Jewish
National Workers Alliance (*Farband*) which also sustained schools and
camps, and the International Workers Order now serve a dwindling
number of surviving members. Efforts to enlist the American-born
children of members have met with little success.

The oldest and largest Jewish fraternal order, B'nai B'rith, established in 1843, has been able to sustain itself by adapting to the
changing needs of the Jewish community. For the first century of its
existence it was an organization of power and influence. It was the first

cultural export of American Jewry, going international in the last decades of the nineteenth century with lodges established in Western Europe and Palestine. The Jerusalem lodge was one of the first organizations in that city with an Ashkenazic and Sephardic membership; and Dr. Sigmund Freud, as cultural chairman of the Vienna lodge, presented some of his ground-breaking ideas to its membership in a series of lectures. It established the Anti-Defamation League in 1913 and sponsored the Hillel Foundations on campus, which aided two generations of Jews in effective integration into academic life. In 1943, it was the national Jewish body powerful enough to convene the American Jewish Conference. The ADL has acquired a life of its own; more and more of the Hillel Foundations are receiving local Jewish Federation sponsorship. In an era of the decline of fraternal orders, B'nai B'rith has become an international Jewish service organization.

The national Jewish organizations, once arbiters of the Jewish communal destiny—the American Jewish Committee and the American Jewish Congress—have become largely service agencies for social and cultural needs in the Jewish community. They serve the Jewish community with skill and effectiveness, but are no longer spokesmen for it. The effective power in the Jewish community has shifted to the local Jewish federations and through them to the Council of Jewish Federations and Welfare Funds. On matters of national and international import, the Conference of Presidents of Major American Jewish Organizations speaks for American Jewry.

The most active national Jewish organizations in America today are Hadassah and the National Council of Jewish Women. Hadassah has concentrated its work on health and educational services in Israel and cultural activities at home; NCJW has for almost ninety years contributed social services and worked with the successive Jewish immigrant groups arriving in America. These women's organizations have to an extraordinary degree been able to utilize the talents of a large corps of volunteers who accomplished their unpaid tasks with professional expertise and high devotion. The movement of America's women into the labor force has depleted the pool of voluntary workers that constituted the strength of these organizations, as well as that of Women's Ort, Pioneer Women, AMIT Women and the women's divisions of the UJA, the synagogal bodies and the local federations and synagogue sisterhoods.

The most significant development in Jewish organizational life in the 1970s and 1980s has been the entry of women into positions of leadership in national organizations and local federations and synagogues which had traditionally been male preserves. To be sure, much of Jewish organizational life and institutional service had long been sustained by an army of volunteer women, but it was always as secondary support battalions—the ubiquitous "women's divisions" of philanthropic organizations and the "ladies auxiliaries" of religious institutions.

The change to egalitarian participation has been dramatic. The percentage of women on boards of Federations and Federation-supported agencies increased from 14 percent in 1972 to 40 percent a decade later. Women have served as presidents of the Federations of New York, Los Angeles, Boston, Baltimore, Milwaukee, Houston and Dallas. Esther Leah Ritz serves as president of the National Jewish Welfare Board, Jacqueline Levine of the National Jewish Community Relations Advisory Council, Ruth B. Fein of the American Jewish Historical Society, Muriel M. Berman of the Jewish Publication Society and Evelyn E. Handler of Brandeis University.[1]

"Our readership," the editors of "The Jewish Women's Magazine" *Lilith* wrote, "is clearly concerned about Jewish life and eager for changes to enable all of us to participate in it fully and equally." It drew a profile of its readership:

Nearly 44% have graduate degrees and another 20–24% have done graduate study. Most (84%) have had some Jewish education. . . . The majority (57%) belong to Jewish organizations. More than half our readers had been to Israel and 48% belong to synagogues.[2]

The magazine is a vigorous proponent of full egalitarianism in all aspects of Jewish life, a subject which has become commonplace in Jewish periodicals. Fully two-thirds of the Winter 1984 issue of *Judaism,* the American Jewish Congress sponsored scholarly journal, is given to a symposium on "Women as Rabbis"; the April 1984 issue of *Genesis 2,* "an independent voice for Jewish renewal," is devoted to a "Special Focus On Judaism and Feminism"; the Spring 1984 issue of American Jewish Committee sponsored *Present Tense* features "Feminism Is Good For Women—and Men Too"; and the June-July 1984 issue of *Hadassah Magazine* announces on its cover "Spiritual Frontiers/Women In Ritual/ Women Cantors." The feature article "Women of Spirit" proclaims:

Inspired by the feminist movement as well as the *baal teshuva* movement [the Jewish phenomenon of return to religion], these women are working for innovation in all denominations in Judaism. As Reform and Conservative women become cantors and rabbis, Orthodox women also are beginning to study Gemara and Mishnah and to pray in their own groups—a practice considered shocking 10 years ago.[3]

THE RELIGIOUS ESTABLISHMENT

A survey of religious preference among American Jews conducted in the late 1970s by the National Jewish Population Study placed the percentages: Conservative, 40.4 percent; Reform, 30.0 percent; and Orthodox, 11.4 percent; with 12.2 percent "Just Jewish." An age distribution analysis indicates that the lower the age of the respondents the more liberal their religious preference. The national Jewish religious movements, their constituent bodies and their affiliated congregations have retained remarkable viability in the seventies and eighties (if not the vitality of the fifties and sixties) in an age in which ethnic designation has replaced religious identification, but each group faces serious problems, as does the synagogue itself.

During the first two decades of the century, Reform continued its drift away from tradition. A return to Traditionalism then began, at first hardly perceptible, then developing slowly, and finally bursting into great activity in the years following World War II. An increasing number of rabbis ordained by the Reform seminary, Hebrew Union College, came from East European Traditionalist background, and under the influence of Zionism, focused their interest on Jewish peoplehood and Jewish culture.

The Columbus Platform, adopted by the CCAR in 1937, affirmed "the obligation of all Jewry to aid in (Palestine's) upbuilding as a Jewish homeland," and called for "the preservation of the Sabbath, festivals and Holy Days, the retention and development of . . . customs, symbols and ceremonies . . . and the use of the Hebrew language in our worship and instruction."

Mass influx of sons and daughters of East European immigrants into the Reform congregations stimulated return to traditional forms in the temple and reintroduction of ritual into the home. The late Sabbath evening service on Friday night replaced the Sunday worship as the main service in almost all congregations. Use of Hebrew in the liturgy increased. *Bar* and *Bat Mitzvah, kiddush* and even *havdalah* became part of Reform practice. The formerly proscribed head-covering for men was made optional in many congregations; some even reintroduced the *tallit* for pulpit wear, and permitted it in the pews.

In 1976 the Central Conference of American Rabbis reassessed the "spiritual state of Reform Judaism," calling for a renewal of obligation to Jewish religious practice and to the surrvival of the Jewish people:

> The past century has taught us that the claims made upon us may begin with our ethical obligations but they extend to many other aspects of Jewish living including: creating a Jewish home centered on family devotion; life-long study; private prayer and public de-

votion; daily religious observance; keeping the Sabbath and holy days.

We have learned again that the survival of the Jewish people is of highest priority and that in carrying out our Jewish responsibilities we help move humanity toward its messianic fulfillment.[4]

Reform's turn to traditional forms has evoked organized resistance by a group of rabbis advocating the retention of classic Reform "verities" in ideology and practice. Ideological differences have resulted in political confrontation, and there is ferment beneath the placid waters of organizational unity. Of substantive concern is the phenomenon illustrated by the following, which appeared in *The New York Times* in July 1981:

> The marriage of F.F. . . . to Dr. L.S. . . . took place yesterday in Bethpage, L.I. The Rev. R.O'C. . . . and Rabbi D.B. performed the ceremony in St. Martin of Tours Roman Catholic Church.

Rabbi W. Gunther Plaut, president of the CCAR, in his report to the 1983 Biennial Convention of the Union of American Hebrew Congregations, complained that a "significant number of congregations judge the eligibility of a rabbi . . . first and foremost by the fact of whether he or she does not officiate at mixed marriages"—rejecting those who do not. The number of Reform rabbis who perform such religious ministration seems to be growing, yet so is the number of those who are turning to *halachic* guidance. Similar trends are evident in the laity. How long institutional unity will be able to encompass such growing polarity is the problem facing organized Reform Jewry.

In the era of Solomon Schechter, 1902–15, Conservative Judaism was an ideological reaction to Reform. It was a reaffirmation of the authority of *halacha*, as a living albeit changing system of law, custom and tradition. It emphasized the total historical religious experience of the Jewish people. Later, Conservative Judaism came into competitive confrontation with Orthodoxy. Orthodox congregations turned Conservative in hope of retaining the interest and loyalty of the new generation attracted by the Conservative emphasis on family worship and the congregational school. The movement adopted Mordecai M. Kaplan's definition of Judaism as "the evolving religious civilization of the Jewish people" and built synagogues which were cultural, spiritual and social centers.

Marshall Sklare, who published his study of the movement, *Conservative Judaism,* in 1955, took another look in 1970 and reported that, "Conservative Judaism has flourished during the past two decades." He further notes that the movement had achieved "primacy on the American Jewish religious scene," and that its synagogues have emerged particularly in the suburbs, "as the leading congregations in their communities." Yet, he notes, "the morale of the Conservative movement is on the decline. . . . It has lost its older confidence of being in possession of a formula that can win the support of younger Jews."

He attributes this erosion in morale and confidence in part to Conservatism's misreading of the future of Orthodoxy in America. It expected Orthodoxy's strength and influence to wane, when it in fact has risen. Another cause for the crisis in morale, especially among the rabbis, was what Sklare termed "Conservatism's defeat on the ritual front which can be demonstrated in almost every area of Jewish observance."[5]

A 1979 study of Conservative Jews disclosed that while twenty-nine percent kept kosher homes, only 7 percent claimed that they were "totally kosher." Sixty-five percent attended synagogue less than once a month and only 32 percent recited *kiddush* on Sabbath eve.[6]

An issue recently agitating Conservative Judaism has been the division within the rabbinate, the laity and the Jewish Theological Seminary faculty on the ordination of women. A vote of the faculty in October 1983 to accept women into the rabbinical school (two decades after the Hebrew Union College had done so) resulted in the formation of the Union for Traditional Conservative Judaism, a body of rabbis and laymen opposing "revolutionary change." Conservative Judaism, like Reform, seems to be facing a growing polarization.

Some Conservative and Reform congregations attempted to intensify the religious life of their congregants through the introduction of the *havurah,* created by Jewish students in the 1960s who saw it as their "duty to increase the positive elements in the community . . . to build a Jewish community that is creative." Bill Novak, editor of the student journal *Response,* described the *havurah* in 1970: "Merging the old idea of a small religious society with the new experiments in small communal groups with shared life-styles, the *havurot* have attempted to combine religious, social and educational aspects of one's personal life."[7]

Rabbi Harold M. Schulweis describes his synagogue, Valley Beth Shalom, Encino, California:

> In our congregation, a *havurah* is comprised of a minyan of families who have agreed to meet together at least once a month to learn together, to celebrate together and hopefully to form some surrogate for the eroded extended family. . . .
>
> From my pulpit I have never succeeded in getting many of my congregants to build a Succah. The *havurah* has succeeded. One needs the encouragement and help of other families and the goal of a family dinner in the Succah to motivate such activity. . . .
> There was a death in the *havurah*. The widow had few members

of the family around her; most were back East. I saw who was at the funeral, who took care of the children during the black week of the *shivah*. The widow remained within the *havurah*. . . . The *havurah* offers the synagogue member a community small enough to enable personal relationships to develop.[8]

The earliest experiences of East European Orthodoxy in America had been calamitous. The immigrants transplanted Old World synagogal forms to the New. Though these answered the immigrants' spiritual needs, they did not win the interest or allegiance of their children. The Orthodox reaction was to withdraw into self-contained communities and spiritual and cultural isolation. Forward-looking leaders, taking example from the neo-Orthodoxy of Samson Raphael Hirsch of Frankfurt am Main, launched an attempt at making the traditional faith at home in the modern world. Their efforts took the form of a *yeshiva*-university, where young men would receive modern high-school and college training while studying the sacred texts in the traditional manner, in an Orthodox religious atmosphere.

Yeshiva University and its Rabbi Isaac Elchanan Theological Seminary graduated a generation of rabbis, teachers and lay leaders who have given renewed vitality to Orthodoxy. Orthodox Jews are found on college faculties, in the laboratories and in communal and cultural life. The Orthodox congregations have taken on new life, though the price has sometimes been the adoption of new forms borrowed from more liberal coreligionists. In the post–World War II years, there was a growth of fundamentalist Traditionalism in Orthodoxy, largely occasioned by the immigration of Hasidim from Central Europe, and a new militancy on the part of native-born Orthodox leaders, who were critical of what they considered Yeshiva University's religious liberalism.

Dr. Samuel Belkin, president of Yeshiva University, saw in 1956 "religious life on this continent divided into three parts." One group, despairing of the possibility of traditional Jewish life in America, offers an "easygoing *translated Judaism,* a Judaism which requires no great sacrifices, a Judaism which may be acquired with little effort." Another, certain that Judaism can only be lived apart and separate from the contemporary environment, "*transfers,* without the slightest change, the traditional Jewish way of life that their forefathers lived for centuries on the European continent." And there is what their critics call "enlightened Orthodoxy." Its aim is not merely to *transfer* the European model of piety to the American soil. Says Dr. Belkin: "Our philosophy is one of integration and we firmly deny that our integration in the American community in any way implies the abrogation of even one iota of our sacred tradition."[9]

Rabbi Oscar Z. Fasman, who had served as president of the

Hebrew Theological College (Chicago), wrote in 1979: "From the gloom of '29 to the zoom of '79—this has been my experience with American orthodoxy."[10]

Already in 1965 Charles S. Liebman asserted in his study of Orthodoxy published in the *American Jewish Year Book* that "there is a recognition and admiration for Orthodoxy as the only group which today contains within it a strength and will to live that may yet nourish all the Jewish world."[11] There is today a triumphalism in the fundamentalist sectors of the Orthodox community occasioned by their ability to retain the religious loyalty of even their academically trained children and to attract "converts" to Traditionalism—*baalei t'shuvah* they call themselves—who come from nontraditional Jewish backgrounds. To the studies which point to decreasing numbers of Orthodox they answer that most traditional Jews do not respond to pollsters, and that in a voluntary society intensity of commitment is more an indication of health and strength than numbers. But Orthodoxy, for all its increasing visibility, constititutes a diminishing percentage of American Jewry. Splintered by ideological and *halachic* differences which now and again flare up into political conflict, Orthodoxy is moving away from the main-line community into a self-imposed isolation, which may insulate it against corrosive influences, but which in turn vitiates its influence on the Jewish community at large.

"The Synagogue must become a Beth-Am," Mordecai M. Kaplan urged in 1927, "a neighborhood center where Jews may foster their social and cultural as well as religious interests."[12] On West Eighty-sixth Street in New York, he had built the prototype of the synagogue center he espoused, with a synagogue, classrooms, dining and lecture halls, clubrooms, a gymnasium and a swimming pool. In the years between world wars, the synagogue-center replaced the temple and the *shul* as the representative American synagogue, and in post–World War II America the synagogue attained the position of centrality and power in the Jewish community.

The move to the suburbs and the need for the new "suburban immigrants" to establish their presence made the founding of congregations necessary. Jews became part of their new community through their synagogue, which was welcomed as part of the suburban landscape.

The rabbi as leader and representative of a religious community had status in the Jewish and general communities. Consequently a corps of gifted men were attracted to the rabbinate and the challenge of their office developed latent talents and energies. From the twenties to the fifties, rabbis occupied positions of influence on the national Jewish scene and in local Jewish and general communities. Stephen S. Wise, Abba Hillel Silver, Solomon Goldman, James G. Heller and Israel Goldstein played central roles in the development of Zionism in America. Wise had entrée to the White House when the incumbent was a Democrat; Silver was respected by members of the highest echelons of the Republican party. Joshua Loth Liebman's best-selling *Peace of Mind* raised him to national prominence as a religious teacher, and the books and lectures of Milton Steinberg made him a spokesman to American Jewish intelligentsia. In their communities, Solomon B. Freehof in Pittsburgh, Morris Adler in Detroit, Philip S. Bernstein in Rochester and many others were counted among the most distinguished citizens. All were pulpit rabbis, their pulpits providing a forum from which to ascend to national prominence.

In 1960, Marshall Sklare pointed out that the visible success of the synagogue in terms of affiliation was a source of danger to it as a religious institution. Those filling its rolls were in large measure secularized Jews who had departed "in attitudes and life patterns from religious norms." [13] Their presence might well turn the synagogue into an institution serving the desires of its members rather than the demands of the Jewish religious tradition.

Added to the spiritual problem is the sociological fact that the local Jewish Community Federation is now replacing the synagogue as the central institution in Jewish communal life. Much of the lay leadership of a community is attracted to the federation where, because of its control of large sums of money, the exercise of power is greater. The able young people looking for a career of Jewish social service, and who in times past could find it almost solely in the rabbinate, now have the option of the university faculty where tensions are less and satisfactions greater, or federation service, where, as one put it, "the action is." The relocation of population from city to suburb, from the North to the Sunbelt, imposes increasing financial burdens on synagogues which are edifice and facilities-centered: to maintain the existing buildings and programs in the face of decreasing membership and income.

Still, for reasons both Jewish and American, American Jewry defines itself as a religious community. The synagogue is its most enduring and pervasive institution; Jewishness is expressed through religious celebrations and observance, which are viewed as simultaneously cultural and national. This is not to say that the community is defined by piety. Though there are pious Jews in America, those who are less pious consider themselves no less Jewish. Whether less or more devout, American Jews have found that ritual observance and liturgy add dimension to their Jewish identity and being. For some, *mitzvot,* the Sabbath, the festivals and Holy Days mark the rhythm of life; for others they offer meaning and uplift; for nearly all, they serve as a bond with the Jewish people, past and present.

The National Jewish Population Study (NJPS) on Jewish Identity found that while 83.4 percent of America's Jews observed Passover and 75.2 percent celebrated Hanukkah, only 36.7 percent kept the Sabbath and only 25.9 percent the laws of *kashrut*.[14] (The percentages refer to some form of observance, not necessarily to the full traditional ways.) The study further indicated that "discipline observances," i.e., those of the Sabbath and of *kashrut,* were diminishing, while "celebration observances" seemed to retain their hold. For the great majority of American Jews, Jewishness is evidently a leisuretime activity, expressing itself more in celebrations than in duties and disciplines, more through shared activities with fellow Jews than through ritual obedience.

DEMOGRAPHIC PROBLEMS: BIRTHRATE AND MOBILITY

A 1972 study of comparative population distribution in America by age levels disclosed:

Age Group	Percentage of Population	
	Total	Jewish
10–14	10.0	9.7
5–9	9.7	6.8
0–4	8.4	4.0

The National Jewish Population Study figures for the Jewish youngest age group are not quite so low, but they are still some 30 percent below the corresponding figure for the total population.

In 1977, Elihu Bergman of the Harvard Center for Population Studies predicted, "When the United States celebrates its Tricentennial in 2076 the American Jewish community is likely to number no more than 944,000 persons. . . ."[15] Bergman attributed present and projected population losses to two causes: a birthrate below replacement level, and assimilation, due mainly to intermarriage. A critique of Bergman's prognosis by Samuel Lieberman and Morton Weinfeld[16] projects a slow rise in U.S. Jewish population up to the year 2000, then a steady decline to 3.9 million by 2070. The slump in the Jewish birthrate is so severe that it may well be the single most serious threat to Jewish survival in America.

Among American Jews in their late twenties in 1980 three-quarters of the men and one-half of the women had completed university studies; over one-third had postgraduate professional degrees. Increasingly America's Jews are becoming a community of professionals— either self-employed, such as doctors, lawyers, accountants, or salaried, such as teachers, scientists, engineers and workers in communications fields. The salaried group is steadily increasing, and is one of the most mobile population segments. Self-employed professionals generally relocate only once, from their birthplace to wherever they can best use their training; but salaried professionals tend to move from position to position and from city to city. Figures from an NJPS[17] study in the late seventies illustrate the high mobility prevalent in the Jewish community, especially among its younger members. Among persons aged 30 to 34, some 29 percent expected to move within five years; among those aged 25 to 29, the figure was 61 percent. In the 30 to 34 age group, 58 percent had already moved at least once in the last ten years.

Mobility tends to weaken the extended family; the nuclear family relocates, leaving older generations behind. (Fully 87 percent of American Jews above 65 live alone or with only their spouses.) Mobility can disrupt the nuclear family itself; there is a marked rise in the divorce rate after moving. The effects on the quality of Jewish life, on Jewish loyalty, are serious, particularly because so much of the Jewish living is family-centered. In a disrupted family, grandparents—and in cases of divorce, fathers or mothers—are no longer steadily present to convey Jewish ways of life to the children.

Mobility also weakens communal structure. Communities need stability; loyalty to institutions grows from long usage and family tradition. A mobile population, often avid consumers of communal services, rarely gives adequate support to communal institutions.

The majority of present-day American Jews were either raised in immigrant homes or were themselves immigrants. More than one-quarter are foreign-born and fewer than one-fifth have American-born grandparents. A century ago, the community, now well over five and one-half million strong, numbered about a quarter of a million. In the course of the century the Jewish population multiplied by a factor of twenty-two (while the general population of the United States increased four and one-half fold).

Long a host community, American Jewry is faced with the challenge of integrating into its communal life two new immigrant groups, from Israel and from the Soviet Union. Each presents an unprecedented problem. Unlike preceding immigrants who hastened to become Americans, many Israelis retain their Israeli nationality, asserting they are temporary residents. They therefore feel no compelling need to become integrated into American Jewish communal life. Unlike earlier newcomers, the great majority of Russian immigrants arrive with minimal Jewish knowledge and little or no experience of Jewish communal living. They view integration into Jewish life with ambivalence.

Since the days of mass migration, American Jewry has been one of the world's major Jewish communities. For over two generations, it has been the largest. It constitutes, however, only a small minority of the American nation, and that is diminishing—from a high of some 3.7 percent in the 1930s to 2.5 percent in the 1980s. (In 1983, America's 5,728,000 Jews constituted 2.47 percent of the population.) There is concern about the loss of influence which may result from such attrition. The concentration of over three-fourths of America's Jews in ten urban areas is viewed with some apprehension. These areas are the loci of greatest social tensions and would be the first to be torn by strife in times of serious economic stress or political upheaval.

INTERMARRIAGE

In 1845, Mordecai M. Noah warned that if marriage between Jews and Gentiles would be permitted, the American Jew would disappear within two or three generations.[18] In 1872, W. M. Rosenblatt, as we have noted, wrote in *The Galaxy* that "the second generation born on American soil . . . will be indistinguishable from the mass of humanity which surrounds them,"[19] because of intermarriage. Rabbi David Einhorn declared in 1870 that to lend a hand to mixed marriage was "to furnish a nail to the coffin of the small Jewish race,"[20] and in 1934, Mordecai M. Kaplan sounded the alarm: "Intermarriage . . . if left uncontrolled is bound to prove Judaism's undoing."[21]

What has been the incidence of intermarriage in American Jewry? What does it mean? and what are its implications?

Malcolm H. Stern's genealogical work, *Americans of Jewish Descent,* records that of 699 marriages contracted by Jews between 1776 and 1840, 201 (28.7 percent) were out marriages.[22] This high percentage may be attributed to the small size of the Jewish community: 1500 in 1776, some 10,000 in 1840. Throughout the nineteenth century, intermarriage occurred in inverse proportion to the size of the Jewish community; the larger the number of Jews grew, the fewer people chose non-Jewish mates. In the large East European immigrant community that developed after 1880, intermarriage was rare; in 1912, an estimate placed the rate for all Jews in America at only 2 percent.

Two sets of statistics might have alerted American Jewry to an impending upturn in the rate. In 1920, Julius Drachsler published a table of intermarriage rates among New York Jews by country of origin, which indicated that those who had lived longest under emancipation and had attained a degree of social integration had the highest intermarriage rates from 0.45, 0.62, 0.8 per one hundred marriages for those born in Romania, Russia and Turkey, to 4.26, 5.16, 6.54 for those born in the United States, Germany and France. [23] Similarly, in 1957, Aryeh Tartakower cited strikingly high intermarriage rates between 1920 and 1930 in certain large cities in Central Europe where freedom and integration had long obtained. The figures ranged from 25 percent in

Vienna and 28 percent in Budapest to 45 percent in Berlin and no less than 71 percent in Trieste.[24]

When in 1957 the U.S. Census Survey disclosed a rate of 7.2 percent, little concern was voiced. But only six years later a lead article by Erich Rosenthal in the 1963 *American Jewish Year Book*[25] cited intermarriage rates of 42 percent for the state of Iowa and 13 percent for Washington, D.C., and indicated that over 70 percent of the children of intermarried couples in Washington were being raised as non-Jews. Though some observers pointed to the small number of Jews in Iowa and argued that Washington was an atypical community, Rosenthal's article placed intermarriage high on the agenda of Jewish concerns, where it has remained.

What most disturbed those concerned with Jewish survival was the thought, then generally accepted, that the great majority of children born of intermarriage were certain to be lost to the Jewish community. Intermarriage was—or was perceived as—an act of alienation, defiance, rejection or upward social mobility. One remembers the Schoenberg who became a Belmont, the Goldwasser who became a Goldwater, and wonders what had become of the descendants of the Jewish families of great wealth: Seligman, Guggenheim, Lewisohn, Straus, Lehman? Obviously, persons marrying out for such reasons could not be expected to raise their children in the cultural traditions of the group from which they had cut themselves loose. By the 1960s and 1970s, the chief factor in marrying out was no longer rebellion; it was proximity. Exodus to the suburbs, resulting social integration of the young in schools and neighborhoods, and the influx of Jews into more fully integrated universities led to interdating, which in turn often led to marriage.

If marrying out was not caused by defiance or rebellion, it might be expected that many Jews married to non-Jews would want their children to be raised in their own religious or cultural traditions, and the data of the National Jewish Population Study seem to bear out this expectation.[26] Between 1966 and 1972, 31.7 percent of Jews who married chose a non-Jewish mate. (Intermarriage was defined as any marriage where one partner had been identified as a non-Jew at the time of meeting the other, even if either partner subsequently converted to Judaism before marrying.) Jewish men married non-Jewish women twice as often as vice versa; more than one-quarter of non-Jewish women but few non-Jewish men who married Jews converted to Judaism; virtually no Jews converted to other religions; and nearly half of the non-Jews married to Jews without converting eventually came to identify themselves as Jewish.

As for the religious orientation of children, where the wife was the Jewish partner, a "very high proportion" of the children were raised as Jews; where the husband was the Jewish partner, "more than one-third of the children . . . are being raised outside a Jewish religious-cultural viewpoint." The true figures are probably lower, because intermarried families who opt for a non-Jewish identity are likely to be left out of a Jewish population study. Even so the indications are, as Lieberman and Weinfeld conclude, that there may well be no significant loss of Jewish population due to intermarriage.

Quantity is, of course, not the only consideration. How much Jewish loyalty can an intermarried couple transmit to the children, and how much Jewish commitment can be expected of children who have non-Jewish extended families? A study on intermarriage, sponsored by the American Jewish Committee and directed by Dr. Egon Mayer, makes a distinction between mixed marriage, where no conversion has taken place, and *conversionary marriage,* where the non-Jewish partner has converted to Judaism. It discloses that:

> In most mixed marriages, the born-Jewish spouse affirms a Jewish identity, but does little to act on this affirmation. Only a minority . . . provide formal Jewish education for their children. . . .
> On every index of Jewish attitudes and practice, couples whose born-Gentile spouses have converted to Judaism scored higher than other intermarried couples. Indeed, based on what is known about the religious and ethnic life in endogamous marriages, the family life of conversionary marriages is more consciously Jewish, both in religious practice and in formal and informal Jewish acculturation of children.[27]

The study concludes:

> Since intermarriage is likely to increase, rather than decrease . . . the greatest counterbalance to the assimilationist thrust of such marriages, in the short run, would seem to be an increase in the conversion rate among born-Gentile spouses . . . the Jewish community would do well to examine what steps it can take to encourage such moves.[28]

Shlomo Riskin, a popular Orthodox rabbi, in a letter soliciting contributions for his Ohr Torah Institute in 1984, raises the alarm of "the scourge of assimilation" which threatens the Jewish community with a Holocaustlike devastation. He lists as its signals: an intermarriage rate "approaching 47%"; that "82% of our children do not attend synagogue"; and the "declining figures for congregational affiliation, Hebrew school enrollment, and membership in Jewish communal organizations."

Charles E. Silberman reported at the 1983 General Assembly of the Council of Jewish Federations:

After four and a half years of research that have taken me the length and breadth of this continent, I am persuaded that the end is *not* at hand, that Judaism is *not* about to disappear in the United States. The overwhelming majority of American Jews are choosing to remain Jews. . . . We are, in the early stages of a major revitalization of Jewish religious, intellectual and cultural life. . . . Young Jews freely choose to be observant . . . with a seriousness, vitality, imagination, elan . . . and a fund of Jewish knowledge that are wholly new to American Jewish life.

The American Jewish scene offers ample documentation for both the fear of Riskin and the faith of Silberman. American Jews, like other Jews before them, live within a paradox of faith and fear—the faith that theirs is an eternal people, and the fear that their generation may be the last. Survival of the Jewish community is conditional. Do not God's assurances of the eternity of this people begin with an "If . . ."?

American Jews' morale for survival is bolstered by their historic experience in America. They are here despite the prophecies of doom pronounced in every generation. And they can look back to ideologies and strategies of survival which made possible the ongoing enterprise of creative Jewish survival in a free and open society.

15.

Survival in a Free Society

IN AMERICA, THE JEW HAS EXPERIENCED EMANCIPATION AND ENLIGHTEN-ment to their furthest reaches. A common citizenship tended to erase distinctions of creed and nationality in the unfolding social and cultural scene. Whereas in the European community, assimilation had demanded an act of disassociation from one's own group—usually apostasy—in America one would become assimilated into the larger community unless he or she expressed, in word or deed, identification with the community into which he or she was born.

Assimilation was facilitated by many factors in America: No governmental designation of "Jew," small isolated communities, continued movement of immigrants uninhibited by communal or family restraints, no ancestral memories evoked by neighborhood, no webs of social relationships extending over generations. The maverick spirit, the social mobility of a frontier society and the overriding ideology of a unified America, which later observers termed the melting pot, further facilitated smooth entry into the larger society. In the context of such an America, the Jews who wished to retain their Jewishness had to fashion an identity which would be acceptable to America and which would prove vital to themselves. In this enterprise, they could look to the solution to the similar challenge worked out by Jews in Europe entering the modern world.

EUROPEAN PRECEDENTS

Jews of Western Europe learned early in their experience of enlightenment and emancipation that the society which was beginning to open its doors to them was asking that they justify their continued corporate existence; and that the national state which was haltingly extending civic and political rights was asking for a public group identity which would fit comfortably into the body politic and would be compatible with fullest loyalty to the nation. These twin demands were given dramatic expression in the Swiss clergyman Reverend Johann Casper Lavater's challenge to Moses Mendelssohn in 1769 to refute Christianity or to accept it, and by Napoleon's twelve questions to the Assembly of Jewish Notables convened in 1806, which asked: Can Jews abiding in their Jewishness be full participants in the life of the modern state? More pointedly, Lavater suggested the need for Jews to justify their continued existence, and Napoleon pointed to the need for a new definition of Jewish corporate identity. The response to the latter challenge was direct and immediate. Abraham Furtado well expressed it: "We no longer are a nation within a nation." Joseph Marie Portalis *fils,* a commissioner of Napoleon, described it: "The Jews ceased to be a people and remained only a religion."

Their new definition as a "religious community," the emancipated Jews felt certain, would make their status more comprehensible and more acceptable to their neighbors. But the need to explain, to justify continued Jewish existence persisted. Of what benefit is it to the nation, of what value to the Jew? Why should the modern world tolerate Jewish survival? Why should a Jew remain a Jew?

Ideological justification for Jewish survival in the modern world was formulated by Reform Judaism in Germany early in the nineteenth century. Seizing upon the then popular theory—which nationalism made emotionally acceptable and intellectually respectable—that each people is endowed with a unique native genius, Rabbi Abraham Geiger applied it to the Jews. The ancient Greeks, he noted, possessed a national genius for art, philosophy and science. The Jewish people, he asserted, are likewise endowed with a religious genius, which it is obligated to use in service to mankind. Rabbi Samuel Holdheim, among others, expressed what came to be known as the Mission Idea.

> It is the destiny of Judaism to pour the light of its thoughts, the fire of its sentiments, the fervor of its feelings, upon all the souls and hearts on earth . . . It is the Messianic task of Israel to make the pure law of morality of Judaism the common possession and blessing of all the peoples on earth.[1]

The Mission Idea, which held that Israel is a *religious community* charged with the divine task to bring the knowledge of the One God and the message of ethical monotheism to the world, made Jewish group survival acceptable in the modern national state. It provided the ideological justification for continued communal existence: the world needs this "priest-people" and its "God-ordained mission" of spiritual service; the Jew, as a Jew, in undertaking this divine mission fulfills the noblest of purposes in life, service to mankind.

THE MELTING POT

The challenge posed by emancipation and enlightenment was altered in the New World by the new context of Jewish existence. In the European experience emancipation was the end product of a long struggle, in part a victory won, in part a gift granted. The declaration which announced American nationhood proclaimed liberty not as a gift but as an unalienable right. In the unfolding social and cultural climate of the New World there were, in theory, no doors barring entry into mainstream America; one assimilated into the larger society, unless one chose voluntarily to retain his group identity.

Throughout the nineteenth century, the melting pot concept (though the term was used only in the twentieth) demanded cultural assimilation of immigrants. As early as 1782, Michel Guillaume Jean de Crèvecoeur had noted:

> He is an American, who leaving behind him all his ancient prej-
> udices and manners, receives new ones from the new mode of life
> he has embraced, the new government he obeys, and the new rank
> he holds . . . Here individuals of all nations are melted into a new
> race of men.

In 1845 Ralph Waldo Emerson wrote in his Journal: "In this continent-asylum of all nations . . . all the European tribes . . . will construct a new race, a new religion, a new state."

Later, the Anglo-Jewish writer Israel Zangwill, in his play *The Melting Pot* (1908), would apply this concept to the Jewish experience in America. A young Russian-Jewish composer is writing an "American" symphony, celebrating an America where a new nation is being forged. The symphony completed and performed, David Quixano speaks his vision:

> America is God's crucible, the Great Melting Pot, where all races
> of Europe are melting and reforming . . . Celt and Latin, Slav and
> Teuton, Greek and Syrian, black and yellow, Jew and Gentile . . .
> How the great Alchemist melts and fuses them with his purging
> flame! . . . Here shall they all unite to build the Republic of Man
> and the Kingdom of God. Peace, peace unto ye unborn millions
> fated to fill this giant continent—the God of our children give you
> Peace.[2]

This was America as perceived by immigrant Jews. It demanded of them that they divest themselves of their distinctive ways, and absorb and adopt the language, the values, the ways of native American culture. It was an enticing invitation, an opportunity to rise above minority status and become members of God's new Chosen People—the American nation. If it was difficult for the immigrant to cast off the known and the habitual which provided them with stability in the new and threatening environment, it was easy and alluring for their children to wash away the marks of Old World peculiarity and become *Americans*.

The same America which called for ethnic and cultural assimilation accepted religious differentiation. The retention of a particular religious identity was viewed as a contribution to the well-being of a nation which was a gathering of peoples. The sense of continuity and security which the immigrants needed to feel at home in their new home could be provided by a transplanted church. "The immigrants thought it important," Oscar Handlin noted, "to bring their churches to the United States." For the sake of national unity, the nation willed the immigrant to take on new political loyalties, new cultural ways, but for the sake of social well-being it permitted religious diversity.

Organized religion was esteemed in nineteenth-century America because, as Louis B. Wright concluded, it was the most effective "of all the agencies utilized by man in maintaining traditional civilization on the successive frontiers in America."[3] It was not lost on the Jews, newly arrived in America, that here churches and other religious institutions were favored, those who supported them respected, and that the synagogue was viewed as an American religious institution. They therefore maintained the synagogue not only in support of their own Jewish interests, but also as an expression of patriotic obligation. Dr. Jacob De La Motta expressed it at the dedication of the Mikveh Israel synagogue in Savannah, Georgia in 1820: "Were we not influenced by religious zeal, a decent respect to the custom of the community in which we live should actuate us to observe public worship."[4]

Building a house of worship in America was not so much an act of piety as an expression of good citizenship; maintaining it was bearing witness to America as a land of freedom and opportunity.

Identity as a religious community established the appropriate corporate status for Jewish survival in America; justification for that survival required an ideology with roots in Jewish ideals and experience, as well as a promise of service to America and the world. The Mission Idea of Reform Judaism served well the West European immigrant Jew. It lifted the difficult and anxiety-filled experience of relocation to an enterprise of high, selfless purpose. It fit in well with the rhetoric used to vindicate America's national expansion in the language of "mission" and "manifest destiny."

The rabbinic conferences which formulated the ideology of Classic Reform affirmed these emphases. The Philadelphia Conference of 1869 stressed the messianic goal of Israel, defining the dispersion of the Jews in terms of divine purpose; the Pittsburgh Conference of 1885 proclaimed: "We consider ourselves no longer a nation, but a religious community." Such a status enabled the Jews to retain communal identity, while becoming integrated into the American nation.

The Jewish religious community proclaimed itself a partner and co-worker with other religious denominations in "doing God's work," and allied itself with progressive forces outside the religious establishment. The Pittsburgh Conference stated:

> We acknowledge that the spirit of broad humanity of our age is our ally in the fulfillment of our mission, and therefore we extend the hand of fellowship to all who operate with us in the establishment of the reign of truth and righteousness of men.[5]

As a religious community whose dominant ideology was the Mission Idea, and which sought alliances with the forces of "broad humanity," it was closer in spirit and practices to liberal Christianity than to traditional Judaism. There were, of course, factors which bound Jews of all persuasions one to another, factors such as national and historic identity, but these were precisely those which Reform chose to suppress. By the end of the nineteenth century American Jews had evolved a public identity which, they were certain, America would understand and accept: a religious community in a larger setting of cultural assimilation.

By the beginning of the twentieth century, it became apparent that, while such an identity might be acceptable to America, it could not serve Jewish survival needs. It deprived Judaism of the cultural-national vitality which gave it viability, and it made no provision for the growing number of Jews who defined their Jewish identity as cultural rather than religious.

The first serious call for a redefinition of identity came from a venerated leader of Reform Judaism, Rabbi Bernhard Felsenthal. In his "Fundamental Principles of Judaism," published in the first issue of the Zionist periodical *The Maccabean* (November 1901), he states:

> *Judaism* and *Jewish Religion* are not synonymous . . . *Jewish religion* is only part of *Judaism* . . . *Judaism* is the sum of all ethnological characteristics which have their roots in the distinctively Jewish national spirit . . . The Jewish People is the fixed, the permanent, the necessary substratum, the essential nucleus. Judaism is not a universal religion. There would be no Judaism without Jews.[6]

Felsenthal shifted the definition of identity from religious concepts to the living community of Jews. To be sure, Judaism contains "certain universal elements, certain absolute and eternal truths," but "Judaism does not limit itself to these universal elements." It requires "a certain characteristic ritual, certain established national days of consecration, certain defined national symbols and ceremonies." Survival demands an acceptance of Jewish distinctiveness and the fostering of those elements of culture and nationality which constitute the "national Jewish religion." How does a national religion serve larger humanity? Felsenthal suggested that as each national religion strengthens its inner wisdom and truth, and "exerts beneficial influence upon its particular nation, it also adds to the adornment of all humanity."

The realities of American life led Felsenthal to accept the organization of American Jewry as a religious community, with the synagogue as its central institution. But, he reminded, "The Jews are *not only* a religious community, and Judaism is *not only a religion.*"[7] As implementation of his broader definition of Judaism, he urged commitment to Zionism and greater emphasis on Jewish culture and folkways. What was crucial to him was that the Jews organized as a religious community accept a broad cultural-national definition of Judaism, and that this be reflected in the life—purpose, programs, activities—of the congregation and community.

From the camp of traditional Jewry in the first decades of the twentieth century came a voice calling for reassertion of *national* Jewish identity. Israel Friedlaender, professor at the Conservative Jewish Theological Seminary, and a founder of the Young Israel movement in Orthodoxy, argued that a religion divorced from nationality and culture was false to authentic Judaism, and could therefore neither save nor survive.[8] If Judaism is to continue in America, he argued,

> it must break the narrow frame of a creed and resume its original function as a culture, as the expression of the Jewish spirit and the whole of Jewish life. The Jew must have the courage to be different, to think his own thoughts, to feel his own feelings, to live his own life . . . but with the consciousness that only in this way does he fulfill his destiny, for the benefit of mankind.

Friedlaender envisioned a Judaism "that does not confine itself to synagogues and hospitals, but endeavors to embrace the breadth and width of modern life." He urges a reassessment of the possibilities of Judaism in the American environment—a Judaism comprised of national and cultural as well as religious elements. "The true American spirit," he observes, "understands and respects the traditions and associations of other nationalities." The American idea of liberty "signifies liberty of conscience, the full, untrammeled development of the soul." Judaism owes it not only to itself but to America to become the center "of the spiritual life of the Jewish people in the dispersion," for in doing so it will become "a most valuable and stimulating factor in the public and civic life." Friedlaender questioned the melting pot concept as being truly reflective of the American spirit, and rejected the implication that "Americanization" demands cultural assimilation. He laid the foundation for what was later termed cultural pluralism by pointing to the receptivity of America to national cultures, and to the contribution which an ethnic culture, sustained and developed, would make to American civilization.

Both Felsenthal and Friedlaender recognized that the realities of American life mandated that American Jewry be organized as a religious community, but they argued for a definition which was based not on American models but on the Jewish historic tradition. Religious leaders could plead for attention to inner Jewish spiritual and cultural needs, but immigrant Jews and their children had a higher priority, the need to be accepted by America—an America still conceived as a melting pot. What was needed was a new image of America—an America which would approve of a distinctive Jewish identity and welcome Jewish cultural creativity and expression.

CULTURAL PLURALISM

The danger to Jewish survival in the melting pot vision of America was attacked by two secular ideologists, Chaim Zhitlowsky and Horace M. Kallen. Each, from his own viewpoint, called the concept inimical to American civilization.

Zhitlowsky, the leading proponent of secular Yiddish cultural life in America, argued that the melting pot was neither desirable nor possible, for it robbed American civilization of the richness which variety bestows, and the ethnic groups in response to their own needs would turn from such an America. He called upon America to harbor the "united nationalities of the United States." He proposed a "nationality-brotherhood," where "each individuality unfolds and brings out into the open all the richness with which its soul may be blessed by nature."

Such a peaceful, creative unity of national cultures would lead to mutual enrichment. The individual nationalities would become channels which would carry to their homelands, and thus to the world, the most precious gift America could give, a model for a United States of the World. His is a secular restatement of the mission idea in the context of America. To the Jews it proclaimed that retaining their cultural national identity was a service to America, helping America to fulfill its world mission.[9] Zhitlowsky failed, for he made the vehicle of national expression the Yiddish language, but he prepared the immigrant generation for acceptance of the practical application of cultural pluralism.

It was Kallen, Harvard-educated disciple of William James, who gave currency to the concept "cultural pluralism." His article "Democracy *Versus* the Melting Pot" appeared in *The Nation* on February 18 and 25, 1915, its argument that true democracy demands a vision of America other than a melting pot. Kallen concluded his seminal essay with "the outlines of a possibly great and truly democratic commonwealth":

> Its form would be that of the federal republic; its substance a democracy of nationalities, cooperating voluntarily and autonomously through common institutions in the enterprise of self-realization through the perfection of men according to their kind. . . . "American civilization" may come to mean . . . multiplicity in a unity, an orchestration of mankind. As in an orchestra every type of instrument has its specific *timbre* and *tonality* . . . so in society, each ethnic group may be the natural instrument, its temper and culture may be its theme and melody and the harmony and dissonances and discords of them all may make the symphony of civilization . . . and the range and variety of the harmonies may become wider and richer and more beautiful.[10]

As Kallen later stated, his vision of America grew out of his Jewish cultural milieu. In his 1910 essay, "Judaism, Hebraism, Zionism," he had declared his commitment "to the persistence of a 'Jewish separation' that shall be national, positive, dynamic and adequate." Critical of those who would take from the Jewish group its group identity and uniqueness, he rejected Reform's recasting the nature of corporate Jewish existence. Kallen's concept of cultural pluralism, his vision of an America enriched by its distinctive ethnic groups, provided justification for continued Jewish communal life. What Zhitlowsky was saying to his immigrant, Yiddish-speaking, European-oriented audiences, Kallen was advocating for the "Americanized" Jew: the individual's need of life-giving cultural sustenance within his own ethnic group, and the benefit of such corporate cultural activity to the nation.

In American Jewish life, the period between the two world wars was the era of cultural pluralism, in which Jewish life underwent significant change. The "Americanizing" settlement houses were replaced by Jewish community centers. The communal Talmud Torah became the most prominent and successful Jewish educational institution. Hebrew, Zionist and Yiddish culture found expression in synagogue, center, school and summer camp programs. In response to the new definition

of Judaism and the new understanding of American democracy, synagogues began to transform themselves from "houses of worship" to
"synagogue-centers," offering a broad spectrum of activities "for every
member of every family."

JUDAISM AS A CIVILIZATION

The chief philosopher of the redefinition of Judaism was Mordecai M. Kaplan and the title of his magnum opus, *Judaism as a Civilization,* sums up his definition.

Judaism is "the evolving religious civilization of the Jewish people." The Jewish people is the enduring, creative constant. Civilization
includes "peoplehood, history, language, music, literature and art."
The motive force of this civilization is religion, and like the civilization
itself, religion is evolving, growing, changing. Yet basic forms persist:
"The conservation of form with the reconstruction of meaning has been
the history of the Jewish civilization."[11] The citizen of a modern state,
Kaplan argued, "is not only permitted but encouraged to give allegiance
to two civilizations; one, the secular civilization of the country in which
he lives, and the other the Christian which he has inherited from the
past."[12] Thus the American Jew lives at one and the same time in two
civilizations, that of America and that of his group.

Kaplan felt no need to offer justification for Jewish group survival, because, "if Jewish life is a unique way of experience, it needs
no justification."[13] But the need for justification was felt, nonetheless,
and it was provided by Kaplan's most gifted disciple, Rabbi Milton
Steinberg. In *To Be or Not to Be a Jew,* Steinberg made an eloquent plea
for *living in two civilizations.* He recognized that Jews "are accustomed
to the circumstance that Americans will be identified with minority
churches. After all, every religious denomination in our country is of
such a character *vis-à-vis* the total population." But the Jew, he argued,
is "associated with a cultural tradition as well." Thus, the American
Jew has two cultural traditions, the primary American and the ancillary
Jewish. To the question: "Can a person live happily, without stress and
strain, in two cultures?" Steinberg answered, "Yes," and proposed that
"Out of such husbandry of the spirit may well emerge a cultural life
richer than any the human past has heretofore known." Steinberg offered yet another justification for Jewish group survival, one which
foreshadowed the emphasis on the fulfillment of the individual that
would characterize American society in the 1970s.

> If the only effects . . . were to bolster the shaken morale of the
> Jews and to enrich their personalities with the treasures of a second
> heritage, the whole effort would have justified itself from the point

of view of American interests. Quite obviously America will be benefited if its Jews, who constitute one segment of its citizenry, respect themselves, if they are psychologically adjusted rather than disaffected, if they are richer rather than poorer in spirit.[14]

Kaplan's concept of Judaism as a religious civilization came to be accepted as "normative" in Conservative Judaism. It also influenced Reform's own redefinition of Judaism, as "the historical religious experience of the Jewish people." From Felsenthal, Friedlaender and others, the survivalist American Jew had learned that Judaism demanded a definition deeper in tradition and broader in meaning than a "religious community." The concept of cultural pluralism made the broader definition proposed by Kaplan acceptable in the American context.

Kallen concluded his essay with the query: "But the question is, do the dominant classes in America want such a society?"

With the wisdom of hindsight, we can assert that the more relevant question would have been, "Do the ethnic groups want such a society, which would continue their ethnic identity?" Hindsight permits us also to provide the answer: The children of the "ethnic" immigrants did not want to remain "ethnics."

Cultural pluralism had its able ideologists and zealous devotees, but it was becoming clear that America as a "nation of nationalities" was being rejected by those most affected. The proponents of cultural pluralism then seized upon a felicitous sentence of the historian of immigration, Marcus L. Hansen, and gave it the status of a sociological law: "What the son wishes to forget, the grandson wishes to remember." If the second generation rejected cultural pluralism and ethnic identity, the third generation, more secure and at home in America, less in need to "Americanize," would retain or reestablish ethnic identity. C. Bezalel Sherman points out, however, "Alone of all the white ethnic groups do American Jews supply proof for the correctness of the Hansen thesis. Only among them do the grandchildren manifest a greater desire to be part of the community than the children of immigrants."[15] Will Herberg offers an explanation.

We can account for this anomaly by recalling that the Jews came to this country not merely as an immigrant group but also as a religious community; the name "Jewish" designated both . . . When the second generation rejected its Jewishness, it generally, though not universally, rejected both aspects at once . . . The young Jew for whom the Jewish immigrant-ethnic group had lost all meaning because he was an American and not a foreigner, could still think of himself as a Jew, because to him being a Jew now meant identification with the Jewish religious community.[16]

Part of the "religious revival" which marked American life in the decades following World War II, third-generation Jews did not return to the *folkways* of their immigrant forefathers, but they did return to the *faith* of their grandparents.

Sherman noted, "Contrary to secularist prophecy, America has manifested no desire to become a nationality state and religion has shown no inclination to die, a lesson not lost on the acculturated Jew."[17] Quite the opposite, "acculturation" spurred Jews to retain their particularistic identity, to affiliate and participate in that which the American culture esteemed—their religious heritage.

The melting pot still operated, but not as had been theorized. As minorities entered it, their ethnic distinctiveness was indeed melted away, but their religious tradition—Protestant, Catholic, Jewish—was stressed. America became as Herberg termed it the land of the three great faiths.

No one accepted this terminology with greater alacrity than did the Jew. American Jewry, viewed as a religious community, was lifted out of the constellation of ethnic minorities: from the status of 3 percent of the population to one-third of the nation. Symbols of this new status abounded. A minister, a priest and a rabbi sat on the dais at every civic function, including the inauguration of a president; radio and television apportioned time equally to each of the three faiths. Small wonder that American Jews accepted once again the identity of a religious community. (They delighted most of all in the use of the term "Judeo-Christian heritage." This concept raised the Jew to full partnership—and senior partner at that!)

It was noted, however, that the posture of a religious community did not reflect a true religious revival, such as transforms the life of the individual. It was more an expression of organization and form than a way of life or commitment.

American Jewry designated itself a religious community, while at the same time holding on to its own self-identification as a people. The establishment of the State of Israel, and the ready identification of American Jewry with its destiny, indicated an identity beyond that of a "faith" group.

DUAL-IMAGE IDENTITY

What had developed was a new corporate posture which we may term a *dual-image identity*. Having neither an initiator nor an ideologist, it was fashioned by the folk wisdom of the people. In simple words it says: Before the world, in our relationship with the larger society and with other groups, we retain the identity of *a religious community*. Internally, in our understanding of ourselves, in assessing our needs, in ordering our priorities, in fashioning our institutions, we are a *people,* possessed of our own unique *civilization.* When we address America, we do so as one of its religious communities; in relating to other Jewish communities, we do so as a component segment of a world people and civilization.[18]

This dual-image identity persisted into the new image of America which emerged in the sixties and seventies, a land of *ethnic identity.*

Once again, the Jewish community seems to be the exception. In the midst of a serious crisis which beset the Christian religious establishment, Jews retained the posture of a religious community. Jewish seminaries expanded their student bodies and a new one, the Reconstructionist, was founded; synagogues have retained their membership to a remarkable degree. There was little evidence that American Jews were anxious to call themselves an ethnic minority. There was a significant increase in the influence and activities of local Jewish federations and community councils, and of the Council of Jewish Federations and Welfare Funds on the national scene. This might have seemed a move from religious to communal identification. But, as in the 1920s the congregations became miniature communities in function, so in the 1970s the community councils were becoming expanded congregations. In their relations with the larger community they present the posture of representing a religious group, and they sponsor programs of culture and education which heretofore had been deemed the province of the synagogues. The dual-image identity was maintained in the "decades of the ethnics." American Jews utilized structure and symbols recognized as religious to express their national, "peoplehood" identity.

Some might agree with the sardonic observation that the children of the immigrants wanted to be like Gentiles, without becoming Gentiles, while the grandchildren of the immigrants want to be like Jews, without becoming real Jews.

American Jews, whose life span has been in the era of emancipation, have attempted to fashion a corporate identity which would make for their full integration into the American nation, while at the same time retaining their identification with the people-civilization called Israel. They drew optimism for the possibility of such an identity from America's commitment to political federalism, which posits multiple political associations and loyalties. They saw this as giving legitimacy to a pluralistic society, and argued that religious, ethnic, cultural pluralism is not only permissible but mandatory if America was to be a truly democratic society. Their quest for a corporate identity which would make for group survival began with all emphasis on "objective public identity," but has become increasingly influenced by the need to give fullest expression to "self-identity."

Practical viability has been given higher priority than ideological consistency—as in the separation of form and content in the dual-image identity. Long-range hazards have been mitigated by apparent present well-being. American Jews have been so intent in their faith that "America is different," that they have rarely sought to assess their situation in the context of world Jewish experience, or consider seriously lessons which could be drawn from the accounts of other communities in similar quest. They continue to believe, buoyed by the historic memory, as Arthur A. Cohen noted, that the American tradition and the American environment "made it possible for the Jew to become an American without ceasing to be a Jew."

American church historian Winthrop S. Hudson notes that for two thousand years Jews have been faced with the challenge, "to maintain the integrity of their faith while meeting demands for coexistence within a non-Jewish culture and society." It was a difficult task to accomplish, especially in the modern era of emancipation and enlightenment, but it was done, "even in America where the temptation to abandon a dual allegiance was greatest."

Because American Jews are heirs to a two-millennial experience in the world, and a tricentennial experience in America of bearing "the burden of both commitments," they can make a signal contribution to America. Says Hudson:

> Perhaps one of the greatest contributions of Judaism to the United States will be to help other Americans understand how the United States can be a truly pluralistic society in which the pluralism is maintained in a way that is enriching rather than impoverishing, a society of dual commitments which need not be in conflict but can be complementary. . . . From the long experience of Judaism, Americans of other faiths can learn how this may be done with both grace and integrity.[19]

There has been in America a turning away from group concerns to the needs of the individual. Formerly, the group, be it ethnic or religious, would justify its existence by demonstrating its worth to American institutions; today, a group is esteemed to the degree by which it enhances the life of its individual members. The sentiment is abroad that America's real strength is rooted in the well-being, psychological as well as physical, of its individual citizens.

The pledge and promise of America was *life, liberty,* and *the pursuit of happiness.* The first was secured by economic expansion and opportunity; the second was assured by democratic institutions; the third, the pursuit of happiness, remains the continuing challenge. There is a growing feeling that this challenge can best be met by religioethnic groups that nurture the well-being of the individual. To the extent, then, that the Jewish community in America provides its members those

components of religious vision, cultural expression and group association which strengthen purpose and fulfillment, it contributes to the
preservation of a pluralist and democratic America. To strengthen such
a group, to enhance its effectiveness, can only contribute to America's
well-being. American Jews can thus view their participation in the
Jewish enterprise as both a response to their own individual and community needs, and a civic contribution to the nation in which they have
found both haven and home.

Appendix 1

Jewish Population in the United States
Compared to Total United States Population: 1790–1980

Year	U.S. Population	U.S. Jews	% of Population
1790	3,929,214	1,350	0.03
1800	5,308,483	1,600	0.03
1810	7,239,881	2,000	0.03
1820	9,638,453	2,700	0.03
1830	12,866,020	4,500	0.03
1840	17,069,453	15,000	0.09
1850	23,191,876	50,000	0.22
1860	31,443,321	150,000	0.48
1870	38,558,371	200,000	0.52
1880	50,155,783	250,000	0.50
1890	62,947,714	450,000	0.71
1900	75,994,575	1,050,000	1.38
1910	91,972,266	2,043,000	2.22
1920	105,710,620	3,600,000	3.41
1930	122,775,046	4,400,000	3.58
1940	131,669,275	4,800,000	3.65
1950	150,697,361	5,000,000	3.32
1960	179,323,175	5,500,000	3.07
1970	203,235,298	5,850,000	2.88
1980	226,545,805	5,920,000	2.61

Appendix 2

United States Jewish Population Compared to World Jewish Population: 1800–1980

Year	World Jewish Pop.	U.S. Jews	% of World Jewry
1800	2,500,000	1,600	0.06
1825	3,280,000	3,500	0.11
1850	4,750,000	50,000	1.05
1880	7,650,000	250,000	3.27
1900	10,600,000	1,050,000	9.91
1910	12,840,000	2,043,000	15.91
1920	15,745,000	3,600,000	22.86
1930	15,050,000	4,400,000	29.24
1940	15,757,000	4,800,000	30.46
1950	11,500,000	5,000,000	43.48
1960	12,800,000	5,500,000	42.97
1970	13,951,000	5,850,000	41.93
1980	14,527,000	5,920,000	40.75

Appendix 3

General and Jewish Immigration
into the United States: 1881–1943

I. 1881–1898*

Year	General	Jewish	% Jews
1881–84	2,580,337	74,310	2.9
1885	395,346	19,610	4.9
1886	334,203	29,658	8.8
1887	490,109	27,468	5.6
1888	546,889	31,363	5.7
1889	444,427	23,962	5.3
1890	455,302	34,303	7.5
1891	560,319	69,139	12.3
1892	579,663	60,325	10.4
1893	439,730	32,943	7.5
1894	285,631	22,108	7.7
1895	258,536	32,077	12.4
1896	343,267	28,118	8.2
1897	230,832	20,684	8.9
1898	229,299	27,409	11.9
Total	7,613,841	533,478	7.0

II. 1899–1943†

Year	General	Jews	% Jews
1899	311,715	37,415	12.0
1900	448,572	60,764	13.5
1901	487,918	58,098	11.9
1902	648,743	57,688	8.9
1903	857,046	76,203	8.9
1904	812,870	106,236	13.1
1905	1,026,499	129,910	12.7
1906	1,100,735	153,748	14.0
1907	1,285,349	149,182	11.6
1908	782,870	103,387	13.2
1909	751,786	57,551	7.7
1910	1,041,570	84,260	8.1
1911	878,587	91,223	10.4
1912	838,172	80,595	9.6
1913	1,197,892	101,330	8.5

*Jewish figures are for the ports of New York, Philadelphia, and Baltimore.

†Fiscal year figures.

II. 1899–1943[†] (Cont.)

Year	General	Jews	% Jews
1914	1,218,480	138,051	11.3
1915	326,700	26,497	8.1
1916	298,826	15,108	5.1
1917	295,403	17,342	5.9
1918	110,618	3,672	3.3
1919	141,132	3,055	2.2
1920	430,001	14,292	3.3
1921	805,228	119,036	14.8
1922	309,556	53,524	17.3
1923	522,919	49,719	9.5
1924	706,896	49,989	7.1
1925	294,314	10,292	3.5
1926	304,488	10,267	3.4
1927	335,175	11,483	3.4
1928	307,255	11,639	3.8
1929	279,678	12,479	4.5
1930	241,700	11,526	4.8
1931	97,139	5,692	5.9
1932	35,576	2,755	7.7
1933	23,068	2,372	10.3
1934	29,470	4,134	14.0
1935	34,956	4,837	13.8
1936	36,329	6,252	17.2
1937	50,244	11,352	22.6
1938	67,895	19,736	29.0
1939	82,998	43,450	52.3
1940	70,756	36,945	52.2
1941	51,776	23,737	45.8
1942	28,781	10,608	36.9
1943	23,725	4,705	19.8
Total	20,031,406	2,082,139	10.4

[†]Fiscal year figures.

Appendix 4

Largest Jewish Urban Centers
in the United States in 1905 and 1983

1905 Cities		1983 Metropolitan Areas	
New York	672,000	New York	1,734,800
Chicago	80,000	Los Angeles	522,380
Philadelphia	75,000	Miami	388,000
Boston	45,000	Philadelphia	295,000
St. Louis	40,000	Northern New Jersey	288,600
Baltimore	25,000	Chicago	248,000
Cleveland	25,000	Boston	170,000
Newark	20,000	Washington	160,000
Cincinnati	17,500	San Francisco-Oakland	140,000
San Francisco	17,000	Baltimore	92,000
Pittsburgh	15,000	Cleveland	70,000
Detroit	8,000	Detroit	70,000
Milwaukee	8,000	St. Louis	53,500
Louisville	7,000	Pittsburgh	46,000
Buffalo	7,000	Palm Beach	45,000
Jersey City	6,000	Denver	40,000
Kansas City	5,500	San Diego	34,000
New Haven	5,500	Atlanta	32,000
Minneapolis	5,000	Phoenix	32,000
New Orleans	5,000	Minneapolis-St. Paul	29,500
Rochester	5,000	Houston	28,000
Syracuse	5,000	Hartford	26,000
Scranton	5,000	San Jose	25,000
Albany	4,000	Milwaukee	23,900
Denver	4,000	Dallas	22,000

Notes

Chapter 1. In Colonial America

1. Christopher Columbus, *Journal of the First Voyage to America* (New York, 1924), p. 2.
2. Morris U. Schappes, *Documentary History of the Jews in the United States* (New York, 1950), p. 1.
3. Samuel Oppenheim, "The Early History of the Jews in New York 1654–1664," *Publications of the American Jewish Historical Society (PAJHS)* 18 (1909): 73–74.
4. Ibid., p. 2.
5. Ibid., p. 3.
6. Ibid., p. 5.
7. Ibid., p. 12.
8. Cited, Jacob R. Marcus, *The Colonial American Jew 1492–1776* (Detroit, 1970), vol. I, p. 247.
9. Ms. document in possession of author. Cited by Edwin Wolf 2d and Maxwell Whiteman, *The History of the Jews of Philadelphia . . .*, (Philadelphia, 1957), p. 61; and Marcus, *Colonial American,* pp. 881–82.
10. Malcolm Stern, "Jewish Settlement in Savannah," *American Jewish Historical Quarterly (AJHQ)* 52 (March 1963): 184
11. Ibid., pp. 185–86.
12. Malcolm Stern, "Two Jewish Functionaries in Colonial Pennsylvania," *AJHQ* 57 (September 1967): 42.
13. Ibid., p. 45.
14. Leon Huhner, "Daniel Gomez, A Pioneer Merchant of Early New York," *PAJHS* 41 (December 1951): 107 ff.
15. William Vincent Byars, "The Gratz Papers," *PAJHS,* no. 23 (1915):5.
16. Cited, George Alexander Kohut, *Ezra Stiles and the Jews* (New York, 1902), pp. 138–39.
17. Cited, Herbert Friedenwald, "Jews in the Journal of the Continental Congress," *PAJHS,* no. 1 (1892): 87–88.
18. Henry D. Gilpin, ed., *The Papers of James Madison* (Washington, 1840), vol. 1, pp. 63, 178. Cited by Wolf and Whiteman *Jews of Philadelphia,* p.108.
19. Schappes, *Documentary History,* p. 65.
20. *The Literary Diary of Ezra Stiles* (New York, 1901), vol. 1, p. 354.
21. See Abraham J. Karp, *Beginnings, Early American Judaica* (Philadelphia, 1975), pp. 11–16, for an account of the "Emissary From Hebron" and a facsimile of the Sermon pamphlet.

22. Ira Rosenswaike, "An Estimate and Analysis of the Jewish Population of the United States in 1790," *PAJHS* 50, no. 1 (September 1960): 23–67.

23. For text of letters see Joseph L. Blau and Salo W. Baron, *The Jews of the United States 1790–1840: A Documentary History* (New York, 1963), vol. 1, pp. 8–11.

24. M. Kayserling, "A Memorial Sent by German Jews to the President of the First Continental Congress," *PAJHS*, no. 6 (1897): 5–8; Hans Lamm, "The So-called 'Letter of a German Jew . . ., ' "*PAJHS*, no. 37 (1947): 171–84.

25. Schappes, *Documentary History*, pp. 68–69.

26. Ibid., pp. 79–80.

27. Ibid., pp. 80–81.

28. Jacob Marcus, *American Jewry, Documents, Eighteenth Century* (Cincinnati, 1959), pp. 51–54.

Chapter 2. The Early Republic

1. Reverend G. Seixas, *Discourse, Delivered in the Synagogue in New York on the Ninth of May, 1798* (New York, 1797 [*sic*], 1798). For facsimile of pamphlet see Karp, *Beginnings*.

2. Jacques J. Lyons and Abraham De Sola, *A Jewish Calendar for Fifty Years* (Montreal, 5614—1854).

3. Jacob R. Marcus, *Memoirs of American Jews* (Philadelphia, 1955), pp. 6–7.

4. Adams devotes chap. 34, vol. 2, pp. 204–21 to an account "of the Jews in America." Her work was republished in London, 1818; in German, Leipzig, 1820; and in French, Paris, 1826 (where her name is omitted as author).

5. Mordecai Manuel Noah, *Travels in England, France, Spain, and the Barbary States in the Years 1813–1814 and 15* (New York and London, 1819), p. 376.

6. Blau and Baron, *Jews of the United States*, vol. 2, p. 320.

7. Wolf and Whiteman, *Jews of Philadelphia*, p. 97.

8. Schappes, *Documentary History*, pp. 92–96.

9. Isaac Fein, *The Making of an American Jewish Community* (Philadelphia, 1971), pp. 25–26.

10. Ibid., p. 252.

11. For facsimile of Speech, see Karp, *Beginnings*.

12. *The North American Review*, no. 52, New Series no. 37 (July 1826): 74.

13. *The Sabbath Service and Miscellaneous Prayers . . .*, (Charleston, 1830), pp. 5–6.

14. Mordecai M. Noah, *Discourse . . .* (New York, 1818), p. 27.

15. *The Occident* 17, no. 14 (June 30, 1859): 80–81.

16. For facsimile, see Karp, *Beginnings*.

17. Blau and Baron, *Jews of United States*, p. 929.

18. Noah, *Discourse . . .*, 1818, pp. 27–28.

19. For text of the *Proclamation*, see Blau and Baron, *Jews of United States*, pp. 894–905.

20. Mordecai M. Noah, *Discourse . . .* (New York, 1837), p. 38.

21. Mordecai M. Noah, *Discourse . . .* (New York, 1845). For facsimile, see Karp, *Beginnings*.

22. Ibid., p. v.

23. Ibid., passim, pp. 35–51.

24. *The Occident* 2, no. 12 (March 1845): 603.

25. Ibid. 3, no. 1 (April 1845): 33.

26. Ibid., p. 34.

27. Ibid. 1, no. 1 (April 1843): 1. For facsimile of vol. I, no. 1 issue, see Karp, *Beginnings*.

Chapter 3. The Emerging Community

1. *Die Deborah* 1, no. 1 (August 24, 1855): 2. The English translation by N. appeared earlier in *The Israelite*, Cincinnati, 1, no. 33 (February 22, 1855): 3 (259).

2. Cited in Rudolf Glanz, *Studies in Judaica Americana* (New York, 1970), pp. 25–26.

3. Ibid., p. 36.

4. Ibid., p. 24.

5. Ibid., p. 75.

6. Ibid., p. 52.

7. *The Occident* 15, no. 6 (September 1857): 277, 279.

8. Abram Vossen Goodman, "A Jewish Peddler's Diary," *American Jewish Archives* 3, no. 3 (June 1951): 101 ff.

9. Glanz, *Judaica America,* pp. 22–23.

10. I. J. Benjamin II, *Drei Jahre in Amerika, 1859–1862* (Three Years in America), (Hanover, 1862), II Teil, Part 2, p. 134.

11. Gustav Gottheil, "Position of the Jew in America," *North American Review,* no. 243 (May–June 1878).

12. *The Occident* 8, no. 11 (February 1851): 575–76.

13. Alexis De Tocqueville, *Democracy in America* (New York, 1899), 1:313.

14. Benjamin, *Drei Jahre,* I Teil, Part 1, pp. 87–88.

15. For the Call and the Resolutions of the Conference: W. Gunther Plaut, *The Growth of Reform Judaism* (New York, 1965), pp. 29–31.

16. L. Maria Child, *Letters from New York,* 3d ed. (New York, 1845), p. 42.

17. *The Occident* 14, no. 12 (March 1857): 599–601.

18. Ms., New York Colonial Manuscripts, vol. 54, p. 64, New York State Library, Albany, N.Y., *The Documentary History of the State of New York* (Albany, 1850), vol. 3, p. 434.

19. Charles Reznikoff and Uriah Z. Engelman, *The Jews of Charleston* (Philadelphia, 1950), pp. 252–55.

20. Letter ms., I. M. Wise to Simon Tuska, Cincinnati, April 21, 1859, *American Jewish Archives.*

21. See Abraham J. Karp, "Simon Tuska Becomes a Rabbi," *PAJHS* 50, no. 2 (December, 1960): 79–97.

22. Simon Tuska, *The Stranger in the Synagogue* (Rochester, N.Y.: Darrow & Bros., 1854).

23. *The Israelite* 3, no. 7 (August 22, 1856): 53.

24. Ibid.

25. Ibid. 4, no. 27 (January 8, 1858): 212.

26. Ibid. 5, no. 15 (October 15, 1858): 118.

27. Ibid. 5, no. 31 (February 4, 1859): 243.

28. Ibid., p. 242.

29. Letter, Wise to Tuska, 1859, *American Jewish Archives.*

30. Hyman B. Grinstein, *The Rise of the Jewish Community in New York* (Philadelphia, 1947), p. 243.

31. *PAJHS* 42, no. 4 (June 1953): 399 ff.

32. See Abraham J. Karp, "America's Pioneer Prayerbooks," *Jewish Book Annual* (New York, 1976), vol. 34, pp. 15–25.

33. *First Annual Report of the Jewish Foster Home Society of Philadelphia* (Philadelphia, 1856), p. 4.

34. Bertram W. Korn, *American Jewry and the Civil War* (Philadelphia, 1951), pp. 28–29.

35. M. J. Raphall, *Bible View of Slavery* (New York, 1861), pp. 28–29.

36. G. Gottheil, *Moses versus Slavery* (Manchester, England, 1861).

37. *Sinai* 6, no. 1 (February 1861): 2 ff; no. 2 (March 1861): 45 ff. The first was reprinted as a pamphlet, *Die Prosklaverei-Rede des herren Dr. Raphael [sic] 20 New York* (Baltimore, 1861).

38. Korn, *American Jewry and the Civil War,* p. 22.

39. Ibid., p. 122.

40. Lloyd P. Gartner, "Roumania, America, and World Jewry: Consul Peixotto in Bucharest, 1870–1876," *AJHQ* 58, no. 1 (September 1968): 52.

Chapter 4. American Judaism

1. Bernhard Felsenthal, *The Beginnings of the Chicago Sinai Congregation* (Chicago, 1898).

2. See Abraham J. Karp, "An East European Congregation on American Soil: Beth Israel, Rochester, N.Y., 1874–1886," *A Bicentennial Festschrift for Jacob R. Marcus,* ed. Bertram W. Korn (New York, 1976): 263–302.

3. *The Occident* 13, no. 9 (December 1855): 467.

4. Minutes (MS) Beth Israel Congregation, July 10, 1884.

5. *Rochester Union-Advertiser,* April 5, 1895, p. 10.

6. *Hayehudim V'hayahadut B'New York* (New York, 1887), p. 4.

7. James Parton, *Topics of the Times* (Boston, 1871), p. 311.

8. Jacob Goldman, *The Voice of Truth* (Philadelphia, 1870), pp. 93–95.

9. W. Gunther Plaut, *The Growth of Reform Judaism* (New York, 1965), p 30.

10. Ibid., pp. 33–34.

11. *Proceedings of Chicago Sinai Congregation* . . . (Chicago, 1885).

12. Sigmund Hecht, *Epitome of Post Biblical History* (Cincinnati, 1882), p. 113.

13. *Proceedings of the First Biennial Convention of the Jewish Theological Seminary Association* (New York, 1888), pp. 19–20.

14. Marcus Jastrow, *A Warning Voice* (Philadelphia, 1892), pp. 6–7.

15. *The American Hebrew* 29 (January 7, 1887): 136.

16. *Proceedings First Biennial*, p. 6.

17. Ibid., p. 9. From the Preamble of the Constitution of the Jewish Theological Seminary Association, adopted at its founding convention, May 6, 1886.

18. *New York Herald*, July 21, 1888.

19. *Proceedings First Biennial*, p. 11.

20. Ibid., p. 20.

21. Ibid., p. 18.

22. *Students' Annual, Jewish Theological Seminary of America, Schechter Memorial* (New York, 1916), p. 61.

23. See Abraham J. Karp, "Solomon Schechter Comes to America," *AJHQ* 53, no. 1 (September 1963): 44–62.

24. Norman Bentwich, *Solomon Schechter* (Philadelphia, 1938), p. 169.

25. Cyrus Adler, ed., *The Jewish Theological Seminary of America* (New York, 1939), pp. 9–10.

26. *Students' Annual*, p. 161.

27. Cyrus Adler, "Solomon Schechter," *American Jewish Yearbook*, 5677 (Philadelphia, 1916), p. 52.

28. Letter, Schechter to Sulzberger, June 26, 1898, Library JTSA.

29. *The American Hebrew (AH)* 65, no. 8 (June 23, 1899): 231.

30. Ibid. 70 (March 8, 1902): 484.

31. See Abraham J. Karp, "New York Chooses a Chief Rabbi," *PAJHS* 44, no. 3 (March 1955): 129–98.

32. Judah D. Eisenstein, "History of the Association of American Orthodox Hebrew Congregations," *Ner Ha-Ma'arovi* (Hebrew) 1, no. 11 (1897): 4.

33. For text of charter see Karp, "New York Chooses," pp. 189–90.

34. Abraham Cahan, *Bleter Fun Mein Leben* (Yiddish) (New York, 1926), vol. 2, pp. 402–3.

35. *Jewish Messenger*, July 13, 1888.

36. *Jewish Tidings*, August 17, August 24, 1888.

37. *American Israelite (AI)*, March 30, 1888.

38. *New York Sun*, August 12, 1888, p. 5.

39. *AI*, August 3, 1888.

40. *AH*, August 10, 1888.

41. *Jewish Exponent*, September 5, 1888.

42. *AH*, August 10, 1888, p. 2.

43. *AI*, October 5, 1888; for Yiddish version see *Der Volksadvocat*, September 19, 1888.

44. *Der Volksadvocat*, October 5, 1888.

45. *AH*, April 12, 1889.

46. *Jewish Daily Forward*, July 29, 1902.

47. *Jewish Gazette*, English Supplement, August 15, 1902.

Chapter 5. The Great Wave

1. [Charles Reznikoff], *By the Waters of Manhattan* (New York, 1929), p. 173.

2. Benjamin L. Gordon, *Between Two Worlds* (New York, 1952), p. 134.

3. "Jewish Immigrants to the United States, 1881–1900," *YIVO Annual of Jewish Social Science* 6 (New York, 1951): 158.

4. Zosa Szajkowski, "The Attitude of American Jews to East European Jewish Immigration," *PAJHS* 40, pt. 3 (March 1951): 232.

5. Ibid., pp. 264–71 (text of letter).

6. *Second Annual Report of the Association of Jewish Immigrants of Philadelphia* (Philadelphia, 1886), pp. 5–6.

7. *Third Annual Report* . . . (Philadelphia, 1887), pp. 27–28.

8. Mary Antin, *From Plotzk to Boston* (Boston, 1899), pp. 78–80.

9. Ephraim E. Lisitsky, *In the Grip of Cross-Currents* (New York, 1959).

10. Hoffman, B., *Fufzig yahr klockmacher union* (New York, 1936), p. 22.

11. Matthew Hale Smith, *Sunshine and Shadow in New York* (Hartford, 1868), p. 452.

12. Ibid., p. 453.

13. Ibid.

14. James Parton, *Topics of the Times* (Boston, 1871), p. 315.

15. Israel Kasovich, *The Days of Our Years* (New York, 1929), pp. 173–78.

16. Jacob A. Riis, *How the Other Half Lives* (New York, 1890), p. 128.

17. *The Jewish Alliance of America* (New York, 1891), p. 24.

18. Morris Rosenfeld, *Songs of Labor*, trans. from the Yiddish, Rose Pastor Stokes and Helena Frank (Boston, 1914), p. 7.

19. Eliakum Zunser, *Fir Vemen Die Goldene Land? For Whom Is the Gold Country?*, words and music (New York, 1894). Trans. by author.

20. Quoted by Abraham Cahan, "The Russian Jew in America," *The Atlantic Monthly*, July 1898, p. 130.

21. Jacob Lestschinsky, "Jewish Migrations," *The Jews*, ed. Louis Finkelstein (Philadelphia, 1949), vol. 4, pp. 1225–26.

22. Abraham Cahan, "Russian Jew," p. 132.

23. Hutchins Hapgood, *The Spirit of the Ghetto* (New York, 1902), pp. 113; 115–16.

24. Cahan, "Russian Jew," p. 132.

25. For text see *YIVO Bletter*, vol. 39 (New York, 1955): 276. Trans. by author.

26. Sholom Aleichem (Shalom Rabinowitz), *Kleine Menshelech* (New York, 1918), pp. 248–51.

27. Anzia Yezierska, *Hungry Hearts* (Boston and New York, 1920), pp. 261–62.

28. Ibid., pp. 263–65.

29. *News of YIVO*, no. 150 (September 1979): 7.

30. Rosenfeld, *Songs*, pp. 10–11.

31. See note 19.

32. Heard by author from Mrs. Abraham Burstein.

33. Eliakum Zunser, *Zwanzig Yiddishe Folks Lieder: Twenty Popular Songs* (Brooklyn, N.Y., n.d.): 114–120. Trans. by author.

34. Broadside in Yiddish: *Hanokem Et Nikmatenu* (New York, 1899). Trans. by author.

Chapter 6. Americanization

1. *American Jewish Yearbook (AJY)*, 5662 (Philadelphia, 1901), pp. 15 ff.

2. George E. Barnett, "A Method of Delineating the Jewish Population of Large Cities of the United States," *PAJHS*, no. 10 (1902): 41.

3. Charles S. Bernheimer, *The Russian Jew in the United States* (Philadelphia, 1905), pp. 9–18. This book, a collection of reports on demographic, economic, cultural, religious and social aspects of Jewish life in New York, Philadelphia, Chicago, edited by Bernheimer, was reprinted a year later as *The Immigrant Jew in America*, "Issued By the Liberal Immigration League." The books are identical, except that in the latter the names of the Jewish editor and all twenty-nine Jewish contributors are deleted. Only the names of the four non-Jewish authors are listed, and a new preface by Edmund J. James, president of the University of Illinois, is added.

4. Stephen Birmingham, *The Grandees* (New York, 1971), p. 265.

5. *The Galaxy* 13, no. 1 (January 1872): 47–60.

6. For the Jewish interests of Emma Lazarus, see Philip Cowen, *Memories of an American Jew* (New York, 1932), pp. 332–45.

7. *The Century* 24, no. 1 (May 1882): 48–56.

8. Ibid. 25, no. 4 (February 1883): 602–11.

9. *American Hebrew*, November 10, 1882–February 24, 1883.

10. *Judaism at the World's Parliament of Religions* (Cincinnati, 1894), p. 303.

11. Josephine Lazarus, *The Spirit of Judaism* (New York, 1895).

12. *A Letter to Hon. Moritz Ellinger from the Hebrew Emigrant Aid Society* (New York, 1882), 4 pp.

13. For an account of the meeting see: *The New York Times*, April 24, 1901, p. 3, col. 5.

14. Stephen Birmingham, *Our Crowd* (New York, 1967), p. 239.
15. *New York Herald,* July 22, 1879.
16. Plaut, *The Growth of Reform Judaism,* p. 40.
17. Richard G. Gottheil, *Zionism* (Philadelphia, 1914), p. 208.
18. Madison C. Peters, *Justice to the Jew* (New York, 1899), p. 359.
19. *The Spirit of the Ghetto,* p. 177.
20. *The Spirit of the Ghetto* was reissued three times in the 1960s.
21. *The Autobiography of Lincoln Steffens* (New York, 1931), p. 243.
22. Jacob A. Riis, *Children of the Poor* (New York, 1892), p. 44.
23. Mary Antin, *The Promised Land* (Boston and New York, 1912), pp. 202–5.
24. Trans. by author.
25. Arthur Mann, *Growth and Achievement: Temple Israel, 1854–1954* (Cambridge, Mass., 1954), pp. 59–61.
26. For full text see *American Hebrew and Jewish Messenger* 88, no. 23 (April 7, 1911).
27. Jacob David Willowsky, *Nimukei Ridbaz* (Chicago, 1904).
28. Trans. by author.
29. Quoted in Ze'ev Shraga Kaplan, *Edut B'Yaakov* (Warsaw, 1904), p. 49.
30. For text of address see Israel Friedlaender, *Past and Present* (Cincinnati, 1919), pp. 159–84.

Chapter 7. New Arrivals
1. *YIVO Bletter,* vol. 39, p. 278.
2. Esther Panitz, "In Defence of the Jewish Immigrant," *AJHQ* 55, no. 1 (September 1965): 57.
3. *Official Correspondence Relating to Immigration of Russian Exiles* (Washington, 1891), pp. 6–7.
4. "New Light on the Jewish Question," *North American Review* 417 (August 1891): 141–42.
5. Cited in Maldwyn Allen Jones, *American Immigration* (Chicago, 1960), p. 259.
6. Charles Reznikoff, ed., *Louis Marshall: Champion of Liberty* (Philadelphia, 1957), pp. 113–14.
7. "Eastern and Western Civilization," *American Hebrew,* March 6, 1903, p. 592.
8. Isaac Max Rubinow, "The Jewish Question in New York City (1902–1903)," trans. Leo Shpall, *PAJHS* 49, no. 2 (December 1959): 121.
9. Samuel Joseph, *History of the Baron de Hirsch Fund* (Philadelphia, 1935), p. 129.
10. Max Vorspan and Lloyd P. Gartner, *History of the Jews of Los Angeles* (Philadelphia, 1970), pp. 111–12.
11. Cited in Louis J. Swichkow and Lloyd P. Gartner, *History of the Jews in Milwaukee* (Philadelphia, 1963), pp. 158–59.
12. Cyrus Adler, *Jacob H. Schiff, His Life and Letters* (New York, 1928) vol. 2, p. 98.
13. *Sixth Biennial Session of the National Conference of Jewish Charities in the United States, St. Louis, Mo.,* May 17–19, 1910 (Baltimore, 1910), p. 125.
14. "The Yahudi and the Immigrant, A Reappraisal," *AJHQ* 42, no. 1 (September 1973): 13.
15. Adler, *Jacob H. Schiff,* vol. 2, p. 106.
16. *Sixth Biennial Session,* pp. 146–47.
17. *PAJHS,* no. 22 (1914): 226.
18. *Hebrew Technical Institute of New York, Twenty-fifth Anniversary, 1884–1909* (New York, 1909).
19. Joseph, *Baron de Hirsch Fund,* p. 235.
20. Rubinow, "Jewish Question," pp. 118–19.
21. Miriam Blaustein, ed., *Memoirs of David Blaustein* (New York, 1913), pp. 133–36.
22. Ibid., p. 267.
23. Thomas Kessner, *The Golden Door* (New York, 1977), p. 173.

Chapter 8. Making a Living
1. Rubinow, "Jewish Question," pp. 94–95.
2. Beckless Willson, *The New America* (London and New York, 1903), pp. 172–73.
3. Jacob Lestschinsky, "Economic and Social Development of American Jewry," *The Jewish People, Past and Present* (New York, 1955), vol. 4, p. 80.
4. Ibid., p. 78.

5. *The Russian Jew in the United States*, p. 135.

6. Kaplan, "Wages and Unemployment in New York," *Der Jüdischer Emigrant* (St. Petersburg) 5, no. 22 (1911): 1–3.

7. Rubinow, "Jewish Question," pp. 95, 125–26.

8. *Russian Jew in United States*, p. 136.

9. Vorspan and Gartner, *Jews of Los Angeles*, p. 120.

10. Harry Germanow, *My Own Story* (Rochester, N.Y., 1967), pp. 19–21.

11. Oscar Handlin, *The Americans* (Boston, 1963), p. 274.

12. Lestschinsky, "Economic and Social Development," p. 75.

13. Isaac A. Wile, "History of the Jews of Rochester," *The History of the Jews in Rochester* (n.p., 1911), p. 51.

14. Riis, *How the Other Half Lives*, 125 ff.

15. Sylvia Kopald and Ben Selekman, "The Epic of Needle Trade," *The Menorah Journal* 15, no. 4 (October 1928): p. 306.

16. Ibid., p. 307.

17. Cited by Selig Perlman, "Jewish American Unionism," *PAJHS* 41, no. 4 (June 1952): 304.

18. See Louis Levine, *The Women's Garment Workers* (New York, 1924).

19. Joel Seidman, *The Needle Trades* (New York, 1942), p. 121.

20. Will Herberg, "The Jewish Labor Movement in the United States," *AJYB* 53 (1952): 31.

21. S. M. Melamed, "Jews in the Needle Trade Industry," *Jewish Experiences in America*, ed. Bruno Lasker (New York, 1930): 120–22. (Extracts from an article in *The Reflex*, August 1927.)

22. Lestschinsky, "Economic and Social Development," p. 85.

23. Published by Funk and Wagnalls Co., 1901–6, with Isidor Singer as Projector and Managing Editor.

24. Jacob Kabakoff, "Hebrew Culture and Creativity in America," *Judaism* 3, no. 4 (Fall 1954): 404.

25. Eisig Silberschlag, "Hebrew Literature in the United States: Record and Interpretation," *The Jewish Quarterly Review* 45, no. 4 (April 1955): 430–31.

26. Cited in Samuel Niger, "Yiddish Culture," *The Jewish People Past and Present*, vol. 4 (New York, 1955): 274.

27. Hapgood, *The Spirit of the Ghetto*, p. 113.

28. *The Menorah Journal* 15, no. 1 (July 1928): 32.

Chapter 9. The Shaping of the Jewish Community

1. Cyrus Adler, *The Voice of America on Kishineff* (Philadelphia, 1904), p. 472.

2. Ibid., pp. 242–43.

3. Ibid., pp. 270, 272.

4. Ibid., p. 338.

5. Ibid., p. 481.

6. For text of Roosevelt statement: ibid., pp. 472–76.

7. Reznikoff, *Louis Marshall*, p. 19. Letter dated December 26, 1905.

8. Ibid. Letter, Marshall to Cyrus Adler, December 30, 1905.

9. Letter accompanying *The American Committee Seventh Annual Report* (New York, 1913).

10. Adler, *Jacob H. Schiff*, vol. 2, pp. 151–52.

11. "The Passport Question," *AJYB*, 5672 (Philadelphia, 1911), p. 79.

12. Ibid., p. 23.

13. Quoted, Naomi W. Cohen, *Not Free to Desist* (Philadelphia, 1972), p. 61.

14. "The Passport Question," pp. 76 ff.

15. Cohen, *Not Free to Desist*, p. 69.

16. Ibid., p. 77.

17. Ibid., p. 79.

18. Ibid., pp. 78–79.

19. Reznikoff, *Louis Marshall*, pp. 509–10, letter dated June 12, 1915.

20. Louis Lipsky, *Memoirs in Profile* (Philadelphia, 1975), pp. 341–42. Reprinted from *The Maccabean*, June–July 1917.

21. Ibid., p. 342.

22. Quoted Melvin I. Urofsky, *A Voice That Spoke for Justice* (Albany, N.Y.: 1982), pp. 130–31.

23. *North American Review* 168 (September 1908): 383–84.

24. Cahan, "Russian Jew," p. 133.

25. Adolph M. Radin, *Asirei Oni U'Varzel* (New York, 1893), Yiddish section, p. 4.

26. *Judische Tageblatt*, September 18, 1908, p. 6. Cited Arthur A. Goren, *New York Jews and the Quest for Community* (New York, 1970), p. 35.

27. *The New York Times*, September 18, 1908, p. 16. Cited Goren, *New York Jews*, p. 36.

28. Ibid., p. 39.

29. *New York Tribune*, September 18, 1898.

30. Goren, *New York Jews*, pp. 97–98, from *Jewish Education* 20 (1949): 110.

31. Mordecai M. Kaplan, "Affiliation with the Synagogue," *The Jewish Communal Register* (New York, 1918), pp. 120–21.

32. Goren, *New York Jews*, p. 158.

33. Ibid., p. 198.

34. Ibid., p. 252.

35. "Eighth Annual Report of the American Jewish Committee," *AJYB*, 5676 (Philadelphia, 1915), p. 360.

36. Morris Engelman, *Four Years of Relief and War Work by the Jews of America, 1914–1918* (New York, 1918).

37. Quoted by Joseph C. Hyman, "Twenty-five Years of American Aid to Jews Overseas: A Record of the J.D.C.," *AJYB* (Philadelphia, 1939), p. 179.

Chapter 10. After the Armistice

1. Melvin I. Urofsky, *American Zionism from Herzl to the Holocaust* (New York, 1975), p. 246.

2. Solomon Schechter, *Seminary Addresses and Other Papers* (Cincinnati, 1915), pp. 93, 97, 99–100.

3. *Brandeis on Zionism* (New York, 1942), pp. 49–50.

4. Ibid., p. 10.

5. Ibid., p. 68.

6. Letter to Robert Kesselman, Jerusalem, May 8, 1930, in Carl Herman Voss, ed., *Stephen S. Wise, Servant of the People* (Philadelphia, 1970), pp. 167–68.

7. Naomi W. Cohen, *American Jews and the Zionist Idea* (New York, 1975), p. 43.

8. See Abraham J. Karp, "Reaction to Zionism and the State of Israel in the American Jewish Religious Community." *Jewish Journal of Sociology* 8, no. 2 (December 1966): 150–74.

9. *The American Hebrew*, June 11, 1897, p. 189.

10. Ibid., May 21, 1897, p. 64.

11. Ibid., September 17, 1897, p. 572.

12. Ibid., October 17, 1897, p. 712.

13. Ibid., June 10, 1898, p. 172.

14. *Central Conference of American Rabbis (CCAR) Yearbook* (Cincinnati, 1898), vol. 7, p. xli.

15. *The American Hebrew*, May 28, 1897, p. 126.

16. Stephen S. Wise, "The Beginnings of American Zionism," *Jewish Frontier*, August 1947, p. 7.

17. *The Maccabean*, January, 1918, p. 21.

18. Samuel Halperin, *The Political World of American Zionism* (Detroit, 1961), p. 102.

19. *CCAR Yearbook* (1918), vol. 28, pp. 133–34.

20. *Ha-Ivri* 7, no. 42 (November 16, 1917): 1.

21. Shalom Dov Baer Schneersohn, *Haktav V'Ha-Michtav* (New York, 1917).

22. Baruch Meir Klein, *Sha'alu Sh'lom Yerushalayim* (New York, 1917).

23. November 30, 1947, p. 2.

24. *Proceedings of the Rabbinical Assembly of America* (New York, 1948), vol. 12, p. 65.

25. *CCAR Yearbook* (1948), vol. 58, pp. 93–94.

26. *Council News* 1, no. 11 (December 1947).

27. *CCAR Yearbook*, vol. 58, p. 199.

28. *Orthodox Jewish Life* 15, no. 3 (February 1948); no. 2 (December 1947).

29. *Morgen Zhurnal,* December 4, 1947.

30. Yosef Eliyau Henkin, *Perushei Lev Ibra* (New York, 1957), p. 138.

31. Maurice Samuel, *Jews On Approval* (New York, 1931), pp. 97, 110.

32. *AJYB,* 5696 vol. 37 (Philadelphia, 1935), p. 212.

33. *AJYB,* 5697 vol. 38 (Philadelphia, 1936), p. 243.

34. Burton J. Hendrick, *The Jews in America* (New York, 1923), pp. 1–2.

35. Josephus Ben Gorion, *The Wonderful and Most Deplorable History of the Latter Times of the Jews; with the Destruction of the City of Jerusalem* (Leominster, Mass., 1803), pp. iv, v.

36. Hannah Adams, *The History of the Jews from the Destruction of Jerusalem to the Present Time* (Boston, 1812), vol. 2, p. 219.

37. *The Protocols and World Revolution* (Boston, 1920), pp. 1–2.

38. *Jewish Influences in American Life, The International Jew—The World's Foremost Problem,* vol. 3 (Dearborn, Mich., 1921), pp. 3–4.

39. *Western States Jewish Historical Quarterly* 15, no. 1 (October 1982): 82–83.

40. Letter, Marshall to A. C. Ratchefsky, Boston, June 17, 1922, in Reznikoff, *Louis Marshall,* pp. 266–67.

41. Morton Rosenstock, *Louis Marshall, Defender of Jewish Rights* (Detroit, 1965), p. 252.

42. *Father Coughlin: His "Facts" and Arguments* (New York, 1939), p. 5.

43. T. W. Adorno, Else Freukel-Brunswik, Daniel J. Levinson, R. Nevitt Sanford, *The Authoritarian Personality* (New York, 1950), p. VII.

44. Bruno Lasker, "Jewish Handicaps in the Employment Market," *Jewish Social Service Quarterly,* March 1926, pp. 170 ff.

45. Harry Shneiderman, "The Kings County Hospital Case," *Jewish Experiences in America,* ed. Bruno Lasker (New York, 1930), pp. 72 ff.

Chapter 11. From Dusk to Darkness

1. Quoted in Louis Berg, "American Public Opinion on Palestine," *The Menorah Journal* 17, no. 1 (October 1929): 72.

2. Ibid., p. 73.

3. Ibid., p. 70.

4. Melech Epstein, *The Jew and Communism* (New York, n.d.), p. 226.

5. Berg, "Opinion on Palestine," p. 75.

6. Epstein, *Jews and Communism,* p. 231.

7. Ben Hecht, *A Child of the Century* (New York, 1954), p. 382.

8. *AJYB,* 5701 (Philadelphia, 1940), vol. 42, pp. 269–70.

9. *AJYB,* 5702 (Philadelphia, 1941), vol. 43, p. 95.

10. Joseph Schwartz, "The United Jewish Appeal, 1939–1955," typescript in the UJA Archives, p. 4. Cited in Abraham J. Karp, *To Give Life* (New York, 1981), p. 85.

11. Ibid., p. 114.

12. "Bankrot," (Bankrupt) vol. 21, no. 486 (February 12, 1943): 1–3, trans. in Hayim Greenberg, *Anthology,* ed. Marie Syrkin (Detroit, 1968), pp.198–202.

13. Alex Grobman, "What Did They Know? The American Jewish Press and the Holocaust," *American Jewish History* 68, no. 3 (March 1979): 327–52.

14. *The Menorah Journal* 31, no. 3 (Autumn 1943): 284–95.

15. *Hitler's Ten Year War on the Jews,* ed. Boris Shub (New York, 1943), pp. 155, 300.

16. *The Black Book of Polish Jewry,* ed. Jacob Apenszlak (New York, 1943).

17. William Zuckerman, "A Review of 1943," *The Jewish Ledger* (Rochester, New York), January 7, 1944.

18. Ibid., January 14, 1944.

19. Ibid., March 31, 1944.

20. Typescript, Archives of the Jewish Community Federation of Rochester, New York.

21. Ibid.

22. Culled from *Beth El Bulletin* in Archives of Congregation Beth El, Rochester, New York.

Chapter 12. At the Tercentenary

1. *Jewish Quarterly Review* 45, no. 4 (April, 1955), p. 316.

2. *Judaism* 3, no. 4 (Fall 1954): 301.

3. *The Two Hundred and Fiftieth Anniversary of the Settlement of the Jews in the United States* (New York, 1906), pp. 18–19.

4. Charles S. Liebman, *The Ambivalent American Jew* (Philadelphia, 1973), p. vii.

5. Salo W. Baron, *The Jewish Community* (Philadelphia, 1942), p. 405.

6. Michael Novak, *The Rise of the Unmeltable Ethnics* (New York, 1972).

7. Demographic data culled from *American Jewish Yearbook*(s), reports issued by the National Jewish Population Study, and Marshall Sklare, *America's Jews* (New York, 1971). See especially: Sidney Goldstein, "Jews in the United States: Perspectives from Demography," in *AJYB 1981,* vol. 81 (New York and Philadelphia, 1980), pp. 3–59.

8. *The Jewish Population of Rochester, New York* (Rochester, New York, 1961, 1981).

9. Franklin Hamlin Littell, *From State Church to Pluralism* (New York, 1962), pp. 168–69.

10. James Baldwin et al., *Black Anti-Semitism and Jewish Racism* (New York, 1969).

11. *Commentary* 47, no. 1 (January 1969): 32.

12. Ibid., p. 33.

13. *Encyclopedia Judaica,* vol. 2, p. 826.

14. Alfred Kazin, "The Jew as Modern American Writer," *Commentary Reader,* ed. Norman Podhoretz (New York, 1966), p. xxi.

15. *The New York Times,* October 22, 1976, sec. I, p. 3.

Chapter 13. Zionism, Philanthropy and Politics

1. Daniel J. Elazar, "The Rediscovered Polity," *AJYB* 70 (1969): 172–73.

2. "United States of America: Overview," *The Yom Kippur War,* ed. Moshe Davis (New York, 1974), pp. 34–35.

3. Marie Syrkin, "United States of America: Perspectives," *Yom Kippur War,* p. 82.

4. *Yom Kippur War,* p. 90, "Letter to the Editor," *The New York Times,* December 14, 1973.

5. Ibid., p. 90, Irving Howe, "Thinking the Unthinkable: A Personal Statement," *New York* magazine, December 24, 1973.

6. Cited in Abraham J. Karp, *To Give Life* (New York, 1981), p. 148.

7. Interview with Joseph Meyerhoff (September 9, 1975) UJA Oral History Project.

8. Daniel J. Elazar, *Community and Polity* (Philadelphia, 1976), pp. 341–77.

9. W. M. Rosenblatt, "The Jews . . ." p. 58.

10. Myer Moses, *An Oration Delivered Before the Hebrew Orphan Society* (Charleston, 1807), p. 7.

11. Earl Raab, "The Deadly Innocence of American Jews," *Commentary* 50, no. 6 (December, 1970): 32.

Chapter 14. Changes and Challenges

1. See Aviva Cantor, "The Missing Ingredient—Power and Influence in the Jewish Community," *Present Tense* 11, no. 3 (Spring, 1984): 8–12.

2. *Lilith* 1, no. 3 (Summer, 1977): 2.

3. Diana Katcher Bletter, "Women of Spirit," *Hadassah Magazine* 65, no. 10 (June–July, 1984): 14.

4. *CCAR Yearbook* 86 (1976): 174–78.

5. Marshall Sklare, "Recent Developments in Conservative Judaism," *Midstream* 17, no. 1 (January, 1972): 3–19.

6. Charles S. Liebman and Saul Shapiro, "A Survey of the Conservative Movement and Some of its Religious Attitudes," September, 1979, mimeo.

7. Bill Novak, "The Making of a Jewish Counter Culture," *Response* no. 7 (Spring–Summer, 1970): 10.

8. Harold M. Schulweis, "Restructuring the Synagogue," *Conservative Judaism* 27, no. 4 (Summer, 1973): 21–23.

9. Samuel Belkin, *Essays in Traditional Jewish Thought* (New York, 1956), p. 69.

10. Oscar Z. Fasman, "After Fifty Years, An Optimist," *American Jewish History* 69, no. 2 (December, 1979): 173.

11. Charles S. Liebman, "Orthodoxy in American Jewish Life," *AJYB,* 1965 (New York and Philadelphia, 1965): 92.

12. Mordecai M. Kaplan, "Toward A Reconstruction of Judaism," *Menorah Journal* 13 (April, 1927): 125.

13. Marshall Sklare, "Church and Laity Among Jews," *Annual of the American Academy of Political Science* (November, 1960), p. 69.

14. *NJPS, Jewish Identity* (New York, 1974), p. 11.

15. Elihu Bergman, "The American Jewish Population Erosion," *Midstream*, October 1977, pp. 9 ff.

16. "Demographic Trends and Jewish Survival," *Midstream*, November 1978, pp. 9–19.

17. The National Jewish Population Study was sponsored by Council of Jewish Federations and conducted under the direction of Fred Massarik.

18. Mordecai M. Noah, "The Restoration of the Jews," *The Occident* 3, no. 1 (April 1845): 34. "Break down the barrier and allow Jews and Christians to marry, and in two or three generations we shall no longer be heard of."

19. W. M. Rosenblatt, "The Jews . . .": 60.

20. David Einhorn, "Noch ein Wort über gemischte Ehen," *Jewish Times* 1 (January 28, 1870): 10.

21. Mordecai M. Kaplan, *Judaism as a Civilization* (New York, 1934): 418.

22. See Malcolm H. Stern, "Jewish Marriage and Intermarriage in the Federal Period (1776–1840)," *American Jewish Archives* 19 (November 1967): 142.

23. Julius Drachsler, *Democracy and Assimilation* (New York, 1920), 121 ff.

24. Aryeh Tartakower, *Ha-Hevra Ha-Yehudit* (Tel Aviv, 1957), p. 217.

25. Erich Rosenthal, "Studies in Jewish Intermarriage in the United States," *AJYB* 64 (1963): 3–53.

26. *NJPS, Intermarriage*.

27. Egon Mayer and Carl Sheingold, *Intermarriage and the Jewish Future* (New York, 1979), p. 29.

28. Ibid., p. 32.

Chapter 15. Survival in a Free Society

1. W. Gunther Plaut, *The Rise of Reform Judaism* (New York 1963), p. 138.

2. Israel Zangwill, *The Melting Pot* (New York, 1909), pp. 198–99.

3. Louis B. Wright, *Culture on the Moving Frontier* (New York, 1961), p. 168.

4. Blau and Baron, *Jews of United States*, vol. 2, p. 576.

5. Plaut, *The Growth of Reform Judaism*, p. 34.

6. *The Maccabean* 1, no. 2 (November 1901): 66.

7. Emma Felsenthal, *Bernhard Felsenthal* (New York, 1924), p. 233.

8. Israel Friedlaender, *Past and Present* (Cincinnati, 1919), pp. 159–84: "The Problem of Judaism in America," a lecture before the Mickveh Israel Association, Philadelphia, December 8, 1907.

9. Chaim Zhitlowsky, *Gesamelte Schriften* (New York, 1912), vol. 2, pp. 187–286. Anarchist leader Emma Goldman wrote of Zhitlowsky in her *Living My Life* (p. 370): "An ardent Judaist, he never tired of urging upon me that as a Jewish daughter I should devote myself to the cause of the Jews."

10. Horace M. Kallen, *Culture and Democracy in the United States* (New York, 1924), pp. 124–25.

11. Mordecai M. Kaplan, "Judaism as a Civilization, Religion's Place in It," *The Menorah Journal* 15, no. 6 (December 1928): 511.

12. Kaplan, *Judaism as a Civilization* (New York, 1934), p. 513.

13. Ibid., p. 182.

14. Milton Steinberg, *To Be or Not To Be a Jew* (New York, 1941), from *Common Ground*, Spring 1941, p. 15.

15. C. Bezalel Sherman, *The Jew Within American Society* (Detroit 1961), p. 208.

16. Will Herberg, *Protestant—Catholic—Jew* (New York, 1955), pp. 201–2.

17. Sherman, *Jew Within American Society*, p. 223.

18. See Abraham J. Karp, "The American Jewish Community—Union Now or Ever?" *Proceedings of the Rabbinical Assembly of America* (New York, 1961), vol. 25, pp. 55–66.

19. Winthrop S. Hudson, *Religion in America*, 2d ed. (New York, 1973), pp. 440–41.

Index